SAMS
Teach Yourself

Microsoft® Office 2003

Greg Perry

SAMS 800 East 96th St., Indianapolis, Indiana, 46240 USA

Sams Teach Yourself Microsoft Office 2003 in 24 Hours

Copyright © 2004 by Sams Publishing

International Standard Book Number: 0-672-32553-5

Library of Congress Catalog Card Number: 2003103645

Printed in the United States of America

First Printing: September 2003

06 05 04 03   4 3 2 1

Trademarks

All terms mentioned in this book that are known to be trademarks or service marks have been appropriately capitalized. Sams Publishing cannot attest to the accuracy of this information. Use of a term in this book should not be regarded as affecting the validity of any trademark or service mark.

Warning and Disclaimer

Every effort has been made to make this book as complete and as accurate as possible, but no warranty or fitness is implied. The information provided is on an "as is" basis. The author and the publisher shall have neither liability nor responsibility to any person or entity with respect to any loss or damages aris-ing from the information contained in this book.

Bulk Sales

Sams Publishing offers excellent discounts on this book when ordered in quan-tity for bulk purchases or special sales. For more information, please contact

> **U.S. Corporate and Government Sales**
> **1-800-382-3419**
> corpsales@pearsontechgroup.com

For sales outside of the U.S., please contact

> **International Sales**
> **1-317-428-3341**
> international@pearsontechgroup.com

ASSOCIATE PUBLISHER
Greg Wiegand

ACQUISITIONS EDITOR
Michelle Newcomb

DEVELOPMENT EDITOR
Kevin Howard

MANAGING EDITOR
Charlotte Clapp

PROJECT EDITOR
Elizabeth Finney

COPY EDITOR
Kris Simmons

INDEXER
Mandie Frank

PROOFREADER
Suzanne Thomas

TECHNICAL EDITOR
Lovisa Bedwell

TEAM COORDINATOR
Sharry Lee Gregory

INTERIOR DESIGNER
Gary Adair

COVER DESIGNER
Alan Clements

PAGE LAYOUT
Michelle Mitchell

Contents at a Glance

	Introduction	1
Part I	**Working with Office 2003**	**5**
1	Getting Acquainted with Office 2003	7
Part II	**Processing with Word 2003**	**27**
2	Welcome to Word 2003	29
3	Formatting with Word 2003	47
4	Managing Documents and Customizing Word 2003	67
5	Advanced Word 2003	83
Part III	**Computing with Excel 2003**	**103**
6	Understanding Excel 2003 Workbooks	105
7	Restructuring and Editing Excel 2003 Worksheets	121
8	Using Excel 2003	145
9	Formatting Worksheets to Look Great	161
10	Charting with Excel 2003	171
Part IV	**Presenting with Flair**	**183**
11	PowerPoint 2003 Presentations	185
12	Editing and Arranging Your Presentations	197
13	PowerPoint 2003 Advanced Features	211
14	Animating Your Presentations	225
Part V	**Organizing with Outlook 2003**	**237**
15	Communicating with Outlook 2003	239
16	Planning and Scheduling with Outlook 2003	257
Part VI	**Tracking with Access 2003**	**275**
17	Access 2003 Basics	277
18	Entering and Displaying Access 2003 Data	295
19	Retrieving Your Data	309
20	Reporting with Access 2003	325

Part VII Combining Office 2003 and the Internet 339

21 Office 2003 and the Internet 341

22 Creating Web Content with Word, Excel, Access, and PowerPoint 351

Part VIII Publishing with Office 2003 363

23 Publishing with Flair Using Publisher 2003 365

24 Adding Art to Your Publications 381

Part IX Appendixes 391

A Sharing Information Between Office 2003 Programs 393

B Business Contact Manager and Office Extras 405

Part X Bonus Hours 415

25 Using FrontPage 2003 for Web Page Design and Creation 417

26 Managing Your Web with FrontPage 433

Index 443

Contents

Introduction   **1**

Part I Working with Office 2003   **5**

Hour 1 Getting Acquainted with Office 2003   **7**

What's in Office 2003? 8
   Office Is Fully Integrated 10
   Introducing Word 11
   Introducing Excel 12
   Introducing PowerPoint 14
   Introducing Outlook 14
   Introducing Access 16
   Introducing Publisher 17
Starting Microsoft Office 18
The Office Assistant 19
   Customizing the Office Assistant 20
Typing Your Question 23
Making Office Easier to Use 23
Get Ready for the Internet and Office 24
   The Web Toolbar 24
Summary 25
Q&A 25

Part II Processing with Word 2003   **27**

Hour 2 Welcome to Word 2003   **29**

Beginning Words About Word 29
Documents and Disks 33
Entering and Editing Text 34
   Entering Text 34
   Navigating Word Documents 35
   Selecting Text 36
   Deleting Text 37
   Copying, Cutting, and Pasting 38
   To Do: Find and Modify Text 40
   To Do: Find and Replace Text 40
   Advanced Find and Replace 41
   AutoCorrecting and AutoFormatting 43
   To Do: Use the AutoCorrect Feature 44

Correcting Mistakes 45
Initial Spelling and Grammar Correction 45
Summary 45
Q&A 46

HOUR 3 Formatting with Word 2003   **47**

Simple Character Formatting 48
    Applying Fonts 49
    Applying Color 49
To Do: Insert Numbers and Bullets 51
Paragraph Formatting 52
    Justifying Text 53
    Setting Margins and More 53
    Using Tab Settings 54
    Setting Indentation and Spacing 55
    Making the Ruler Work for You 57
    Inserting Line and Page Breaks 57
    Viewing Your Document's Formatting 59
Formatting with Styles 60
Format Painter 60
    To Do: Use the Format Painter to Copy Formatting 60
Preview for Printing 61
Controlling View Size 62
A Word About Word's Wizards 63
Word Themes 64
Summary 65
Q&A 66

HOUR 4 Managing Documents and Customizing Word 2003   **67**

Understanding Document Properties 68
Using Word's Advanced Proofreaders 69
    Using the Spell-Checker 70
    Using the Grammar Checker 73
    Using Automatic Hyphenation 75
    Using the Thesaurus 77
Simple Translation 77
Customizing Word to Work for You 78
    Using the Customize Features 78
    Using the Options Settings 79
Summary 80
Q&A 80

Hour 5 Advanced Word 2003   **83**

Using Special Characters 84

Inserting Dates and Page Numbers 85

Inserting Pictures, Video Clips, and Sounds 86

To Do: Add Clip Art 86

Inserting Scanned and Digital Camera Images 87

To Do: Create and Use AutoText Entries 88

Adding Tables to Your Documents 89

To Do: Create a New Table 89

Traversing the Table 91

Inserting New Columns and Rows 92

Drawing Tables Freehand 92

Creating Multiple Columns 93

Creating Headers and Footers 95

To Do: Add a Header and Footer 95

Adding Footnotes and Endnotes 97

To Do: Insert a Footnote 97

Introducing Mail Merge 98

Preparing for Mail Merge 98

To Do: Step Through the Mail-Merge Process 99

Summary 100

Q&A 100

Part III Computing with Excel 2003   **103**

Hour 6 Understanding Excel 2003 Workbooks   **105**

Starting Excel 106

Understanding Worksheets and Workbooks 106

Entering Worksheet Data 109

Entering Text 109

Entering Numbers and Formulas 112

Entering Dates and Times 113

Navigating in Excel 114

To Do: Create Your First Worksheet 115

To Do: Format the Worksheet 116

To Do: Complete the Worksheet's Format 118

Summary 119

Q&A 120

Hour 7 Restructuring and Editing Excel 2003 Worksheets   **121**

Worksheet Editing 122

Selecting Cells 122

Editing Cell Contents 123

To Do: Correct Cell-Entry Mistakes 123

Inserting and Deleting 123

    Inserting Entire Cells 123

    To Do: Insert a Cell into a Worksheet 124

    To Do: Insert Rows and Columns 124

    To Do: Delete Rows and Columns 124

Working with Worksheet Ranges 126

    To Do: Name a Range 127

Using Formulas 128

    Excel's Primary Math Operators 129

    Using Range Names in Formulas 129

    Relative Versus Absolute Cell Referencing 130

    Copying Formulas 132

Recalculating Worksheets 133

Working with Functions 134

    To Do: Use AutoSum for Efficiency 135

    Common Functions 137

    Advanced Functions 138

Introduction to Worksheet Formatting 140

    Justification 140

    Row and Column Height and Width 140

    Font Changes 141

Making Format Changes 142

Summary 143

Q&A 143

Hour 8 Using Excel 2003   145

AutoCorrect Worksheets 146

    Finding and Replacing Data 146

Reviewing Cut, Copy, and Paste in Excel 148

Clearing Data 149

Speed Data Entry 151

    To Do: Use Data Fills 151

Smarter Fills with AutoFill 152

Designing Your Own Fills 154

    To Do: Create a Custom List 154

    To Do: Enter Large Amounts of Series Data 155

A Word About Printing 156

Adding Comments 157

Summary 158

Q&A 158

Hour 9 Formatting Worksheets to Look Great   161

AutoFormatting Worksheets 161
Modifying Styles 163
  To Do: Modify the Default Style 163
Additional Formatting Options 164
  Special Alignment 165
  Special Cell Borders 166
  Special Cell Shades 167
Conditional Formatting 168
Separating Worksheets with Tab Colors 168
Summary 169
Q&A 169

Hour 10 Charting with Excel 2003   171

Creating Custom Graphs 172
  Choosing the Chart Type 172
  Selecting Data for Your Graph 173
  Modifying the Graph 176
A Quick Chart 177
  To Do: Create a Quick Chart 177
Making Your Chart Fancy 178
  To Do: Add a Background Picture to Your Chart 179
Summary 180
Q&A 181

Part IV Presenting with Flair   183

Hour 11 PowerPoint 2003 Presentations   185

Presenting PowerPoint 185
Understanding Presentations and Slides 186
Creating a New Presentation 187
  The AutoContent Wizard and Presentation Design 189
  To Do: Use the AutoContent Wizard 189
  Creating Presentations Using Design Templates 191
  Presenting Your Work 194
Summary 194
Q&A 195

Hour 12 Editing and Arranging Your Presentations   197

Getting Acquainted with PowerPoint's Views 198
Using the Outline 200
  Adding and Importing New Items 200
  Promoting and Demoting Elements 201

Working on the Slide 201
    To Do: Edit a Slide's Text 203
        Using the Slide Sorter View 205
        Using the Notes Page View 206
    Saving and Printing Your Work 207
    Summary 208
    Q&A 208

HOUR 13 PowerPoint 2003 Advanced Features   211

    Changing Your Entire Presentation's Design 212
        To Do: Modify a Design Template 212
    Changing a Single Slide's Design 213
    Editing Individual Slides 214
        Putting Comments in Your Presentations 217
        To Do: Add Text and Text Boxes 217
    Adding Art 219
    Ordering Presentations "To Go" 221
    Summary 223
    Q&A 223

HOUR 14 Animating Your Presentations   225

    Using PowerPoint's Slide Show 225
        To Do: Time Transitions 226
        Transition Effects 227
        Setting Up Shows 228
        Rehearsing Your Slide Show 230
    Voice Narration 230
    To Do: Use Action Buttons 231
    Introducing Animation Schemes 233
    Summary 235
    Q&A 235

Part V Organizing with Outlook 2003   237

HOUR 15 Communicating with Outlook 2003   239

    An Outlook Overview 240
    Outlook Is Not Outlook Express 240
    Understanding the Outlook Screen 240
    Outlook's Folders 243
    Viewing Non-Outlook Data 244
    Mastering Outlook Mail 245
        Organizing Messages 246
        To Do: Set Up an Email Account 247

To Do: Create and Send Messages 248

Checking Mail 250

Keeping Contacts 251

To Do: Record Contacts 251

Selecting Contacts 254

Summary 256

Q&A 256

HOUR 16 Planning and Scheduling with Outlook 2003   257

Using the Calendar in Outlook 258

Navigating Times and Dates 258

To Do: Set Appointments 261

Scheduling Meetings 264

To Do: Schedule a Meeting 264

To Do: Schedule an Event 265

Managing a Task List 266

To Do: Create a Task 266

Writing Yourself Notes 267

Expanding the Outlook Bar 268

Keeping a Journal 268

Setting Automatic Journal Entry 269

Adding Journal Entries Manually 270

To Do: Record a Manual Journal Entry 270

Smart Tags 271

Summary 272

Q&A 272

Part VI Tracking with Access 2003   275

HOUR 17 Access 2003 Basics   277

Database Basics 278

Database Tables 279

Records and Fields 280

Using a Key Field 281

Looking at Access 282

Creating a Database 284

Understanding Database Objects 285

To Do: Create a Table 285

Setting Field Properties 287

Setting the Key and Saving the Table 288

Modifying Table Structures 289

Viewing Table Design and Entering Simple Data 291

Summary 293
Q&A 293

HOUR 18 Entering and Displaying Access 2003 Data   **295**

Entering Table Data 296
  Using the Datasheet View 296
  Using Forms to Enter and Edit Data 301
Summary 307
Q&A 307

HOUR 19 Retrieving Your Data   **309**

Using Data Filters 310
  Filter by Selection 310
  To Do: Perform a Filter by Form 312
Using Queries 313
  Creating a Query with the Query Wizard 314
  To Do: Build a Query with the Simple Query Wizard 315
  Using the Query Design View 318
Summary 323
Q&A 324

HOUR 20 Reporting with Access 2003   **325**

Introducing Access Reports 326
  Generating Simple Reports Using AutoReports 327
  To Do: Produce Quick Reports 327
  Generating Reports Using the Report Wizards 329
  To Do: Use the Report Wizard 331
Summary 336
Q&A 336

Part VII Combining Office 2003 and the Internet   **339**

HOUR 21 Office 2003 and the Internet   **341**

How Office Products Combine with the Web 341
  To Do: View Web Pages from Within Office Programs 342
  Viewing Documents in Internet Explorer 342
  Creating Links in Office 344
Keeping Current 345
Word Sends Email 346
  To Do: Send Email from Word 346
To Do: Send Office Documents as Email 347
Summary 348
Q&A 349

Hour 22 Creating Web Content with Word, Excel, Access, and PowerPoint 351

Preparing to Publish Web Pages 352

Office and the Web 353

Word and Web Pages 353

Excel and Web Pages 358

Access and Web Pages 359

PowerPoint and Web Pages 360

Summary 361

Q&A 361

Part VIII Publishing with Office 2003 363

Hour 23 Publishing with Flair Using Publisher 2003 365

All Kinds of Publications 366

Why Publisher and Not Just Word? 368

Getting Acquainted with Publisher 369

To Do: Create Your First Publication 370

Microsoft Gives Some Online Training 373

Filling in the Details 374

Adding Text 374

Importing Text into Your Documents 376

Using Text Boxes 377

Summary 380

Q&A 380

Hour 24 Adding Art to Your Publications 381

Your Publication's Art 382

Extra Shapes 384

Designing with the Design Gallery 385

To Do: Explore the Design Gallery 386

Getting Help with the Design Checker 387

Putting Borders Around Your Publications 389

To Do: Add a Frame 389

Summary 390

Q&A 390

Part IX Appendixes 391

Appendix A Sharing Information Between Office 2003 Programs 393

Sharing Data Between Applications 394

To Do: Drag and Drop 394

Creating Links 395

To Do: Link to a Worksheet 396
Creating Shortcuts 397
To Do: Insert Shortcuts 398
Inserting Hyperlinks 398
To Do: Convert Hyperlinks to Text 399
Turning a Word Document into a Presentation 400
Using Word and Access 400
To Do: Use an Access Table in Word 401
Outlook Letters 402
To Do: Write a Letter from Outlook 402
Summary 403

APPENDIX B Business Contact Manager and Office Extras   **405**

New Office Programs 406
Microsoft Office InfoPath 2003 406
Microsoft Office OneNote 2003 407
Microsoft SharePoint Portal Server 408
Microsoft Office Outlook 2003 with Business Contact Manager 409
The Flavors of Microsoft Office 2003 410
What Is XML? 411
Introduction to XML 411
XML and Its Impact 412
Office and XML 413

Part X Bonus Hours   **415**

HOUR 25 Using FrontPage 2003 for Web Page Design and Creation   **417**

Introduction to FrontPage 2003 418
To Do: Work in FrontPage 419
Preparing for Web-Page Publishing 421
Working with FrontPage 2003 421
To Do: Create Your First Web Page 423
Adding a Title to Your Web Page 425
Web Pages Can Hold Many Kinds of Elements 425
To Do: Finish Your First Simple Web Page 427
Different Views 429
Adding a Background 430
Summary 432
Q&A 432

HOUR 26 Managing Your Web with FrontPage   **433**

Hyperlinking to Other Web Pages 434
To Do: Add a Link to a Web Page 434

To Do: Use a FrontPage Wizard to Create a Web Page 436
Publishing Your Web Page 438
Introduction to XML 439
XML and Its Impact 440
Office and XML 441
Summary 442
Q&A 442

Index   **443**

About the Author

Greg Perry is a speaker and a writer on both the programming and application sides of computing. He is known for his skills at bringing advanced computer topics to the novice's level. Perry has been a programmer and a trainer since the early 1980s. He received his first degree in computer science and a master's degree in corporate finance. Perry has sold more than 2 million computer books worldwide, including such titles as *Sams Teach Yourself Windows XP in 24 Hours*, *Absolute Beginner's Guide to Programming*, and *Sams Teach Yourself Visual Basic 6 in 21 Days*. He also writes about rental property management, creates and manages Web sites, and loves to travel.

Dedication

I dedicate this book to two dear relatives, LaVon and Pat Scott, whose hearts are huge and who bring out the best in everyone they meet.

Acknowledgments

I want to send special thanks to Michelle Newcomb for putting up with me on this project. She was the driving force behind the work. When working with me, she needs all the encouragement she can get!

Lovisa Bedwell had to wade through all the problems I put into this book's first draft. Any problems that might be left are all mine. In addition, the other staff and editors on this project, namely Kevin Howard and Kris Simmons, made this book better than it otherwise could be. Once again, I had the pleasure of working with Elizabeth Finney, one of my many long-time friends at Sams Publishing whom I appreciate very much.

My lovely and gracious bride stands by my side night and day. Thank you once again. You, precious Jayne, are everything that matters to me on earth. The best parents in the world, Glen and Bettye Perry, continue to encourage and support me in every way. I am who I am because of both of them.

—Greg Perry

We Want to Hear from You!

As the reader of this book, *you* are our most important critic and commentator. We value your opinion and want to know what we're doing right, what we could do better, what areas you'd like to see us publish in, and any other words of wisdom you're willing to pass our way.

As an associate publisher for Sams Publishing, I welcome your comments. You can email or write me directly to let me know what you did or didn't like about this book—as well as what we can do to make our books better.

Please note that I cannot help you with technical problems related to the topic of this book. We do have a User Services group, however, where I will forward specific technical questions related to the book.

When you write, please be sure to include this book's title and author as well as your name, email address, and phone number. I will carefully review your comments and share them with the author and editors who worked on the book.

Email: feedback@samspublishing.com

Mail: Greg Wiegand
           Associate Publisher
           Sams Publishing
           800 East 96th Street
           Indianapolis, IN 46240 USA

For more information about this book or another Sams Publishing title, visit our Web site at www.samspublishing.com. Type the ISBN (excluding hyphens) or the title of a book in the Search field to find the page you're looking for.

Introduction

Microsoft Corporation's Office products have an installed base of millions of licensed users. More than 90% of the Fortune 500 companies use Microsoft Office. Microsoft designed the latest Office 2003 to be easier to use than previous versions and added more integration among applications and the Internet. You won't regret your decision to learn and use Office 2003. With the Office 2003 skills that you master in these 24 lessons, you will know the most popular application software on earth.

You probably are anxious to get started with your 24-hour Office 2003 tutorial. Take just a few preliminary moments to acquaint yourself with the design of this book, as described in the next few sections.

Who Should Read This Book?

This book is for *both* beginning and advanced Office 2003 users. Readers rarely believe that lofty claim for good reason, but the design of this book and the nature of Office 2003 make it possible for this book to address such a wide audience.

Readers unfamiliar with Windows–based software will find plenty of introductory help here that brings them quickly up to speed. This book teaches you how to work within Office 2003 as well as how to manage many of the Internet-based Office 2003 elements that you need to use Office 2003 in today's online world. This book talks *to* beginners without talking *down* to them.

This book also addresses those who presently use a Microsoft Office product. With your fundamental Office understanding, you will appreciate the new features and added power of Office 2003. Keep in mind that Office 2003 is similar to previous Office versions but includes new features, improvements, and Web-based add-ons to keep Office gurus intrigued for a long time. This book primarily teaches the Office 2003 Professional Edition, the edition that includes all the Office 2003 products and the one that sells the best.

What This Book Does for You

Although this book is not a complicated reference book, you learn almost every aspect of Office 2003 from a typical user's point of view. Office 2003 includes many advanced technical details that most users never need, and this book does not waste your time with those. You want to get up to speed with Office 2003 in 24 hours, and this book helps you fulfill that goal.

Those of you who are tired of the plethora of quick-fix computer titles cluttering today's shelves will find a welcome reprieve here. This book presents both the background and descriptions that a new Office 2003 user needs. In addition to the background, this book is practical and provides more than 100 step-by-step walkthroughs that you can work through to gain practical hands-on experience. These tasks guide you through all the common Office 2003 actions you need to make Office 2003 work for you.

Can This Book Really Teach Office 2003 in 24 Hours?

Yes. You can master each chapter in one hour. (By the way, chapters are called *hours* throughout the rest of this book.) The material is balanced with mountains of tips, short-cuts, and methods that make your hours productive and hone your Office 2003 skills.

Conventions Used in This Book

Each hour ends with a question-and-answer session that addresses some of the most frequently asked questions about that hour's topic.

This book uses several common conventions to help teach the Office 2003 topics. Here is a summary of those typographical conventions:

- Commands, computer output, and words you type appear in a special `monospaced computer font`.
- To type a shortcut key, such as Alt+F, press and hold the first key, and then press the second key before releasing both keys.
- If a task requires you to select from a menu, the book separates menu commands with a comma. For example, File, Save As indicates that you select the Save As option from the File menu. All menus in this book appear in full even though Office 2003 users can elect to display only the personalized menu options they use most.

In addition to typographical conventions, the following special elements set off different types of information to make them easily recognizable:

Special notes augment the material you read in each hour. These notes clarify concepts and procedures.

You find numerous tips that offer shortcuts and solutions to common problems.

The cautions are about pitfalls. Reading them saves you time and trouble.

Sidebars

Take some time out of your 24-hour tutorial to sit back and enjoy a more in-depth look at a particular feature. The sidebars are useful for exploring unusual Office 2003 features and uses and show you additional ways to utilize the hour's material.

When you learn about a new feature in Office 2003, a New icon will appear in the margin as you can see here. The New icon indicates that the feature is either new in Office 2003 or that the feature is redesigned to work differently from previous versions. Microsoft attempted to make Office 2003 simple to move to from previous Office versions but the new features and simpler tools make Office 2003 better than ever.

Start Your 24-Hour Clock

You are about to begin. Let's synchronize our 24-hour clocks and turn the page to enter the world of Office 2003.

PART I

Working with Office 2003

Hour

1 Getting Acquainted with Office 2003

HOUR 1

Getting Acquainted with Office 2003

Set your sights high because Microsoft's new Office 2003 helps you work more efficiently and effectively. More important, Office is a pleasure to work with. Its colorful interface streamlines your work and makes onscreen items easier to locate. Office offers integrated software tools that are powerful yet easy to learn and use. Offices large and small can use Office–based applications for many of their day-to-day computer needs, as can families and home-based businesses who want simple but robust writing and analysis tools for their computers.

If you have used previous versions of Office, Office 2003 takes you to the next step with an improved user interface that helps you be more productive in the way you use the Office products. You'll get your work done better and more quickly. Office automates many computing chores and provides tools that work in unison and share data between them. This hour shows you how Office tackles many of the standard software requirements of today's offices.

The highlights of this hour include the following:

- What Office contains
- When to use an Office product
- How Office supports different environments

What's in Office 2003?

 Office contains Microsoft's most popular applications, such as Word and Excel, in a single package. Microsoft designed the programs to work well together, and although you might not need every product in Office, you can easily share information between the products that you do want to use. Microsoft offers multiple versions of Office, such as the Office Professional Edition and the Office Enterprise Edition. Program collections such as Office are often called a *suite of programs*. You can still purchase many of the Office programs individually, building a suite of products, but the Office package offers the best deal. If you believe you'll need to use two or more of Office's products in the future, even though you might only use one now, consider getting one of the complete Office suites now to save money. You'll also have all the products handy so you can use them more quickly when you're ready.

The following is a quick overview of the primary Office programs in Office 2003:

- Word 2003 is a word processor with which you can create notes, memos, letters, school papers, business documents, books, newsletters, and even Web pages.

- Excel 2003 is an electronic worksheet program with which you can create graphs and worksheets for financial and other numeric data. After you enter your financial data, you can analyze it for forecasts, generate numerous what-if scenarios, and publish worksheets on the Web.

- PowerPoint 2003 is a presentation graphics program with which you can create presentations for seminars, schools, churches, Web pages, and business meetings. Not only can PowerPoint create the presentation overheads, but it can also create the speaker's presentation notes.

- Access 2003 is a database program with which you can organize data collections. No matter what kind or how much data you must organize, Access can analyze, sort, summarize, and report on that data. Your Web pages can reflect your latest data when you incorporate an Access database into your site.

- FrontPage 2003 is a Web page design and creation program with which you can create Web pages. FrontPage has matured through several generations into one of the most popular Web-designing programs used today. With FrontPage, not only can you design and create Web pages, but you can design, create, and manage entire Web sites and add attention-getting content. Although you can generate Web pages with many of the other Office products, Microsoft designed FrontPage from the ground up to be the best answer for your Web-page creation and editing needs.

- Publisher 2003 is a desktop publishing program that enables you to produce eye-catching documents for all occasions in all kinds of shapes and sizes. With Publisher, you can create newsletters, brochures, catalogs, business cards, and more. Your desktop computer turns into a publishing house!

- Outlook 2003 is a *personal information manager (PIM),* sometimes called a *contact manager,* that organizes your contact addresses, phone numbers, and other information in an address-book format. Use Outlook to track your appointments, schedule meetings, generate to-do lists, keep notes, manage all your Internet email, and keep a journal of your activities.

Depending on the version of Office 2003 you buy, you might or might not get every product listed here. For example, FrontPage 2003 does not come with all versions of Office 2003. When you shop for Office 2003, look through the contents of each suite version to make sure that you get all the tools you need now and will need in the future. For example, if you are fairly sure you'll be creating and editing Web pages, make sure you get an Office suite that contains FrontPage. If you doubt you will need FrontPage, get a suite without it. Fortunately, you can buy FrontPage by itself if you decide you need it later.

All the Office products share common features and common menu choices. Figure 1.1 shows the Word screen, for example, and Figure 1.2 shows the Excel screen. Both screens display the open File menu. As you can see, the two program interfaces look virtually identical even though the programs accomplish entirely different tasks. Once you familiarize yourself with one Office product menu, another Office program's menu is simple to master. The data in each program differs in format due to the nature of the programs, but the interfaces are uniform.

In addition to working with familiar interfaces in the Office 2003 products, you can insert data that you create in one program into another program within the Office suite. If you create a financial table with Excel, for instance, you can put the table in a Word document that you send to your board of directors and embed the table in a PowerPoint presentation to stockholders. After you learn one program in the Office suite, you will be comfortable using all the others because of the common interface.

FIGURE 1.1

The Word interface behaves like that of Excel.

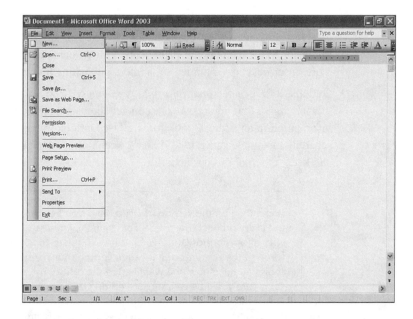

FIGURE 1.2

The Excel interface behaves similar to that of Word.

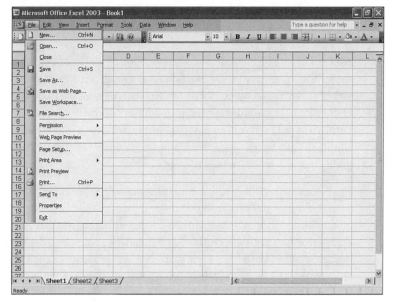

Office Is Fully Integrated

One of the most helpful features of Office is its *personalized menu* capability that adjusts menus and toolbars to work the way you do. For example, you can request that Word not

1

display all menu commands on the File menu but those commands you use most often. You can also keep all menus static so that they retain the same options every time you use them.

If you choose the self-adjusting personalized menu feature, the less often you use a menu option, the more likely Word will remove that option from the menu. Office analyzes the menu options and buttons you use most; those options and buttons you use infrequently begin to go away so that only your common choices remain. You can always access these hidden menu options, but Office puts them out of the way until you need them. The Office products, thus, attempt to keep your screen as free from clutter as possible and yet make available every feature you require.

> This book always displays all menu options although your Office installation might show the personalized menus that reflect the options you use most. You can show the full set of menu commands by selecting Tools, Customize, Options and checking the option labeled Always Show Full Menus.

The Office products are general purpose, meaning that you can customize applications to suit your needs. You can use Excel as your household budgeting program, for example, and also as your company's interactive balance-sheet system.

You can integrate Office into your networked system. This way, Office provides useful features whether you are networked to an intranet, to the Internet, or to both. You can share Office information with others across the network. Office fits well within the online world by integrating Internet access throughout the Office suite of products.

Introducing Word

When you need to write any text-based document, look no further than Word. Word is a word processor that supports many features, including the following:

- Automatic corrections for common mistakes as you type (see Hour 2, "Welcome to Word 2003") using special automatic-correcting tools that watch the way you work and adapt to your needs
- Wizards and templates that create and format documents for you (see Hour 3, "Formatting with Word 2003")
- Advanced page layout and formatting capabilities (see Hour 3)
- Numbering, bulleting, and shading tools (see Hour 3)

- Multiple document views so that you can see a rough draft of your document or the look of the final printed page as you write (see Hour 3)
- Integrated grammar, spelling, and hyphenation tools (see Hour 4, "Managing Documents and Customizing Word 2003")
- Newsletter-style multiple columns, headers, footers, and endnotes in your publications (see Hour 5, "Advanced Word 2003")
- Drawing, border, and shading tools that enable you to emphasize headers, draw lines and shapes around your text, and work with imported art files (see Appendix A, "Sharing Information Between Office 2003 Programs")
- Simple Web-page development so that you can turn your documents into Web pages (see Hour 22, "Creating Web Content with Word, Excel, and PowerPoint")

Figure 1.3 shows a Word editing session. The user is editing a business letter to send to a client. Notice that the letter is well formatted thanks to Word's advanced page layout capabilities.

FIGURE 1.3

Word helps you create, edit, and format letters.

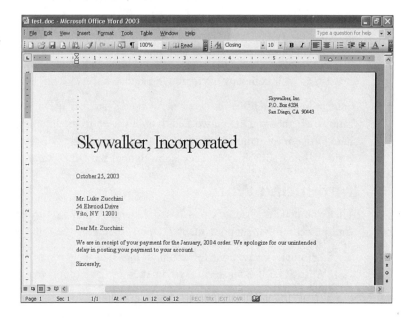

Introducing Excel

Although you can use Excel to organize and sort non-numeric information, the primary goal for Excel is to help you organize and manage financial information such as income statements, balance sheets, and forecasts. Excel is an electronic worksheet program that supports many features, including the following:

- Automatic cell formatting (see Hour 6, "Understanding Excel 2003 Workbooks")
- Automatic worksheet computations that enable you to generate worksheets which automatically recalculate when you make a change to a portion of the worksheet (see Hour 6)
- Built-in functions, such as financial formulas, that automate common tasks (see Hour 7, "Restructuring and Editing Excel 2003 Worksheets")
- Automatic row and column completion of value ranges with AutoFill (see Hour 8, "Using Excel 2003")
- Formatting tools that let you turn worksheets into professionally produced reports (see Hour 9, "Formatting Worksheets to Look Great")
- Powerful charts and graphs that can analyze your numbers and turn them into simple trends (see Hour 10, "Charting with Excel 2003")

Figure 1.4 shows an Excel editing session. The user is getting ready to enter invoice information for a sale. As you can see, Excel can start with a predesigned form. If you have worked with other worksheet programs, you might be surprised at how fancy Excel can get. The wizards make creating advanced worksheets easy.

FIGURE 1.4

Excel helps you create, edit, and format numeric worksheets.

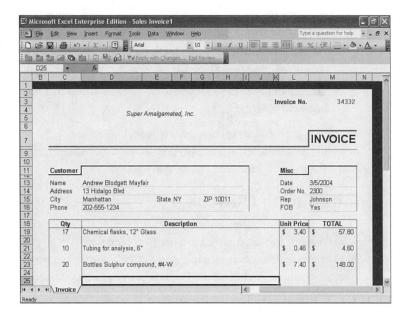

Introducing PowerPoint

Have you ever presented a talk and longed for a better approach to messy overhead slides? Have you seen the pros wow their audiences with eye-catching, professional computerized presentations? With PowerPoint, there is simply no reason why you shouldn't be wowing your audiences as well. Professional presentations are now within your reach. PowerPoint is the recognized presentation leader, and if you've seen great presentations, the chances are overwhelming that PowerPoint was the engine driving them.

PowerPoint supports many features, including the following:

- The capability to turn Word document outlines into presentation notes (see Appendix A)
- Using the AutoContent Wizard to generate presentations automatically (see Hour 11, "PowerPoint 2003 Presentations")
- Sample design templates that provide you with a fill-in-the-blank presentation (see Hour 11)
- A screen display that imitates how a slide projector displays slides (see Hour 12, "Editing and Arranging Your Presentations")
- Complete color and font control of your presentation slides (see Hour 13, "PowerPoint 2003 Advanced Features")
- A collection of clip-art files, icons, sounds, and animations that you can embed to make presentations come alive (see Hour 13)
- Numerous transitions and fades between presentation slides to keep your audience's attention (see Hour 14, "Animating Your Presentations")
- The capability to save presentations as Web pages that you can then present on the Internet (see Hour 22)

Figure 1.5 shows a PowerPoint editing session. The user is getting ready for a presentation and has only a few minutes to prepare six color slides for the meeting. With PowerPoint, a few minutes is more than enough time!

Introducing Outlook

Outlook is simple to use and manages your business and personal meetings, email, to-do lists, contacts, and appointments. Microsoft completely redesigned Outlook for Office 2003 to make the contact manager more closely mirror the way you organize your emails, schedules, and contacts. Outlook provides many features, including the following:

- The capability to track your contact information, including multiple phone numbers and computerized email addresses (see Hour 15, "Communicating with Outlook 2003")

- Management of your email, phone calls, and to-do lists (see Hour 15)

- A journal that tracks your computer activities in a journal (see Hour 16, "Planning and Scheduling with Outlook 2003")

- A communication feature that helps you schedule appointments with other Outlook users (see Hour 16)

- The capability to plan which people and resources you need for meetings (see Hour 16)

- An alarm you can set to sound before an important event (see Hour 16)

FIGURE 1.5

PowerPoint helps you create, edit, and format professional presentations.

The presentation's first slide

The rest of the slides

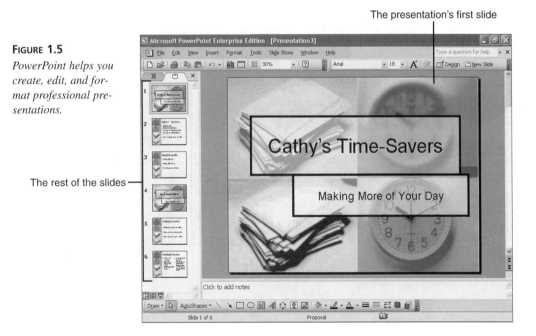

Figure 1.6 shows an Outlook calendar screen. The user is getting ready to schedule a meeting on a particular day. As with all the Office programs, you can modify screen elements in Outlook so that they appear in the format most helpful to your needs.

FIGURE **1.6**

Outlook tracks appointments and events.

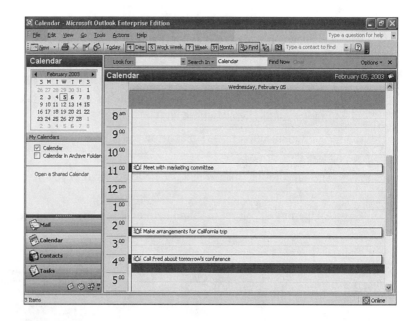

Introducing Access

If you want to organize large collections of data, such as customer and inventory records, Access makes your job simple. Access is known as a *relational database system*, and it is one of the most powerful available today. Access goes far beyond other databases in power and ease of use by supporting features that include the following:

- Simple table-creation wizards and data-entry tools that enable you to set up and enter database information easily (see Hour 17, "Access 2003 Basics")
- Complete relational database support to reduce data redundancies (see Hour 17)
- Form-designing tools to ease data entry chores (see Hour 18, "Entering and Displaying Access 2003 Data")
- Information-retrieval query tools that enable you to quickly get to the data you need (see Hour 19, "Retrieving Your Data")
- The capability to filter data rows and columns so that you see only data you want to see (see Hour 19)
- Report-generation that enables you to track and publish your data (see Hour 20, "Reporting with Access 2003")
- Sorting of data by any value (see Hour 20)

- The capability to produce custom labels for any printer (see Hour 20)
- Automatic summary provisions such as totals, averages, and statistical variances (see Hour 20)
- The capability to save databases in Web pages so that Internet users can view your database's information (see Appendix A)

Figure 1.7 shows an Access session. The user is editing product details. Notice that Access accepts and tracks all kinds of data, including numbers and text.

FIGURE 1.7

Access manages your database data.

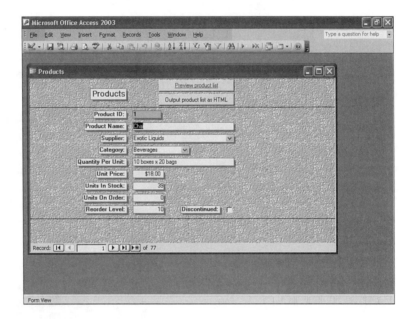

Introducing Publisher

For some Office users, one of the most useful programs in the suite is Publisher 2003. With Publisher, you can create attention-getting publications. You can easily import text and data from other Office programs into your Publisher publications. You can create stunning publications by modifying any of the numerous sample publications that Publisher provides. Publisher brings to you features that include the following:

- Create almost any type of publication from scratch or from one of the many samples, such as advertisements, banners, business cards, calendars, catalogs, envelopes, newsletters, resumes, signs, and even fancy Web pages. (See Hour 23, "Publishing with Flair Using Publisher 2003.")
- Maintain a consistent look in your publications (see Hour 23).

- Easily manage multipage publications such as catalogs and newsletters and wrap text from one page to any other page inside your publication (see Hour 23).

- Change the color scheme for your publication on the fly so that the borders, text, headlines, and other elements take on a correct color-blend (see Hour 23).

- Learn how to place, crop, size, and adjust any art you place in your publications from just about any source. (See Hour 24, "Adding Art to Your Publications.")

- Easily adjust your publication's pictures, borders, and text so your publication takes on the look you want (see Hour 24).

Figure 1.8 shows a Publisher session. FrontPage helped the user place the graphics and text in such a way that visitors to the Web pages will see a professional-looking site.

FIGURE 1.8

With Publisher, you can easily create attention-grabbing publications.

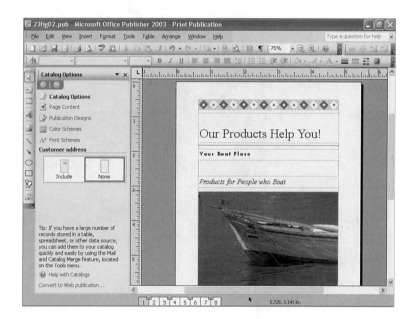

Starting Microsoft Office

Generally, you'll start one of the Office applications by clicking your Windows Start toolbar button and doing one of the following:

- Select New Office Document and select one of the icons that appear in the New Office Document dialog box (shown in Figure 1.9). Windows automatically starts the correct Office program that works with the document you want to create. The New Office Document option might appear when your Windows Start menu first opens, but if not, you'll find it on the Microsoft Office Tools menu.

You can drag the New Office Document menu option from the Microsoft Office Tools menu to your Windows Start menu button. Doing so places this option that you might frequently use on the Start menu so you'll see it immediately when you display the Start menu. You can do the same with the Open Office Document option.

FIGURE 1.9

Select the type of Office document you want to create.

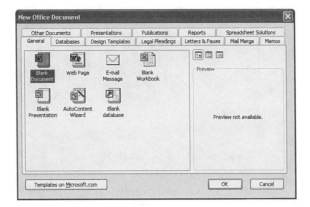

- Select Open Office Document from the Windows Start menu and choose a file you've created already with one of the Office programs.
- From any Windows Explorer-like window that displays a file listing, select any file created by an Office program to start that program and load the file for editing.
- Use the Windows Start menu's Programs option to start a specific Office program and then use that program's File menu to open an existing data file or create a new one.

The Office Assistant

When you start any Office program, one of the first features you notice is the *Office Assistant*, an online cartoon character that hangs around as you work. Figure 1.10 shows the default Office Assistant (named *Clippit*), who appears when you start an Office product.

You might see a different character, and you can change the character if you want. The next section, "Customizing the Office Assistant," explains how to change the Office Assistant's animated character.

FIGURE **1.10**

*Clippit, a helpful
assistant, remains
faithful as you use
Office.*

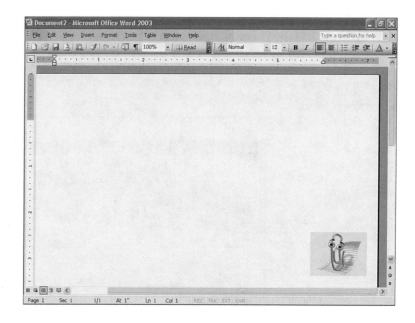

Keep your eyes on the Office Assistant as you work because you will be amused at the
contortions it goes through as it provides advice. If you have your speakers turned on,
the Office Assistant makes noises to draw your attention.

Move the Office Assistant to a different screen location by dragging the character. If the
Office Assistant is covering an area in which you are about to type, it automatically
moves out of the way.

Suppose that you want help italicizing Word text. You can search through the online help
system (via the Help menu), or you can click the Office Assistant, type a question, such
as "How do I italicize text?," and press Enter. The Office Assistant analyzes your
question and displays a list of related topics (as shown in Figure 1.11). Click the topic
that best fits your needs, and the Office Assistant locates that help topic and displays the
Help dialog box.

If you do something and the Office Assistant sees a better method, you see a yellow light
bulb that you can click for shortcut information. If you begin to create a numbered list
using menus, for example, the Office Assistant might display the light bulb to let you
know that you can create a numbered list by clicking a button on the toolbar.

Customizing the Office Assistant

If you work on a slow computer, you might want to disable the Office Assistant to keep
things moving a little faster. Also, many (most?) Office users like the Office Assistant

when they first start using Office but then tire of the assistant always moving around the screen.

FIGURE **1.11**

The Office Assistant offers a lot of advice.

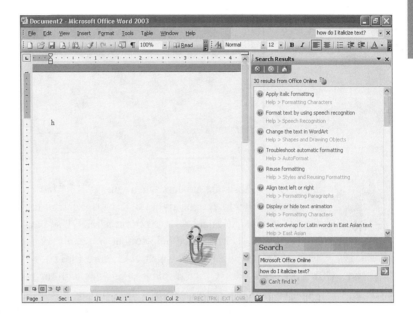

When you right-click the Office Assistant, a pop-up menu appears with these options:

- Hide—Gets rid of the Office Assistant. Display the Office Assistant again by clicking the toolbar's Office Assistant button.

- Options—Displays an Office Assistant dialog box, from which you can control the behavior of the Office Assistant (such as the Office Assistant's response to pressing the F1 key).

- Choose Assistant—Enables you to change to a different animated Office Assistant character from the dialog box shown in Figure 1.12.

- Animate!—Causes the Office Assistant to dance around its window; the Office Assistant likes to show off. Select Animate a few times to see the Office Assistant's contortions.

By default, the Office Assistant does not appear until you activate him. If you don't see an Office Assistant when you start an Office program, select Help, Show Office Assistant, and the Office Assistant appears. In reality, you might grow tired of this fun guy rather quickly. The Office Assistant is cute at first and then becomes a nuisance in many people's opinions. (Those people turn him off right after he turns them off.) Do what you want; Office 2003 is designed to provide what you need and hide what you don't want to see or use.

FIGURE **1.12**
Select a new Office Assistant.

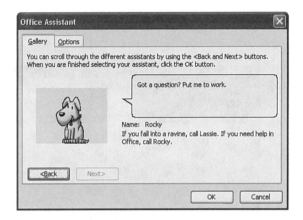

If the Office Assistant appears when you press F1 but you want to use the normal content-based help system, right-click over Assistant to display the pop-up menu. Select Options, and uncheck the option labeled Use the Office Assistant. Office then uses a Web-like, HTML-based help so that you can navigate the online help the same way you might navigate Web pages. As Figure 1.13 shows, when you display non–Office Assistant help, Office displays two panes with the help text in the right pane and a condensed Office program screen in the left pane. (You can drag the center bar left and right to adjust the width of the panes.) With the help shown in a second pane, you can keep working in the left pane while referring to instructions in the right pane.

You can type a question here

FIGURE **1.13**
Office products provide a two-pane help view.

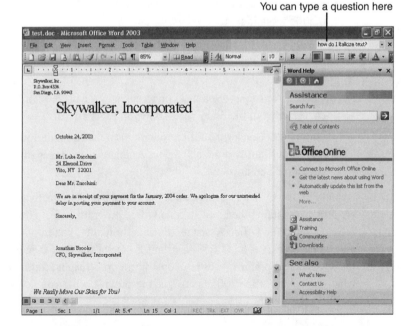

Typing Your Question

1

Figure 1.13 also shows a text box where you can type a question to the help system. When you want help and the Office Assistant is not showing, you can type your question, and Office displays a list of topics that attempt to answer your question.

Airbags for Office

In what is sometimes called "airbags for Office," several crash-recovery features are built into the Office products. If a system crash or power outage occurs before you've had a chance to save all your Office data to your disks, you get a chance when you restart the Office product to recover whatever file or files you were working with before the disaster.

Most of the time, the Office 2003 products are all smart enough to recover most, if not all, of your work. At worst, you typically have to save the recovered data under a name that differs from its original name before the problem began. Even early test releases of Office 2003 recovered files very well, which was fortunate considering how often the early Beta test versions of Office 2003 crashed!

Making Office Easier to Use

Several accessibility features make Office easier to use. You will become familiar with many of these features as you work with Office. Following is a sample of some of these features:

- Make toolbar buttons larger so they are easier to find. Right-click on a toolbar and select Customize from the pop-up menu that appears. The Customize dialog box provides access to larger icons on the toolbar buttons.

- The Office programs contain many *AutoComplete* features with which you can begin typing items such as dates, times, days of the week or month, names, and any other AutoText entries you set up. Office completes the entry for you. If you begin typing a month name such as Nov, for example, Word displays a small box with November above your month abbreviation. If you press Enter, Word completes the month name for you! If you type a full month name, such as July, Word offers to complete your entry with the current date, such as July 7, 2004. You can accept the complete date by pressing Enter or ignore it by typing the rest of the sentence as you want it to appear.

- You can rearrange toolbar buttons and customize toolbars so that they contain only the buttons you use most frequently. Office itself analyzes how you use the menus and toolbars and begins to hide any options and buttons you use less frequently to reduce screen clutter. You can always see all menu options and toolbars when you want by displaying a menu for a couple of seconds until the hidden options appear. In addition, you can drag a toolbar left or right to see hidden options. These personalized menus attempt to give you the tools you need when you need them.

• You can assign shortcut keys to just about any task in any Office product. Suppose that you often need to add color and bold to an Excel value. Create a shortcut keystroke and press it whenever you want to apply the special formatting.

Get Ready for the Internet and Office

When you're working in Word and you need to check a Web page, you don't have to start Internet Explorer to do so. Microsoft integrated Office and the Internet. The seamless Web integration lets you get to Internet data much easier than before. The Internet interface between the various Office products differs a little, but the Internet interface is always underneath Office, ready to handle the connection.

The Web Toolbar

All core Office programs contain a Web toolbar that appears when you click a *hyperlink* (underlined text that links to a document or Web page on your computer, on a networked computer, or to an Internet Web page). You can also display the Web toolbar by right-clicking on any toolbar and selecting Web from the list that appears.

If you're logged on to the Internet when you click a Web toolbar button such as the Start Page button, or when you type a Web address in your Office application's Web address bar, Office takes you directly to that Web page, substituting your Web browser for the current Office program on your screen. If you're not logged on to the Internet before using the Web toolbar buttons, Office initiates your logon sequence for you. When you click the browser's Back button, you return to Word or Excel or to whatever Office program you were running.

This back-and-forth nature of Office is a little-used but tremendous tool. Why should your workplace be littered with multiple windows, one for your Excel worksheet and a separate one for your Internet browser? Just display your Web toolbar, and you can go back and forth between your own computer's documents and data and the Web's information without ever having to start a Web browser or click buttons on your Windows taskbar.

> If you happen to be working in Internet Explorer and decide you need to refer to an Excel worksheet on your own computer, don't start Excel; just select File, Open from the Internet Explorer menu and open your Excel worksheet. Internet Explorer's menus change to reflect Excel's menu, and your worksheet replaces the Web page you were viewing! Just click Back when you're done with Excel, and you'll be right back to the Web page.

As you use Office more and more, you'll find many ways to integrate Office and the Web. For example, suppose you're giving a PowerPoint presentation and you need to reference something on the Web. Simply insert a hyperlink to that Web site and click it during the presentation. PowerPoint jumps to the Web and displays the page (assuming you're online).

A Web site does not even have to exist yet for you to insert a hyperlink to it. For example, you might be creating an in-house reference manual for your company's new Web site. You can insert a hyperlink to an address on your company site before the site actually appears on the Internet.

Summary

This hour introduced Office 2003 by showing you a little of what each of the suite's programs can accomplish. Before learning Office specifics, you need to get the big picture. This hour provided that big picture and introduced the Office tools that you will use.

All Office programs share a common interface and help system. After you learn one Office program, the others are easy to master. Some users find that they can use Office for all their computer needs.

Hour 2, "Welcome to Word 2003," introduces Word. You'll soon see why Word is considered the most powerful word processor available.

Q&A

Q I've used Word and Excel. Do I need the other Office products?

A Only you can answer that question because only you know whether you need a program to keep track of your appointments and contacts (Outlook) or your database (Access). Only you know whether you will be called to present a topic in a meeting or at a conference (PowerPoint). For example, you might need to generate simple Web pages, and perhaps Word is all you need because with Word, you can save your documents as Web pages. Nevertheless, for Web pages that you need to customize in greater detail, you'll probably want to utilize the power of FrontPage.

If you need word processing and worksheet computing only, you might not need the other Office products. In that case, you need to install only those programs that you want to use. If you have truly mastered Word and Excel, however, you will be glad that Microsoft kept the same uniform interface throughout all the Office products. This uniformity enables you to use what you already know.

Q Suppose that I want to keep track of names and addresses. Which Office product do I use?

A This is actually a trick question. Word, Excel, Access, and Outlook all track names and addresses! Word keeps track of names and addresses for mail merging (sending the same letter to many people); Excel includes a simple database feature that can track items such as names and addresses; Access's primary purpose is to track virtually any data in an organized list; and Outlook records all your name and address records. Generally, use Outlook for your names and addresses (all the other Office products can read Outlook's data), and save the other Office products for their primary purposes.

Q Is it true that the Office programs are simple after I learn one well?

A The Office programs share common interfaces, such as uniform menus and dialog boxes. After you learn how to use one Office program, you already understand the basic interface of the others. Therefore, you can concentrate on the specifics of each product instead of learning a new interface in each program.

PART II

Processing with Word 2003

Hour

2 Welcome to Word 2003

3 Formatting with Word 2003

4 Managing Documents and Customizing Word 2003

5 Advanced Word 2003

HOUR 2

Welcome to Word 2003

This hour readies you for Microsoft Word 2003. You will soon see why Microsoft Word is the most popular word processor on the market. With Word 2003, you can create documents of any kind with amazing ease. Word helps you painlessly create letters, proposals, Web pages, business plans, résumés, novels, and even graphics-based multicolumn publications, such as fliers and newsletters.

The highlights of this hour include the following:

- Why Word is considered the most powerful word processor available today
- How to enter text and navigate through your document
- When to enable Word's Find and Replace operation
- How Word's advanced AutoCorrection features help eliminate common editing tasks for you

Beginning Words About Word

Given that Word is probably the most advanced word processor ever produced for a computer, you might think that Word's interface would be complicated. Although some of Word's more advanced features can seem tricky at first, you'll be using Word's most popular and regular features quickly. Microsoft made a huge effort to streamline Word's (and all the Office 2003 products') interface so that you can get to the most common features without a fuss.

Figure 2.1 shows Word's typical screen during the editing of a document. Your screen might differ slightly depending on the options currently set on your installation.

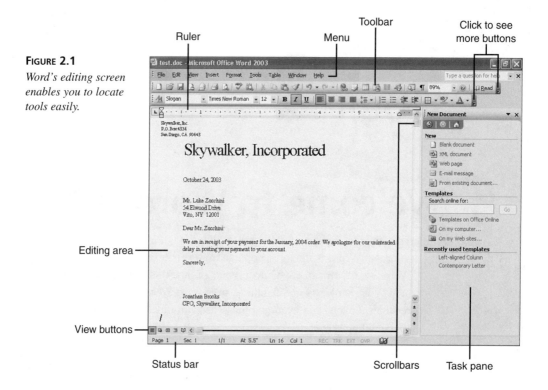

The most important area of Word's screen is the editing area. That's where the document you want to edit appears. If the document does not all fit on one screen, you can use the scrollbar to scroll down the page. Word offers several ways to view your document, but you'll almost always work inside Normal view (as shown in Figure 2.1) or Print Layout view. In Normal view—chosen from the View menu or by clicking the Normal view button in the lower-left part of the screen—more of your document's text fits on the screen than in any other view. In Print Layout view (selected also from the View menu or by clicking the Print Layout button), you gain a better perspective of how your document's text fits onto a printed page, in addition to seeing header and footer text such as page numbers if any appear.

Just rest your mouse pointer over any toolbar button, and a ScreenTip displays, identifying the button.

Word 2003 offers a new view called Reading Layout that presents documents that you want to read but not edit. Figure 2.2 shows the same letter that appears in Normal view in Figure 2.1. In Reading Layout view, Word attempts to display the letter in two readable columns, with no regard for how the letter is actually to appear when finally printed. This view is designed to display as much text on your screen as possible while still maintaining readable margins.

2

Toolbar changes
to fit current view

Click to return to previous view

FIGURE 2.2

The new Reading Layout view displays as much text as possible from your document so you can read without clutter on the screen.

Reading area

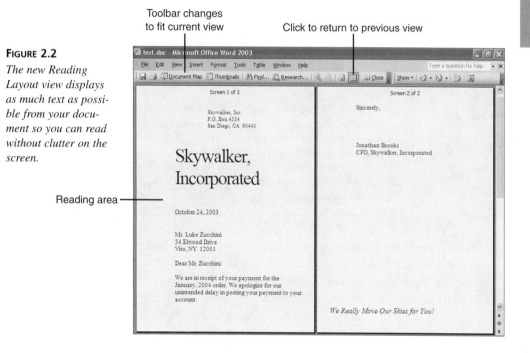

If you download *eBooks*, that is, books online that you can download in a Word-compatible format, use Reading Layout view to read them. Just click the toolbar's Read button to convert to Reading Layout. Click Close to return to your previous view.

The *task pane* is an area to the right of Word's screen that you can display or hide. You can close the task pane by clicking its Close button (the X in the task pane's upper-right corner). The task pane keeps editing tools that you might need nearby during your editing session. You can always turn the task pane back on when you want to use it. (Subsequent sections in this and later chapters explore ways to take advantage of the task pane.)

The toolbar actually consists of two separate toolbars next to each other, the Standard toolbar and the Formatting toolbar. Some users prefer these to reside on two separate rows on the screen. You can change to the more common two-row setup by right-clicking the toolbar, selecting Customize, and checking the option marked Show Standard and Formatting toolbars on Two Rows. When you separate these toolbars, the top one is the Standard toolbar with typical file and editing commands, and the second toolbar is the Formatting toolbar in which common character, paragraph, and document formatting tools await your click.

As with most Office features, you can do the same thing from different areas of the program. Use whatever way you prefer. As an example, you can save a mouse click by clicking on either of the two small down arrows (one appears in the middle and one at the right of the single-line toolbar as Figure 2.1 pointed out) and selecting Show Buttons on Two Rows. These arrows are called *toolbar options* arrows. The View, Toolbars, Customize menu option also provides the same option.

Working with the Word and other Office menus is simple. Either press Alt followed by an underlined menu key or point and click with your mouse to open any of the pull-down menus. Office 2003 features personalized menus that, over time, change as you use Word and the other Office products. The often-used menu commands appear, and those you don't use much or at all do not show up when you first display a menu. If you double-click a menu name, keep a menu open for a few moments, or click the arrow at the bottom of a drop-down menu, all of that menu's options appear.

By keeping the most-used commands on the menu and hiding the others (for a short period), Word keeps your screen clutter down but sometimes makes locating a more obscure menu option harder. You can elect to keep the personalized menus on. You also can turn on all menu options at all times (the option set for this book's figures) by selecting Tools, Customize and checking the option labeled Always Show Full Menus.

Documents and Disks

You have a lot of ways to create new documents. Most of the time, however, you select File, New to display the New Document task pane. You then can click Blank Document to create an empty Word document or select from one of the templates Word offers, such as several legal, letter, and fax templates. A *template* is a predefined page, sometimes with accompanying artwork, such as a standard letter format or a fax cover sheet that gives your document a predefined look.

2

> If you click inside Templates on the Microsoft.com area of your task pane, you can search and select from hundreds of Word templates on Microsoft's Web site. The template you select determines how your document will look; once you select a template, just type the document's content.

Word typically hides the task pane after you make a selection from it to give you more editing room. As you work, a different task pane might appear to help you with a different feature.

When you are ready to save your document for the first time, select File, Save and specify a location and filename before clicking Save. After the first time you save a document, you only need to select File, Save (or press Ctrl+S) to update your changes. To save the document using a different name or location, select File, Save As and enter a new name.

> Word documents normally end with the .doc filename extension as in Proposal.doc. Filenames can have spaces in them. You don't have to type the extension when opening or saving documents; all Office products automatically attach the correct extension.

Once saved, you can load any document into memory to make further changes or to print the document by selecting File, Open (or pressing Ctrl+O) and selecting the file you want to edit.

Editing Multiple Documents

If you want to work on two documents at the same time, perhaps to cut and paste information from one into the other, use File, Open to open a second (or even a third, fourth, or more) document. Press Ctrl+F6 to switch between the documents. You can also switch between documents by clicking the appropriate Windows taskbar button.

With several documents open, the taskbar can get cluttered with Word icons. You can clean up the taskbar by selecting Tools, Options, View and unchecking the Windows in Taskbar option. Your Windows taskbar at the bottom of your screen then shows only one Word session even if you edit multiple documents at the same time in that session.

If you're new to Word or to word processing, master editing with a single document before you tackle multiple documents at once.

Entering and Editing Text

This section reviews fundamental Word editing skills and brings you up to speed even if you are new to word processing. In this section, you learn how to do the following:

- Type text into a document and maneuver around the screen
- Copy, cut, and paste text from one location to another
- Locate and replace text

Entering Text

The blank editing area is where you type text to create a new document. Of course, Word supports more than just text because you can add graphics and even Web page elements to a Word document. The best way to become familiar with Word, however, is to start with straight text.

Two pointers appear in Word: the mouse's pointing arrow and the insertion point, which is the flashing vertical bar (also called the *text cursor*) that shows where the next character will appear. As you type, remember these basic editing hints:

- Don't press Enter at the end of each line. As you type close to the right edge of the screen, Word automatically wraps the text to the next line for you.
- Only press Enter at the end of each paragraph. Each subsequent press of the Enter key adds an extra blank line before the next paragraph. (If you type a list of items, you press Enter at the end of each item.)
- If you make a typing mistake, press the Backspace key to erase the last character you typed. You can also erase any text you've typed, not just the most recent character. If you press one of the arrow keys, you can move the *insertion point* (the text

cursor) all around the document until you get to text you want to erase. At that point, you can press the Delete key to erase whatever character follows the insertion point.

Insert mode is Word's default editing mode. When you are using Insert mode, new text you type appears at the text pointer, pushing existing characters to the right (and down the page if needed). When in *Overtype mode*, new text replaces existing text.

The Word status bar shows the current insertion mode. If the letters OVR are visible, Word is in Overtype mode. If OVR is grayed out, Word is in Insert mode. You can switch between the two modes by pressing the Insert key.

Navigating Word Documents

When you first type a document, you might enter the rough draft all at once and edit the text later, or you might be the kind of writer who edits as you go. No matter how you write, you need to be able to move the insertion point around a Word document quickly, locating just the text you want. Often, you navigate through a Word document using these general practices:

- Use the four arrow keys to move the insertion point within the current editing area.
- Click the scrollbars to scroll through the display until you view the text you want.
- Click your mouse pointer anywhere inside the editing area to set the insertion point in that location.
- If you type more text than fits in the editing area, use the scrollbars; arrow keys; and PageUp, PageDown, Ctrl+Home, and Ctrl+End keys to scroll to the portions of text that you want to see.

> Any time you start Word and want to return to what you were doing in your previous session, open the document and press Shift+F5 to jump directly to your last edit. You then can pick up right where you left off.

To quickly navigate many pages in a document, press Ctrl+G (the shortcut for Edit, Go To) to display Figure 2.3's Find and Replace dialog box and enter a page number to jump to that page. The Find and Replace dialog box is great for jumping not only to specific page numbers, but also to specific text that you want to read or edit. You will learn more about the Find and Replace dialog box as well as how the task pane helps you search for text.

FIGURE 2.3

You can quickly jump to any place in your document.

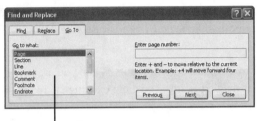

You can jump to several places

The navigation skills you learn here also apply to the other Office 2003 products. Excel, for example, has a similar Find and Replace dialog box.

Selecting Text

Earlier in this hour, you learned how to insert and delete individual characters; you will now learn how to select entire sections of text you can move or delete.

When you highlight (*select*) text, you can perform tasks on that selection. For example, you can select two sentences and underline them for emphasis. You can select text using your keyboard or mouse. Table 2.1 shows the mouse-selection operations.

TABLE 2.1 Word Makes Easy Work of Text Selection

To Select	Do This
Any text	Click the mouse on the first character of the text and drag the mouse to the last character. (Figure 2.4 shows a partial paragraph selection.)
A single word	Double-click anywhere on the word.
A sentence	Press Ctrl and click anywhere within the sentence.
A line	Click the white margin area at the left of the line.
A paragraph	Double-click the white margin area at the left of the paragraph, or triple-click anywhere inside the paragraph's text.
The entire document	Press Ctrl and click the white margin area at the left of the document's text.

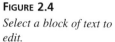

FIGURE 2.4

Select a block of text to edit.

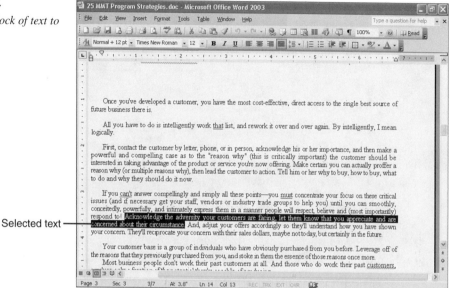

Selected text ——

If you want to select different sections of text at the same time, press Ctrl before you select each section of text. By using Ctrl, you can select a sentence at the top of your document and one at the bottom at the same time and then apply a special format to both sentences at once. Hour 3, "Formatting with Word 2003," explains how to format text you select.

To select text with your keyboard, move the insertion point to the beginning of the selection, press the Shift key, and move the insertion point to the final selection character. Release the Shift key when you're finished selecting the text.

> You can press Ctrl+A to select your entire document.

Deleting Text

Press Delete to erase a single character to the right of the insertion point. Any characters to the right of the deleted character shift left to close the gap. You can also press Delete to delete all your selected text. Furthermore, you can press Backspace to erase text characters to the left of the insertion point.

Here's a tip that even advanced Word gurus often forget: Ctrl+Backspace erases the word to the left of your insertion point, and Ctrl+Del erases the word to the right of your insertion point.

Copying, Cutting, and Pasting

After you select text, you can *copy* or *cut* (move) that text to a different location. One of the most beneficial features that propelled word processors into the spotlight in the 1980s was their capability to copy and move text. In the medieval days (before 1980), people had to use scissors and glue to cut and paste. Now, your hands stay clean.

Windows utilizes the *clipboard* concept to hold text that you want to cut, copy, or move, and Office takes the concept of the clipboard further with the *Office Clipboard*. The Office Clipboard is where text resides during a copy, cut, or paste operation. It shows itself in Office as a task pane. Select View, Task Pane, and if one of the non-clipboard task panes appears, click the arrow toward the top of the task pane and select Clipboard to display the Office Clipboard contents. The Office Clipboard can hold 24 selected items (text, graphics, hyperlinks, or any other kind of Office data), and a special Clipboard task pane automatically appears as you select text (see Figure 2.5). If you don't want to see the task pane when you use the Office Clipboard, click the task pane's Options button and select Collect Without Showing Office Clipboard. You can always redisplay the task pane by selecting from the View menu.

To copy text or other document elements such as graphics from one place to another, first select the item. Next, copy the selected text to the Office Clipboard by selecting Edit, Copy. (You can also press Ctrl+C or click the Copy button.) Then, paste the Office Clipboard contents in their new location by selecting Edit, Paste. (Alternatively, you can press Ctrl+V or click the Paste button.) You can paste the same text again and again wherever you want it to appear. If you've copied several items to the Office Clipboard (by performing a copy operation more than once during the current editing session), click where the pasted item is to appear in your document and then click the item in the Office Clipboard task pane.

When you paste an item into your document, a small Paste Options button (similar to the one on the Paste toolbar button) appears under the pasted text. You can ignore the button by continuing with your typing and the icon goes away. But if you click on the Paste button's drop-down list arrow, Word displays several formatting options that control the way your text pastes into the document.

FIGURE 2.5

The Clipboard task pane displays items you've cut or copied.

Office clipboard

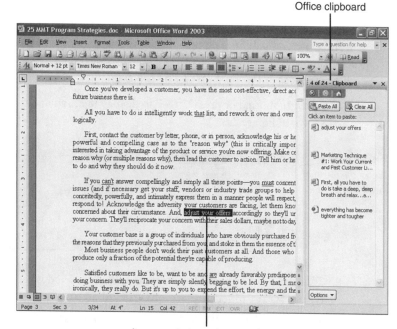

Items copied or cut appear here.

2

When you cut text from your document (select Edit, Cut; click the Cut toolbar button; or press Ctrl+X), Word erases the text from your document and sends it to the Office Clipboard so you can paste the Office Clipboard contents elsewhere. In effect, cutting and pasting moves the text. As with copying text, you don't have to paste the most recent item you've copied to the Clipboard if you've copied multiple items. Simply click the item you want to paste in the Office Clipboard task pane. You can paste the same item into several different locations.

You can also move and copy by using your mouse. This technique is called *drag and drop*. To use this method to move text, select the text to move and hold the mouse button while dragging the text to its new location. To copy (instead of move) with your mouse, press and hold Ctrl before you click and then drag the selected text. Word indicates that you are copying by adding a small plus sign to the mouse pointer while you are performing the operation.

To Do: Find and Modify Text

Use Word to locate text for you. When searching through extremely long documents, Word's search capabilities come in handy. Suppose that you are writing a political letter, for example, and you want to correct a congressional district's seat name. Let Word find all occurrences of the word *district* by following these steps:

1. Select Edit, Find or press Ctrl+F to display the Find and Replace dialog box, as shown in Figure 2.6.

FIGURE 2.6

Enter the text that you want Word to locate.

2. Type the word or phrase you want to find in the Find what text box. For example, type **district** to locate that word. Click Find Next.

3. When Word locates the first occurrence of the search text, it highlights the word.

4. If the selected text is the text you want to edit in some way, click the Cancel button (or press Esc) to get rid of the Find and Replace dialog box. Word keeps the selected text highlighted. Make your changes to the selected text. If the selected text is not the text you wanted to modify in some way, click the Find Next button in the Find and Replace dialog box to search for the next occurrence of the text.

If you click the Find and Replace dialog box's option labeled Highlight All Items Found in, and then click Find All, Word immediately highlights all occurrences of the text. This option is useful when you want to see where all instances of the text occur without locating each individual one using the Find and Replace method.

> Be careful, however, because if you click your mouse or press any key other than the mouse buttons and keyboard keys that scroll your document, Word instantly removes all the highlighted words.

To Do: Find and Replace Text

As you probably can guess from the name of the Find and Replace dialog box, Word not only finds but can also replace text. Suppose that you wrote a lengthy business proposal to an associate whom you thought was named Paul McDonald. Luckily, before you sent the proposal over your corporate network (using Outlook), you realized that Paul's last name is spelled *Mac*Donald.

Use Word to change all instances of *McDonald* to *MacDonald* by following these steps:

1. Select Edit, Replace or press Ctrl+H. Word displays the Find and Replace dialog box with the Replace tab displayed.

2. Type **McDonald** in the Find What text box.

3. Press Tab to move the insertion point to the Replace with text box.

4. Type the replacement text (in this case, **MacDonald**).

5. If you want Word to replace all occurrences of the text, click the Replace All button. After Word finishes replacing all the occurrences, it indicates how many replacements were made in a message box.

   If you want to replace only one or a few of the occurrences (for example, there might be another person with the name McDonald in the business plan whose name is spelled that way), click the Find Next button again. Upon finding a match, Word selects the text and gives you a chance to replace it. To skip an occurrence, click Find Next rather than Replace after a match is found that you want to ignore.

6. Press Esc or click Cancel when you are finished.

> If you want to delete all occurrences of a word or phrase, leave the Replace with text box blank before clicking Replace All.

Advanced Find and Replace

The Find and Replace dialog box contains more buttons. If you want more control over how Word searches for and replaces text, click the More button on either the Find or Replace tab. The dialog box expands to show more options, as Figure 2.7 shows.

> After you click the More button and the dialog box expands, the More button becomes a Less button that you can click to return to the simpler Find or Replace pages.

2

FIGURE 2.7

*Advanced options
enable you to control
your find-and-replace
operations.*

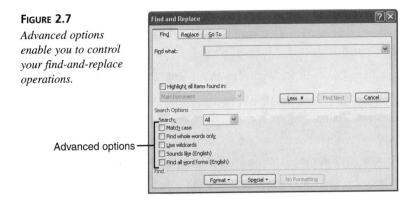

Advanced options

Table 2.2 describes each of the advanced find-and-replace options.

TABLE 2.2 The Advanced Find and Replace Dialog Box Options

Option	Description
Search	Determines the scope of the find and replace. Select All to search the entire document starting from the beginning, Down to search the document from the insertion point's current position down in the document, or Up to search the document from the insertion point's current position up through the document.
Match Case	Finds text only when the text exactly matches the capitalization of your search text.
Find Whole Words Only	Matches only when complete text words match your search phrase. If this box is checked, Word does not consider *McDonald* a match for *McD*, for example. If unchecked, *McD* matches *McDonald*, *McDonald's*, and *McDonalds*.
Use Wildcards	Uses an asterisk (*) to indicate zero or more characters or a question mark (?) to indicate a single character in your search. If you search for *Mc** and click this option, for example, Word matches on *Mc*, *McDonald*, and *McDonald's*. If you search for *M?cDonald*, Word considers *MacDonald* a match but not *McDonald*.
Sounds Like	Bases the match on words or phrases that phonetically match the search phrase but are not necessarily spelled the same way as the search phrase. Therefore, Word would consider both *to* and *too* matches for the search phrase *too*.
Find All Word Forms	Matches on similar parts of speech that match the search phrase. Therefore, Word would not consider the verb *color* to be a match for the noun *color* when you check this option.

Word cannot conduct a Word Form search if you have checked either the Use Wildcards or Sounds Like option.

AutoCorrecting and AutoFormatting

Word is smart. Often, Word fixes problems without you ever being aware of them, thanks to Word's AutoCorrect feature. As you type, Word analyzes the errors and makes corrections or suggested improvements along the way. If you select Tools, AutoCorrect and select Replace Text As You Type and Automatically Use Suggestions from the Spelling Checker options, Word makes spelling corrections as you type.

The Office Assistant is always there to guide you, but AutoCorrect is integral to Word as well as to many of the other Office 2003 products. If AutoCorrect recognizes a typing mistake, it immediately corrects the mistake.

Following are just a few of the mistakes AutoCorrect recognizes and corrects as you type:

- AutoCorrect corrects two initial capital letters at the beginning of sentences. "LAtely, we have been gone" becomes "Lately, we have been gone."

- AutoCorrect capitalizes the names of days and months that you forget to capitalize.

- AutoCorrect corrects a sentence that you accidentally typed in the Caps Lock key mode. For example, "lATELY, WE'VE BEEN GONE" becomes "Lately, we've been gone."

- AutoCorrect replaces common symbols with predefined characters. When you type **(c)**, for example, Word converts the characters to a single copyright symbol (©).

- AutoCorrect replaces common spelling transpositions, such as *teh* with *the*.

If AutoCorrect corrects something that you don't want corrected, press Ctrl+Z (Alt+Backspace also works) and AutoCorrect reverses its action. If you type an entry in the AutoCorrect list that you do not want corrected in the future, such as *QBasic* that Word incorrectly changes to *Qbasic*, press Backspace as soon as Word first corrects the word. A small bar appears beneath the correction. When you rest your mouse pointer over the bar for a moment, the AutoCorrect option buttons appear so that you can control the way the correction works.

The initial AutoCorrection word list and AutoCorrect options are preset. However, you can add your own frequently misspelled (or mistyped) words to the list. You will most certainly want to add your initials to the AutoCorrect table, for example, so that you need only type your initials when you want to enter your full name in a document.

To Do: Use the AutoCorrect Feature

To add your own AutoCorrect entries to the list, perform these steps:

1. Select Tools, AutoCorrect Options. Word displays the AutoCorrect dialog box, as shown in Figure 2.8.

2. Type the AutoCorrect shortcut, such as an abbreviation, in the Replace text box.

3. Press Tab.

4. Type the AutoCorrect replacement text in the With text box.

5. Press Enter.

FIGURE 2.8

Add your own AutoCorrect entries.

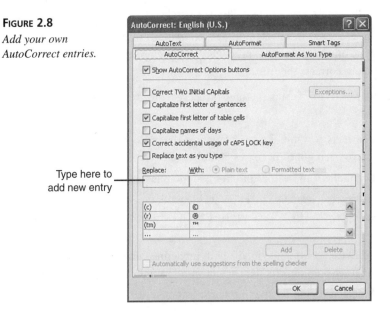

Type here to add new entry

After you enter a new AutoCorrect entry, you can begin using the AutoCorrect feature immediately.

In addition to AutoCorrect entries, Word also automatically formats special character combinations within your document as you type. For example, Word converts common typed fractions, such as 1/2, to their single character equivalents. You can control exactly which AutoFormat features Word uses by selecting Tools, AutoCorrect Options and then clicking the AutoFormat as You Type tab.

Correcting Mistakes

At any point you can *undo*, or reverse, your most recent edit or edits. Click the toolbar's Undo button. (This performs the same action as selecting Edit, Undo and is easier to use in most cases.) If you delete a character or even an entire paragraph, for example, click Undo. Word puts the deleted text right back where it was originally!

As you edit documents, Word changes its Edit, Undo menu option to reflect your last change. If you delete text, for example, the Edit menu's first option becomes Undo Clear, indicating that you can undo the clearing of text that you previously performed.

2

Word keeps track of multiple edits. Therefore, if you realize that the last three modifications you made were wrong, click Undo three times and Word reverses those three edits no matter what they were. If you reverse too many of your changes, just click the Redo toolbar button, and Word replaces the undo—in effect, undoing the undo! It gets confusing. If you click the arrows next to either the toolbar's Undo or Redo buttons, Word displays a list of as many as 100 or more recent changes, which you can choose to undo or redo as a group from that point forward.

Initial Spelling and Grammar Correction

As you type, you soon notice red and green wavy lines. The red and green wavy lines indicate that Word found a spelling or a possible grammatical error. Word is not perfect, just helpful, and sometimes Word incorrectly flags such errors when they are not really errors. This hour is already up, so for now just understand that the wavy lines mean that possible misspellings or grammar problems occur in your text. In Hour 4, "Managing Documents and Customizing Word 2003," you'll learn how to use the spelling and grammar checker.

Summary

This hour introduced Word, Office 2003's word processing product. As you saw in this hour, Word makes entering and editing text simple. In fact, Word can even correct mistakes as you type. One of Office's many productivity boosters is that all the products in the Office 2003 suite often work in a similar manner. Therefore, many of the skills you learned in Word this hour carry over to the other products. Furthermore, if you have used Word in the past, you have already seen some of the improvements Microsoft made with Word.

The next hour delves more deeply into Word and shows you how to format your document's text. In addition, you see how you can use Word templates and wizards to practically create your documents for you.

Q&A

Q Does it matter whether I press Tab or several spaces when I want to move text to the right?

A In some cases, pressing Tab and the spacebar several times seem to produce the same visual results, but you should reserve pressing Tab for those times when you want to indent or align several lines of text. You can more easily adjust tab spacing later if you want to change the indention.

Q How can I remove items from the Office Clipboard task pane?

A Either click Clear All to erase the entire clipboard or right-click over the Clipboard task pane item that you want to remove and select Delete. Remember that if you've hidden the Clipboard task pane, you need to select Edit, Office Clipboard to display the Office Clipboard task pane once again.

Hour 3

Formatting with Word 2003

This hour demonstrates Word's formatting features, which add style and flair to your writing. Not only can Word help your writing read better, but also it can help your writing look better.

Word supports character, paragraph, and even document formatting. If you don't want to take the time to format individual elements, Word can format your entire document automatically for you. When you begin learning Word, type your text before formatting it so that you get your thoughts in the document while they are still fresh. After you type your document, you can format its text.

The highlights of this hour include the following:

- Which character and paragraph formats Word supports
- Why you should not get too fancy with document formats
- When different views are helpful
- How to see a preview of your printed document

Simple Character Formatting

When you want to make a point, you can *format* your text to modify the way the text looks. The three standard character formatting styles are underline, boldface, and italicized text. Figure 3.1 shows a document with boldfaced and italicized text on the top half and underlined text on the bottom half.

FIGURE 3.1

Character formatting adds flair to your documents.

Bold   Italicized

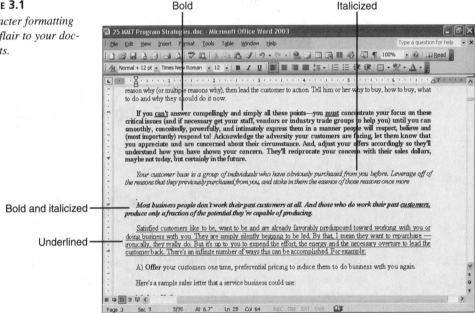

Bold and italicized

Underlined

These special formatting styles are called *character formats* even though you can apply them to multiple characters, paragraphs, and complete documents as easily as you can apply them to single characters. The character formatting styles are applied to whatever text you select for the formatting.

Express but don't impress. Too many different kinds of characters make your documents look busy and distract the reader from the main ideas in your document.

For example, select the text that you want to format and click the Bold, Italic, or Underline toolbar buttons. Alternatively, you can apply the same commands by pressing Ctrl+B, Ctrl+I, or Ctrl+U. The text you select before applying the format or the text you type after selecting a format style takes on that format. So, to underline a sentence you've already typed, highlight the sentence and press Ctrl+U. To underline the next sentence you want to type, press Ctrl+U before typing the sentence.

Applying Fonts

One of the most common formatting changes you can make is to change the *font*, or typeface, in your document. A font determines the way your characters look, whether curly or elegant. Fonts have different names, such as Courier New and Times New Roman.

Consider a daily newspaper. The banner across the top of the page probably looks similar to old Gothic letters; the headlines are more standard type. Either might or might not be boldfaced, underlined, or italicized (although a newspaper rarely applies underlining styles). Throughout your paper, the articles might contain the same font as the headline, but the headline font might be larger and heavier than the articles' font.

The size of a font is measured in *points*. One point is approximately 1/72nd of an inch. As a standard rule of thumb, a 10- or 12-point size is standard and readable for most word processing. As you type and move your insertion point throughout a document, Word displays the current font name and size on the Formatting toolbar. To change any selected text's typeface, click the drop-down arrow to the right of the Font box and select a new font. To choose a new size for selected text, use the Font Size drop-down list.

Instead of using the toolbar to apply font and other format changes, you can set formats in the Font dialog box. When you select Format, Font, Word displays the Font dialog box, as shown in Figure 3.2. You can also display the Font dialog box by right-clicking selected text and choosing Font from the pop-up menu.

Not only can you set multiple character formats using the Font dialog box, but also Word displays a preview of the font in the dialog box's Preview area. Therefore, you can select various font names, sizes, and styles and see the results before actually closing the dialog box to apply those changes. When the previewed text looks the way you want, click OK to apply those changes to your selected text.

Applying Color

You can change the color of your text. To do this, click the drop-down arrow next to the Font Color toolbar button to see the Font Color palette, as shown in Figure 3.3. Click a color on the palette to change your selected text to that color.

3

FIGURE 3.2

The Font dialog box provides many charac-ter formats.

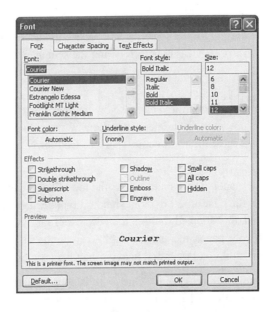

Click here to open color box

FIGURE 3.3

You can change the color of text.

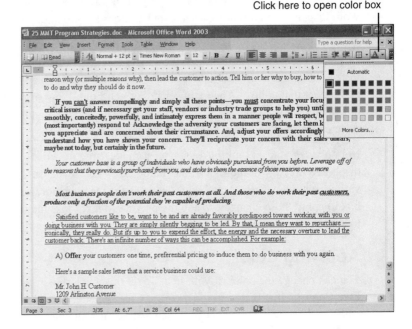

Use the Formatting toolbar's Highlight button to add color to the area behind your text. The Highlight button works well for marking important text that you want to reference later or emphasize for other readers. To use the button, select the text and then click the Highlight tool: Word highlights the text as though you marked your screen with a yellow highlighter pen.

To Do: Insert Numbers and Bullets

Word makes numbered and bulleted lists easy to produce. Assuming that the typical AutoFormat options are set (select Tools, AutoCorrect Options, AutoFormat as You Type and make sure that the options labeled Automatic Bulleted Lists and Automatic Numbered Lists are checked), follow these steps to create a formatted and indented numbered list:

1. Press Tab to start the first numbered item.

2. Type the number and punctuation, such as 1. (following the number with a period).

3. Press Tab.

4. Type the text for the first numbered item.

5. Press Enter. Word converts your previous text to a numbered list and starts the next item in the list with the number 2.

   If you don't want the next numbered item that automatically appears, you can click the icon that appears next to the first number to stop the automatic numbering or cancel it altogether for the rest of the document.

6. Keep entering numbered items. When you finish, press Enter without typing any text after a number, and Word stops creating the numbered list at that point.

In other words, to create a well-formatted numbered list, just start typing the list! Word formats and numbers your list after you enter the first item.

If you want to convert a series of paragraphs or lines into a numbered list, select the text and then click the Numbering toolbar button. Figure 3.4 shows a numbered list.

Here's another numbering trick: Before you begin typing the numbered list, click the Numbering toolbar button. Word types the first number for you and inserts a tab. You only have to complete the numbered item. Word continues to add the numbers as you type the list.

One of the best features of Word is that you can delete and insert numbered items from and to numbered lists, and Word automatically renumbers the remaining items.

FIGURE 3.4

Word helps you create numbered lists.

The numbered list ——

> Surprisingly, if you contact 100% of your customers within 10 to 20 days after buying their initial purchase, 10% to 25% will buy something else from you on the spot. Just do it as a regular follow-up aspect of your business.
>
> The additional benefits of contacting the customer are many...
>
> **It gives you the opportunity to resell your product, your service and your company to the customer —** reassuring the purchaser that he or she made a shrewd buy.
>
> By doing that for your customer:
>
> 1. You allay any "post-purchase dissonance" (buyer's remorse) that may be lurking in the mind of your customer, his/her family or associates.
> 2. You dramatically reduce — and perhaps eliminate — the refunds, exchanges or costly service expenses that disenchantment always produces.
> 3. You make the customer more receptive to your next offer.
> 4. You develop a closer relationship with your customers and satisfy their cravings to be acknowledged.
> 5. You give yourself an opportunity to recommend a buying strategy that includes continuous repurchasing.
> 6. You can solicit a customer sales referral.
> 7. You can often turn the initial sale into a renewable annual contract by adding more products or services at a discount.
> 8. You can explain the use of the product so it will be used more often and re-ordered sooner.

If you want to create a bulleted list, type the items to be bulleted, select the items, and then click the Bullets button. Again, when you add and delete items, Word automatically adds or removes the bullets.

> You can control the size of the bullets as well as the styles used for your bulleted and numbered lists by selecting Format, Bullets and Numbering.

Often, you might want to indent a numbered or bulleted list differently from Word's default location. To do so, simply highlight the list and click the Increase Indent toolbar button. You can move the list back to the left by clicking the Decrease Indent toolbar button. If you first highlight one item in the list, Word increases or decreases the indention for that one item.

Paragraph Formatting

You can change the format of entire paragraphs of text, such as the line spacing, justification, and indention of text. You can apply that format to selected paragraphs or to all the paragraphs in your document. This section describes the essentials for formatting your paragraphs so that your documents look the way you want them to look.

As with all the formatting commands, you can set up a paragraph format before typing the paragraph, and Word applies the format to the newly typed paragraph. In addition, you can change the format of existing paragraphs of text.

Justifying Text

Perhaps the most common way to format a paragraph is to justify it. When you *justify* text, you determine the text's alignment in relation to the right and left margins. Word supports these justification options:

- Left-justification aligns (makes even) text with the left margin.
- Center-justification centers text between the left and right margins.
- Right-justification aligns text with the right margin.
- Full-justification aligns text with both the left and right margins.

The simplest way to justify existing text is to click anywhere inside the paragraph that you want to justify (or select multiple paragraphs if you want to justify several) and then click the toolbar's Align Left, Center, Align Right, or Justify (for full justification) buttons. Before you start a paragraph, you can click at the left, middle, or right of an empty line of text to justify the text that you then type there.

Newspaper, magazine, and newsletter columns are usually fully justified. The text evenly aligns with the left and right margins.

Setting Margins and More

Display the Page Setup dialog box (shown in Figure 3.5), by selecting the File, Page Setup command. In addition, you can double-click the top gray area of the ruler. This dialog box enables you to control your paragraph and page margins. Enter values for your top, bottom, left, and right margins so that your text does not extend past the margin limits.

Many printers, especially laser printers, cannot print flush with the edge of the paper. Generally, one-half inch is the minimum margin size these printers allow.

FIGURE 3.5

The Page Setup dialog box enables you to set margins, page size, and page layout.

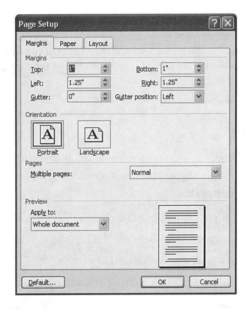

Using Tab Settings

A *tab stop* controls the horizontal placement of text on a line. When you place a tab stop at a particular location on a line, Word moves the insertion point to that point when you press the Tab key. To set tab-stop values, click the Tabs command button in the Format, Paragraph dialog box to display the Tabs dialog box, as shown in Figure 3.6. The bottom line is that a tab keeps you from having to press your spacebar many times when you want to insert multiple spaces in your text. In addition, a tab is more accurate when aligning text.

FIGURE 3.6

The Tabs dialog box enables you to specify multiple tab settings.

Table 3.1 describes each of the options in the Tabs dialog box. After you set tabs, press your Tab key as you enter paragraph text to move the insertion point to the next tab stop.

TABLE 3.1 Tabs Dialog Box Options

Option	Description
Tab Stop Position	Enables you to enter individual measurement values, such as .25" to represent one-fourth of an inch. After you type a value, press Set to add that value to the list of tab settings. To clear a tab stop, select the value and click Clear. Click Clear All to clear the entire tab list.
Alignment	
Left	Left-aligns text at the tab stop (the default).
Center	Centers text at the tab stop.
Right	Right-aligns text at the tab stop.
Decimal	Aligns lists of numbers so that their decimal points align with each other.
Bar	Inserts a vertical bar at the tab stop.
Leader	
None	Removes *leader* characters. A leader is a character that provides a path for the eye to follow across the page within a tab stop. By default, Word displays nothing (blanks only) for tab areas.
....	Displays a series of periods inside the tabs (often used for connecting goods to their corresponding prices in a price list).
-------	Displays a series of hyphens between the tabs.
_____	Displays a series of underlines between the tabs.

Later in this hour, the section titled "Making the Ruler Work for You" explains how to use the ruler to set and adjust tab settings.

Setting Indentation and Spacing

If you need to change *indentation* (the space between the page margin and where the text aligns) or *line spacing* (the amount of blank space between lines), select Format, Paragraph to display the Paragraph dialog box, as shown in Figure 3.7.

3

FIGURE 3.7

The Paragraph dialog box holds indentation and spacing values.

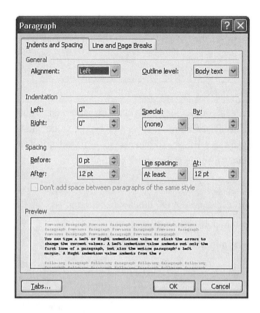

You can type a Left or Right indentation value or click the arrows to change the current values. A Left indention value indents not only the first line of a paragraph but also the entire paragraph's left margin. A Right indention value indents from the right. You can set off a particular paragraph from surrounding paragraphs, such as a quoted paragraph, by indenting the paragraph by specifying either a Left, Right, or Full (using both) indention value. As you change the indentation, Word updates the Preview area at the bottom of the Paragraph dialog box to show your setting results.

Do not use the spacebar to indent text on multiple lines because the text will not align properly. Use tab stops to ensure that text aligns at the tab.

You can determine how indentation applies itself to the paragraph by clicking the Special drop-down list arrow and then choosing (none), First Line, or Hanging. If you leave (none) selected, Word indents the complete paragraph by the Left and Right indentation values that you supply. If you select First Line, Word uses the value in the By field to indent only the first line of the selected paragraph. If you select Hanging, Word indents all the lines of the paragraph except the first line.

If you indent the first line or apply a hanging indent, your Left and Right indentation values still apply to the entire paragraph. The First Line and Hanging Indent values specify the *additional indenting* you want Word to perform on the first or subsequent paragraph lines.

The Spacing section enables you to specify exactly how many points you want Word to skip before or after each paragraph. You can also request that Word double-space, triple-space, and perform other multispacing options by changing the value under Line Spacing.

Increase or decrease a paragraph's indentation by clicking the Decrease Indent and Increase Indent buttons on the Formatting toolbar.

3

Making the Ruler Work for You

As you specify indentation and tab information, the ruler updates to indicate your settings. Not only does the ruler show settings, but you can also make indentation and tab changes directly on the ruler without using dialog boxes.

Figure 3.8 shows the ruler's various tab stops and indentation markers. Click anywhere on the ruler to add a tab stop after you select the appropriate tab from the tab selection area. To remove a tab, drag the tab stop off the ruler into the document area before releasing the mouse. By dragging an indentation handle, you can change a paragraph's indentation on-the-fly.

You can double-click the gray bar across the top of the ruler to display the Page Setup dialog box.

Inserting Line and Page Breaks

Lines and pages do not always break the way you need them to because they break according to Word's default. For example, you might want to end a page early because you want to insert a chart at the top of the next page or start a new chapter. Or perhaps you want to put a sentence on a line by itself to make it stand out from the surrounding text. The Format, Paragraph dialog box's Line and Page Breaks page enables you to control the way your document's lines and pages start and stop. When you click the Paragraph dialog box's Line and Page Breaks tab, Word displays the settings shown in Figure 3.9.

FIGURE 3.8

Use the ruler to set and change tabs and indents.

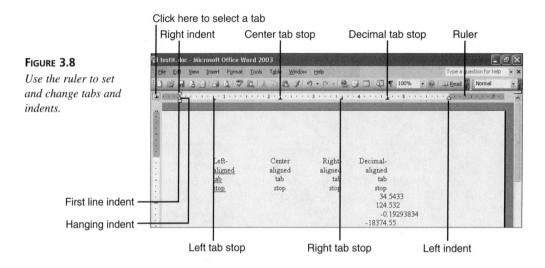

Click here to select a tab
Right indent   Center tab stop   Decimal tab stop   Ruler

First line indent

Hanging indent

Left tab stop   Right tab stop   Left indent

FIGURE 3.9

Control the way your paragraph lines break.

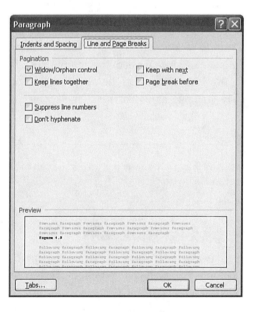

Here's a quick run-through of the options: A *widow* is the last line of a paragraph that prints at the top of the next page, and an *orphan* is the first line of a paragraph that prints at the bottom of a page. Usually, widowed and orphaned lines look incomplete. If you click the Widow/Orphan control option, Word adjusts page breaks, if necessary, so that two or more paragraph lines always begin a page and so that two or more paragraph lines always end a page.

The Keep Lines Together check box ensures that a page break never splits the selected paragraph. The Keep with Next check box ensures that a page break never appears between the current paragraph and the next. The Page Break Before check box forces a page break before the selected paragraph even if a page break would not normally appear for several more lines.

By enabling the Suppress Line Numbers check box, law pleadings and other documents with line numbers will not print the numbers on the selected paragraph lines. If you have set up automatic hyphenation, the Don't Hyphenate option deactivates automatic hyphenation for the selected paragraph.

Viewing Your Document's Formatting

You can view the existing format on text that you've already typed. Click anywhere within a paragraph and press Shift+F1. The mouse pointer changes to a question mark. When you click over text, Word displays all the information about that selected text, including the character and paragraph formatting, inside the Reveal Format task pane. This feature is neat! (Figure 3.10 shows an example.) To get rid of the formatting description, click the task pane's Close button.

List of formats

FIGURE 3.10

You can find out a lot about formats!

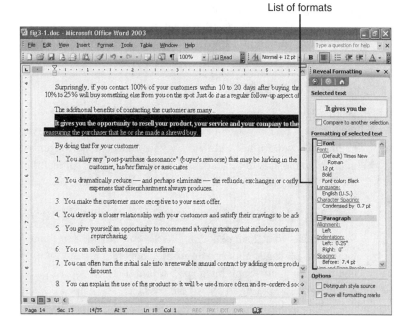

Formatting with Styles

A *style* is a collection of character and paragraph formats you can apply to selected text. Each Word document includes several default styles, and you can modify those and add your own. Each style has a name. Word comes with several styles, and you can also create your own.

Click the drop-down arrow on the Style box. (You might have to click the More Buttons button at the right of the toolbar to see the Style box drop-down list arrow.) You will see the names of the document's styles. After you select a style, Word applies it to the current paragraph and subsequent paragraphs that you type.

If you want to change a style's formatting or create a new style, select Format, Styles and Formatting to show the Styles and Formatting task pane. (You can also click the Styles and Formatting button to display the task pane.) To modify the current style, click on a style and open the style's drop-down list to choose Modify. If you want to create a new style, click the New Style button.

Suppose that you routinely write résumés for other people. You might develop three separate sets of character and paragraph formats that work well, respectively, for the title of a résumé and an applicant's personal information and work history. Instead of defining each of these formats every time you create a résumé, format a paragraph with each style and store the styles under their own names (such as Résumé Title, Résumé Personal, and Résumé Work). The next time you write a résumé, you need only to click the Style box's drop-down list arrow and select Résumé Title from the style list. When you then type the title, the title looks the way you want it to look without your having to designate any character or paragraph format.

Format Painter

Word's *Format Painter* feature too-often goes ignored but provides one of the easiest ways to replicate any kind of character, paragraph, or other style throughout your document. After you format text the way you want, you no longer have to apply the set of formatting commands to format another area of your document the same way. Instead, you use the Format Painter to, well, *paint* the format where you want to apply it.

To Do: Use the Format Painter to Copy Formatting

Suppose that your document contains several passages of quoted text throughout. Where the quoted passages appear, you want to separate it from the surrounding text by indenting, italicizing, and applying a special font to those quoted passages. All you need to do is apply the formatting to one of the passages and paint the rest as follows:

1. Click anywhere within the formatted passage.

2. Click the Format Painter button. Your mouse pointer changes to a brush icon.

3. Select the next quoted paragraph by clicking and dragging the brush until you've selected the entire text to format.

4. Release the mouse button. Word formats the second paragraph the same as the first. All margins, indents, tab stops, and character and paragraph styles now apply to both paragraphs.

To paint several nonconsecutive paragraphs throughout your document, click on the paragraph that contains the style you want to select and then double-click the Format Painter button. When you click on subsequent text to convert the style to the original paragraph's style, the Format Painter remains active. Keep clicking on paragraphs to format. Press Esc when you format the final paragraph to deactivate the Format Painter.

> The choice of creating a special quoted passage style versus applying the Format Painter depends on your preferred way of working. If you take the time to create a quoted paragraph style, you only then need to select that style before typing the next passage or apply that style to the already-selected passages. The Format Painter feature allows you to format several areas of text the same without requiring that you first create a style, but the Format Painter requires a little more work each time you use it than simply selecting a style from the Style drop-down list box.

Preview for Printing

In the previous hour's lesson, you saw how the Normal view differs from the Reading Layout and Print Layout views. The Normal view provides a larger editing area, but in the Print Layout view, your onscreen document looks closer to the way it will appear when you eventually print the document. Some people prefer to use the Print Layout view if they use headers and footers. These items otherwise remain hidden while working inside the Normal view during an editing session.

Print Preview shows how your document will look on paper. Select File, Print Preview to display the preview screen. By default, Word shows you how the current page will look on the printed page. As Figure 3.11 shows, you can click Print Preview's Multiple Pages button to display several pages. You get a bird's-eye view of your printed document, which enables you to predict print format problems without wasting time or paper. Although you cannot edit text inside the Print Preview, you can drag the ruler's left and right symbols to change the margins of the page.

Click the Close button or press Esc to exit Print Preview.

Multiple pages   Margin markers

FIGURE 3.11

View how your printed document's pages will look.

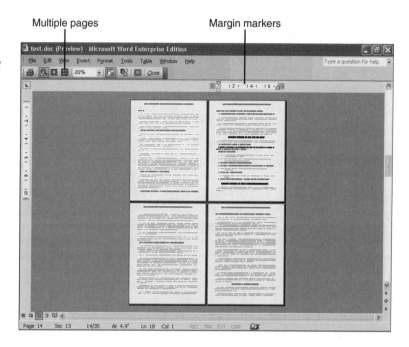

If you want a closer view of your document in Print Preview, click the magnifying glass mouse pointer anywhere on the preview screen to take a closer look at that section of the printed page.

Controlling View Size

A full page probably won't entirely fit on your screen. You can adjust the amount of text that you see by changing the size of the displayed document. When you need to see as much of your document as possible, select View, Full Screen. Word hides the toolbars, status bar, and menu bar to give more screen real estate to your document. Click the Close Full Screen button or press Esc to return to the preceding viewing state.

You can also determine just how much of your document will fit on your screen by selecting from the Zoom dialog box (shown in Figure 3.12). Select View, Zoom to display it. The Zoom dialog box enables you to adjust the display size of your characters onscreen so that you can see more text on the screen. If your margins and font size make your document's text wider than your screen size but you want to see entire lines, shrink the percentage shown in the Zoom dialog box to squeeze more text onto your screen. You can enable Word to adjust the size to fill your entire screen by selecting the Page Width option.

FIGURE 3.12

Display as much of your text as you need to.

3

A Word About Word's Wizards

This hour has discussed various ways to format text within your documents. Word's wizards, however, help you create documents with much of the formatting and styles already in place, ready to use. When you select File, New and click the General Templates hyperlink, Word displays a list of wizards and templates from which you can select.

Templates contain formatting that you can use, as well as automated buttons that you can click to format certain text elements. Wizards are more interactive and produce more customized documents than do templates.

For example, select File, New to display the New Document task pane. Select the On My Computer hyperlink on the New Document Task Pane. Click the Publications tab, and double-click the Brochure Wizard icon. Word walks you through a step-by-step procedure to create a brochure. Obviously, Word does not know the specific text you'll use in the brochure, but Word's wizard sets up a standard template-based style for the brochure's headlines, titles, column placement, and font. You then can add the specific text and format the brochure further to match your needs.

Word Themes

A *theme* is a set of predefined and unified elements that often appear in documents. Here are some of the elements defined within a theme:

- Background colors
- Heading and regular paragraph styles
- Horizontal lines
- Web hyperlinks
- Bulleted and numbered lists
- Table borders and colors

Notice that some of the theme elements apply to documents you create for Web pages, graphic presentations, and reports. In a nutshell, a theme is like a personality that your document takes on.

When you use a template or a template-based wizard to create a document, Word adds the template's formatting and styles to the blank document. When you apply a theme to a document, every theme-defined element within your document changes instantly—even after you've completed the document.

To apply a theme, either before, during, or after you create a document, select Format, Theme. Word displays the Theme dialog box, such as the one in Figure 3.13.

FIGURE 3.13

A theme changes elements within your document.

Many themes are tied to standard styles that are available within all Word documents, such as Heading 1 (for major headlines), Heading 2 (for titles), and regular text. If you utilize styles, you will learn which styles are most beneficial to your work and you'll begin to apply those styles to your documents to maintain a uniform appearance. For example, you can apply the Heading 1 style to your themed document's major title or headline, and later you could apply a different theme. Word then updates your headline to match the new theme.

Styles, Templates, or Themes?

Word and the other Office products offer so many choices; even Office gurus get confused. A *style* is a specific set of formats you can apply to text. A template is a predefined set of styles that you request when you first create a document. Until you change one of the specific template styles, that style will apply to any text that uses the style. If you want to change the look of a document that you create with a template (or with a template wizard), you must redo all the styles by hand.

A *theme* is a predefined set of styles for a document. When you change an existing document's theme (or apply a theme to a document that never had one), Word does all the work for you by reformatting all the theme's predefined styles. You can change a theme over and over until your document looks the way you want.

3

Summary

This hour explained the various format options available to Word users. Keep your audience in mind; don't overdo formats or your documents will look cluttered. Keep your documents readable as you format.

You can apply the character formats to individual characters as well as to selected text or even the entire document. Paragraph formats control the spacing and justification of paragraphs. By using styles, templates, and themes, you help streamline the overall uniform look and personality of your documents.

The next hour moves into document management and Word customization. Depending on how you use Word, you might want to change the way Word behaves in certain situations—and you will learn how to do just that.

Q&A

Q How can I type an italicized paragraph?

A Before typing the paragraph, set up the formatting. If you want to italicize a word, phrase, or an entire document that you are about to type, press Ctrl+I (or click the Formatting toolbar's Italic button) before you type, and Word will italicize the text as you type it.

Q How can I see my entire page on the screen at once?

A If you have an extremely high-resolution monitor and graphics adapter card, you can probably see an entire document page when you select the full-screen view with View, Full Screen. If you want to see the toolbars, menu, and status bar, however, you probably have to adjust the display by selecting View, Zoom. After you display the Zoom dialog box, click the Page Width option to enable Word to fit the text within your screen width, or you can control the width using the Percent option. The only other way to see an entire page is to select File, Print Preview to enter the Print Preview mode; in Print Preview mode, you can make simple margin adjustments but no text changes.

HOUR 4

Managing Documents and Customizing Word 2003

This hour teaches you how to work more globally with your documents than the previous two hours. Instead of concentrating on specific editing skills, you learn how to manage your document properties. Word manages your documents well and tracks changes that are made to the document. This tracking really comes in handy if you work in a group environment.

The proofing tools in Word are powerful and work as you type. You learned a little about the spelling checker in Hour 2, "Welcome to Word 2003," but in this hour you'll learn to control the spell-checker as well as use Word's grammar, hyphenation, and synonym features.

The highlights of this hour include the following:

- What document properties are
- Where to locate and change a document's properties
- How to use the spelling and grammar checkers
- Why you need to proof documents manually despite the proofing tools in Word
- How to customize Word to behave the way you want

Understanding Document Properties

Each Word document (as well as the other Office 2003 documents) has properties. A *property* is information related to a particular document, such as the author's name and creation date. If you do not specify properties, Word adds its own to your document. You see the Properties dialog box when you select File, Properties (see Figure 4.1).

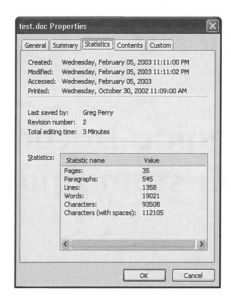

The pages in the Properties dialog box provide the following information:

- *General*—Contains the document's file information, including the date and time you created, last modified, and last accessed the document.
- *Summary*—Tracks a document title, author (the name to which the software is registered by default), keywords, and comments you enter about the document.
- *Statistics*—Tracks the document's numeric statistics, such as character, word, page counts, and total editing time.
- *Contents*—Describes the parts of your document, such as the header, body, and footer.
- *Custom*—Keeps track of customized information that you specify and want to track. You can use this page to monitor customized properties such as the department responsible for creating or maintaining the document, the name of a project group that works on the document, and the person responsible for typing the document's information.

As you add items to the Properties Custom tab, indicate the item's data type (such as text or date) so that Word can properly format the property value that you want to track. The Custom page is great for using in departments in which many people see and edit the same set of documents.

Some properties are available elsewhere in Word. You can find a document's statistics, such as word and paragraph counts, for example, by selecting Tools, Word Count. Often, you can select from a menu option more quickly than you can display the document properties.

You might find that the Word Count toolbar comes in handy. When you select Tools, Word Count and click the Show Toolbar button, Word displays a floating toolbar that enables you to keep track of the word count as you type. Every time you click the Word Count's Recount button, the word count is recalculated. The Word Count toolbar can also display a count of the lines, pages, and paragraphs, depending on your selection.

If you create numerous documents and continually search through your files for particular ones, consider adding search keywords to the Properties Summary tab. Then, you can more quickly find that document using the Advanced Search option in the Open dialog box.

4

Using Word's Advanced Proofreaders

Word offers these proofreading features for your writing:

- *Spell-checker*—Checks your document's spelling either from beginning to end after you finish creating your document or while you type.
- *Grammar checker*—Checks your document's grammar either from beginning to end or as you enter text into the document.
- *Thesaurus*—Provides synonyms for the selected word.
- *Hyphenation*—Automatically hyphenates words at the end of lines, when appropriate, either from beginning to end or as you enter the text into the document.

Word's built-in proofreading tools do not eliminate your proofing responsibilities! No matter how good Word is, Word cannot match human skills when deciphering the written language. Word's spell-checker has no problem with this sentence, for example:

Wee road two the see too sea the waives.

The proofreading tools work only as guides to find those problems you might have missed during your own extensive proofing.

Another important reason to learn the proofreading tools is that the other Office products use similar features. Therefore, after you learn how to use Word's proofreading tools, you also know how to use the tools for an Excel worksheet or an Access database.

Using the Spell-Checker

By default, Word automatically checks your spelling and your grammar as you type your document. You can turn off this option (or turn it back on if it's off) by selecting Tools, Options, Spelling and Grammar. Click the options labeled Check Spelling as You Type and Check Grammar as You Type. Any time you see red wavy underlines or green wavy underlines as you type, Word is letting you know about a possible spelling problem (the red line) or grammar problem (the green line).

Occasionally, you will be typing text inside Word (and the other Office products) and a blue dotted line appears beneath the word. The blue line indicates a *smart tag*, which often is a proper name (such as a person's first name or a city) or date. You will learn more about smart tags in Part V, "Organizing with Outlook 2003." The smart tags indicate actions that you might want to perform on the tagged word or phrase, such as add a person to your Outlook contact list.

Depending on the options you (or someone else) have set, your version of Word might not check both spelling and grammar as you type. Therefore, if you don't see any wavy lines, you should check your document's spelling and grammar after you have typed the document so that you don't miss anything. In addition, you might not see wavy lines if Word's AutoCorrect feature automatically replaced all your misspellings with corrected entries.

To turn on and off the Check Spelling as You Type option, choose Tools, Options, and then click the Spelling & Grammar tab. On that page, check the Check Spelling as You Type check box.

When you see a red wavy line, you can correct the problem in these ways:

- Edit the misspelling manually.
- Right-click the misspelling to display the pop-up menu shown in Figure 4.2. Word offers you the following options:

FIGURE 4.2

Right-click to select your spell-correction choice when Word finds a misspelling.

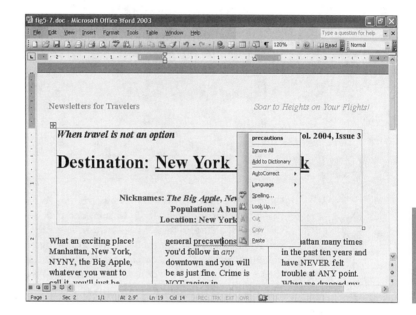

- *Suggested corrections*—Word displays a list of possible spellings at the top of the pop-up menu. When you select one, Word replaces the incorrect spelling with your selected word.
- *Ignore All*—Ignore all subsequent similar misspellings (in case you want to type foreign words or formal names, but you don't want to add those words to Word's spelling dictionaries).
- *Add to Dictionary*—Add the word to Word's dictionary so that Word no longer flags the word as misspelled.
- *AutoCorrect*—Select AutoCorrect and choose a correct word to add the misspelling to the AutoCorrect entries so that Word subsequently corrects the word for you on-the-fly.
- *Language*—Specify a different language dictionary to use (useful if you write for the medical or a technical community and you maintain several dictionaries for each subject).

- *Spelling*—Display Word's more comprehensive Spelling dialog box, as shown in Figure 4.3.

FIGURE 4.3

The Spelling dialog box offers more options than the pop-up menu.

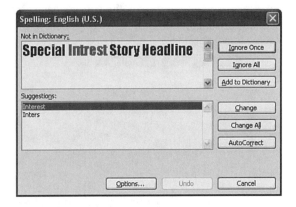

> Word enables you to easily remove words that you accidentally add to your spelling dictionary. Select Tools, Options and click the Spelling & Grammar tab. Click the Custom Dictionaries button. Select the dictionary from which you want to delete (most probably the Custom dictionary, which is the default unless you have created a new customized dictionary), and then click the Modify button. Word displays the dictionary's words in a text box so that you can delete the word or words you no longer want. (You can also edit any existing words or add new words.) Click the Save toolbar button. You must also turn on automatic spell-checking by displaying the Spelling & Grammar page once again, clicking the option labeled Check Spelling as You Type, and then clicking OK in each of the displayed dialog boxes.

- Ignore the misspelling and leave the red wavy line.
- Ignore the misspelling, but check the entire document's spelling after you finish typing the document.

The Spelling dialog box appears when you click the pop-up menu's Spelling option. In addition, the dialog box appears when you select Spelling and Grammar from the Tools menu. Table 4.1 lists the options in the Spelling dialog box.

> When you check the spelling of your document by choosing Tools, Spelling and Grammar, Word checks from the cursor's current position down to the end of your document. Word then shows a message box asking whether you

want to check starting at the beginning of the document. If you want Word to check your entire document's spelling in one step (assuming that you have turned off the automatic spell-checking that occurs as you type), move your cursor to the top of your document (by pressing Ctrl+Home) before launching the spell-checking to check from the beginning to end of the document in one step.

TABLE 4.1   Spelling Dialog Box Options

Option	Description
Ignore Once	Tells Word to ignore this misspelling but continues to flag the misspelling in the future if it occurs.
Ignore All	Tells Word to ignore all occurrences of this misspelling in this document.
Add to Dictionary	Adds the word to Word's spelling dictionary. This is the same dictionary that you add to when you select the Add to Dictionary option on a word that Word thinks is misspelled.
Change	Corrects only this occurrence of the misspelled word.
Change All	Corrects all occurrences of this misspelled word.
AutoCorrect	Adds the misspelling and selected correction to your collection of AutoCorrect entries. You can also select AutoCorrect option to add the correction to your list of AutoCorrect entries so that Word corrects the spelling automatically in subsequent editing sessions.
Options	Displays the Spelling & Grammar options page (shown in Figure 4.4), which you can use to modify the behavior of the spelling and grammar checker.

Using the Grammar Checker

When you see a green wavy line beneath a word, Word is warning you about a possible grammar problem. Figure 4.5 shows the pop-up menu Word displays when you right-click a green wavy-lined word.

If you don't want Word to flag possible grammatical problems as you edit your document, select Tools, Options, Spelling & Grammar and uncheck the option labeled Check Grammar as You Type. Word will not mark grammar problems as you enter text. However, after you finish your document, select Tools, Spelling and Grammar (F7 is the shortcut key) to check the grammar for your entire document. You might want to keep Office Assistant turned on if you check grammar all at once. Microsoft added a lot of plain-spoken, grammar-correcting advice to the Office Assistant's repertoire of helpful topics.

FIGURE 4.4
Change the Spelling &
Grammar options in
this dialog box.

 Although many people consider the Office Assistant a nuisance, the Office
Assistant shines when used in conjunction with the grammar checker.

FIGURE 4.5
Word displays a pop-
up menu when you
right-click a word with
a green wavy under-
line.

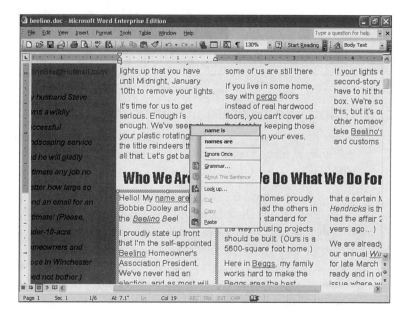

As with the spelling pop-up menu, you can replace a grammar problem with the suggested word or words or ignore the suspected problem (just because Word indicates a problem does not necessarily mean that one exists), or you can start the full grammar-checking system to correct that problem as well as the rest of the document.

When you check a document's grammar from the Tools, Spelling and Grammar option (to check the entire document) or by selecting the full grammar check from the pop-up menu, Word displays the same Spelling & Grammar dialog box you see when you check for spelling only. As Figure 4.6 shows, however, the Office Assistant can chime in with its advice as well.

FIGURE 4.6

Select your grammar-correction choice when Word finds a problem.

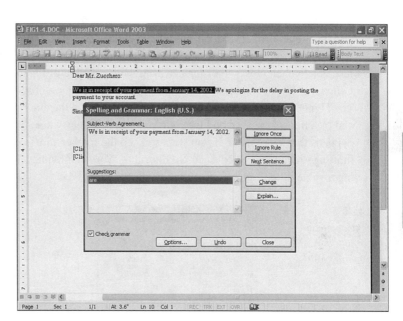

Using Automatic Hyphenation

As long as you turn on automatic hyphenation from the Tools, Language, Hyphenation menu option, Word can hyphenate your text as you type, or you can manually hyphenate your entire document. Word supports three kinds of hyphens:

- *Regular hyphens*, which Word uses to break words at the end of lines (when needed) to maintain proper document formatting. You must turn on automatic hyphenation by selecting Tools, Language, Hyphenation and checking the option labeled Automatically Hyphenate Document.

- *Optional hyphens*, which break special words (AutoCorrect becomes Auto-Correct, for example) only if those words appear at the end of lines. (Press Ctrl+- (hyphen) to indicate where you want the optional hyphen as you type the word.)
- *Nonbreaking hyphens*, which keep certain hyphenated words together at all times; if the hyphenated name Brian-Kent appears at the end of a line and you want to prevent Word from breaking apart the names at the end of a line, for example, press Ctrl+Shift+- (hyphen).

You need to indicate optional and nonbreaking hyphens only when you type special words that Word would not typically recognize, such as company names and special terms.

The area that Word checks for possible hyphenation, toward the end of a line, is called the *hyphenation zone*. You can adjust the size of the hyphenation zone so that Word inserts a hyphen closer to or further from the right edge of the line. Select Tools, Language, Hyphenation to display the Hyphenation dialog box, as shown in Figure 4.7. The Hyphenation Zone field enables you to determine the amount of space between the end of a line's last word and the right margin. A higher value reduces the number of hyphens that Word adds. If you want to keep the hyphenation to a minimum, consider limiting the number of consecutive lines that Word can hyphenate at one time by specifying a value in the Limit consecutive hyphens to text box.

FIGURE 4.7

Specify automatic hyphenation to let Word do the work.

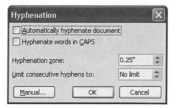

To hyphenate your document manually after you have created it, select Tools, Language, Hyphenation and click Manual. Word prompts for your approval at each hyphen location.

If you want to stop Word from hyphenating particular paragraphs, select those paragraphs, and then select Format, Paragraph, click the Line and Page Breaks tab, and check the Don't Hyphenate option.

If you export your document text to another program (such as to a Web page), do not have Word hyphenate your document. The target system that produces the final output should control the hyphenation, if possible. If you have Word hyphenate your document, hyphens might appear in the middle of lines if the typesetter fails to eliminate all of Word's hyphens.

Using the Thesaurus

When you just can't seem to think of a particular word, type a *synonym*, which is a different word whose meaning is similar to the meaning you want. Then, solicit Word's thesaurus for a suggestion. To see a list of synonyms, first click anywhere in the word and then choose Tools, Language, Thesaurus. Alternatively, press Shift+F7. Either way, Word displays the Thesaurus task pane, as shown in Figure 4.8.

FIGURE 4.8

Find synonyms fast using the task pane.

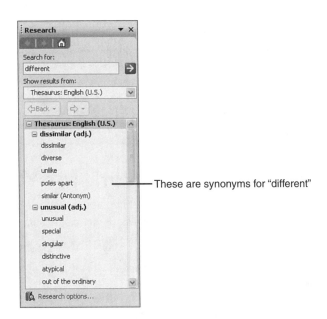

These are synonyms for "different"

4

From the Thesaurus task pane, you can select a replacement word. Word automatically inserts the synonym when you click the down arrow next to the task pane's synonym. Alternatively, use the replacement word list to look up additional synonyms. If you cannot find a good synonym for dissolve but one of the replacement words for dissolve is liquefy, for example, look up synonyms for liquefy. Do so by clicking liquefy in the task pane. Through this link of related words, you might find the synonym for which you are looking.

Simple Translation

Word provides simple translation of words, phrases, and even your entire document. Depending on which dictionaries were installed on your system, you can translate between your default language and several others such as Spanish and French.

To translate, highlight a word or phrase, right-click over the selection, and select Translate from the pop-up menu. Word displays the Translate task pane. (If you want to translate a word not found in your document, you can enter the word to translate at the top of the Translate task pane window.) Select the translation you desire from the Dictionary list, such as English to Spanish. Word translates the text and displays the result in area below; just click the word in the lower pane to see its translated offerings. Typically, a word has several translations depending on its context.

> Computer translation is helpful but certainly not guaranteed to be 100 percent accurate. So many idioms, phrases, and word combinations exist that computer technology simply cannot yet translate perfectly. In addition, be warned that the first time you use translation, Word pauses and installs the feature. Depending on the options you chose when you installed Office, you might need your Office CD-ROM for the install procedure.

Customizing Word to Work for You

If you don't like the way Word does something, you can usually customize Word to act the way you want. The Tools menu contains options that enable you to customize Word:

- *Customize*—Enables you to change the layout of Word's toolbars and menus
- *Options*—Enables you to control the behavior of most of Word's automatic and manual editing features

Using the Customize Features

Figure 4.9 shows the dialog box that appears when you select Tools, Customize and click the Options tab.

The Toolbar tab enables you to specify exactly which toolbars you want to see, if any, during your editing sessions. Too many toolbars can clutter your screen and take away editing space, but different toolbars are useful at different times. Display the Tables and Borders toolbar, for example, any time you want to create or edit tables in your documents. (The toolbar selection is also available from the View, Toolbars menu option.)

Most people modify the options on the Commands tab when they want to add or remove an item from the menus in Word. To do this, select the menu from the Categories list, and Word displays that menu's items in the Commands list. You then can change a menu label or add one from the list.

FIGURE 4.9

Customize toolbars and menus.

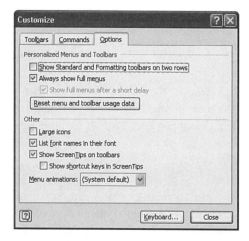

The Options tab includes controls that enable you to increase the size of the toolbar icons to read them more easily, to determine whether you want to see ScreenTips, and to determine whether you want shortcut keys attached to those ScreenTips. From the Options page of the Customize dialog box, you can control the way Word displays menu options and the two most common toolbars, the Standard and Formatting toolbars.

Using the Options Settings

You can choose Tools, Options to display the Options dialog box. This dialog box is the Library of Congress of Word options. Using the Options dialog box, you can modify the behavior of these Word features:

- *View*—Changes the way Word displays documents and windows.
- *General*—Determines colors, animation, behavior, and the measurement standard (such as inches or centimeters).
- *Edit*—Changes the way Word responds during your editing sessions.
- *Print*—Determines several printing options.
- *Save*—Specifies how you want Word to save document changes.
- *Spelling & Grammar*—Lists several spell-checking and grammar-checking settings that you can change. This is one place where you can turn these options on or off.
- *File Locations*—Enables you to set disk-drive locations for common files.
- *Compatibility*—Lists a plethora of options you can change to make Word look and feel like other word processors, including previous versions of Word.

- *User Information*—Holds the name, initials, and address of the registered party for use with document summaries and automatic return addresses.
- *Security*—Enables you to specify passwords for encryption and for sharing the document.
- *Track Changes*—Determines the format Word uses when you make changes to documents in a group environment or when you want to track several revisions for the same document. (Word can keep track of multiple versions of a document.)

Summary

This hour explained how to better manage your Word documents through the use of document properties. The document properties contain count statistics as well as other pertinent information that stays with your documents. If you work in an office environment, the properties help maintain order when many people edit the same document.

Part of managing your documents is proofing them to make them more readable and correct. The proofing tools in Word include a spell-checker, grammar checker, hyphenation capabilities, and thesaurus. Although these tools don't replace human proofreading, they can help you locate problems.

Finally, you can customize almost any part of Word. This hour gave you just a glimpse of the many modifications that you can make to Word's settings. Take the time to peruse the pages inside the Options dialog box. Even advanced Word users forget some of the options that can make their editing lives simpler. Check these Options dialog box screens frequently as you learn Word, and you will make Word work the way you want it to.

The next hour wraps up Word as you learn about its more advanced capabilities.

Q&A

Q Does Word update my document-property values for me?

A In some cases, Word updates your document's property values. As you type words into your document, for example, Word updates that document's word count. You must specify other user-specific properties, such as the document-search keywords and comments.

Q Why should I wait until after I create a document to proof it?

A Most Word users prefer to turn on the automatic spell-checker but wait until their documents are finished before hyphenating and checking the grammar. During the editing process, edits frequently change hyphenation locations; depending on your

computer's speed, Word might slow down considerably to update changed hyphens when you change lines. Additionally, the grammar checker has to work constantly as you create your document, not only slowing down your edits but also indicating bad grammar in the places where you might be typing rough-draft material.

Q Should I modify Word settings if several people use the same computer?

A If you share a computer with others, you should not customize Word without telling the others what you have done. As a group, you might determine that certain Word options are better defined than others, but be sure to make customization changes only with the consent of others. Otherwise, the next person who uses Word might think Word no longer can check spelling, when in fact you have only turned off the spell-checker temporarily.

4

HOUR 5

Advanced Word 2003

This hour wraps up your Word coverage by giving you an idea of Word's uncommon features and advanced capabilities. Despite being advanced, these features are not difficult to use.

You will find a lot of tidbits throughout this chapter that you will use as you write. From inserting special characters to creating multiple-column newsletters, Word offers something for everybody's writing needs.

The highlights of this hour include the following:

- How to type special characters that don't appear on your keyboard
- How to insert the date, time, and page numbers in your documents
- When to add AutoText entries and when to add AutoCorrect entries
- How to prepare tables in your documents
- How to convert a single-column document into multiple columns
- What headers, footers, footnotes, and endnotes are all about
- What mail merge is all about

Using Special Characters

Symbols are special characters that don't appear on the standard keyboard, such as ¿ and £. To enter special symbols, select Insert, Symbol to display the Symbol dialog box, shown in Figure 5.1.

Click here to display other sets of symbols

FIGURE 5.1

Find a symbol you want to insert.

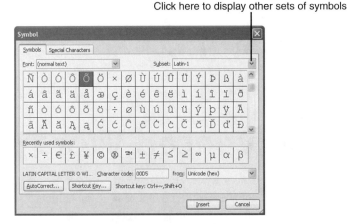

If you don't see the symbol you want to insert, select a different font from the Font drop-down list. Many fonts, such as *Wingdings*, supply special symbols from which you can choose.

> If you find yourself inserting the same symbol over and over again, consider adding that symbol to your AutoCorrect list. Click the Insert, Symbol dialog box's AutoCorrect button to see the AutoCorrect dialog box (in which Word has already inserted the symbol). Type the AutoCorrect entry that you will use to produce the special symbol, press Enter, and you have created the AutoCorrect entry for that symbol.

You can assign a shortcut key to any symbol. Click the Symbol dialog box's Shortcut Key button, type a shortcut keystroke (such as Alt+Shift+S), and press Enter. Word then assigns that shortcut keystroke to the special symbol. Subsequently, you won't have to display the Symbol dialog box to insert special symbols but will only have to press the appropriate keystroke.

Many special characters already have AutoCorrect and shortcut-key entries. If you want to see these predefined symbols, click the Symbol dialog box's Special Characters tab to display the Special Characters page, as shown in Figure 5.2. Scroll through the list to see which symbols already have a keyboard shortcut assigned.

FIGURE 5.2
Word comes predefined with many shortcuts for symbols.

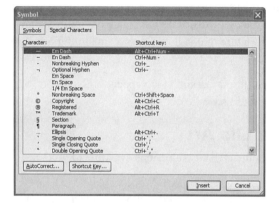

Inserting Dates and Page Numbers

In addition to special characters, you can insert the date and time at the cursor's current position. To do this, select Insert, Date and Time and then click the date and time format from Word's selection list. If you click the Update Automatically option, Word constantly updates the date and time. If you leave the Update Automatically option unchecked, Word maintains the original date and time in the document.

Press Shift+Alt+D to insert the date at the cursor's location.

5

If you want Word to insert page numbers at the top or bottom of the document's printed pages, select Insert, Page Numbers. Word displays the Page Numbers dialog box. Select from the Position list to indicate whether you want the page numbers to appear at the top or bottom of the document pages. In addition, you can control the left, center, right, or inside facing-page alignment from the Alignment list box.

Word can format page numbers in several formats, such as 1, -1-, use Roman numerals, and even letters of the alphabet. Click Format to select from the various page-number format options.

Inserting Pictures, Video Clips, and Sounds

A *clip* or *clip art* is an image, audio, or video file that you can add to your documents to spruce them up. To add a clip to a document, select Insert, Picture, From File to display the Insert Picture dialog box. Locate the image on your disk and click Insert to insert the image. The Insert Picture dialog box shows a small thumbnail sample of your graphic image.

Several collections of images and video appear both on your computer and on the Web. You can search and use specific clips.

To Do: Add Clip Art

To add a clip from the clip-art collections available to you, perform these steps:

1. Select Insert, Picture, Clip Art. Word displays the Clip Art task pane. As you familiarize yourself with the clip-art collections and add clips and graphics to your own computer, you will begin to utilize the Insert Clip Art task pane's search features to more quickly locate the media object you want to insert.

2. Type a subject, such as house, in the Search field.

3. Open the Search In list to select your own computer or the Web to locate a clip you want to use. If you leave the option showing All Collections, Word searches your computer as well as the Web for any available clips that match the subject you're looking for.

4. Click the Go button to display a list of pictures, video clips, and sounds that match your search criteria, as shown in Figure 5.3.

5. Select the image or clip to insert into your document.

> If your own computer has several picture, video, and sound clips, you can add your computer's clips to the list that the Office programs search by clicking the Organize Clips link at the bottom of the Clip Art task pane and instructing the Clip Organizer to search your computer and include those clips in future clip-art searches.

You can display inserted graphic images from the Print Layout view or from the Print Preview screen. If you insert a sound or video clip, Word places an appropriate icon at the location. When you or someone else views your document in Word (or on the Internet even if you create Web pages inside Word), that clip plays.

Search subject

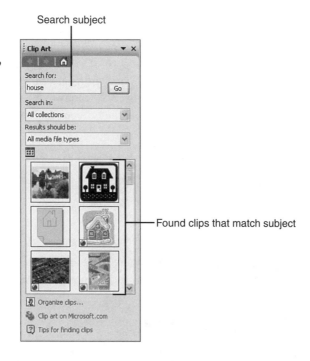

FIGURE 5.3
Select an image or clip to add to your document.

Found clips that match subject

Watercolor Pictures

A *watermark* is a faded graphic image that appears behind text in a document. With Word, a watermark can appear in color (assuming that you have a color printer) or in a grayscale tone. Watermark images are so faded they do not interfere with the text in any way. Yet, a watermark image does lightly appear in the background on the page and prints behind the text. Some of the Office themes contain such watermark images.

A watermark might be a company logo or a design that adds personality to your printed documents. To add a watermark, select Format, Background, Printed Watermark. Click the Picture watermark option and then click Select Picture. Choose an image and click Insert. Word inserts the watermark behind your document's text.

5

Inserting Scanned and Digital Camera Images

Technology is rapidly changing, and Office does its best to keep up with that hurried pace. You can easily insert images that you scan on a scanner or take with a digital camera. Office makes inserting pictures from these devices as easy as inserting graphics from a file.

For example, suppose that you want to scan a child's drawing to insert into a letter to relatives. Simply select Insert, Picture, From Scanner or Camera. Word displays a scanner collection dialog box or digital camera dialog box from which you can control your scanner or digital camera's transfer of the picture to your document.

To Do: Create and Use AutoText Entries

In addition to AutoCorrect, *AutoText* enables you to quickly insert completely formatted multilined text. AutoText is often called *boilerplate text*, which is a publishing term used for text that appears frequently.

Suppose, for example, that you often place your boldfaced, 16-point name and address centered across the top of your personal letters. Instead of typing and formatting this text each time you need it, follow these steps to add the text as an AutoText entry:

1. Type and format the text you want to add to the AutoText entries. Make sure that it is exactly as you want it to be reproduced.

2. Select the text.

3. Select Insert, AutoText, AutoText. Word displays the AutoText tab, which shows the AutoText entries currently in effect, as shown in Figure 5.4.

FIGURE 5.4

Adding an AutoText entry makes subsequent typing easier.

4. Type an abbreviation for the AutoText entry in the field labeled Enter AutoText Entries Here. You can either type this text to activate the AutoText entry, or you can select from the available options listed.

5. Press Enter.

When you subsequently type the AutoText entry's abbreviation and press F3, Word replaces the abbreviation with your expanded, formatted AutoText entry. AutoText entries require the F3 keystroke. Nevertheless, AutoText entries can be more complex and longer than those of AutoCorrect, which allows only 255 characters.

After you create an AutoText entry, check the Show AutoComplete check box on the AutoText dialog box before closing the dialog box. Afterwards, when you type that AutoText entry's abbreviation, a ScreenTip appears that shows your entry beneath the abbreviation. If you press Enter at that point, Word replaces your abbreviation with the expanded entry so that you don't have to press F3. If you want to ignore the AutoText instead, just keep typing and the ScreenTip will go away.

Adding Tables to Your Documents

Word's report-creation power shines when you see how easily you can compose customized tables of information in Word documents. *Tables* are collections of information organized in rows and columns. Tables might contain numbers, text, even graphics, or combinations of any of these. Each row and column intersection is called a *cell*. As you begin to use both Word and Excel, you might want to embed part of an Excel worksheet into a Word table. Embedded worksheets enable you to report financial data from within Word. (Hour 6, "Understanding Excel 2003 Workbooks," introduces Excel.)

5

To Do: Create a New Table

To create a new table, perform these steps:

1. Select Table, Insert, Table. Word displays the Insert Table dialog box, as shown in Figure 5.5.

2. Specify the number of columns and rows your table will need. You can change these values later if you need to. Estimate on the high end, however, because it is easier to delete additional rows and columns than to add them.

3. Enter a column width, or leave the Column Width field set to Auto if you want Word to guess the table's width. You can change a table's column width at any time—even after you enter data. You can request that Word automatically adjust each column's width to the widest data in the column by selecting the AutoFit to Contents option. The AutoFit to Window option adjusts the column widths equally within the table's size if you resize the window that holds the table.

FIGURE 5.5

Use the Insert Table dialog box to prepare the new table.

4. When creating your first table, press Enter or click OK. After you get used to creating tables, you can click the AutoFormat button to select from a list of predefined table formats, as shown in Figure 5.6.

Categories group similar styles

FIGURE 5.6

Word can format your table automatically.

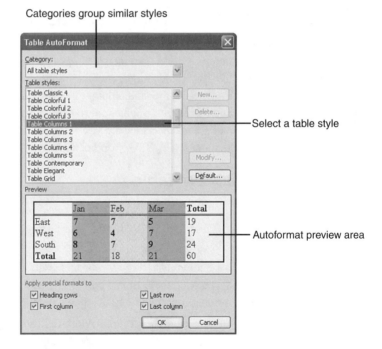

Select a table style

Autoformat preview area

5. Click OK (or press Enter) to close the Insert Table dialog box. Word creates your table and outlines the table's cells in a grid format.

Word contains another tool that helps you build more customized tables. You can draw your tables by clicking the Insert Table toolbar button and dragging the resulting table of cells down and to the right until you outline the table size you prefer. In addition, you can draw tables freehand using the Word tools available (described later this hour in a section entitled "Drawing Tables Freehand").

Traversing the Table

One of the easiest ways to enter data in a table's cell is to click the cell (which moves the cursor to the cell) and type. As you type past the cell's right margin, Word wraps the cell and increases the row height (if needed) to display the complete cell contents.

When you begin typing data, notice that Word's automatic formatting might not match the table's data; perhaps one of the columns is too narrow or too wide. Use your mouse to adjust the size of a row or a column's width by clicking and dragging one of the table's four edges in or out. You can also expand or shrink individual columns and rows by dragging their edges.

Although you can click a cell with your mouse every time you want to enter or edit the contents of that cell, the cursor-movement keystrokes come in handier because you can traverse the table without ever removing your hands from the keyboard. Table 5.1 describes how to traverse a table's rows and columns.

When you move your cursor to a table's row or column edge, Word changes the mouse pointer to a table-adjuster cursor. When the mouse cursor changes, you can drag your mouse to resize the column or row.

TABLE 5.1 Moving Around a Table

Press This...	To Move the Table's Cursor Here
Tab	The next cell
Shift+Tab	The preceding cell
Alt+PageUp	The column's top cell
Alt+PageDown	The column's bottom cell
Alt+Home	The current row's first cell
Alt+End	The current row's last cell

To select a row or column, click the margin to the left of the row or in the area above the column. The Table, Select menu also provides a row and column selection option if you find that easier to use. When you select a column or row, Word highlights the selected item. After Word selects a row or column, you can drag your mouse down, up, left, or right to select additional rows or columns.

Inserting New Columns and Rows

Not creating enough rows or columns for your table is one of the first table problems you will encounter. To insert or delete rows or columns, select a row or column and right-click your mouse in the margin to the left of the row or directly above the column. The menu that appears enables you to add rows or columns.

Suppose that you need to insert a column. Select the column that will appear after the new column by pointing above the column until the mouse pointer changes to a down arrow. Select multiple columns by dragging your mouse to the right after you select one column. Right-click your mouse to display a pop-up menu. The menu differs, depending on whether you select a row or column first. Select Insert Columns, and Word inserts a new column to the left of the selected column. The right-click menu also contains a Delete Columns command. Keep in mind that the Table, Insert menu provides additional row and column insertion options that you can explore.

> After you create a simple table, click in the table and then select Table, Table AutoFormat to select a style, such as a shaded style. Word formats your table professionally.

Drawing Tables Freehand

As you have seen, the Tables menu option gives you complete control over tables you create. Word goes one step further to help you create exactly the table you want. The Standard toolbar's Tables and Borders button enables you to draw tables freehand the way you might draw using a pencil and paper. The Tables and Borders button enables you to quickly draw tables that don't necessarily have an equal number of columns for each row.

Follow these steps to use the Tables and Borders button:

1. Click the location in your document where you want the new table.

2. Click the Tables and Borders button. (You might have to click the More Buttons toolbar button first to locate the Tables and Borders button on your toolbar.) Your mouse pointer turns into a pencil shape, and the Tables and Borders toolbar appears.

3. Click and drag the pencil pointer diagonally down and across the page. A rectangular table outline appears. When you release the mouse, the outline becomes your table's outline.

4. Continue adding rows and columns by dragging the mouse. Notice that you can draw (by dragging) a partial row or partial column. If you draw a row or column you don't want, click the Tables and Borders Eraser tool and drag over the table lines you want to delete.

After you draw the table's basic outline, use the Border Color, Outside Border, and Shading Color tools to modify the table's colors. The remaining tools enable you to modify the table in many ways, including the following:

- Merging two or more cells into one
- Splitting long cells into multiple cells
- Changing a cell's text alignment (as you might do with border columns)
- Equally distributing columns or rows within an area
- Sorting (alphabetically or numerically) cells within a selected row or column
- Summing a selected row or column automatically

Creating Multiple Columns

5

When you want to create newspaper-style columns—such as those that appear in newsletters and brochures—configure Word to format your text with multiple columns. You can assign multiple columns to the entire document or to only a selected part of your document. Figure 5.7 shows a document with three columns and a single column at the top for the title area. Generally, you should type your document's text before breaking the document into multiple columns.

When you want to set multiple columns, follow these steps:

1. Select the text you want to convert to multiple columns. If you want to select your entire document, press Ctrl+A.

2. Select Format, Columns to display the Columns dialog box shown in Figure 5.8.

FIGURE 5.7
You can use multiple columns for newsletters, brochures, and other pamphlets.

Single-column lines ——

Three-column area

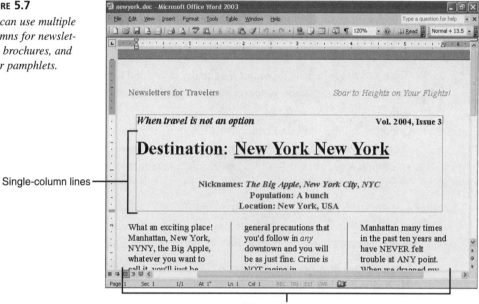

Click to determine columns

FIGURE 5.8
Set up multiple columns with the Columns dialog box.

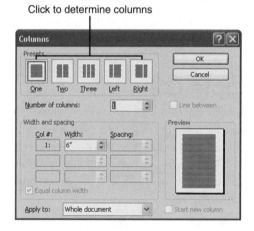

3. In the Presets area, click the column format you want and then enter the number of columns you want to produce.

4. In the Width and Spacing area, adjust the column width and spacing between columns or accept Word's default. Generally, the default measurements work well. As you adjust the columns, Word updates the Preview area to give you an idea of the final result.

5. If you want a line between the columns, click the option labeled Line Between.

6. When you click OK, Word formats your selected text into multiple columns.

To add multiple columns quickly and let Word handle the spacing (which Word generally does well), select the text that you want to format into multiple columns and then click the toolbar button's Columns button. Drag your mouse to the right to select the number of columns (from one to four). When you release the mouse, Word formats the multiple columns.

If you format your document into multiple columns that are fully justified, you will probably need to hyphenate the document. Thin, justified columns often contain a lot of extra spaces that Word inserts to maintain the right-justification. You might want to select File, Print Preview to see how your overall document looks with the narrow columns before printing.

Creating Headers and Footers

A *header* is text that appears at the top of each page (or the pages you select, such as all even pages) in your document. A *footer* appears at the bottom of your pages. You might want to add page numbers to the top or bottom of a document, and you can do so from the header or footer area. You don't have to add headers and footers to each page: Word enables you to type them just once, and it automatically adds them to each page.

To Do: Add a Header and Footer

To add a header or footer, follow these steps:

1. Select View, Header and Footer to display the Header and Footer toolbar and display an entry area in which you can type the header and footer text. Figure 5.9 shows a document that displays this toolbar and the header entry area in a document.

2. Type your header text. If you want to type footer text, click the toolbar's Switch Between Header and Footer button to display the footer entry area and type your footer text. If you want to add page numbers, the date, or the time to your header or footer text, click the appropriate buttons on the Header and Footer toolbar.

3. Click the Close button to anchor the header or footer in your document.

5

FIGURE 5.9

Use the Header and Footer toolbar to develop your document's header and footer.

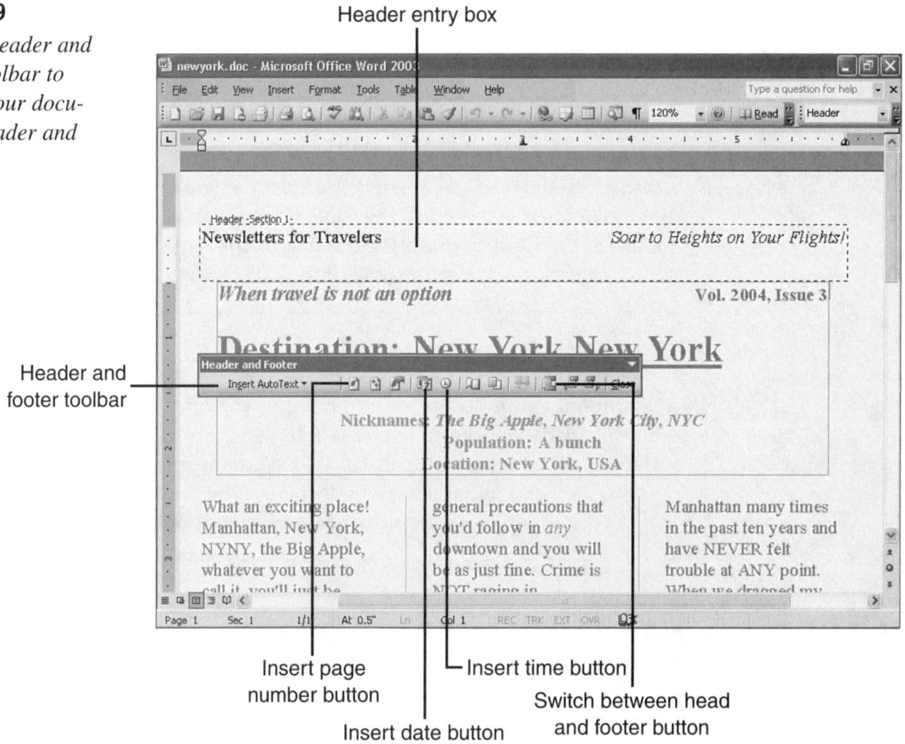

Header entry box

Header and footer toolbar

Insert page number button

Insert date button

Insert time button

Switch between head and footer button

Word normally dims header and footer text so that you can easily distinguish between the header, footer, and the rest of your document. You can see these items when editing your document within the Print Layout view, but they remain dimmed while in Normal view. If you want to specify that the header (or footer) are to appear only on certain pages such as odd- or even-numbered pages, select File, Page Setup, Layout and check the Different Odd and Even or Different First Page check box. You must be in the Print Layout view to see headers, footers, footnotes, and endnotes in their proper places on the page.

If you want to edit a header or footer, display your document in Print Layout view and then double-click the dimmed header or footer text. Word opens the Header and Footer toolbar and enables you to edit the header or footer text.

Adding Footnotes and Endnotes

A *footnote* differs from a footer in that a footnote appears only at the bottom of the page on which you include it. Word inserts a footnote reference in the text where you choose to insert the footnote. If you later add text to the page so that the footnote reference moves to the next document page, Word automatically moves the footnote as well. Therefore, the footnote always appears on the same page as its reference. *Endnotes* are footnotes that appear at the end of your document rather than at the bottom of each page.

To Do: Insert a Footnote

To insert a footnote, follow these steps:

1. Select Insert, Reference, Footnote. Word displays the Footnote and Endnote dialog box shown in Figure 5.10. Click the option you want to add, Footnotes or Endnotes.

FIGURE 5.10

Add footnotes and endnotes with this dialog box.

2. If you want Word to number the footnote (or endnote) sequentially starting with 1, click Insert. If you want to use a different symbol for the number, click the Symbol button, choose a symbol, and then select that symbol from the Custom Mark text box.

3. Click Insert to add the footnote. Word adds a separating line between your document and the note, adds the reference number to your document text where you inserted the footnote, and places the cursor at the bottom of the page next to the footnote reference number.

4. Type the footnote (or endnote) and click your mouse on the body of the document to resume editing.

5

Remember that you must display the Print Layout view to see headers, footers, footnotes, and endnotes in their proper places on the page.

Introducing Mail Merge

Word provides many tools for those who want to mail personalized mail to family, friends, and customers. Although explaining all the ins and outs of Word's mail-merge techniques could fill an entire book, which could show how you to use other Office products such as Access to add to your mail-merge power, these 24 hours only give you time for a quick overview. Yet a quick overview is enough to get you started because Word makes things easy.

> Although this book is aimed to introduce Office 2003, once you complete these 24 hours you will have mastered most of the common techniques and skills necessary to use the Office programs effectively. Having said that, this section does not teach you the step-by-step procedures necessary for mastering mail merging. With this introduction and Word's help system, however, you should have little trouble filling in the gaps and producing your own mass mailing as soon as you need to do so.

Preparing for Mail Merge

You must create a *main document* and locate or create a *data source* before you can accomplish mail merging with Word. The main document is a form letter, envelope, label, or some other document, large or small, that contains the formatted text that will be the same across the entire print run. In a way, the main document contains placeholders (called *merge fields*) for the data that changes, such as each customer who you're mailing to or each inventory part number that you're printing labels for.

The data source contains the data that changes between each item you print. Therefore, the data source might hold the customer names, addresses, and phone numbers, or perhaps the data source is your inventory file from which you'll pull data for your inventory labels.

Before you begin the actual mail-merge process, you use Word to create your main document, such as the form letter you want to send to clients. Now that you've worked through your first five hour lessons, that should be simple! Just don't include any name after your salutation and don't include an address for the recipient.

End all your main document filenames with *main* and store them in their own folder so that you can locate them more easily.

To Do: Step Through the Mail-Merge Process

Here is a quick run-through of the steps you'll take when you're ready to produce a mass mailing:

1. Open your main document.

2. Select Tools, Letters and Mailings, Mail Merge Wizard to open the Mail Merge task pane. Word asks you to select in the task pane the type of main document you're working on, such as letters or labels.

3. Select Letters and click Next at the bottom of the task pane.

4. Word then asks you to select the main document. You'll be using the currently open main document, so click Next to move to the next step.

5. Word now must know the data source you're going to use. One of the most obvious places to locate your contacts is Microsoft Outlook. Although you haven't yet mastered Outlook, if you've upgraded to Office 2003 from a previous version of Office, you might already have several names in your Outlook contacts list. Click the second option to select the data source from your Outlook contacts and then click Next to continue.

You can enter new data into a new data source or click the Browse button to locate data from another source such as an Access database.

6. Word locates your data and allows you to sort the list or remove some from the list before you use that data source. Click Next to continue.

7. The Mail Merge task pane shown in Figure 5.11 is where you tell Word exactly where to insert each field from your data source. For example, if you want your letter to include the recipient's address, click where that information is to appear on each letter and then click the Address block section of your task pane.

8. Click Next to preview your letter. Word gives you the chance to step through each and every document that will print in the mailing if you want to see each one. If you run across one that you don't want to send, even though that person was in your data source, you have one final chance to exclude that recipient from this mailing.

5

9. Clicking Next completes the merge and the printing can begin.

FIGURE 5.11

You must tell Word exactly where to place the data on each letter printed for the mass mailing.

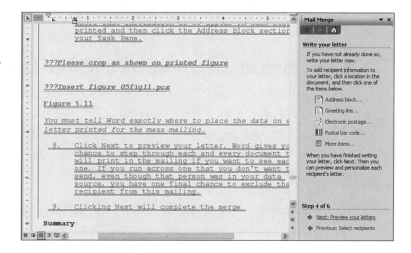

Summary

This hour wrapped up this book's discussion of Word. You learned how to add the document extras that often turn simple writing into powerful cross-referenced published works.

If you need to display tabular information, let Word create and format your tables so that your data presentation looks clean. In addition, multiple columns work well for newsletters and brochures to keep the reader's attention.

To speed up your writing, use as many AutoCorrect and AutoText entries as you can. If you repeatedly type a phrase, sentence, or block of information, that text is a good candidate for AutoCorrect or AutoText.

Hour 6 introduces you to Excel 2003. As you will see, Excel enables you to present numeric data as professionally as Word presents your documents.

Q&A

Q Should I use AutoText or AutoCorrect?

A You must decide how much formatting and effort the boilerplate text requires. If you need to type the same text often but the text consists of only a word or two and requires no special formatting, use AutoCorrect (Tools, AutoCorrect).

With AutoCorrect, Word makes changes for you as you type the AutoCorrect abbreviations. (Be careful not to create AutoCorrect entries from common words, or Word might replace text that you don't always want replaced.) If the text is lengthy or requires special formatting that spans multiple lines, however, add the text as an AutoText entry. After you type the AutoText abbreviation, press the F3 key to expand the abbreviation into the formatted full text. Keep in mind that AutoCorrect imposes a 255-character limit on entries you make there.

Q Why can't I see my headers and footers while editing my document?

A Perhaps you are displaying your document in Normal view. Select View, Print Layout to see headers and footers in their correct positions on the page.

Q What is the difference between a table and a document formatted with multiple columns?

A Both tables and multicolumn documents have multiple columns. The multicolumn document, however, is useful when you want to create a newspaper-style document with flowing columns of text and graphics. Tables have both columns as well as rows, making cells at each row and column intersection for specific data. A multi-column document might contain a table in one of its columns.

Use tables when you want side-by-side columns of related information. Use multiple columns when you want your text to snake from the bottom of one column to the top of another.

5

Part III

Computing with Excel 2003

Hour

6 Understanding Excel 2003 Workbooks

7 Restructuring and Editing Excel 2003 Worksheets

8 Using Excel 2003

9 Formatting Worksheets to Look Great

10 Charting with Excel 2003

HOUR 6

Understanding Excel 2003 Workbooks

This hour introduces you to Excel 2003, Microsoft's spreadsheet program. Microsoft Excel is to numbers what Word is to text; Excel has been called a *word processor for numbers*. With Excel, you can create numerically based proposals, business plans, business forms, accounting worksheets, and virtually any other document that contains calculated numbers.

If you are new to electronic worksheets, you will probably have to take more time to learn Excel's environment than you had to learn Word's. Excel starts with a grid of cells in which you place information. This hour takes things slowly to acquaint you with Excel and explains the background necessary for understanding how an Excel working area operates.

The highlights of this hour include the following:

- What worksheets and workbooks are
- How to enter various kinds of Excel data
- How to navigate in an Excel worksheet

Starting Excel

When you start Excel, you see a screen similar to the one in Figure 6.1. The task pane is called the *home* task pane, and it is similar to the task pane all Office products display when you first start the programs. With the home task pane, you can create new Excel documents (called *worksheets*) and open documents you've recently worked on.

FIGURE 6.1

Familiarize yourself with Excel's opening screen.

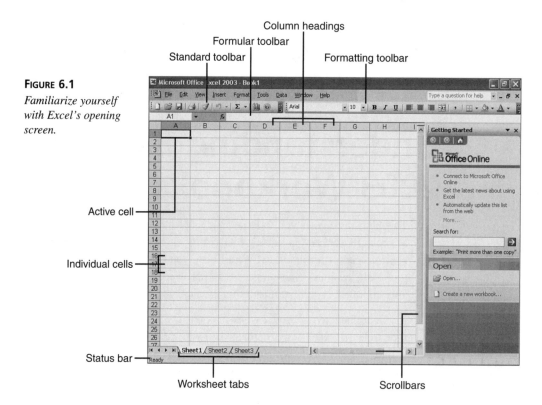

Understanding Worksheets and Workbooks

Excel enables you to create and edit worksheets that you store in workbooks. Typically, people work with a single worksheet (sometimes called a *spreadsheet* or just *sheet*). A *worksheet* is a collection of rows and columns that holds text and numbers, as you see in Figure 6.1. Typically, Excel helps users prepare financial information, but you can manage other kinds of data in Excel, such as a project timeline. If your project requires multiple closely linked worksheets, you can store the worksheets in one large workbook file. A *workbook* is a collection of one or more worksheets stored in the same file. A company with several divisions might create a workbook with annual sales for each division, and each division might be represented with its own tabbed worksheet inside the workbook.

Any time you create, open, or save an Excel file, you are working with a workbook. Often, that workbook contains only one worksheet. When that's the case, the terms worksheet and workbook are basically synonymous. To open a new Excel worksheet (in a new workbook), select File, New to display the New Document task pane, which is virtually identical to Word's New Document task pane that you learned about in Hour 3, "Formatting with Word 2003."

All Excel files end in the .xls filename extension. Your workbook name is the Excel name you assign when you save a file. You can save Excel worksheets and workbooks in HTML and other formats (such as Lotus 1-2-3 for compatibility and older versions of Excel). When you save your worksheet as an HTML file, you can embed your worksheet data inside a Web page. To save your work, select File, Save; name your Excel workbook and specify the location; and click OK. To load an existing Excel file, use File, Open.

A worksheet is set up in a similar manner to a Word table, except that Excel worksheets can do much more high-end, numeric processing than Word tables can.

Initially, blank Excel workbooks contain three worksheets named Sheet1, Sheet2, and Sheet3, as shown at the bottom of Figure 6.1. When you click a sheet's tab, Excel brings that sheet into view. Again, most of the time you'll stick with one worksheet file per workbook, so you'll typically never have to click on the secondary worksheet tabs to bring the other worksheets into view.

Give your worksheet a name other than Sheet1. Doing so is a good idea to help you keep track of what data is on each worksheet. Right-click the worksheet tab labeled Sheet1, select Rename from the shortcut menu, and enter a different name. By giving your worksheet a meaningful name, such as 2004 Payroll, you can more easily distinguish that worksheet from others that you might use later.

6

Each worksheet column has a heading; heading names start with A, B, and so on. Each row has a heading, starting with 1, 2, and so on. The intersection of a row and column, called a *cell*, also has a name that comes from combining the column number and row name, such as C4 or A1. A1 is always the top-left cell on any worksheet. The gridlines throughout the worksheet help you to distinguish between cells.

> No matter how large your monitor is, you see only a small amount of the worksheet area. Use the scrollbars to see or edit information in the off-screen cells, such as cell M200.

Every cell in your workbook contains a unique name or address to which you can refer when you are tabulating data. This name is called the *cell reference*, and it is unique for each cell in the worksheet. The *cell pointer* (the cell with the dark border around it, the active cell that will receive the next character that you type) indicates the active cell, and you learn to select multiple cells later this chapter. The cell pointer's location, also known as the cell reference, appears at the left of the formula bar. (Some refer to the cell reference as the *cell address*.) In Figure 6.1, the box reads A1 because the mouse pointer is in cell A1.

When you move your mouse pointer across Excel's screen, notice that the pointer becomes a cross when you point or click over a cell. The cross returns to its pointer shape when you point to another part of Excel, such as a toolbar or task pane.

Figure 6.2 shows a worksheet used to create an invoice for a company. Excel's automatic calculation features are perfect for applications, such as invoices, that require totals. With Excel's advanced formatting tools, your worksheets don't have to look as though they conform to a rigid row-and-column grid system.

> Many of Excel's tools and options are similar to Word's, so you already understand many of them. This uniformity applies as well to the basic features in each of the Office products.

FIGURE 6.2

Your Excel worksheets don't have to appear dull and boring.

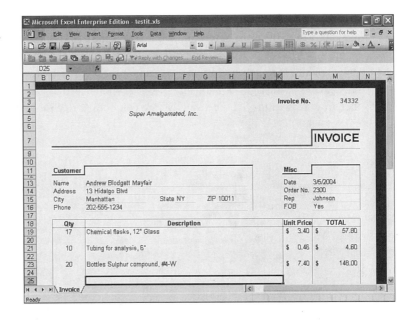

Entering Worksheet Data

Often, entering worksheet data requires nothing more than clicking the correct cell to select it and then typing the data. The various kinds of data behave differently when entered, however, so you should understand how Excel accepts assorted data.

Excel can work with the following kinds of data:

- Labels—Text values such as names and addresses, as well as date and time values.
- Numbers—Numeric values such as 34, –291, 545.67874, and 0.
- Formulas—Expressions that compute numeric results. (Some formulas work with text values as well.)

Excel also works well with data from other Office 2003 products as well as integrates into the online Internet world by supporting hyperlinks that you can embed into your worksheets. Additionally, you can *import* (transfer) worksheet data from other non-Microsoft products, such as Lotus 1-2-3.

Entering Text

If you want to put text (such as a title or a name) in a cell, just click the cell to select it and then type the text. By default, Excel left-justifies the text in the cell. As you type, the

6

text appears both in the cell and in the formula bar (see Figure 6.3). Remember that the name box to the left of the formula bar displays the name of the cell into which you are entering data, such as C7. When you press Enter, Excel moves the cell pointer down one row. In addition to pressing Enter, you can click the Enter button (indicated by a green checkmark) to the right of the name box to keep the current cell selected, or press one of the arrow keys or the Tab key to move the cell pointer to a different cell adjacent to the current one.

FIGURE 6.3

Excel might or might not display all of a cell's contents.

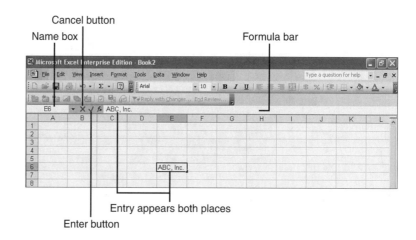

As you type text into a cell, you can press Backspace to erase what you've typed before anchoring the contents in the cell with Enter or another cursor-movement key. If you press Esc or press the Cancel button at any point during your text entry but before you move to another cell, Excel erases the text you typed in the cell and restores the original cell contents. In addition, you can click the Undo button or press Ctrl+Z to back up to a cell's previous state.

When you create a new worksheet, the cell sizes take on the width and height size specified by the template you specify or by the default template if you don't specify a different one. If the width of your text is greater than a cell's original width, Excel does one of two things, depending on the contents of the next cell to the right:

 Press Tab to move the cell pointer to the right or the arrow keys to move the cell pointer in any direction after you enter data.

- If the adjacent cell is empty, Excel displays the entire contents of your entry, with the overflow spilling into the next cell to the right.
- If the adjacent cell contains data, Excel *truncates* (cuts off) the wide cell to show only as much text as fits in the cell's width. Excel does not remove the unseen data from the cell; however, if the adjacent cell contains data, it always displays instead.

Figure 6.4 shows two long labels in cells C5 and C10. The same label, which is longer than standard cell width, appears in both cells. Because no data resides in D5, Excel displays all the contents of C5. The data in D10, however, overwrites the tail end of C10. C10 still contains the complete label, but only part of it is visible.

FIGURE 6.4

Excel might or might not display all of a cell's contents.

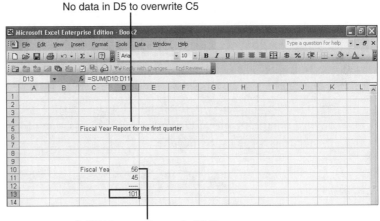

No data in D5 to overwrite C5

Cell D10 overwrites part of C10.

> You can increase and shrink the width and height of columns and rows by dragging the right edge of a column heading or the bottom edge of a row heading. If you drag the right edge of column D to the right, for example, all rows in the entire column D widen.

Excel usually recognizes any entry that begins with an alphabetical character as text. Some textual data, such as price codes, telephone numbers, and ZIP Codes, can fool Excel into thinking you are entering numeric data because of the initial numeric value. As you see in the next section, Excel treats numeric data differently from text data when you type the data into cells. If you want Excel to treat a number (such as a ZIP Code) as a text entry so that it does not perform calculations on the cell, precede the contents with a single apostrophe ('). For example, to type the ZIP Code 74137, type '**74137**; the apostrophe lets Excel know to format the value as text.

When you enter what would otherwise be a valid number but use the apostrophe prefix, Excel places a small green triangle in the cell's upper-left corner. This triangle is a small warning that cautions you about the apostrophe where possible numeric data should appear. If you click the cell, Excel displays an icon you can click to open a pop-up menu with the following options:

- *Convert to Number*—Converts the number to a numeric format by removing the apostrophe. (You would choose this if you accidentally typed the apostrophe or changed your mind later.)

- *Help on This Error*—Displays online help about entering numeric and text data.

- *Ignore Error*—Keeps the apostrophe and removes the green triangle tag.

- *Edit in Formula Bar*—Places the value in the formula bar with the insertion-point text cursor at the end of the data so that you can edit the data.

- *Error Checking Options*—Displays the Options dialog box, shown in Figure 6.5, from which you can change the way Excel reacts to a possible data-entry error such as numeric values that you enter with an apostrophe.

- *Show Formula Auditing Toolbar*—Displays a toolbar with which you can trace all cell references related to a formula to help you repair formulas that don't produce the results you expect them to.

FIGURE 6.5

Specify how you want Excel to handle common errors.

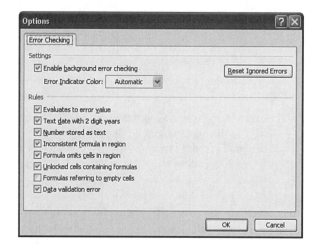

Entering Numbers and Formulas

Excel accepts numeric values of all kinds. You can type positive numbers, negative numbers, numbers with decimal points, zero-leading numbers, numbers with dollar signs, percent signs, and even *scientific notation* (a shortcut for writing extremely large and small numbers).

If you type a number but see something similar to 3.04959E+16 appear in the cell, Excel converted your number to scientific notation to let you know that the cell is not wide enough to display the entire number in its regular form. Excel does not extend long numbers into adjacent cells. Excel converts most numbers that contain more than 12 digits to scientific notation.

Excel right-justifies numbers inside cells. You can change the format for a single cell, a group of cells, or the entire worksheet, as you will see in Hour 8, "Using Excel 2003."

Perhaps the most important task in learning Excel is mastering formulas. You never have to do math in Excel because Excel does it for you. The trick is getting your formulas correct. Hour 7, "Reconstructing and Editing Excel 2003 Worksheets," explains the ins and outs of Excel formulas. Later in this lesson, you get a chance to create a simple worksheet. As you will see, if your data changes, Excel automatically recalculates the entire worksheet for you. Therefore, once you create a worksheet and enter all the formulas, you can concentrate on the data and let Excel do the calculating.

Entering Dates and Times

Excel supports almost every national and international date and time format. Excel uses its AutoFormat feature to convert any date or time value that you type to a special internal number that represents the number of days since midnight, January 1, 1900. As with all Office 2003 products, Excel automatically displays all dates the user enters with four-digit year values by showing the full year. Although this strange internal date representation of days since 1-1-1900 might not make sense now, you use these values a lot to compute time between two or more dates. You can easily determine how many days an account is past due, for example, by subtracting the current date from the cell in the worksheet that contains the due date.

Excel uses a 24-hour clock to represent time values unless you specify a.m. or p.m. To convert p.m. times to 24-hour times, add 12 to all time values after 12:59 p.m. Thus, 7:54 p.m. is 19:54 on a 24-hour clock.

6

You can type any of the following date and time values to represent 6:15 p.m., July 4, 1976, or a combination of both 6:15 p.m. and July 4, 1976:

```
July 4, 1976
4-Jul-76 6:15 p.m.
6:15 p.m.
```

```
18:15
07/04/76 18:15
07-04-76 18:15
```

If you enter any of these date and time values, Excel converts them to a shortened format (such as 7/4/76 18:15). You can enter a date, a time value, or both. The shorter format often helps worksheet columns align better.

Navigating in Excel

Your mouse and arrow keys are the primary navigation keys for moving from cell to cell. Unlike Word, which uses an insertion point, Excel uses a cell pointer to show you the currently *active* cell. The active cell has a darkened border around it and accepts whatever data you enter next. As you press an arrow key, Excel moves the cell pointer in the direction of the arrow to a new cell, making the new cell the active one.

If you work with a rather large worksheet, you might find the Go To command useful. Press F5 to display the Go To dialog box, where you can select a range of cells that you might have previously named or type a cell reference value such as C141 to jump to that cell.

Table 6.1 lists the most commonly used navigational keystrokes within Excel. Use your mouse to scroll with the scrollbars. To scroll long distances, press Shift while you scroll with the mouse.

TABLE 6.1   Using the Keyboard to Navigate Excel

Press This Key...	To Move To
Arrow keys	The direction of the arrow one cell at a time
Ctrl+up arrow, Ctrl+down arrow	The topmost or bottommost cell that contains data or, if at the end of the range already, the next cell that contains data
Ctrl+left arrow, Ctrl+right arrow	The leftmost or rightmost cell that contains data or, if at the end of the range already, the next cell that contains data
PageUp, PageDown	The previous or next screen of the worksheet
Ctrl+Home	The upper-left corner of the worksheet cell A1
End, arrow	The last blank cell in the arrow's direction
Ctrl+PageUp, Ctrl+PageDown	The next or previous worksheet within the current workbook

To Do: Create Your First Worksheet

The next hour's lesson presents the details of creating, editing, and understanding specific areas of an Excel worksheet. For practice, however, work through the following steps to try Excel now. To do so, you will create a simple test-tracking worksheet for a professor. By working with a hands-on example now, you'll have a better feel for the overall Excel concept as you work the rest of this section of the book.

Follow these steps to create your first worksheet:

1. Select File, New and select Blank Workbook from the New Worksheet task pane to create a new workbook.

2. Click on cell C4 to move the cell pointer there and make it the active cell. The cell name, C4, appears in the formula bar.

3. Type **Student Gradebook**. The text is wider than the cell, but Excel extends the text label over into the right cell (D4).

4. Click on cell B6 and type **Name**.

5. Press Tab to move the cell pointer to C6. (You can also click in C6 or press the right-arrow key to move the cell pointer to C6.)

6. Enter the labels **Test 1**, **Test 2**, **Test 3**, and **Average** in cells C6 through F6.

7. Move to B8 and enter these values across row 8: **Mary Bee**, **77**, **89**, and **86**. (The 86 ends up in cell E8.)

8. Enter these values underneath the previous ones to add the second row of data for your worksheet: **Paul North**, **89**, **87**, and **94**.

9. Enter the following data for the next row: **Terry Smith**, **93**, **100**, and **95**. Notice that cell B10 is not wide enough to hold Terry Smith's entire name. As soon as you enter data in C10, the right portion of Terry Smith's name is truncated. You will fix this problem in a moment.

10. Enter the following for the row 11: **Sue Willis**, **64**, **79**, and **83**.

11. Type **Class Average:** in cell D13. (The label will flow into E13.) Your worksheet should resemble the one in Figure 6.6.

6

Name box   Formula bar

FIGURE 6.6

*You are on your way to
creating your first
Excel worksheet!*

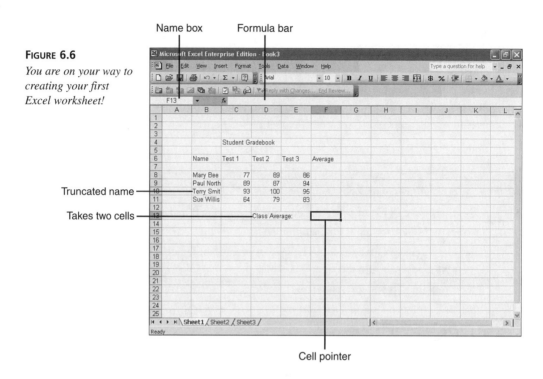

Truncated name

Takes two cells

Cell pointer

To Do: Format the Worksheet

The worksheet requires some formatting to look better, but you've already used Excel to
enter text and numbers. The averages now need computing via a formula. Additionally, a
little formatting would greatly improve the look. Follow these steps to complete the
worksheet:

1. Move the cell pointer to F8 and type this: **=(C8+D8+E8)/3**. Then, press the down
   arrow to move to cell F9. Notice that Excel computed the average of Mary Bee's
   test scores. You just entered a formula that requests the average. The formula tells
   Excel to add the contents of cells C8, D8, and E8 and then divide the sum by 3.
   Several methods exist for creating such a formula, and you'll learn even better
   ways throughout the next three hours' lessons.

2. Excel is smart and guesses at a lot of tasks to make life easier for you. Instead of
   typing the same formula all the way down column F, you only need to copy and
   paste the formula you just entered to F9, F10, and F11 to calculate the other three
   student averages. Click on cell F8 (the cell to copy), and press Ctrl+C to copy the
   cell to the Clipboard. Excel highlights the cell to show the selection.

3. Click cell F9 and do this: Hold down the Shift key while pressing the down arrow twice. Excel highlights three cells. These cells are the target of your copy.

4. Press Ctrl+V (or select Edit, Paste) to paste the Clipboard contents into the high-lighted cells. When you do, Excel instantly updates the averages for the remaining three students. Excel even changes the formula you copy to reflect the new row numbers. This is called *relative cell referencing* because the formulas are copied relative to their new locations. You can ignore the Paste icon that Excel displays after the paste. When you paste data into a document, the Paste icon appears and enables you to modify the way the paste is performed. You can, for example, elect to paste the formula as text, and if you do, the result does not show in the cell but the formula itself does.

> If Excel refused to change the row numbers when you copied the formula from F8, all four students would reflect Mary Bee's average. You can click on cell F10 and look at the formula in the formula bar (beneath the standard toolbar) to see that all references now indicate row 10 and no longer row 8 even though you copied the formula from row 8. Fancy? You bet.

5. You now must compute the average for the class. That's simple: just type the fol-lowing formula in cell F13: **=(F8+F9+F10+F11)/4**. The class average appears instantly. Your worksheet now looks like the one in Figure 6.7.

FIGURE 6.7

Excel calculates all the averages for you.

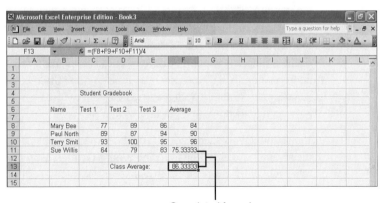

Completed formulas

Now that you've finished entering text, numbers, and formulas, you can improve a work-sheet's look with a little formatting. In addition, you might be interested in knowing how Excel can improve the functionality of the worksheet. If you insert new blank rows into the worksheet, Excel changes the average calculations at the end of the displaced student rows to reflect their new row location. You also can insert new columns in case the students take additional tests, and the formulas update to reflect new column names.

To Do: Complete the Worksheet's Format

One problem exists, however, with the formulas in their present state. If you add tests, you have to change each calculated average to reflect the additional test scores. As you might expect, Excel supports other ways to enter formulas so that the formulas update automatically even if you add new test columns. You'll learn about some of these features as you progress through the next two hours.

For now, follow these steps to complete the worksheet's format:

1. Although you will often format individual cells, you can use Excel's AutoFormat feature to create an interesting worksheet look. Select the entire Student Gradebook table by clicking on cell B4 and dragging your mouse to cell F13 to highlight the entire table.

2. Select Format, AutoFormat to display the AutoFormat dialog box.

3. Scroll down to the Colorful 2 format and select it. Instantly, Excel makes your table appear as though you slaved away for an hour over a hot computer!

4. The two average calculations produce answers with too many decimal places for this worksheet. You should format the numbers so that they show only two decimal places. Highlight cells F11 through F13 by clicking and dragging your mouse.

5. On the Formatting toolbar, you see a comma (,) that indicates, with the ScreenTip pop-up description, that it is called the Comma Style button. Click that comma toolbar button, and Excel changes the two cells to look better, displaying only two decimal places. (You might have to click the far-right toolbar button that shows additional options if you do not see the Comma Style button.) As Figure 6.8 shows, your Student Gradebook worksheet now looks truly professional. Excel even increased the Name column so that plenty of room exists for each name.

6. Rename the worksheet by right-clicking over the Sheet1 tab name at the bottom of the screen, selecting Rename, and typing **Grades**. Don't worry about naming the other two worksheets because you are not using them at this time.

By default, Excel creates new workbooks with three worksheets. You can remove extra worksheets by right-clicking over any worksheet tab and selecting Delete. In addition, you can insert additional worksheets by right-clicking over a tab and selecting Insert from the shortcut menu. Excel

> displays the Insert window, and you then can select Worksheet to insert a blank worksheet. When you insert new worksheets, Excel inserts a new worksheet to the left of the one on which you right-clicked.

7. You can save your creation by selecting File, Save and entering a name such as **Gradebook** for the document name. Excel automatically appends the .xls filename extension if you do not supply it. You've just saved a workbook with three worksheets, but only one has anything valid in it, the first one with the name of Gradebook.

FIGURE 6.8

Your simple worksheet now looks more exciting.

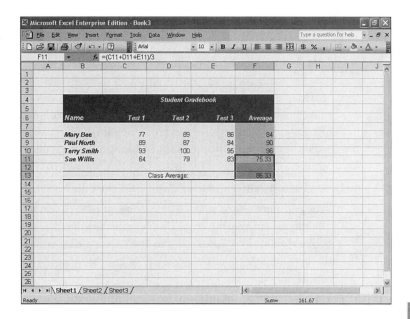

Now that you've got some hands-on experience with Excel, you're ready to master some of the more detailed aspects of the program. The next hour will take you through a more involved look at formulas and cell data.

6

Summary

This hour introduced Excel and covered elements on Excel's application screen. It also explained the concept of workbooks and worksheets. The workbook files contain your worksheets, and your worksheets hold data, such as numbers and labels. As you see throughout this part of the book, Excel supports a tremendous number of formatting options so that you can turn your numeric data into eye-catching, appealing output.

Although Excel works best with numeric data, Excel works with text (called labels) such as names, addresses, titles, dates, and time values. The true power of Excel shows itself in its manipulation of numeric data. Excel works with formulas that you enter as well as several internal functions that perform calculations. In the next hour's lesson, you will learn more about how to specify formulas to produce accurate results.

Q&A

Q I'm not good at math. Can I use Excel?

A Don't worry: Excel does all the calculating. Your job is to place the numeric data on the worksheets so that Excel can do its thing. You also must specify formulas so that Excel can compute results for you, which does require at least some knowledge of math. Many people use Excel for common household actions, such as tracking exercise routines and grocery lists. Excel is not just for accounting and mathematical applications. You will learn in the next hour how to specify formulas. There, you will see that Excel provides a lot of help along the way and can even guess at many calculations, such as totals, that you routinely need in your worksheets.

Q Do I always enter the time along with the date?

A You can enter a time value, a date value, or both. Excel turns the information into an internal shortened format. (You can change the display format if you want to make the data look better.) If you don't enter a date with a time value, Excel accepts the time value only and tracks just the time. If you enter a date, Excel tracks only the date.

HOUR 7

Restructuring and Editing Excel 2003 Worksheets

This hour teaches you how to manage and organize your Excel 2003 worksheets to make them really work for you. You'll be surprised how Excel follows and updates formulas as you modify worksheet data. If you really want to master Excel, you must understand how to set up and work with cell ranges. Therefore, this hour's material will greatly enhance your Excel expertise. You will learn to use range names and references to produce more powerful Excel formulas and functions.

In addition to using the editing tools, you also learn how to format worksheets to make them look better. This hour teaches the formatting essentials so you will be ready for even more fancy stuff in the next hour.

The highlights of this hour include the following:

- How to insert and delete rows and columns
- How to work with ranges of cells
- When range names are important
- How to write formulas so that they compute in the order you want them to
- How to format cells to add eye-catching appeal to your worksheet

Worksheet Editing

The better you are at editing worksheets, the more Excel will enhance your productivity. You already know that entering numeric data is error-prone at its best; the faster you edit cell values accurately, the faster you complete accurate worksheets. The following sections show you the primary editing techniques in Excel and explain how you can leverage those techniques to produce more accurate worksheets.

Selecting Cells

You can select a cell, a row of cells, or a column of cells just by clicking and dragging your mouse. As you drag your mouse, Excel selects a rectangular region, called a *range*. You notice as you drag your mouse that Excel displays the number of rows and columns you have selected. You see the message 10R X 4C appear in the toolbar's name box as you select 10 rows and 4 columns, for example. When you release your mouse, Excel displays the selection's upper-left corner cell name inside the name box, as Figure 7.1 shows.

FIGURE 7.1

Drag your mouse to select multiple cells.

Upper-left selected cell name

Selected cells

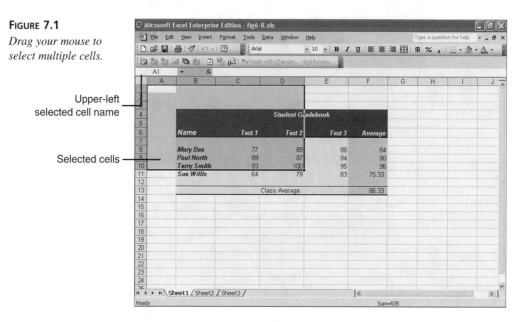

Not only can you select an adjacent rectangular region of cells, but you can also select nonadjacent regions. Select the first area, and then press Ctrl while you click another cell and drag the mouse to select the second region. The highlighted selection appears in both places on your screen. Remove any selection (either adjacent or nonadjacent) by clicking your mouse on any cell or by pressing an arrow key.

Editing Cell Contents

Much of your Excel editing requires that you correct numeric data entry. Of course, if you begin to type a number (or a formula) into a cell but realize you have made a mistake, press Backspace to erase your mistake or press the arrow keys to move the cell pointer back over the entry to correct something.

To Do: Correct Cell-Entry Mistakes

If you have already moved to another cell when you recognize that you have entered an error, quickly correct the mistake as follows:

1. Move the cell pointer to the cell you need to correct. (Click the cell to move the pointer there.)

2. Press F2, which is the standard Windows editing shortcut key. (If you still have your hand on the mouse, you can double-click the cell to edit the cell's contents.) You know Excel is ready for your edit when you see the cell pointer appear in the cell.

3. Use the arrow keys to move the cell pointer from the end of the cell to the mistake.

4. Press the Insert key to change from Overtype mode to Insert mode or vice versa. As with Word, Overtype mode enables you to write over existing characters, whereas Insert mode shifts all existing characters to the right as you type the correction.

5. Press Enter to anchor the correction in place.

If you want to reverse an edit, click the Undo button. To reverse an undo, click the Redo button. As you can see, after you have mastered one Office product (as you have Word), you know a lot about the other products.

Inserting and Deleting

As you saw in the preceding hour, you edit Excel worksheets somewhat differently from Word documents, even though both programs perform tasks in a similar manner and with similar menu commands and dialog boxes. The nature of worksheets makes them behave differently from word-processing documents. The next few sections explain how to insert and delete information from your worksheets.

Inserting Entire Cells

Inserting cells, as opposed to inserting data inside a cell, requires that the existing worksheet cells move to the right and down to make room for the new cell. Perhaps you created a worksheet of employee salaries and failed to include the employees who work at

7

another division. You can easily make room for those missing entries by inserting new cells. You can insert both new rows and new columns in your worksheets.

To Do: Insert a Cell into a Worksheet

When you want to insert a cell into an existing worksheet, you perform these steps:

1. Select the cell that should appear *after* the inserted cell.
2. Select Insert, Cells to display the Insert dialog box.
3. Click either the Shift Cells Right option or the Shift Cells Down option to determine the direction of the shift. The shift makes room for your new cell.
4. Click OK to begin the shift.

You can use the mouse to move cells right or down to make room for new data by using the *fill handle*, the small black box that appears in the bottom-right corner of a cell. (Figure 7.1 shows the selected range's fill handle.) Press Shift and drag the cell's fill handle (or the selection's fill handle if you have selected a group of cells) down or to the right. Excel grays out the areas that are left blank by the shifting.

To Do: Insert Rows and Columns

To insert a row or column (and thus move the other rows down or other columns to the right), perform these steps:

1. Select the row or column that appears *after* the inserted rows or columns by clicking its header to select the entire row or column. If you want to insert more than one row or column, select that many existing rows or columns by dragging the row or column selection.
2. Select Insert, Rows or Insert, Columns. Excel shifts the existing rows or columns to make room for the new empty row or column. Instead of selecting from the menu bar, you can point to the selected row or column and display the shortcut menu shown in Figure 7.2 by right-clicking the mouse to insert the new row or column. (Excel inserts multiple rows or columns if you first selected more than one row or column.)

To Do: Delete Rows and Columns

You can use the Delete dialog box not only to delete cells, but also to delete entire rows and columns.

FIGURE 7.2

The shortcut menu offers Insert, Delete, and several other options.

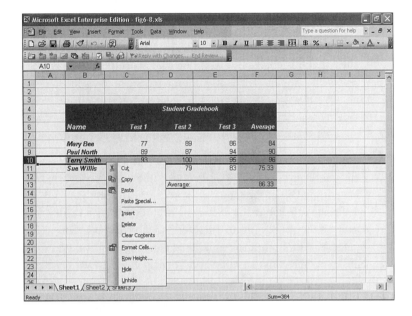

To delete a row or column, perform these steps:

1. Select a cell in the row or column you want to delete.

2. Select Edit, Delete to display the Delete dialog box.

3. Select either the Entire Row or Entire Column option.

4. Click OK to perform the deletion. Excel shifts columns to the left or shifts rows up to fill in the missing gap.

> If you want to delete multiple rows or multiple columns, select cells from each column or row you want to delete before displaying the Delete dialog box.

Deleting rows and columns differs from deleting specific contents inside cells. When you want to erase a cell's specific contents, the other cells to the right and below that cell don't shift to fill in the empty space. To erase a cell's contents, click on the cell to move the cell pointer there and press F2 to edit the cell's contents. Press Backspace to erase the cell. Even quicker, you can press Ctrl+X or select Edit, Cut to remove the contents and send them to the Office Clipboard where you can paste them elsewhere or ignore them.

7

Working with Worksheet Ranges

A *range* is a group of cells. A selected group of cells composes a range. A range is always rectangular, and it might be a single cell, a row, a column, or several adjacent rows and columns. The cells within a range are always contiguous, but you can select multiple ranges at the same time. You can perform various operations on ranges, such as moving and copying. If, for example, you want to format a row of totals in some way, you first select the range that includes the totals and then apply the format to that range.

Figure 7.3 shows three ranges on a worksheet. You can describe a range by the cell reference of the upper-left cell of the range (the anchor point) and the cell reference of the lower-right cell of the range. As you can see from Figure 7.3, multiple-celled ranges are designated by listing the *anchor point*, followed by a colon (:), followed by the range's lower-right cell reference. Therefore, the range that begins at B3 and ends at F4 has the range of B3:F4. To select more than one range, in case you want to apply formatting to different areas of your worksheet at once, hold Ctrl while selecting the ranges.

FIGURE 7.3

Three ranges appear on this worksheet.

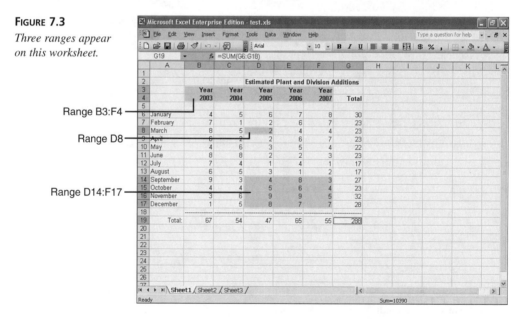

In Excel, you often work with ranges. One of the ways to make your worksheets more manageable is to name your ranges. Range names are far easier to remember than range references. You might assign the name Titles to your column titles, for example, Months to your column of month names, and so on.

To Do: Name a Range

To name a range, perform these steps:

1. Select the cells that you want to include in the named range.

2. Click the name box at the left of the formula bar (the text box that displays cell references).

3. Type the range name. The name can be as long as 255 characters, and the first character must be a letter or the underscore character. The rest of the name can contain letters, numbers, a period, and the underscore character but no spaces or other special characters such as a question mark. The name cannot be the same as a possible cell reference, so R2D2 would not count as a valid range name.

4. Press Enter. When you subsequently select the range, you will see that Excel displays the range name rather than the range reference in the name box.

Range names are easier to remember than range references. If you create a payroll worksheet and assign the names GrossPay, NetPay, HoursWorked, TaxRate, and PayRate to the ranges holding that data, for example, you never again have to type the range references. When you want to move or copy one of the ranges or use the range as a formula, just refer to the range name and let Excel figure out the correct references. You learn how to use ranges (including range names) in formulas in the section called "Using Formulas."

Here's an even better reason to name ranges: If you move a range, Excel moves the name with the cells! If you track range references and not names, you often must track down the latest references when you refer to the range. By naming ranges, you never have to worry about keeping track of references because the names won't change even if the references do.

Use meaningful names. Although AAA works as a name for a column of net sales figures, Net Sales (not pw) makes a lot more sense and is easier to remember.

If you create a large worksheet and you need to return to a named range to make some changes, click the name box's drop-down list arrow and select the name. Excel instantly displays and selects that range for you. Moving around Excel is much simpler once you set up a set of named ranges.

7

Using Formulas

Without *formulas*, Excel would be little more than a simple row- and column-based word processor. When you use formulas, however, Excel becomes an extremely powerful time-saving planning, budgeting, and general-purpose financial tool.

On a calculator, you typically type a formula and then press the equal sign to see the result. In contrast, all Excel formulas *begin* with an equal sign. For example, the following is a formula:

=4*2-3

The asterisk is an operator that denotes the times sign (*multiplication*). This formula requests that Excel compute the value of 4 multiplied by 2 minus 3 to get the result. When you type a formula and press Enter or move to another cell, Excel displays the result and not the formula on the worksheet.

As Figure 7.4 shows, the answer 5 appears on the worksheet, and you can see the cell's formula contents right on the formula bar area. When entering a formula, as soon as you press the equal sign, Excel shows your formula on the formula bar as well as in the active cell. If you click the formula bar and then enter your formula, the formula appears in the formula bar as well as in the active cell. By first clicking the formula bar before entering the formula, however, you can press the left- and right-arrow keys to move the cell pointer left and right within the formula to edit it. When entering long formulas, this formula bar's editing capability helps you correct mistakes that you might type.

Cell's formula appears here

FIGURE 7.4

Excel displays a formula's result on the worksheet.

Formula's answer

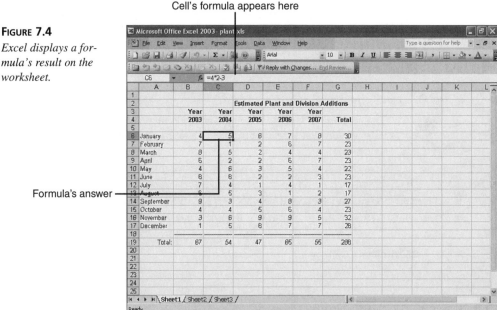

Excel's Primary Math Operators

Table 7.1 lists the primary math operators you can use in your worksheet formulas. Notice that all the sample formulas begin with the equal sign.

TABLE 7.1   The Primary Math Operators Specify Math Calculations

Operator	Example	Description
^	=7 ^ 3	Raises 7 to the power of 3 (called *exponentiation*)
/	=4 / 2	Divides 4 by 2
*	=3 * 4 * 5	Multiplies 3 by 4 by 5
+	=5 + 5	Adds 5 and 5
−	=5 − 5	Subtracts 5 from 5

You can combine any and all the operators in a formula. When combining operators, Excel follows the traditional computer (and algebraic) *operator-hierarchy* model. Therefore, Excel first computes exponentiation if you raise any value to another power. Excel then calculates all multiplication and division in a left-to-right order (the first one to appear computes first) before addition and subtraction (also in left-to-right order).

The following formula returns a result of 14 because Excel first calculates the exponentiation of 2 raised to the third power, and then Excel divides the answer (8) by 4, multiplies the result (2) by 2, and finally subtracts the result (4) from 18. Even though the subtraction appears first, the operator hierarchy forces the subtraction to wait until last to compute.

```
=18 - 2 ^ 3 / 4 * 2
```

If you want to override the operator hierarchy, put parentheses around the parts you want Excel to compute first. The following formula returns a different result from the previous one, for example, despite the same values and operators used:

```
=(18 - 2) ^ 3 / 4 * 2
```

Instead of 14, this formula returns 2,048! The subtraction produces 16, which is then raised to the third power (producing 4,096) before dividing by 4 and multiplying the result by 2 to get 2,048.

Using Range Names in Formulas

The true power of Excel shows when you use cell references and range names in formulas. You learned in an earlier section, "Working with Worksheet Ranges," how to name

7

your worksheet ranges. Instead of referring to the range F2:G14, you can name that range MonthlySales and then refer to MonthlySales in your formulas by name.

All the following are valid formulas. Cell references or range names appear throughout the formulas.

```
=(SalesTotals)/NumOfSales
=C4 * 2 - (Rate * .08)
=7 + LE51 - (Gross - Net)
```

When you enter formulas that contain range references, you can either type the full reference or point to the cell reference. If you want to include a complete named range in a formula (formulas can work on complete ranges, as you see later this hour), select the entire range and Excel inserts the range name in your formula. Often, finding and pointing to a value is easier than locating the reference and entering it exactly.

If, for example, you are entering a formula, when you get to the place in the formula that requires a cell reference, don't type the cell reference; instead, point and click on the cell you want to use in the formula, and Excel adds that cell reference to your formula. If you enter a formula such as =7 +, instead of typing a cell reference of LE51, you can point to that cell and press Enter or type another operator to continue the formula. Immediately after typing the cell reference for you, Excel returns your cell pointer to the formula (or to the formula bar if you are entering the formula there) so that you can complete it.

After you assign a name to a range, you don't have to remember that range's reference when you use it in formulas. Suppose that you are creating a large worksheet that spans many screens. If you assign names to cells when you create them—especially to cells that you know you will refer to later during the worksheet's development—entering formulas that use that name is easier. Instead of locating that cell to find its address, you need only to type the name when entering a formula that uses that cell.

Relative Versus Absolute Cell Referencing

When you copy formulas that contain cell references, Excel updates the cell references so that they cite *relative references*. For example, suppose that you enter this formula in cell A1:

```
=A2 + A3
```

This formula contains two references. The references are relative because the references A2 and A3 change if you copy the formula elsewhere. If you copy the formula to cell B5, for example, B5 holds this:

```
=B6 + B7
```

The original relative references update to reflect the formula's copied location. Of course, A1 still holds its original contents, but the copied cell at B5 holds the same formula referencing B5 rather than A1.

An absolute reference is a reference that does not change if you copy the formula. A dollar sign ($) always precedes an absolute reference. The reference B5 is an absolute reference. If you want to sum two columns of data (A1 with B1, A2 with B2, and so on) and then multiply each sum by some constant number, for example, the constant number can be a cell referred to as an absolute reference. That formula might resemble this:

```
=(A1 + B1) * $J$1
```

J1 is an *absolute reference*, but A1 and B1 are relative. If you copy the formula down one row, the formula changes to this:

```
=(A2 + B2) * $J$1
```

Notice that the first two cells changed because when you originally entered them, they were relative cell references. You told Excel, by placing dollar signs in front of the absolute cell reference's row and column references, not to change that reference when you copy the formula elsewhere.

$B5 is a partial absolute cell reference. If you copy a formula with $B5 inside the computation, the $B keeps the B column intact, but the fifth row updates to the row location of the target cell. If you type the following formula in cell A1:

```
=2 * $B5
```

and then copy the formula to cell F6, cell F6 holds this formula:

```
=2 * $B10
```

You copied the formula to a cell five rows and five columns over in the worksheet. Excel did not update the column name, B, because you told Excel to keep that column name absolute. (It is always B no matter where you copy the formula.) Excel added 5 to the row number, however, because the row number was relative and open to change whenever you copied the formula.

The dollar sign keeps the row B absolute no matter where you copy the formula, but the relative row number can change as you copy the formula.

The bottom line is this: Most of the time, you use relative referencing. If you insert or delete rows, columns, or cells, your formulas remain accurate because the cells that they reference change as your worksheet changes.

7

Copying Formulas

Excel offers several shortcut tools that make copying cells from one location to another simple. Consider the worksheet in Figure 7.5. The bottom row needs to hold formulas that total each of the projected year's 12-month values.

How do you enter the total for column B in cell B19? You can type the following formula in cell B19:

```
=B6+B7+B8+B9+B10+B11+B12+B13+B14+B15+B16+B17
```

There are better ways to total a column of numbers, but for now this way will suffice. As you enter formulas, Excel color-codes cells that you refer to as you type the formula. Therefore, if you create Figure 7.5's worksheet and start typing =B6+B7+ into the total area, Excel colors each cell starting with B6, as well as that cell reference in the formula, a unique color. By color-coding the cells to match the formula references, you can more easily spot mistakes in long formulas.

FIGURE 7.5

A total row is needed for the project's yearly values.

A total goes here

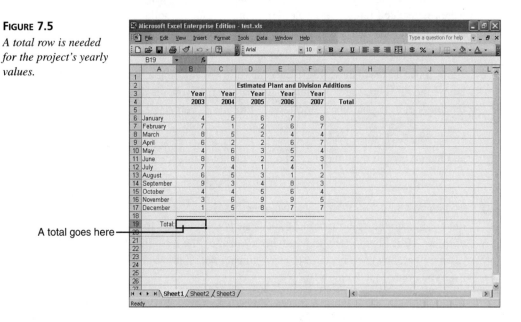

After you type the formula in B19, you then can type the following formula in cell C19:

```
=C6+C7+C8+C9+C10+C11+C12+C13+C14+C15+C16+C17
```

You then can type the values in the remaining total cells. Instead of doing all that typing, however, copy cell B19 to cell C19. Hold Ctrl while you drag the cell edge of B19 to C19. When you release the mouse, cell C19 properly totals column C! Press Ctrl and copy C19 to D19 through F19 to place the totals in all the total cells. The totals are accurate, as Figure 7.6 shows.

After you drag one or more cells to fill data in other cells, Excel displays the AutoFill Options button at the right of the fill that you can click to specify how you want the new cells to be formatted (the same as the original cell without bringing the original cell's format to the new ones). Generally, the default fill method works well and you'll often never click the AutoFill Options button to change the way Excel completed your cells.

FIGURE 7.6

Relative references make totaling these columns simple.

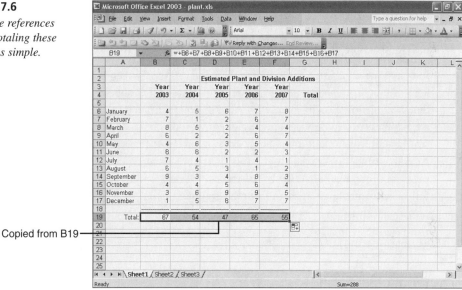

Copied from B19

Recalculating Worksheets

After you set up formulas, your job is done; Excel's job has just begun, however. If you change any value in the worksheet, Excel recalculates all formulas automatically! Therefore, Excel keeps your worksheet fresh and accurate as you modify values. You can use the same worksheet each month and change only the monthly data. If you leave the formulas intact, Excel computes and displays the correct answers.

You can turn off the automatic recalculation and manually recalculate when ready if you use a slow computer and want to save time when editing a large worksheet. Select Tools,

7

Options and click the Calculation tab. Click the Manual option to force manual recalculation. If you now change the data, Excel does not recalculate your worksheet until you press F9 (the Calculate Now shortcut key).

Working with Functions

The previous sections explained how to enter a formula once, using relative cell referencing, and copy that formula to other cells. Although you only have to type the formula one time, this kind of totaling formula is tedious to type and introduces greater chance for error:

```
=B6+B7+B8+B9+B10+B11+B12+B13+B14+B15+B16+B17
```

Fortunately, Microsoft includes several built-in *functions* that perform many common mathematical calculations. Instead of writing a formula to sum a row or column of values, for example, use the Sum() function.

Function names always end with parentheses, such as Average(). A function accepts zero or more *arguments*, and an argument is a value that appears inside the parentheses that the function uses in some way. Always separate function arguments with commas. If a function contains only a single argument, you do not use a comma inside the parentheses. Functions generally manipulate data (numbers or text), and the arguments inside the parentheses supply the data to the function. The Average() function, for example, computes an average of whatever list of values you pass in the argument. Therefore, all the following compute an average from the argument list:

```
=Average(18, 65, 299, $R$5, 10, -2, 102)
=Average(SalesTotals)
=Average(D4:D14)
```

> When you begin to enter a formula, ScreenTips pop up after you type the formula's name to help guide you through the formula's required contents.

As with many functions, Average() accepts as many arguments as needed to do its job. The first Average() function computes the average of seven values, one of which is an absolute cell reference. The second Average() function computes the average of a range named SalesTotals. No matter how many cells compose the range SalesTotals, Average() computes the average. The last Average() function computes the average of the values in the range D4 through D14 (a columnar list).

The following formula computes the average of seven arguments, one of which (F14) is a cell reference and one of which (R5) is an absolute cell reference:

=Average(18, F14, 299, R5, 10, -2, 102)

The Sum() function is perhaps the most common function because you so often total columns and rows. In the preceding section, you entered a long formula to add the values in a column. Instead of adding each cell to total the range B6:B17, you could more easily enter the following function:

=Sum(B6:B17)

If you copy this Sum() function to the other cells at the bottom of the yearly projections, the total appears at the bottom of those columns.

> When you insert rows within the Sum() range, Excel updates the range inside the Sum() function to include the new values.

To Do: Use AutoSum for Efficiency

Before looking at a table of common functions that you can use in your worksheets, consider that one of the activities you'll do the most is adding numbers in formulas. You'll need to add to compute totals, count items, and compute days between activities. Excel helps you add values by analyzing ranges that you select and automatically inserting a Sum() function if needed, thus computing the total. Here's how to do that:

1. Select the range that you want to sum. If you want to sum the months over the projected years for this hour's sample worksheets, for example, select the row with the January label, as shown in Figure 7.7.

2. Click the AutoSum toolbar button. If you don't see the AutoSum button on your toolbar, click the Toolbar Options button to locate it. Excel guesses that you want to sum the selected row and inserts the Sum() function in the cell to the right of the row.

3. Make any edits to the summed value if Excel included too many or not enough cells. You can click the cell and press F2 to edit the sum. Usually, no edits are required.

After Excel generates the Sum() function, you can copy the cell down the rest of the column to add the monthly totals. However, can you see another way to perform the same monthly totals with one selection? Select the *entire set* of monthly values with one extra blank column at the right (the range B6:G17). Excel sees the blank column and fills it in

7

with each row's sum when you click AutoSum. You now can select the new column of totals and let AutoSum compute them. Figure 7.8 shows the result of the new sums after you add underlines and a title to the row.

FIGURE 7.7
Getting ready to request a sum.

AutoSum button

Excel places
Sum function here

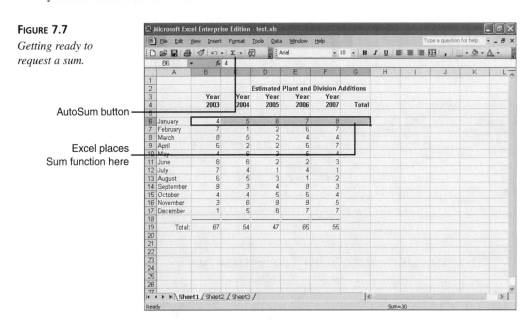

FIGURE 7.8
AutoSum in action.

AutoSum totaled
the entire column

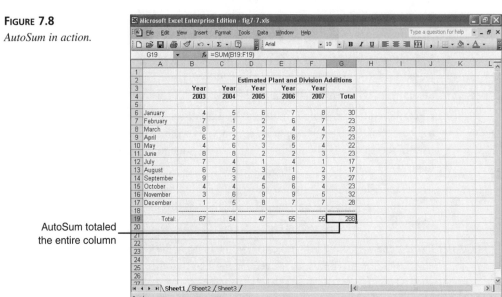

Common Functions

Functions improve your accuracy. If you want to average three cell values, for example, you might type something such as

```
=C2 + C4 + C6 / 3
```

This formula does not compute an average! Remember that the operator hierarchy forces the division calculation first. If you use the `Average()` function, as shown next, you don't have to worry as much about the calculation's hierarchy.

```
=Average(C2, C4, C6)
```

Another advantage of using functions is that you can modify them more easily than long calculations. If you want to include another cell value into the previous average, for example, you only need to add the extra cell to `Average()`; if you use a formula, you must remember to change the 3 to 4.

Table 7.2 describes common Excel built-in functions that you find a lot of uses for as you create worksheets. Remember to start every formula with an equal sign and to add your arguments to the parentheses, and you are set!

TABLE 7.2 Common Excel Functions

Function Name	Description
Abs()	Computes the absolute value of its cell argument. (Good for distance- and age-difference calculations.)
Average()	Computes the average of its arguments.
Count()	Returns the number of numerical arguments in the argument list. (Useful if you use a range name for the argument list.)
CountBlank()	Returns the number of blank cells, if any exist, in the argument range. (Useful if you use a range name for the argument list.)
Max()	Returns the highest (maximum) value in the argument list. (Useful if you use a range name for the argument list and you need to pick out the highest value.)
Min()	Returns the lowest (minimum) value in the argument list. (Useful if you use a range name for the argument list and you need to pick out the lowest value.)
Pi()	Computes the value of mathematical pi (requires no arguments) for use in math calculations.

continues

7

TABLE 7.2   Continued

Function Name	Description
Product()	Computes the product (multiplicative result) of the argument range.
Roman()	Converts its cell value to a Roman numeral.
Sqrt()	Computes the square root of the cell argument.
Stdev()	Computes the argument list's standard deviation.
Sum()	Computes the sum of its arguments.
Today()	Returns today's date (requires no arguments).
Var()	Computes a list's sample variance.

Excel supports many functions, including complex mathematical, date, time, financial, and engineering functions. Click F1 or type a question in the Ask a Question box for Help to supply more details on all the functions you can use.

Advanced Functions

Some of the functions require more arguments than a simple cell or range. Excel contains many financial functions, for example, that compute loan values and investment rates of return. If you want to use one of the more advanced functions, click on an empty cell and select Insert, Function or click the Insert Function button to display the Insert Function dialog box, as shown in Figure 7.9.

You can select from a category of functions in the drop-down list box or describe what you want to do at the top of the dialog box and let Excel locate a function that might work. When you decide on a function (you can simply scroll the list of function names at the bottom of the dialog box and select one), Excel displays an additional dialog box with text box areas for each of the function arguments, such as the one shown in Figure 7.10. As you continue entering arguments that the function requires, Excel builds the function in the cell for you. As you get more proficient, you no longer need the help of the Insert Function dialog box as often.

FIGURE 7.9

Let Excel help you enter complex functions.

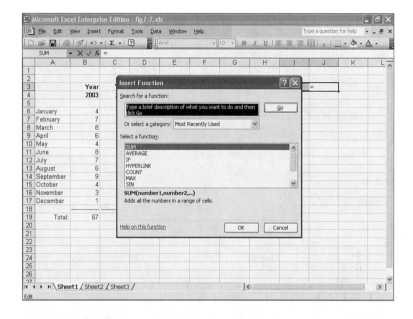

FIGURE 7.10

You can quickly enter arguments in the Function Arguments dialog box.

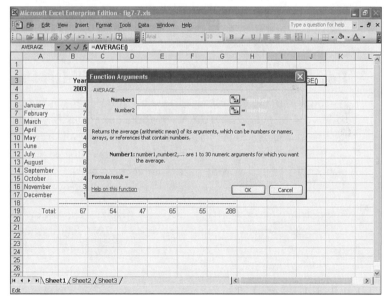

7

Introduction to Worksheet Formatting

It is now time to show you how to pretty things up. This hour is about to come to a close, but you still have time to learn some cell-formatting basics and you can continue with Excel's more advanced formatting features in the next hour's session.

Justification

Excel right-justifies numbers (and formulas that result in numbers) and left-justifies text labels. You don't have to accept Excel's default justification, however. To left-, center-, or right-justify the contents of any cell (or range), select the cell (or range) and click the Align Left, Center, or Align Right toolbar buttons. Using these buttons, you can center titles above columns and adjust your numbers to look just right.

> Excel offers a trick that even some Excel gurus forget: If you want to center a title above several columns of data, type the title in a cell above the data. If you cannot center the title over the values by clicking the Center toolbar button, select all the cells around the title so that you have selected as many columns as there is data. Click the Merge and Center toolbar button. Excel centers the title, even though the title resides in a single cell, across the entire column selection.

Row and Column Height and Width

As you learn more formatting tricks, you will need to adjust certain row and column widths and heights to hold the newly formatted values. To adjust a row's height, point to the line that separates the row number from the previous row. When the mouse pointer changes to a double-pointing arrow, drag the row's top edge up or down. In the same manner, to change the width of a column, point to the column heading's right edge and drag your mouse left or right. Sometimes large titles need larger row heights.

In the same manner, to change the width of a column, point to the column name's left or right edge and drag your mouse left or right. Excel adjusts the column width to follow your mouse movement. When you release the mouse, Excel anchors the new column width where you left it.

If you shrink a column width so that the column can no longer display numerical data, Excel displays pound signs (#####) to warn you that you need to widen the column. Your data is still stored in the cell; it just cannot be displayed.

To adjust the column width so that the column (or range of columns) is exactly large enough to hold the largest data value in the column, select the column (or columns) and double-click the right edge of the column heading. Excel adjusts the column to hold the widest data in the column.

Font Changes

Feel free to change the worksheet's font to add appeal. Simple font changes, such as boldfacing, italicizing, and underlining, greatly improve the look of titles. The Bold, Italic, and Underline toolbar buttons add the proper formatting to your selected cell or range.

If you select Format, Cells and click the Font tab, Excel displays the Font dialog box (virtually identical to that of Word's), in which you can select a new font name and size. As Figure 7.11 shows, simple font changes can make a big improvement on otherwise dull worksheets. The only changes were a different font and size for the title and bold for the months and totals.

New title font

FIGURE 7.11

Already this worksheet looks better.

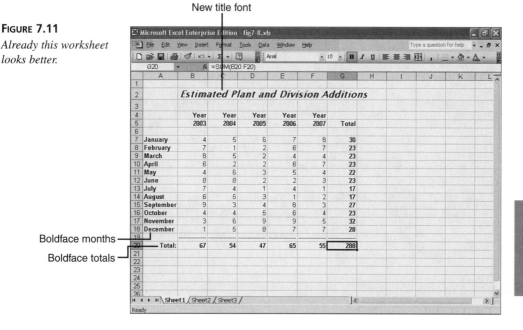

Boldface months

Boldface totals

Of course, you can use the Font and Font Size toolbar buttons to change a typeface or size without displaying the Font dialog box.

Making Format Changes

Now that you have mastered Excel basics, it's time to learn the general format categories Excel uses for worksheet data. Table 7.3 describes each of the format categories. Unless you change the default settings, Excel uses the General format for data of all kinds.

TABLE 7.3 Excel's Fundamental Formats

Format Name	Description
General	Generally appears exactly the way you enter the data with no special formatting for the numeric data.
Number	Displays for all numeric values with the number of decimal places you set.
Currency	Displays a dollar sign and two decimal places for dollar amounts.
Accounting	Aligns currency and decimal points in a column.
Date	Displays date and time values as values whose formats you can change.
Time	Displays only the time portion of a date and time value.
Percentage	Displays a percent sign. If you type 50 into the cell, Excel changes your value to 50%. You can set the number of decimal places Excel displays in the percent.
Fraction	Displays numbers as fractions (great for stock quotes).
Scientific	Uses scientific notation for all numeric values.
Text	Formats *all* data as text. Great for ZIP Codes that are all numbers but that you never use for calculations.
Special	Formats ZIP Codes, phone numbers, and Social Security numbers.
Custom	Lets you define your own cell format. You can decide whether you want to see the plus or minus sign, and you can control the number of decimal places.

Format a selection by choosing Format, Cells and clicking the Number tab to display the formats shown in Table 7.3. If you select the Time format from that list, you must select one of the Time format display variations so that Excel knows how you want the time displayed.

You can also right-click the selection and select the Format Cells command from the shortcut menu. When you do, you see the Format Cells dialog box. You can use this dialog box to assign the formats directly to your data.

> As you saw at the end of the previous hour, Hour 6 "Understanding Excel 2003 Workbooks," you can also use Excel's autoformatting capabilities to easily add style to your worksheet. The next hour, Hour 8, "Using Excel 2003," covers AutoFormat in more detail.

Several Formatting toolbar buttons enable quick formatting of cells using the most common format styles. If you select a cell or a range of cells, you can change the selection's format more quickly with a toolbar button than with the Format, Cells dialog box. Not all Excel's formats are available through the toolbar, but these are: Currency Style, Percent Style, Comma Style, Increase Decimal (to increase the number of decimal places), and Decrease Decimal (to decrease the number of decimal places) .

Summary

This hour extended your knowledge of worksheets by giving you more editing tools with which to insert and delete columns, rows, and cells. After you name important worksheet ranges, you won't have to track specific references in your worksheet; the name is easier to remember, and Excel changes the range if you insert data in or delete it from the range.

One of the most powerful aspects of worksheets is their recalculation capability. If you change data or a formula, Excel recalculates the entire worksheet as soon as you make the change. You are always looking at the computed worksheet with up-to-date information, no matter what kind of data changes you make. When you use formulas, you not only improve your worksheet accuracy, but also you finish your worksheets faster.

The next hour picks up where this one leaves off, going into formatting in more detail. Additionally, you see that graphics spruce up your worksheet and are easy to produce.

Q&A

Q Why would I ever use absolute cell referencing?

A Relative cell referencing seems to make the most sense for the majority of worksheets. If you have to rearrange your worksheet, your relative cell reference updates as well. Absolute references are great when a formula points to a single cell, such as an age or pay value, that rarely changes. You could use dollar signs to anchor the cell reference in the formula that uses that cell but keep the other references relative in case you need to copy the formula around the worksheet.

Q What's the difference between the formatting you get by clicking the Center toolbar button and the formatting you get by clicking the Merge and Center button?

A If you need to center the contents of one cell, both buttons perform the same task. If want to center data (such as a title) above a range of cell columns, however, select the range the centered cell is to go over and click Merge and Center; Excel completes the centering across the multiple columns.

HOUR **8**

Using Excel 2003

Make your worksheets more accurate by mastering the techniques in this hour's lesson. You can easily edit cell contents with the tools Excel 2003 provides.

After you master worksheet-editing skills, you are then ready to see how Excel's AutoCorrect feature works to improve the accuracy of your worksheets. Excel is smart and can even enter cell values for you. When you ask Excel to fill in a series of cell values, it uses some intuitive guesswork to complete any series that you begin. If you often enter a special series of numbers or labels, you can teach Excel to recognize that series. This feature eliminates typing when you use the series again.

The highlights of this hour include the following:

- Why AutoCorrect is important to numeral-based worksheets
- How Excel fills in series for you
- When (and how) to teach Excel a new series
- How to find and replace worksheet data
- How to print worksheets more effectively
- How to use comments to describe a cell

AutoCorrect Worksheets

Use AutoCorrect as you type Excel entries just as you used AutoCorrect in Word. When you type an abbreviation for an AutoCorrect entry, Excel converts that abbreviated form to the complete AutoCorrect entry for you when you press the spacebar or move the pointer to another cell.

> Word, Excel, and all the other core Office products share the same AutoCorrect and spelling dictionaries. Therefore, when you make changes and additions in the AutoCorrect or spelling dictionaries of Word or Excel, the other products recognize those changes.

To add AutoCorrect entries, perform the same steps that you do with Word; namely use the Tools, AutoCorrect Options menu to display the AutoCorrect dialog box and add your entries there.

Finding and Replacing Data

Like Word, Excel contains a powerful search-and-replace operation that can search your worksheet for values and replace those values if needed. Although Word users often use Word's search-and-replace, the feature gets less use in Excel. Nevertheless, the feature is extremely beneficial for worksheets. Imagine that you have a worksheet that tracks the payroll for your company, and the minimum wage increases. Instead of laboriously changing each and every cell that includes the minimum wage, you can use Excel's find-and-replace feature to quickly update the data.

> The find-and-replace feature in Excel works a little differently from that in Word. The numeric nature of Excel requires a different type of find and replace. Therefore, read this section even if you have mastered the find-and-replace feature in Word.

You display the Find and Replace dialog box by choosing Find on the Edit menu. Alternatively, you can press Ctrl+F. Figure 8.1 shows the Find and Replace dialog box in Excel, after you click the Options button to show extra details.

FIGURE 8.1

You can use Excel's Find and Replace dialog box to look for text or numbers.

You can request that Excel search by rows or columns. If your worksheet is generally longer than wide (as most are), select By Columns to speed your search. Select the Match Case option if you want Excel to match the uppercase and lowercase letters in your search exactly.

Use Formulas if you are searching for part of a formula (you learn all about formulas in the next hour), use Values if you want Excel to search only the calculated cells (not within formulas), and use Comments if you want Excel to search through cell comments. Generally, you are searching through formulas, so Excel makes Formulas the default search target.

The Match Entire Cell Contents option indicates to Excel that a cell must contain your entire Find value and nothing else before it makes a proper match.

If you want Excel to replace the found value with another value, select the Edit, Replace command to display the Replace page of the Find and Replace dialog box, as shown in Figure 8.2.

FIGURE 8.2

Let Excel replace values for you.

Enter the text you want Excel to locate in the Find What field and type the text you want to replace that with in the Replace with field. Click the Replace All button if you want Excel to replace all occurrences of the found text. (Be sure that you want to replace all occurrences, or you'll possibly overwrite data unexpectedly.) Otherwise, click Find Next to find the next matching value and, if that is a value you want to replace, click Replace. If it is not a value you want to replace, click Find Next to locate the next occurrence.

If you want to find or replace within a limited worksheet range only, select the range before conducting the find or replace operation.

Reviewing Cut, Copy, and Paste in Excel

If you have mastered the Copy, Cut, and Paste commands in Word, those commands in Excel will be a breeze for you. As with Word and the other Office products, Excel uses the Office Clipboard to hold data that you are copying, cutting, and pasting from within or between worksheets. Alternatively, if you open two workbooks at the same time and display both on your screen (by selecting Window, Arrange), you can easily copy, cut, and paste between the two workbooks by dragging content from one worksheet to the other.

To copy data from one location to another, select the cell or cells you want to copy and then click the Copy toolbar button (or press Ctrl+C) to copy the worksheet contents to your Clipboard. The contents stay in the original location because you elected to copy and not cut the cells. To paste the Clipboard contents to another location, click the cell to indicate the upper-left corner of the target range. Then, click the Paste toolbar button (or press Ctrl+V). Excel overwrites the target cells with the pasted contents, so be sure of the paste target when you paste Clipboard data.

As with all Office products, you can send up to 24 distinct items to the Office Clipboard and paste one or more of the copied items into your worksheet. When you copy or cut more than one worksheet item to the Office Clipboard, the Clipboard task pane appears to display the Office Clipboard contents. You can paste any of the Office Clipboard task pane's items to your worksheet. As with Word and the other Office products, you can copy and paste text, numbers, formulas, pictures, Internet hyperlinks, and Media Gallery clips. The Clipboard task pane appears by default. However, if its display has been turned off, you can redisplay it by choosing Edit, Office Clipboard.

You can continue pasting the copied item to other worksheets as long as you keep selecting a target location and pressing Ctrl+V.

8

Excel supports drag-and-drop editing, so after you select the cells to copy, press Ctrl and drag the selection to its new location. You must drag the selection by pointing to one of the selection edges; if you attempt to drag from the center of a range, Excel modifies which cells are selected. When you release your mouse button and the Ctrl key, Excel pastes the contents to the target location. Of course, drag-and-drop editing works only when you can see both the source and the target copy and paste locations.

To cut contents and place them elsewhere, just select the cells that you want to cut and click the Cut toolbar button (or press Ctrl+X). Excel removes the selection from its original location and places the selection on your Clipboard. You then can paste the Clipboard contents elsewhere. In effect, cutting and pasting performs a movement of the selected data. If you want to move the selection with your mouse, drag the selection without first pressing Ctrl as you did when copying the contents.

> If you want to drag and drop data between two workbooks' worksheets but you only have one worksheet displayed, press the Alt key before dragging your selection. When you drag the selection over the target worksheet's tab, Excel opens that worksheet, and you can drop the dragged contents to the open worksheet.

Clearing Data

Because of the nature of worksheets, erasing worksheet data differs from erasing word-processed data. Other information on the worksheet can heavily depend on the erased data, as you saw in the previous hour's lesson. When you want to erase a cell's or selection's contents, first decide which of the following kinds of erasure you want to perform:

- Erase the selection and send the contents to the Clipboard (as you learned in the previous section).
- Clear only a portion of the selection, such as its formatting, comment, or contents.
- Completely erase the selection and all formatting and notes attached to the selection.
- Erase the selected cells and their positions so that other cells in the row move left or cells below move up.

A worksheet's cell contains a lot more than just the numbers and text that you see on the worksheet screen. Not only can the cells contain formulas and comments, but also they often rely on other cells for information. Therefore, when you want to erase the selection, you must keep in mind how the selection affects other worksheet areas.

If you want to delete only the selected cell's data, press Delete. Excel retains any formatting and comments that you had applied before you deleted the data.

If you want to more selectively erase a cell, select the Edit, Clear command and select from one of the four options listed here:

- The All option deletes the entire selection, including the contents, format, and attached comments (but not the actual cell).

- The Formats option erases only the selection's format; you can get rid of a cell's special formatting and revert to a general format without changing or erasing the actual contents of the cell.

- The Contents option deletes the cell data but leaves the formatting and comments intact.

- The Comments option deletes any special comments that appear in the selected cells.

Reverse an accidental deletion with Undo (Ctrl+Z).

To remove the selected cells as well as their contents and close the gap left by the deleted selection, select Edit, Delete to display the Delete dialog box, as shown in Figure 8.3. Select Shift Cells Left or Shift Cells Up so that Excel knows how to close the gap that the deletion leaves.

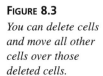

FIGURE 8.3

You can delete cells and move all other cells over those deleted cells.

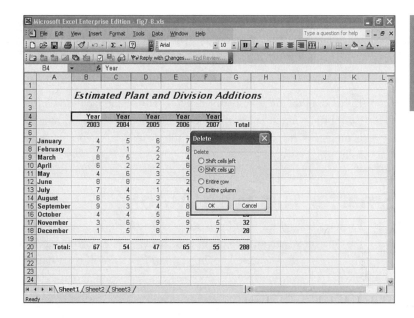

8

Speed Data Entry

Excel can often predict what data you want to enter into a worksheet. By spotting trends in your data, Excel uses educated guesses to fill in cell data for you. Excel uses *data fills* to copy and extend data from one cell to several additional cells.

To Do: Use Data Fills

One of the most common data fills you perform is to use Excel's capability to copy one cell's data to several other cells. You might want to create a pro forma balance sheet for the previous five-year period, for example. You can insert a two-line label across the top of each year's data. The first line would contain five occurrences of the label Year, and the second line would hold the numbers 2003 through 2007. To use the data-fill feature in Excel to create the five similar labels, perform these simple steps:

1. Click the B3 cell to move the cell pointer there.

2. Type **Year**. Don't press Enter or any cell-moving keys after you type the label.

3. Locate the cell's fill handle in the lower-right corner.

4. Drag the fill handle to the right across the next four columns. As you drag the fill handle, Excel displays the pop-up label Year indicating the value that will be automatically entered in the new cells.

5. Release the mouse button. Excel fills all five cells with the label.

If you drag the fill handle down, Excel copies the label down the column. Although the Edit, Fill command performs the same function as the fill handle, dragging the fill handle is much easier than selecting from the menu. Ctrl+D performs the same operation as Edit, Fill, Down.

Smarter Fills with AutoFill

Even if the only fill Excel performed was the copying of data across rows and columns, the data fill would still be beneficial. Excel goes an extra step, however: It performs smart fills with a feature known as *AutoFill*. AutoFill is perhaps the single reason why Excel took over the spreadsheet market a few years ago and has been the leader ever since. When you use AutoFill, Excel examines and completes data you have entered.

The five-year pro forma period you were setting up in the preceding section included the years 2003 through 2007, for example. You can type 2003 under the first Year title and type 2004 under the second title. Select both cells, and then drag the fill handle right three more cells. When you release the mouse button, you see that Excel properly fills in the remaining years (as shown in Figure 8.4).

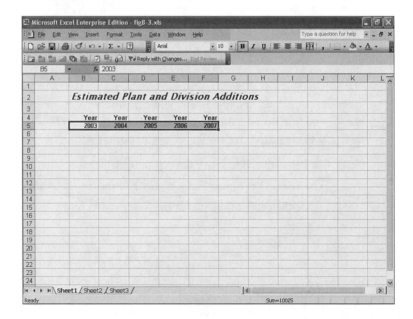

FIGURE 8.4

Excel's AutoFill feature knew which years to fill.

If you had selected only one cell, Excel would have copied that cell's contents across the worksheet. Excel needed to see the two selected cells to notice the trend. Having said that, if you only select one cell with a date such as 2003 and drag the fill handle by clicking the right mouse button instead of the left, a menu pops up that gives you the option of a *Fill Series* that will extend the fill properly by adding one to each year.

The years in Figure 8.4 were right-aligned under the right-aligned titles in the previous row. To do this, you only need to select the year titles and then click the Align Right toolbar button to right-align the years so that they appear directly above the year values.

Excel offers even better tools for automatic cell filling than having to hold the left or right mouse button and then using the drag-and-fill method you just saw. If you want to use AutoFill to increment cells by a single number, as you are doing here with the years, you don't really need to select two cells first. If you select any cell that contains a number, press Ctrl, and drag the fill handle, Excel adds a one to each cell to which you extend. Therefore, you could fill four years from 2003 through 2007 just by pressing Ctrl before you drag the first year's fill handle to the right.

As you know, Excel works with text as well as with numeric values. AutoFill recognizes many common text trends, including the following:

- Days of the week names
- Days of the week abbreviations (such as Mon, Tue)
- Month names
- Month abbreviations (such as Jan, Feb)

Suppose that you want to list month names down the left of the pro forma sheet, starting in cell A5, because you need to report each month's totals for those five years. All you need to do is type **January** for the first month name, and drag that cell's fill handle to the twelfth cell below. Figure 8.5 shows the result.

FIGURE 8.5

*Let Excel fill in the
series of month names.*

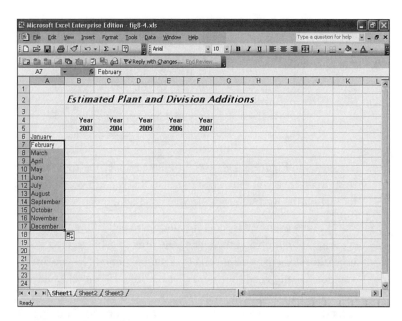

Designing Your Own Fills

In addition to using AutoFill to quickly enter the month and weekday names and abbreviations, Excel can fill in any list of values. You can create a new, customized list with
values that you often use. For example, you can create a custom list for the employees in
your department or for products you sell. After you have shown Excel the new list, any
time you type the first value and drag that cell's fill handle in any direction, Excel fills
the remaining cells with your list.

To Do: Create a Custom List

To add your own custom list to Excel's repertoire of lists, perform these steps:

1. Select Tools, Options.
2. Click the Custom Lists tab to display the current AutoFill lists in effect.
3. Click the Add button.
4. Type the list of values for AutoFill. Excel, in effect, learns your fill values. If you
   have nine departments, you might enter something similar to Dept 1, Dept 2, Dept
   3, Dept 4, Dept 5, Dept 6, Dept 7, Dept 8, and Dept 9. Press Enter after each value.
   Your screen should resemble Figure 8.6.

Figure 8.6

Teach Excel new Custom list entries.

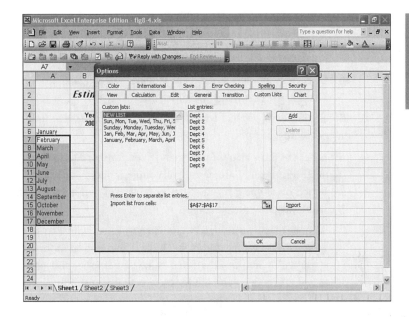

5. Click OK to add your list to AutoFill's current list.

The next time you type the label **Dept 1** in a cell and drag the fill handle to the right or down the worksheet, Excel fills in the remaining departments. If you fill only four cells, Excel uses the first four values. If you fill nine or more cells, Excel fills all nine departments and starts repeating the department names for any number over nine.

If you enter a series in a worksheet and then decide that the series would make a great AutoFill list (in case you want to add the list to another worksheet), Excel doesn't make you re-enter the list. Just select the entire list by dragging the mouse pointer through the list. When you open the Custom Lists tab in the Options dialog box, click Import to add the selected range to the AutoFill entries.

To Do: Enter Large Amounts of Series Data

AutoFill is fine for a typical range of titles and for a series of a dozen or fewer entries, but some data series include numerous entries. When you want to enter a larger number of values in a series, perform these steps:

1. Type the first value of the series in the first cell.

2. Select the cell and all subsequent cells that will receive the rest of the series.

3. Select Edit, Fill, Series to display the Series dialog box.

4. Select Rows if you have selected cells from a row or Columns if you have selected

cells from a column.

5. Select the type of series you are entering. (Table 8.1 describes each of the four types from which you can choose.)

6. Select the subtype. If the Type is Date, select a Date unit. If the series is a series of months, for example, check Month.

7. Enter the Step value, which describes how each value in the series increases or decreases.

8. Enter the Stop value if necessary. (You rarely need to enter one.) If you want to enter a series that increases every three months, for example, you check the Month option, and type **3** for the Step value, Excel will know the final month and you won't need to enter it.

    Although you won't need to indicate to Excel where to stop in most instances, a Stop value is useful if you check the Trend option in the Series dialog box. Excel starts with your initial selected value (if numeric) and estimates the values between that starting value and the Stop value that you supply.

9. Click OK to create and enter the series of values.

TABLE 8.1   Types of Series

Series Name	If You Type...	Excel Can Complete with...
Linear	0	1, 2, 3, 4, 5
	−50, 0, 50, 100	150, 200, 250
Growth	2, 4	8, 16, 32, 64
	10, 100	1000, 10000
Date	1-Jan, 1-Apr	1-Jul, 1-Oct, 1-Jan
AutoFill	Acctg-101, Acctg-102	Acctg-103, Acctg-104
	Year '03	Year '04, Year '05

A Word About Printing

As with the other Office 2003 products, select File, Print to display the Print dialog box for your printer. You can select the number of copies and other print options depending on what features your printer supports. You might want to choose File, Print Preview to

8

display a print preview before printing. This check ensures that the printed worksheet looks the way you prefer.

Excel supports a new feature, called *Intelliprint*, that suppresses the printing of extra, blank worksheet pages that often appear because of the way a worksheet happens to appear on the printed page.

Adding Comments

You can insert *comments* in cells. The comments act like yellow sticky notes onscreen, except that the notes in Excel aren't in the way when you don't want to see them. The comments don't appear in the cell; when you insert a comment, Excel indicates that the comment resides within the cell by flagging the cell's upper-right corner with a red triangle. When you point to the cell, Excel displays the attached comment.

To attach a comment to a selected cell, select Insert, Comment or right-click over a cell and select Insert Comment. Excel opens the box shown in Figure 8.7. Type your comment in the box and press Enter. Excel automatically places your name at the beginning of the comment (assuming that you entered your name when you installed Office). The name indicates who added the comment in case you work in a multiple-user environment. (You can erase the name if you don't want to see it.) You can leave co-workers notes if you edit worksheets as a team. You can also leave yourself a note to fill in data that you might get from an outside source later.

If you select a group of cells and attach a comment, Excel attaches the com-

ment only to the upper-left cell in the selection. Excel cannot attach a comment to an entire selection, only to individual cells.

The section "Clearing Data" earlier in this hour tells you how to remove comments you no longer need.

FIGURE 8.7

Comments help document the worksheet cells.

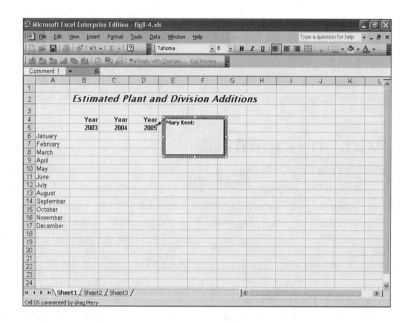

Summary

Excel's Copy, Cut, and Paste commands work much the same as the corresponding operations in Word. This hour focused more on the differences than similarities between the products. Worksheet data differs from a word processor's, and you must handle certain kinds of Excel deletions differently from Word deletions. Remember that deletions in Excel might affect other cells or formulas and result in erroneous data.

This hour taught you how to speed up your data entry by using AutoFill and AutoCorrect. After you teach Excel your own special series, Excel fills in that series of values for you. Although accuracy is more important than speed, you will welcome the speedy data-entry tools Excel provides.

Now that you have covered the groundwork, you are ready to learn about Excel's powerhouse worksheet-formatting features.

Q&A

Q How do I know whether Excel can fill a series I have started?

A Enter the first couple of values, select the cells, and drag the selection's fill handle to the right or down, depending on your desired fill direction. As you drag the fill handle, Excel shows, in a ScreenTips-like pop-up box, which values will fill in the series. If Excel does not recognize the series, the pop-up values won't be correct. You then can teach Excel the new series as explained in this hour or enter the remaining values by hand. In many instances, you will be surprised at the power of Excel; if the first two values in your series are 10 and 20, for example, Excel guesses that you want to extend the series by 10s.

Q Why does Excel sometimes select additional cells when all I want to do is extend a series?

A You must be dragging the cell's contents, *not* the fill handle. Be sure that you drag the fill handle when you want Excel to complete the series. If you drag with one of the cell's straight edges rather than its fill handle, Excel attempts to move the cell contents from their original location to your dragging target; therefore, be careful that you have grabbed the fill handle when you are ready for the fill.

HOUR 9

Formatting Worksheets to Look Great

Excel makes it easy to make even simple worksheets look professional. AutoFormat quickly formats your worksheet within the boundaries you select. If you want to format your worksheet by hand, the formatting commands you learn in this hour will enable you to pinpoint important data and highlight that data. Others can then look at your worksheets and easily find your highlighted information.

The highlights of this hour include the following:

- What AutoFormat can do with your worksheets
- How to apply custom formats to selected cells
- How special orientation and wrapped text can improve your worksheet's appearance

AutoFormatting Worksheets

Before diving into additional formatting commands, remember that the AutoFormat feature in Excel converts an otherwise dull worksheet into a nice-looking, professional one. You saw how simple it is to use AutoFormat in Hour 6, "Understanding Excel 2003 Workbooks," when you applied an AutoFormat to the simple worksheet you created.

Your Excel worksheet's presentation is almost as important as the data within the worksheet. If your worksheet needs sprucing up, try using AutoFormat because it gives a good-looking, consistent dimension to your entire worksheet. After AutoFormat finishes, your worksheet will have a uniform appearance. You can then add finishing touches to the worksheet, such as highlighted totals that you want to make stand out.

To use AutoFormat, select the data in your worksheet that you want to format. AutoFormat works on selected cells, so you need to select your worksheet data first. Select Format, AutoFormat to display the AutoFormat dialog box, as shown in Figure 9.1.

FIGURE 9.1

Let AutoFormat improve your worksheet.

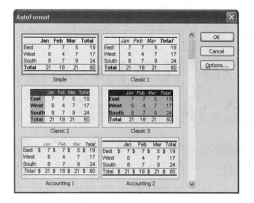

Scroll through the AutoFormat samples and choose any format. When you click OK, Excel applies the format to your selected worksheet cells. Figure 9.2 shows that AutoFormat knows to highlight totals and also knows to separate headings from the data detail.

To omit certain AutoFormat format styles, click the Options button in the AutoFormat dialog box to check or uncheck styles. You can keep AutoFormat from changing your worksheet's font, for example, by unchecking the Font option that appears.

FIGURE 9.2

*AutoFormat improved
the appearance of this
worksheet.*

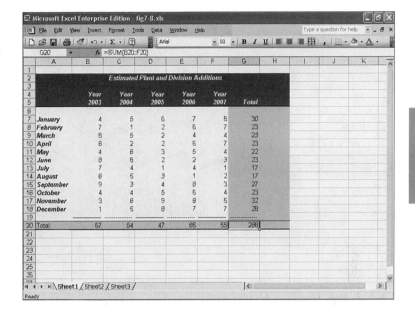

9

Modifying Styles

Suppose that you often print worksheets to fax to others, and your fax requires boldfaced
worksheets so that the recipients can read the numbers. Instead of changing your worksheet text to boldface before faxing the worksheet, you can make boldface the default
font style. Excel enables you to change several of the font defaults. So if you find yourself applying the same font style over and over, consider making that style part of Excel's
default style.

To Do: Modify the Default Style

To modify the default style, follow these steps:

1. Select Format, Style to display the Style dialog box, as shown in Figure 9.3.

FIGURE 9.3

*You can change any
named style.*

2. Select the default style, Normal, from the Style Name drop-down list box. (The Normal style is probably already the style you see when you open the dialog box.)

3. To change the Normal style, click the Modify button. Excel displays the Format Cells dialog box, as shown in Figure 9.4, from which you can modify the named style.

FIGURE 9.4

The Format Cells dialog box allows you to modify any format currently set.

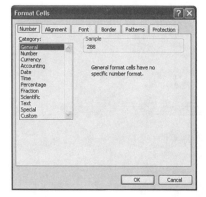

4. Indicate the changes you want to make to the style in the Format Cells dialog box. When you're finished, click OK to close the Format Cells dialog box.

5. Click OK to close the Style dialog box. Excel applies your style to the selected cells. If you made changes to the Normal style, Excel automatically uses that format on future worksheets unless you modify the format or style.

> If you plan to create additional worksheets that are similar to the one you just created, consider saving the worksheet as a template. To do this, choose File, Save As and then select Template on the Save As Type list. When you are ready to create the next similar worksheet, load the template; your formats will already be in place.

Additional Formatting Options

Many of Excel's formatting features are identical to Word's, such as boldface, italics, underline, font color, and fill color (the cell's background color). In addition, you now know how to change the alignment for a range. Excel supports several special formats that go further to improve the look of your worksheets. AutoFormat uses some of these special formats, and you can create your own styles that use these formats as well.

The following sections briefly introduce you to these Excel formatting options, which provide you with additional ways to add impact to your worksheets. You can change any of these formats in the Format Cells dialog box. Open the Format Cells dialog box by selecting Format, Cells or by pressing Ctrl+1.

Special Alignment

Not only can you left-justify, center-justify, right-justify, and justify across selected cells, you can also orient text vertically or to whatever slant you prefer. When you click the Format, Cells, Alignment tab, Excel displays an Orientation box inside the Alignment page, shown in Figure 9.5, in which you can adjust text orientation.

FIGURE 9.5

Align text with the Format Cells dialog box Alignment page.

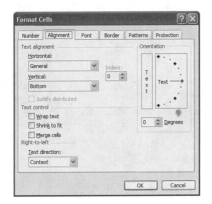

When you click the Alignment page's first orientation text box (the text box with the word Text dropping down the screen), Excel changes all selected cells to vertical orientation. If you want to slant text, such as titles, select a different Degrees value or click the rotating text pointer to the slant you desire. When you click OK, Excel rotates the selected text to your chosen angle. Figure 9.6 shows an example of slanted titles produced by selecting a negative 45-degree angle on the Alignment page of the Format Cells dialog box. The text prints at an angle as well.

If you need to include a lot of text in one or more cells, you already know that Excel either truncates the text or pours the cell's contents into the next cell to the right, depending on whether the adjacent cell includes data. Excel offers several other cell-overflow options as well.

When a cell includes a lot of text, select the Wrap Text option on the Alignment page of the Format Cells dialog box. Excel wraps the text within the cell's width, increasing the cell (and, therefore, row) height to display all the wrapped text. If you click the Shrink to

Fit option, Excel decreases the cell's font size (as much as feasible) to display the entire cell contents within the cell's current width and height. If you click Merge Cells, Excel combines adjacent cells into a single wide cell.

FIGURE 9.6

You can change the vertical alignment of selected text.

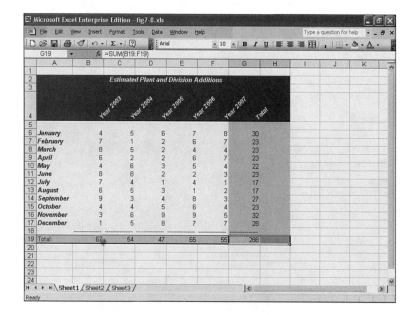

Special Cell Borders

When you select Format, Cells and click the Border tab, the Border page (shown in Figure 9.7) appears. You can use options on this page to apply an outline, or *border*, around selected cells.

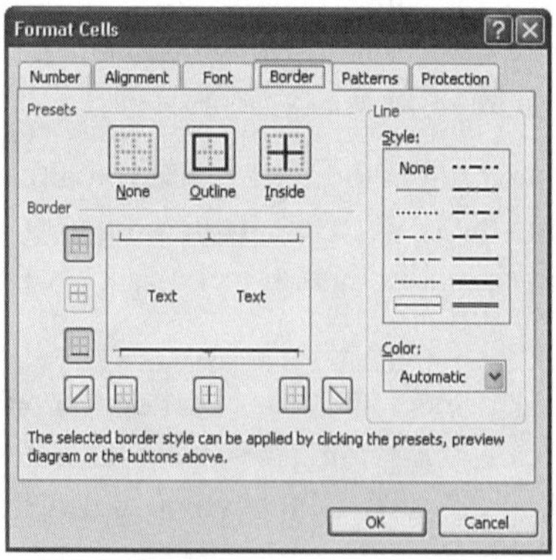

FIGURE 9.7

Add borders around cells to highlight key data.

The Border dialog box enables you to add a border to any side of the selected cells as well as diagonal lines inside the cells so that you can show a cell x'd out or otherwise cross off a cell's contents for a printed report. As you select among the Outline and Inside options, the preview area shows what the resulting border looks like.

> The Draw Borders toolbar button is quicker to use than the Border dialog box, but you cannot control as many border details.

9

Select Style options on the Border page to change the pattern of the border that you choose. If you want to remove any selected cell's border, click None on the Style list. Of course, you can easily change the border's color, which is black by default, from the Color drop-down list box.

Special Cell Shades

When you select Format, Cells and click the Patterns tab, the Patterns page appears and enables you to add color or a shading pattern to selected cells. The Fill Color button colors cell backgrounds more quickly than using the Patterns page options. However, the Patterns page enables you to add a shading pattern to the background in addition to a colored background.

Figure 9.8 shows the Patterns page's extended Patterns palette that is displayed when you click the Pattern drop-down list.

FIGURE 9.8

Choose a pattern for the selected cell.

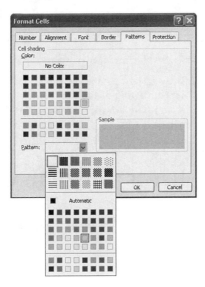

Conditional Formatting

Excel supports *conditional formatting*, whereby you apply a format based on data values and not based on data type or position on the worksheet. Suppose, for example, you are the manager of a company and need to be alerted when sales fall below a fixed level of $500,000. You can set a conditional format on your sales report worksheets to boldface and color the sales values red if any of them fall below 500,000.

Figure 9.9 shows the Conditional Formatting dialog box that appears when you select Format, Conditional Formatting. The Conditional Formatting dialog box uses these parameters:

- The cell value or the formula result of the selected cell (or cells).
- The value or formula between or somehow related to the two values.
- The starting value and the ending value of the condition's range. Click the icons (named the collapse dialog box arrows) to point to cells that form the range if desired.
- The format that Excel is to apply if and only if the condition is met.

You can set multiple conditions for the same selected range by clicking Add and setting up additional conditions.

FIGURE 9.9

Format based on the data value.

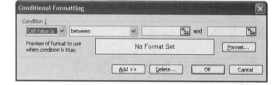

If you have the Office Assistant turned on, the assistant offers to help you with the Conditional Formatting dialog box. Some of the Conditional Formatting options are rather advanced, and the Office Assistant can help get you through them.

Separating Worksheets with Tab Colors

If you need to store multiple worksheets within the same Excel workbook file, you can apply a unique color to each worksheet tab. The colors enable you to more easily distinguish the worksheet tabs at the bottom of the screen.

To apply a color to a worksheet tab, right-click any worksheet tab and select Tab Color. Excel displays a color palette from which you can select.

The tab colors affect only the tab and not the worksheet. After you click a tab to bring that worksheet into focus, the tab color, just as the worksheet (unless you've modified the worksheet's background) becomes white.

9

Summary

Having completed this hour, you can format your worksheets to look any way you want. If you want to let Excel give formatting a try, select your worksheet data and start Excel's AutoFormat feature. Add color, patterns, shading, and borders to your worksheets.

You have learned how to create great looking worksheets, but you have yet to see other ways that Excel can present data to users. In the next hour's lesson, you learn how Excel can display graphs and charts of the data you enter.

Q&A

Q When would I want to create a style?

A If you find yourself applying the same kinds of format commands to cells quite often, consider giving that set of format commands a style name by using the Format, Style dialog box. After you create a style, you can apply it by selecting it from the Style dialog box's list.

Q How can colors help me manage worksheets?

A Apply colors to each worksheet's tab so that you can more easily keep your worksheets separate from each other.

HOUR 10

Charting with Excel 2003

A picture is worth a thousand words—and worth even more numbers! Your worksheet data might contain a ton of numbers, but many times you can present data better with a chart. The actual raw data supplied by a worksheet is accurate and vital information for analysis, but for trends and overall patterns, charts demonstrate the data's nature quickly and effectively. After you create and format your worksheets, use Excel's Chart Wizard to produce colorful charts (also known as graphs). The graphs that the Chart Wizard generates look great, and Excel does all the drawing work for you. After the Chart Wizard creates your charts, you then can customize them to look exactly the way you want.

The highlights of this hour include the following:

- How to use the Chart Wizard to produce graphs that show data trends and comparisons
- When to choose one chart type over another
- How to modify your charts so that they look the way you want them to
- Why an instant chart can come in handy
- How to add graphics to your chart's background area to improve the chart's presentation

Creating Custom Graphs

Luckily, Excel can produce professional-looking graphs from your worksheet data. You don't need to know a lot about graphing and charting unless you want to create extremely sophisticated Excel graphs. Instead you can use Excel's *Chart Wizard* to produce great-looking graphs quickly and easily. When you click the Chart Wizard toolbar button, Excel displays the first Chart Wizard dialog box, as shown in Figure 10.1.

FIGURE 10.1

Excel's Chart Wizard creates graphs for you.

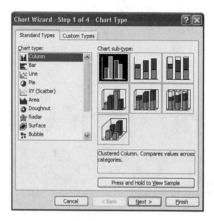

Choosing the Chart Type

Table 10.1 describes each of the chart types that Excel's Chart Wizard can generate. You select an appropriate chart type from the list on the Chart Wizard's first page. To preview the chart, click the Press and Hold to View Sample button. Excel then analyzes your worksheet data and displays a small sketch of the chart in the Sample box. The chart is only a preview of your final worksheet's chart, but a preview is all you need in most cases to know whether the chart is appropriate.

If you don't see the Chart Wizard button (it's the one with the chart icon), click the Toolbar Options button at the far-right edge of the toolbar to display a list of buttons. Once you select the Chart Wizard button, Excel places that button on the toolbar so it's there the next time you need it.

TABLE 10.1   Excel Chart Options

Chart Type	Description
Column	Shows changes over time and compares values.
Bar	Compares data items.
Line	Shows trends and projections.
Pie	Compares the proportional size of items against the parts of the whole.
XY (Scatter)	Shows relationships of several values in a series.
Area	Emphasizes the magnitude of changes over time.
Doughnut	Illustrates the proportional size of items in multiple series.
Radar	Puts in each category an *axis* that radiates from the center of the graph (useful for finding the data series with the most penetration, as needed in market research statistical studies).
Surface	Locates optimum combinations between two data series.
Bubble	Shows relationships between several series values but also (with circles or bubbles of varying sizes) shows the magnitude of data intersections.
Stock	Illustrates a stock's (or other investment's) high, low, and closing prices.
Cylinder, Cone, Pyramid	Indicates trends and comparisons with special 3D cylinder, cone, and pyramid symbols.

> If you are new to charting, you might not know which chart works best for a particular worksheet. If so, you only need to try a chart! If you see that a bar chart does not show a trend that you want to demonstrate, convert the bar chart to a line chart. Excel makes it easy to select among several charts to find the best chart for your needs. Simply right-click the chart and select Chart Type from the shortcut menu that appears.

Selecting Data for Your Graph

A *data series* is a single group of data that you might select from a column or row to chart. Unlike a range, a data series must be contiguous in the row or column with no cells in between. Often, a series consists a time period, such as a week, month, or year. One person's weekly sales totals (from a group of several salespeople's weekly totals) can also form a series. Some graphs, such as pie charts, graph only a single series, whereas other graphs show comparisons between two or more data series.

As you look over your chart, if one of the series looks extremely large in comparison to the others, Excel is probably including a total column or row in the graph results. Generally, you want to graph a single series (such as monthly costs) or several series, but not the totals; the totals throw off the data comparisons. Therefore, if you see extreme ranges at the beginning or end of your graph, select only the data areas (not the total cells) from the Chart Wizard's second screen, shown in Figure 10.2.

Options on the Chart Wizard's second screen provide a way for you to determine exactly what data is to be charted. In a worksheet with a lot of data, Excel cannot be expected to select data automatically. Not only must you inform the Chart Wizard of the data range (or series), but you also need to tell the Chart Wizard which direction the data series flows by clicking either Rows or Columns from the Chart Wizard's second screen.

FIGURE 10.2

Be sure to select only data areas for your graph.

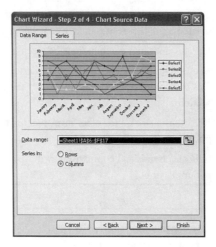

To change the range that the Chart Wizard is to use, click the Collapse Dialog button located to the right of the default Data range, select a different range, and then click the Expand Dialog button.

When you click the Next button to see the third Chart Wizard screen, shown in Figure 10.3, Excel enables you to enter a chart title that appears at the top of the resulting chart as well as axis titles that appear on each edge of your chart.

You find other tabs in the Chart Wizard's third screen that enable you to control the placement of the *legend* and a *data table*. The legend tells the chart's reader what series each chart color represents. A chart's bars and lines appear in different colors to represent the different series being plotted. You can also control the placement of the legend. As you select from the various legend placement options, the thumbnail picture of your chart updates to reflect your selection.

FIGURE **10.3**

Enter titles that you want to see on the chart.

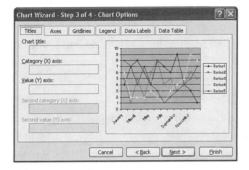

When you click on the Data Labels tab, you can determine how the Chart Wizard selects and places labels on your chart. For example, in addition to a legend, you might want to display the labels next to each piece of a pie chart, as Figure 10.4 illustrates. The Chart Wizard's charting options on the third step's tabbed pages change depending on the type of chart you selected. You might want to try different combinations of legends and labels until you find one that you prefer.

FIGURE **10.4**

The Chart Wizard can place legends and labels where you want them to appear.

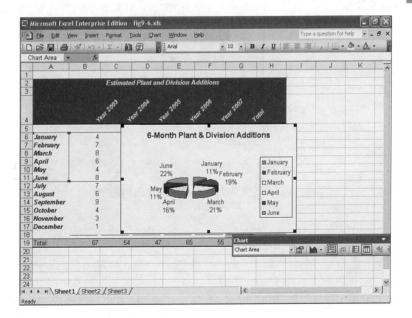

Click Next to see the final Chart Wizard screen, in which you determine exactly where and how to place the generated graph. Excel can create a new worksheet for the graph or embed the graph inside the current worksheet as an embedded object. Each placement has advantages; you might want the chart's data to appear next to the chart, or you might want to use the chart by itself. You can, in turn, embed the chart object in the other Office products, as you will learn in Part VII, "Combining the Office 2003 and the Internet."

Modifying the Graph

Click the Finish button to see your resulting graph. If you have chosen to embed the graph inside your current worksheet, you might have to drag the graph's *sizing handles* to expand or shrink the graph. In addition, you can drag the graph anywhere you want it to appear on your worksheet. Excel displays the Chart toolbar right below the graph in case you want to change it. Figure 10.5 shows a chart embedded as an object in the worksheet, along with the toolbar with which you can modify the graph.

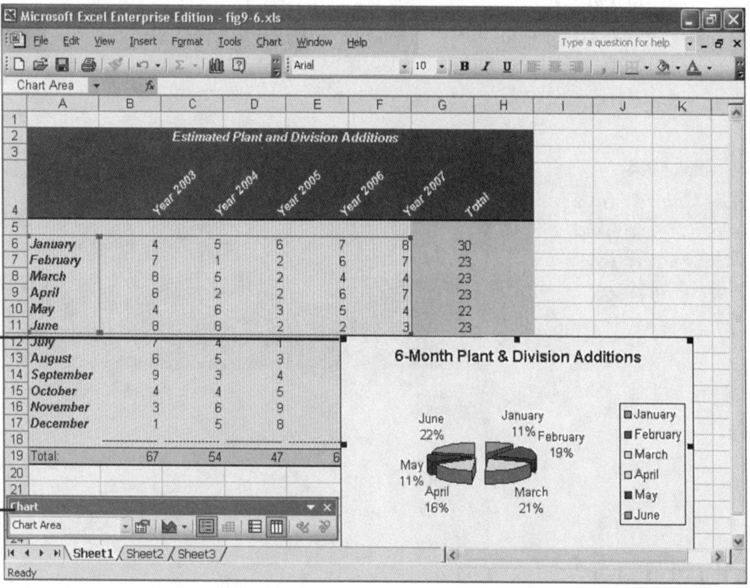

FIGURE 10.5

The worksheet, graph, and Chart toolbar all appear together so that you can make necessary changes.

Sizing handles

Chart toolbar

If your graph does not display data the way you prefer, you can click the Chart toolbar buttons to change the graph's properties. You can even use the Chart toolbar to change the chart type (from a line chart to a bar graph, for instance) without rerunning the Chart Wizard. If you need to make more extensive graph changes, rerun the Chart Wizard.

In addition to using the Chart toolbar, you can often change specific parts of your graph by right-clicking the graph and choosing Chart options on the pop-up menu. If you point to your chart's title and right-click your mouse, for example, Excel displays a pop-up menu from which you can choose Format Chart Title to display the Format Chart Title dialog box.

When you single-click a graph's element, such as the legend or a charted data series, Excel displays sizing handles so that you can resize the element. If you double-click an element, Excel displays the Format dialog box for that element, allowing you to select the formatting options you want.

The mouse makes quick work of the chart's placement as well. You can click and drag within the chart area to move the chart to another location in your worksheet (assuming that you chose to embed the chart in the worksheet at the Chart Wizard's final step). You can also move the chart inside its own enclosing box to make more or less room for the legend.

A Quick Chart

If you want to create a chart in a hurry, Excel lets you with one keystroke as the following To Do task explains.

To Do: Create a Quick Chart

Follow these steps to generate a default column chart:

1. Select a range of values from your worksheet.
2. Press the F11 key or the Alt+F1 key. Excel immediately analyzes the data and instantly presents a generic graph on your screen such as the one in Figure 10.6.

FIGURE 10.6

Excel can generate an instant graph from a range.

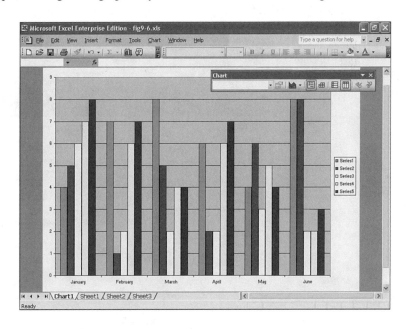

This quick graph won't have proper labels, Excel won't place the graph exactly where you want it (as a matter of fact, the chart will be placed on a newly created, separate chart sheet), and it's possible that Excel will choose a chart type that does not suit your data. That's okay. The instant graphing feature exists to give you a quick glimpse of your selected data.

> If the instant chart that Excel produces is somewhat like the chart you were hoping for, don't run the Chart Wizard to create a similar graph. Instead, right-click the chart's elements that you want to modify, such as the legend, and make your change. Excel already created the chart, so you don't need to go through the Chart Wizard once again to generate another chart.

Making Your Chart Fancy

In spite of the huge assortment of charts, you don't have to limit yourself to the chart types that Excel provides. You can customize virtually any part of the chart, including adding a background image.

Consider the rather simple-looking chart in Figure 10.7. When the user created this chart, she added a chart title and titles for the x- and y-axis descriptions as well. Nevertheless, the chart is lacking in style. It has no personality. It might be fully functional, but if the user wants to use it for a presentation, she might want to pretty it up somewhat.

FIGURE 10.7

Your chart can contain chart titles that you specify.

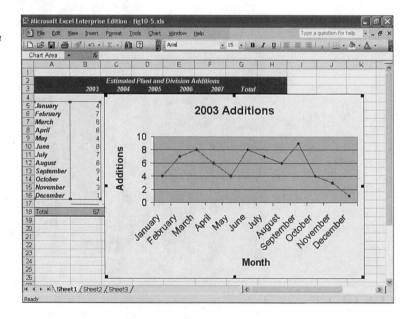

To Do: Add a Background Picture to Your Chart

To add a background picture, you only need to follow these simple steps:

1. Click the chart to display the chart's resizing handles. Increase the size of the chart area by dragging the resizing handles outward.

2. Click the plot area to display its resizing handles and return the plot area to its original size. Move any titles and legend labels back to their places around the graph. You have now added some whitespace inside the graph's area where you can place a picture.

3. Click the Formatting toolbar's (not the Chart toolbar's) Fill Color down arrow to open the Fill Color palette. Make sure that you have the chart area selected and not a label or a title.

4. You could simply select a color and that color would fill the area around your graph. If you'd rather not use a simple color, you can fill your chart's background with a picture by clicking the Fill Color palette's Fill Effects to open the dialog box shown in Figure 10.8. Using the Fill Effects dialog box, you can select many different interesting fills for your chart, such as the Variants area, which gradually changes one color to another.

5. Click the Fill Effects dialog box's Picture tab.

6. Click the Select Picture button and locate a picture on your disk to use as the background of your chart. Depending on how the picture mingles with your legend and graph titles, you might need to reformat the color and font size of those so they appear on top of the picture. Figure 10.9 shows the dramatic difference that a background picture can make as opposed to a chart by itself.

10

FIGURE 10.8

You can create a customized chart using the Fill Effects dialog box.

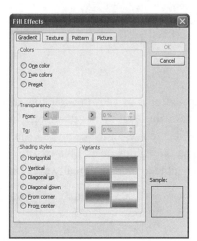

FIGURE 10.9

A background picture makes a dramatic difference in your chart's presentation.

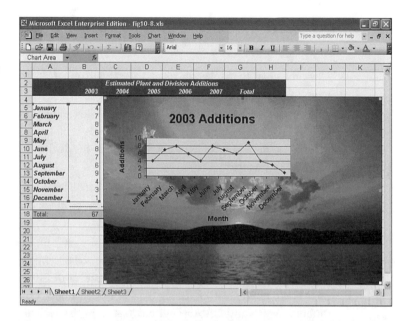

Use the Chart Toolbar

When you work with charts, the Chart toolbar comes in handy. If you don't see the Chart toolbar, select View, Toolbars, Chart. From the Chart toolbar, you can select any element in your chart from the Chart Objects drop-down list box. You can then change any property about that chart object. Here's how: Click the Properties button to display a Properties dialog box with options that control the look of the object.

The remaining toolbar buttons come in handy when you need to modify the chart. Perhaps the most commonly used are the Chart Type and the Legend buttons that allow you to change the chart's type and show or hide the legend.

Summary

This hour augmented your Excel tutorial by showing you how to turn your numeric information into a graph. The numerous chart types that Excel supplies provide you with a wealth of charting options. When you select the data you want to chart, the Chart Wizard takes over and walks you through the rest of the chart's creation. After the Chart Wizard does its job, you still are able to modify virtually every element of the chart.

In the next hour, Hour 11, "PowerPoint 2003 Presentations," you learn about PowerPoint. PowerPoint provides a way for you to present your data to the world by enabling you to create effective presentations.

Q&A

Q Can I add a picture as a background inside the chart's data area itself?

A You can easily add a background to your chart. Whereas Figure 10.9 shows a picture that appears behind the chart's normal gray charting area (called the *fill area*), you can override this background and place a picture behind the actual data lines, bars, and points themselves. To do so, right-click over the fill area's background and select Format Plot Area. Next, select Fill Effects and place the picture just as you did in the final section of this hour.

Q Why would I want an instant graph from the F11 keypress if none of the labels are accurate and if I cannot determine the graph type ahead of time?

A Excel's instant charting feature certainly does not produce final, presentation-ready charts, but that's not the point. When you have data to analyze and you need a quick look at the data, select the data in a range and press F11 (or Alt+F1) to see whether Excel's default Column chart fits the nature of the data. If you want a fancier graph, use the Chart Wizard and specify all the details of the chart. The instant charting feature is available, however, for an initial look at a picture of your data.

10

PART IV

Presenting with Flair

Hour

11 PowerPoint 2003 Presentations

12 Editing and Arranging Your Presentations

13 PowerPoint 2003 Advanced Features

14 Animating Your Presentations

HOUR 11

PowerPoint 2003 Presentations

Have you wanted to wow your audiences with professional presentations? You can with PowerPoint. This hour introduces you to PowerPoint and shows you how to create and design effective presentations. By using the predefined presentation tools of PowerPoint, you generate good-looking presentations without needing to worry about design, format, and color specifics. After PowerPoint generates a sample presentation, you need only follow a few simple procedures to turn the sample presentation into your own.

The highlights of this hour include the following:

- What a presentation is
- How PowerPoint creates new presentations for you
- What kinds of data you can display in a presentation
- When to use the AutoContent Wizard

Presenting PowerPoint

Figure 11.1 shows the opening PowerPoint screen. (Your screen might differ slightly depending on the options that you chose during installation.) As you can see, PowerPoint is ready to begin. You can begin working on the first screen of your presentation right away by clicking and entering a title and subtitle for the presentation. The task pane shows a list of options for creating a new presentation (such as creating a blank presentation or opening a template on which you want to base a presentation).

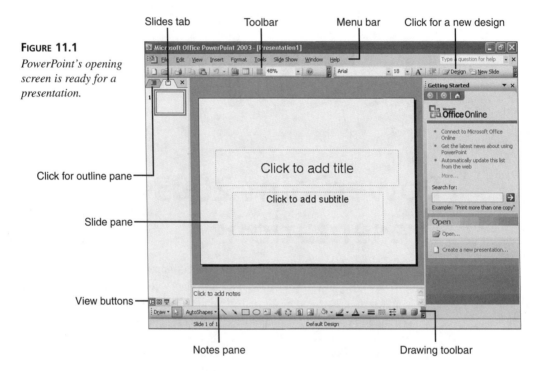

FIGURE 11.1
PowerPoint's opening screen is ready for a presentation.

The next section explains the importance of slides, or individual screens, within your PowerPoint presentation.

Understanding Presentations and Slides

The primary purpose of PowerPoint is to help you design, create, and edit presentations and printed handouts. A *presentation* is a set of screens (called slides) that you present to people in a group. Because PowerPoint provides a wide variety of predefined templates, you don't have to be a graphics design specialist to create good-looking presentations.

Throughout this book, the term *presentation* refers to the entire PowerPoint collection of slides, whereas the term *slide* refers to an individual screen within a presentation.

PowerPoint slides can hold many kinds of information. Here are a few of the things you can add to a PowerPoint presentation:

- Data you insert into PowerPoint, including text, charts, graphs, and graphics
- Word documents
- Live data from the Internet including complete Web pages
- Excel worksheets
- Excel graphs and charts
- Access databases
- Multimedia content such as movies and sound
- Graphics programs that you use to create and edit graphics
- Other software programs whose data you import into PowerPoint

Creating a New Presentation

Figure 11.1 shows the opening window that you see when you start PowerPoint and begin a new presentation. If you close the Slide and Outline tabs window on the left side of the screen, you gain more room to work on the individual presentation slides that appear in the center of the screen.

Select the New Presentation task pane by clicking the task pane's down arrow and selecting New Presentation. This task pane includes an option under the New section labeled From Design Template. Instead of starting to work right away on a blank (and generic) presentation, you can click the option to choose from one of many predefined presentation templates. Click the option now to see your New Presentation task pane change to the Slide Design task pane as shown in Figure 11.2. The task pane displays a list of many presentation style choices, all defined by templates. The idea is that you find the style you like and click that style, and your presentation's elements such as headings, background artwork, and fonts all have a uniform appearance and tone.

The figure shows several design templates that contain layouts you can use. (Templates are stored in files that contain the .pot extension.) For now, don't select a template style, but scroll through the styles to see what is available. Design templates work well for creating PowerPoint presentations one slide at a time, but the design template might not be the best place to begin most presentations.

11

FIGURE 11.2

Templates help you generate uniform presentations.

Now that you've seen some of the ways presentations can look from the styles, you should begin your first PowerPoint presentation by letting PowerPoint help you. The AutoContent Wizard, covered in the next section, is often the best place to begin a new presentation. Once you create a presentation, you can apply a different template if you want to give your generated presentation a different style. If the Slide Design task pane is still showing, click the back arrow at the top of the task pane to return to the previously displayed task pane. There, you will see the AutoContent Wizard option, and you'll be set for the next section.

Planning Is Best Done...in Advance!

Plan your presentations! Think about your target audience. Presenting identical information to two different audiences might require two completely different approaches. A company's annual meeting for shareholders would require a different format, perhaps, from the board of director's meeting.

After you determine your target audience, think about the content of the presentation. Create an outline before you begin. In the next hour, "Editing and Arranging Your Presentations," you will learn about PowerPoint's outlining feature, which you can use to outline a presentation as you create the presentation slides.

The AutoContent Wizard and Presentation Design

Perhaps the best place to begin creating a new presentation, particularly if you are new to PowerPoint, is the AutoContent Wizard. This wizard contains a sample presentation with sample text and a selected design. To use the AutoContent Wizard, you follow a series of screens or pages to select a design and sample content that best suits your needs. After you create the sample presentation, you enter and edit text that replaces the sample's text.

To Do: Use the AutoContent Wizard

To use the AutoContent Wizard to create your presentation, follow these steps:

1. Start PowerPoint.

2. Click the New Presentation task pane's From AutoContent Wizard option to start the AutoContent Wizard's question-and-answer session. Figure 11.3 shows the first of four wizard screens.

3. Answer the AutoContent Wizard's questions to design a presentation that best fits your needs.

FIGURE 11.3

The AutoContent Wizard creates an initial presentation.

11

The AutoContent Wizard helps you create a presentation with content in place. This presentation's design is intended to match the goals of your presentation. As you follow the AutoContent Wizard, you have to determine the answers to these questions: Who is your audience? What message do you want to convey? Are you selling or offering something? Do you want to display your presentation on a computer screen (as you might do via an overhead projection system), over the Internet (your PowerPoint presentations become Web pages if you want), as overheads that you print first (black-and-white or color), or as 35mm slides?

The best approach now might be to run through the wizard once to see the kinds of questions you are asked.

As you recall from the previous section, PowerPoint comes with several predefined style templates. The AutoContent Wizard uses those templates by selecting the one that best suits the goals you indicated by answering the AutoContent Wizard's questions. After the wizard generates the sample presentation, you can change the sample to include the details of your specific presentation.

Here are some of the template styles and presentation types the AutoContent Wizard chooses from:

- Bad news communications
- Business plan
- Corporate financial overview
- Corporate handbook
- Corporate home page
- Employee orientation
- Marketing plan
- Project status
- Reward certificates
- Sales flyers
- Team motivation
- Technical reporting
- Training

All these AutoContent Wizard presentations are available to you even if you don't want the help of the wizard. Instead, you can choose to create a blank presentation directly from a template. PowerPoint supplies two styles for each template: one for an Internet (or company intranet) presentation and one for a standalone PowerPoint presentation.

After you complete the AutoContent Wizard's steps, the wizard generates a sample presentation that matches the style you requested. The wizard generates several slides from that presentation and you can then rearrange, copy, edit, and delete them as needed. Figure 11.4 shows the screen after the AutoContent Wizard was used to generate a sample sales presentation. The left side of the screen shows a list of slide images or a descriptive outline of your presentation, depending on the tab you click. PowerPoint devotes the rest of the screen to whatever slide you select by clicking on a small slide thumbnail to the left.

FIGURE 11.4

The AutoContent Wizard presents you with sample slides that you can edit.

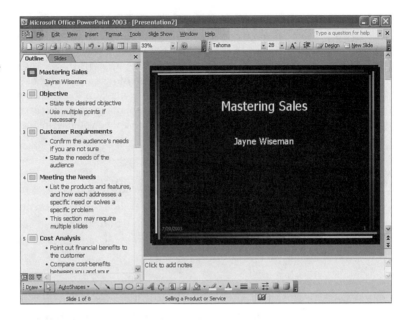

Although your primary editing area for individual slides resides in the center of the screen, you can rearrange the presentation's slide order, delete slides, copy and paste slides to and from the Clipboard, and see a high-level view of your presentation by clicking the Outline or Slide tabs. When you click on any thumbnail slide image on the Slide tab, that slide appears in the slide pane, where you can make specific edits.

11

After the AutoContent Wizard creates the presentation outline, you have to fill in the details. The AutoContent fills the slides with sample text and images, but you change that content to match the presentation you want to give. The remaining lessons on PowerPoint in this part of the book describe how to modify individual slides.

Creating Presentations Using Design Templates

As you learned in this lesson's first section, you can begin working on your presentation's first slide the moment you start PowerPoint. Instead of letting the AutoContent Wizard generate a sample presentation, you can select from one of the templates to get your presentation started with a design and then add slides as you create your presentation using the same template so that your presentation maintains a uniform appearance.

If you click the toolbar's New button, PowerPoint does not open the New Presentation task pane but begins a new presentation with a blank slide and the Slide Layout task pane, as Figure 11.5 shows. The presentation often includes placeholders that you can use to enter your presentation's content. You can choose from among the layouts to generate each slide's look. You won't have the uniformity throughout your presentation that a template would give you, but at the same time you have more flexibility to create exactly the look you require.

When you finish with a slide and you are ready to add the next one, click the New Slide toolbar button and PowerPoint adds a blank slide to your presentation and presents the Slide Layout task pane once more. A presentation contains one or more slides, so you need to click the New Slide button every time you are ready to add the next slide to your presentation.

FIGURE 11.5

You can forgo the AutoContent Wizard and templates and add slides that fit any layout.

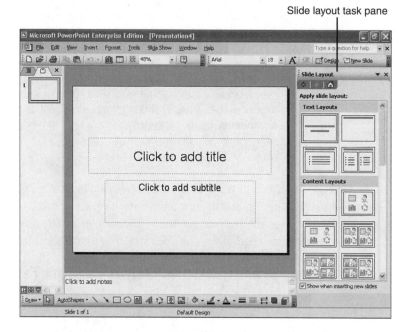

Slide layout task pane

You can change the template design at any point while you're developing your presentation. To do so, just click the toolbar's Design button and the templates appear in the Slide

Design task pane. When you select a template, PowerPoint converts your entire presentation to that template's format. Each slide's background image and standard text such as headings and footers then take on a uniform appearance. If you click another template, PowerPoint converts the entire presentation once again to that new template. You can experiment with different templates to see which, if any, match the tone of presentation you want to achieve.

The instructions on the template's generated slide, as shown in Figure 11.6, indicate what to do next. These preset areas on each slide (placeholders) are designed to accept various kinds of data and make entering information on slides a snap. For example, you can click in a text placeholder and then type your text. In most cases, you edit the text, possibly change colors, and perhaps add a graphic image to the slide. Placeholders help you more easily do this.

FIGURE 11.6

The template's place-holders provide instructions you follow to create a unique slide.

Placeholders with editing instructions

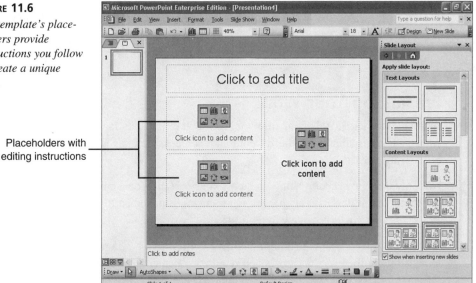

After you add the presentation's final slide, you can save your presentation. You can save the presentation in PowerPoint format or in HTML for embedding into Web pages. Even if your presentation has video and other multimedia content, you can save the presentation as a Web page for viewing from a browser.

You can save a presentation in much the same way as you save a file in Word or Excel. Choose File, Save As and then specify a name for your presentation. PowerPoint automatically adds the filename extension .ppt to your presentation's file.

As you can see, if you start out designing your own slides without the use of a template, you can, at any time later, apply one of the template styles to the slide. Therefore, if you don't like what you generate from scratch, you can redesign the slide or entire presentation without re-entering the slide's text. If you save a presentation as a template file, you can use that presentation's format for subsequent presentations.

Without a template to get you started, presentations require that you manually create every slide element, including the text, titles, and body. Most slides have a title and text, and many have a graphic image. Why not let the AutoContent Wizard or the templates start things off right? The predefined slides work for so many purposes. Resist the temptation to create your slides from scratch until you acquaint yourself with the predefined slides. In most cases, the AutoContent Wizard and templates provide exactly what your presentation needs.

Presenting Your Work

As mentioned earlier this hour, after you create your presentation, you give it to an audience using transparency overheads, computer screens, Web pages, or some other means of presentation.

Not only does PowerPoint help you create your presentations, but also it provides a way to present them. PowerPoint enables you to move from screen to screen, as a slide projector does, at whatever pace you request.

If you do not have access to a high-quality color printer or a 35mm slide printer, many of today's retail office product stores and retail copy centers let you take your PowerPoint presentations, on disk, to their stores where you can request color transparencies and copies of your presentations. In addition, major photography development businesses can turn your disk-based PowerPoint presentations into 35mm slides.

Summary

This hour introduced you to PowerPoint by showing you how to start PowerPoint and how to prepare for your initial slide presentation. PowerPoint prepares all kinds of presentations, all of which have one or more slides (screens). Use PowerPoint to create, edit, and even show your presentations in a slide-projector format.

The AutoContent Wizard is perhaps the best way to start using PowerPoint. Based on your answers to a few simple questions, the AutoContent Wizard creates a presentation with sample text and formatting. To turn the generated presentation into your own, just change the text and, optionally, change the slides' design elements.

The design templates also provide help when you want to add a new slide to a presentation. When you need to create a new slide, select the closest match from the list of design templates. After the design template creates a sample slide, just edit and modify the text.

The next hour shows you how easy it is to turn the AutoContent Wizard or template-designed slides into your own.

Q&A

Q Do I begin with a PowerPoint template, the AutoContent Wizard, or a blank presentation when I want to create a presentation?

A Unlike the other Office products, you almost always create a presentation using the AutoContent Wizard or a template. A blank presentation requires you to lay out all your slide titles and text, which is too much work for most presentations. Unless your presentation requires unusual features, the AutoContent Wizard and templates produce presentations that will be close to your desired presentation.

Basically, all PowerPoint presentation-generation techniques end up producing a new slide on which you must add text, modify colors, change formatting, and add optional graphics. You learn how to apply these slide edits and make specific presentation improvements in the next hour.

Q I'm still confused. What is the difference between the AutoContent Wizard and the design templates?

A The AutoContent Wizard uses the design templates for its slides. The biggest difference between the two presentation-design tools is that the AutoContent Wizard creates a multiple-slide presentation with the sample content and designs in place, whereas the design templates develop a one-slide presentation with design elements present (but no content). You can use either the AutoContent Wizard or a template as a springboard to start your presentation and then customize it to fit your needs.

If you want to add a new slide to a presentation, you might want to use a design template for that individual slide. If you want PowerPoint to generate an entire set of general slides for a specific presentation, such as a corporate business meeting, you can let the AutoContent Wizard generate the entire presentation and then you can fill in the details that your presentation requires.

11

Hour **12**

Editing and Arranging Your Presentations

What do you do once you've generated a sample slide or presentation? PowerPoint's AutoContent Wizard and template samples generate good-looking presentations, but it is up to you to add the specific details inside your slides that teach or show your audience the material you want them to know.

First, you need to change the sample's text. In the process, you might change or add slide titles and formatting or maybe a graphic image for more impact. This hour teaches you a few shortcuts to turn the sample presentations into the presentation you need.

The highlights of this hour include the following:

- When to use the various views that help streamline your PowerPoint work
- Why you work most often using the Normal view
- What editing tools PowerPoint supplies
- How you can use the Slide Sorter view to arrange your slide show
- How to select the presentation printing option you need

Getting Acquainted with PowerPoint's Views

As do all the Office 2003 products, PowerPoint allows you to change the screen's view to make certain tasks more manageable. Therefore, you produce presentations more quickly if you master PowerPoint's views now and learn the advantages and disadvantages of each view.

When you first start PowerPoint and work on a specific presentation, PowerPoint displays a three-pane view (called the *Normal view*) with the presentation's Slide tab and Outline tab in the left pane, a specific slide's content in the top center (called the slide pane), and the notes pane at the bottom of the screen. The notes pane is where you can type notes for the speaker. (Later in this section, you will read about this notes pane.) The task pane is technically not considered part of a view because a different task pane appears depending on what you do within the same view.

The following list not only describes PowerPoint's views but also explains how to use them to convert the template and AutoContent Wizard text to a specific presentation. As you read this section, pay attention to the information that teaches how and when to edit text from the AutoContent Wizard and design templates.

You display PowerPoint's various views from the View buttons in the lower-left of the screen as well as from the View menu. PowerPoint supports the following views:

- *Normal view*—The default, three-pane view from which you can manage your presentation's slide order as well as edit specific slides. In the previous hour's lesson, you worked only from the Normal view. To the left of the large presentation area reside two tabs, the Slide tab that displays thumbnail images of your presentation and the Outline tab that documents your slides' content.

  The Outline tab area enables you to edit and display all your presentation text in one location rather than one slide at a time. Figure 12.1 shows the Normal view that contains a presentation's Outline view in the left pane of a presentation. The large titles (by the slide icons) start new slides, and the details below the titles provide bulleted text for each slide. You can click and drag the dividing line between the presentation area and the outline to see more or less of either side.

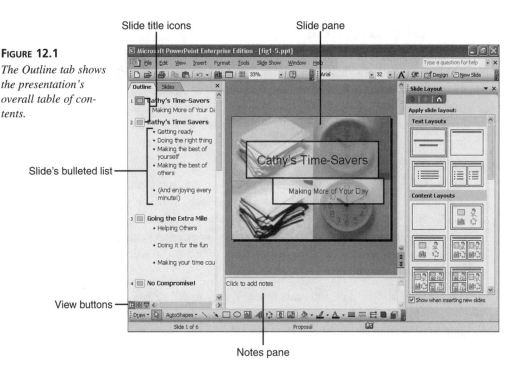

FIGURE 12.1

The Outline tab shows the presentation's overall table of contents.

Slide title icons

Slide pane

Slide's bulleted list

View buttons

Notes pane

12

- *Slide Sorter view*—Displays your entire presentation so that you can easily add, delete, and move slides. The Slide Sorter view acts like a preview tool. You can review your presentation and use the Slide Sorter to present your slides in various ways. For example, you can use the Slide Sorter toolbar to set timings between slides and create special transitional effects when one slide changes to another.

- *Slide Show view*—Displays your presentation one slide at a time without the typical PowerPoint toolbars and menus showing.

- *Notes Page view*—Enables you to create and edit notes for the presentation's speaker. You don't normally have to select the Notes Page view to see the notes pane because a small portion of the notes pane always appears beneath the slide's detail in the Normal view. Click in the notes pane and then add your text.

Change views by selecting the one you want from the View menu. You can also click the Normal view, the Slide Show view, or the Slide Sorter view buttons to the left of the horizontal scrollbar. You work in the Slide Sorter view most often when working with your presentation's layout and slide order, and you work in the Normal view most often when formatting individual slides. Slide Show view displays your presentation as a series of electronic slides.

Using the Outline

An outline helps you organize your presentation and sequence the slides properly. Although PowerPoint makes it easy for you to create the presentation slides themselves, the outline is easier to work with than the full slides, especially when you are still in the process of gathering your thoughts on the presentation's content. If you get in the habit of first working on the presentation's outline (after the AutoContent Wizard generates the presentation), you have less editing and slide rearranging to do later in the development of your presentation.

After you generate a sample presentation by using the AutoContent Wizard or by creating slides from the design templates, use the outline to work on your presentation's details. You can reorganize your slides and edit text in this mode. Click the topic or detail you want to change and edit the text. As you enter and change outline text, PowerPoint updates that individual slide in the slide pane so that you also see the results of your edit to the outline.

All the familiar copy, cut, and paste features work in the outline. If you drag a title's icon or a bulleted list's item down or up the outline area, for example, PowerPoint moves that item to its new location. When you drag a title, all the points under the title move with it. This is a good way to reorganize slides. When you drag an individual bulleted item, PowerPoint moves only that item.

Adding and Importing New Items

To add items to the text in the Slide tab's outline, click at the end or beginning of a bulleted item and press Enter to insert a new entry. If you want to insert a completely new slide, click the New Slide toolbar button, and PowerPoint displays the Slide Layout task pane from which you can select a design and then enter the text. You can also click at the end of an item and press Enter to enter a new slide.

One of PowerPoint's most beneficial text features is its capability to read documents from other Office products. If you create a Word document that you want to include on a slide (or series of slides), select Insert, Slides from Outline and select the Office file that you want to import to your presentation. The file does not have to be in an outline format. For example, you can insert a Word file that is either a Word document or a Word outline file.

As with all Office 2003 products, PowerPoint also recognizes HTML documents so that you can import or save Web page content directly within a presentation.

Promoting and Demoting Elements

From the Normal view, click the Outline tab to display the outline. When you select View, Toolbars, Outlining, the Outlining toolbar appears to the left of the Outline tab area as Figure 12.2 shows. The Outlining toolbar's most important buttons might be its *promotion arrows*. If you type a detail item that you want to become a new slide's title, click the left arrow of the Outline toolbar (the *Promote button*). To convert a title to a bulleted item, click the right arrow of the Outline toolbar (the *Demote button*).

Promote
Demote

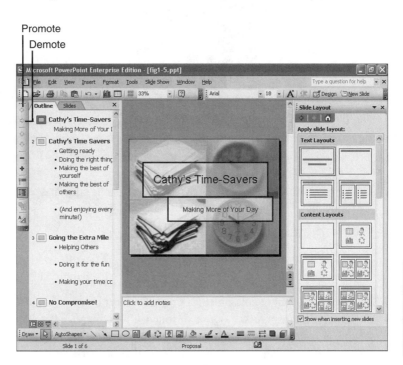

FIGURE 12.2

Buttons on the Outlining toolbar enable you to manipu-late the outline.

12

Working on the Slide

While in Normal view, you can look at and edit the selected slide in the slide pane. As Figure 12.3 shows, the slide's viewing area appears in a full-screen view when you close both the left pane and the task pane. You can make edits directly on the slide and see the results of those edits as you make them. Use the slide pane for viewing changes to your slide's design or for inserting graphical elements into the slide.

FIGURE **12.3**

By closing the sur-rounding panes, you devote more screen area to editing individ-ual slides.

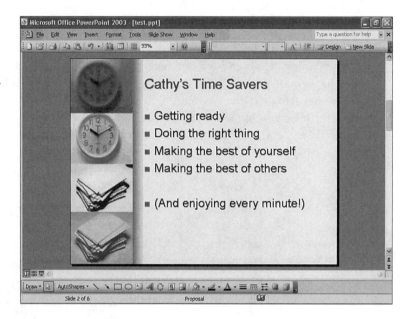

To move from slide to slide while viewing a single slide at a time, perform any of the following:

- Click within the vertical scrollbar area.
- Press the PageUp or PageDown keys.
- Click either the Next Slide or Previous Slide button on the vertical scrollbar.

When you want to edit a text (or graphic) object on an individual slide, click that object. PowerPoint displays the object surrounded by sizing handles. PowerPoint treats a slide's title as a single object and the slide's bulleted set of items as another object. If you've inserted other elements onto the slide, such as a sound or video clip, you can click on that object and move, edit, or delete the object as well. Figure 12.4 shows a busy slide with multiple selections. By holding Ctrl when you click over objects on the slide, you select each of those objects at the same time so that you can apply the same formatting task to the selected items. When you want to change the font or screen size of multiple objects at one time, select them all at once and perform the change only once.

FIGURE 12.4

Select multiple objects to apply a uniform edit to them at once.

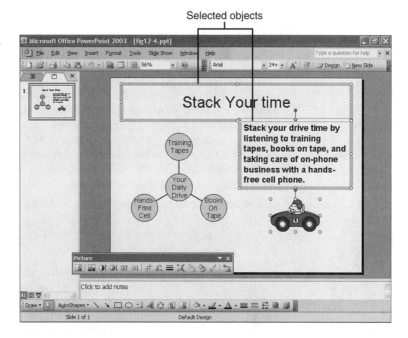

To Do: Edit a Slide's Text

To edit a slide's text, perform these steps:

1. Click the text you want to edit to display the text's sizing handles.

2. To move the text, drag one edge of the text's placeholder in the direction you want to move the text.

3. To shrink or enlarge the selected text object, drag one of the sizing handles in or out to adjust the object's size. (PowerPoint does not shrink or enlarge the actual text inside the placeholder as you resize the sizing box.)

4. After you display the placeholder, click inside the box at the point in which you want to edit text. PowerPoint inserts the text cursor (also called the *insertion point*) at the location of your desired edit. Move the mouse pointer out of the way so you can see the insertion point.

   At the insertion point, you can insert or delete text. You can also change the font, color, size, and style of any text that you select using the Formatting toolbar or the Format, Font menu option. For example, to increase or decrease the font size, use the Font dialog box and select a different size. Displaying the Formatting toolbar

12

makes the most common text formatting tools available, including font, size, bold, and underline.

Select any text, and then click the Increase Font Size toolbar button to quickly increase the font size of the selected text. The Increase Font Size button works faster than opening the Font dialog box. (A Decrease Font Size button is also available.) Depending on your screen size and resolution, you might have to click the toolbar's Toolbar Options button to see the Increase Font Size and Decrease Font Size buttons.

If graphic images appear on the slide, double-click them to edit the images with the graphic-editing tools.

If you right-click an object (such as a graphic image) while editing a slide and select the Action Settings option, PowerPoint displays the Action Settings dialog box, as shown in Figure 12.5. By assigning an Internet hyperlink address, a Windows program, or a sound file to a mouse click or movement, PowerPoint connects to that hyperlink location, runs the program, or plays the sound during the presentation. You can provide pushbutton access to programs and Internet Web pages while delivering your presentation!

FIGURE 12.5

Assign events to mouse clicks and movements.

Using the Slide Sorter View

Use the *Slide Sorter view* to rearrange slides, not to edit text or graphics on individual slides. When you display the Slide Sorter view, PowerPoint presents several of your presentation slides, as shown in Figure 12.6. The Slide Sorter view enables you to quickly and easily drag and drop slides to reorder your presentation. Although you can rearrange slides from the outline, the Slide Sorter view lets you see the overall visual results of your slide movements.

Click to change slide transition
Slide sorter toolbar

FIGURE 12.6

Rearrange slides in the Slide Sorter view.

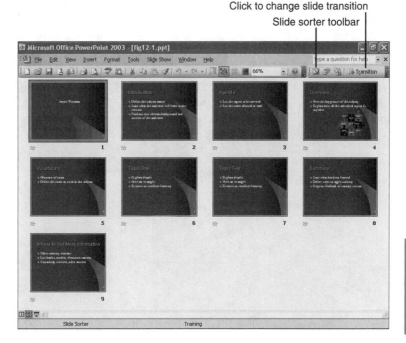

Use your mouse to drag slides from one location to another in the presentation. Remember that the Undo command (Ctrl+Z) reverses any action that you accidentally make. You also can use the Windows Clipboard to copy, cut, and paste, although dragging with your mouse is easier. The Clipboard holds up to 24 entries that you can copy, cut, and paste, as with Word and Excel. To delete a slide, click the slide once and press the Delete key.

One of the more advanced (but useful) slide-sorter features involves the Slide Sorter toolbar, which appears at the top of the Slide Sorter view (refer to Figure 12.6). When you click the Transition button, the Slide Transition task pane appears. These transition effects determine how the slide show feature *transitions* (dissolves) from one slide to the next when you display your presentation. The next two lessons discuss PowerPoint's slide show in more detail. For now, click a Transition button inside the Transition task pane to see the various ways that PowerPoint can move from one slide to the next.

Using the Notes Page View

When you select View, Notes Page, PowerPoint displays your slide, as shown in Figure 12.7, with a blank area at the bottom of the screen for speaker notes. This Notes Page view contains a slide image and, below it, a notes box for the slide. Therefore, the speaker's notes contain the slides that the audience sees as well as notes the speaker wrote to tell the audience about each slide. Your audience does not see the speaker's notes. You click inside the notes box to type or edit slide notes.

FIGURE **12.7**

Prepare speaker's notes using the Notes Page view.

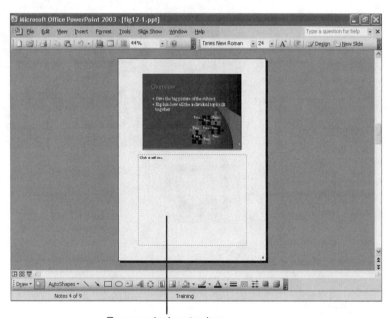

Type speaker's notes here

The Notes Page view is designed to allow printing of the notes for the speaker. However, the speaker can also display the Notes Page view during a presentation to eliminate paper shuffling. If the speaker's computer has two video cards and two monitors, PowerPoint can send the slides to one monitor and the speaker's slides and note pages to the other. When the speaker moves to the next slide, the speaker's notes change as well. When you're ready to return to the Normal view, simply double-click the slide image.

When you display the presentation in Notes Page view, you can use the PageUp and PageDown keys to scroll through the slides and see the speaker's notes at the bottom of each slide. If the text area is not large enough to read the notes, expand the viewing area by using the Zoom command in the View menu.

Saving and Printing Your Work

Be sure to save your presentation after creating and finalizing it. PowerPoint automatically saves your presentation with the .ppt document filename extension unless you override the default file type and save your presentation in another format, such as the Web-based HTML format.

Of course, you also need to print your presentation, either to a color printer or to a printer that supports transparencies. The File, Print dialog box works somewhat differently in PowerPoint than in Word and Excel to take advantage of the special nature of presentations. You can print your entire presentation one slide at a time or elect to print multiple slides on one page for handouts. In addition, you can print only speaker notes and enclose printed slides in framed borders.

When you display the Print dialog box, shown in Figure 12.8, open the Print What drop-down list to view the selection list.

FIGURE 12.8

Decide exactly what you want to print.

Select your printed output

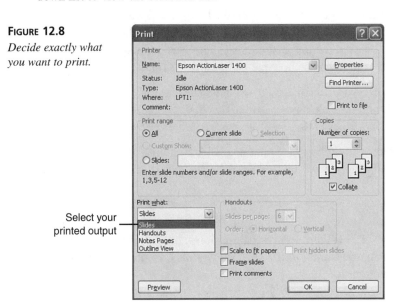

12

The Print Preview feature is new in PowerPoint. You can get an idea of how your presentation will look on paper by selecting File, Print Preview. If you have a black-and-white printer or one that is capable of printing multiple shades of gray (called *grayscale*), the print preview displays in black-and-white or grayscale. If you have a color printer, the print preview displays the presentation's slides in color.

PowerPoint can print your color presentation in grayscale if you don't have a color printer. Select Grayscale from the Print dialog box. In addition, the Print What drop-down list box enables you to print your presentation in any of these styles:

- Slides only for the presentation
- Handouts (which can hold from two to nine slides per page) so that you can give comprehensive notes to the audience
- Notes for the speaker
- The outline for proofreading purposes

If you want to print the entire presentation, you have to select File, Print and select All in the Print range section.

Summary

This hour furthered your PowerPoint knowledge by showing you how to turn a sample presentation into the presentation you want. The views are more critical in PowerPoint presentation development than in Word or Excel. The different views give you a completely new perspective of the presentation. In addition, you use the different views for different functions, such as editing, rearranging slides, and previewing your presentation. Whereas one view is for the audience, another view exists for the speaker.

As you might expect, you can change PowerPoint slide text easily by using the basic text-editing skills you have already mastered. The views enable you to view your slides, outline, and speaker's notes in their most usable form.

The next hour demonstrates how to format your slides with more detail, how to test and start the PowerPoint slide show, and how to spruce up your slides with graphics.

Q&A

Q I want to use PowerPoint to present my slides, but I don't want it controlling the transition and timing of the slide show. Can I use PowerPoint to display my slides manually?

A You learn about the details of the PowerPoint slide show in the next hour, but rest assured that it supports manual slide shows in which you control the appearance of the next slide. Actually, most presenters want complete control over the timing of the slide presentations, and PowerPoint supports such manual transitions. If you want to use PowerPoint to produce Web-based presentations, you can use the slide-show feature as well.

Q Can I print everything (all views) with a single File, Print command?

A No, you can only print individual slide-show components, such as the speaker's notes, audience handouts, or slides from the File, Print menu. If you want to print all presentation elements, select File, Print and print a different component each time.

Q I'm using a bureau service to turn my presentation into individual color slides. Do I need the PowerPoint slide show?

A You will learn about the slide show in the next hour's session. PowerPoint creates individual slides that you can print or display inside PowerPoint, over a Web page, or from any other source that displays PowerPoint presentations. The slide show does not have anything to do with the medium on which you present your final presentation, however, so you can turn your presentation into slides without using the slide show.

12

HOUR 13

PowerPoint 2003 Advanced Features

The more pizzazz and flair you add to your presentations, the more responsive your audiences will be. PowerPoint will help you drive home your point with several advanced features. Your presentations won't be boring. You can format your entire presentation at one time or apply design templates one slide at a time. In addition to applying global presentation and templates, you can edit text and other objects on specific slides. Generally, the AutoContent Wizard and the design templates create presentations that require little editing; if you want to touch up specific parts of your slides, however, PowerPoint provides the tools you need.

The highlights of this hour include the following:

- How to modify your entire presentation's design template
- Why you sometimes need to make minor edits to individual slides
- How to insert art and text from other programs into a slide
- How to insert art and other clip files from the Media Gallery
- What PowerPoint tools you can use to work with text objects
- How to package presentations to work on computers that don't have PowerPoint

Changing Your Entire Presentation's Design

PowerPoint enables you to apply a design template to your entire presentation. No matter whether you develop a presentation with the AutoContent Wizard, with individual design templates, or from scratch, you can easily change the format and look of your entire presentation. You might change your presentation's overall design because you want to give your presentation to a different audience, perhaps one that is more or less formal than the original audience. If you're publishing your presentation on the Internet, you might want to apply a template you've created that incorporates various design elements of your Web site.

An audience change always warrants a review of your overall design. Suppose that you give a seminar to your employees on ethics and morals in the workplace and then learn that your local Chamber of Commerce wants to see your presentation. You would formalize the style when you give your presentation to strangers. You would use a more serious tone provided by another template's design.

To Do: Modify a Design Template

Use the following process to change the entire presentation's design template:

1. With your presentation open, click the Slide Design button on the Formatting toolbar to display the Slide Design task pane as shown in Figure 13.1.

2. Search through the templates for a design you prefer.

3. When you point (not click) your mouse on a template's thumbnail image, an arrow appears to the right of the image that you can then click to provide a menu of choices. You can choose to apply the new template's design to all your slides or to selected slides, and you can even display a larger image of the template to determine whether it's one you want to use.

You can enlarge the thumbnail views of the template's designs by selecting Show Large Previews from any of the template drop-down menus.

4. Instead of selecting from the template menu, simply click any template style once and PowerPoint will change the slides in your presentation to match the style you clicked.

5. After PowerPoint finishes changing the template design for your presentation, page through the slides to see whether you chose a good design. You can always go back through the process to change the design again or undo the change.

FIGURE 13.1

You can apply a completely new design template to your presentation.

Use this task pane.

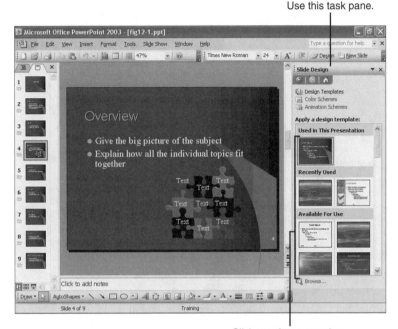

Click to select a template.

Changing a Single Slide's Design

In the previous section, you saw that you could change an entire presentation's design by selecting a new design template without having to edit all the individual slides. Also, by simply selecting Apply to Selected Slide from the Slide Design task pane's drop-down menu, you can change only the current slide.

In either the Normal view or the Slide Sorter view, you can change the design of an individual slide by selecting the Apply to Selected Slides option from the template's drop-down list box of options.

You might be happy with the template but want to change the color set for a slide (or even the entire presentation). When you click on the Color Schemes at the top of the Slide Design task pane, PowerPoint presents you with a list of color schemes for your chosen template, as shown in Figure 13.2. Again, you can apply a color scheme to an

13

individual slide to make that slide stand apart from the crowd, or you can apply the color scheme to the entire presentation by choosing the appropriate option on the drop-down menu.

The preceding section explained how to change the layout of your overall presentation. If you change an individual slide's color or template-based style and then apply a different template or color scheme to the entire presentation, the overall template design takes precedence and changes any individual slide that you might have customized. Therefore, attempt to complete your presentation's overall design and color scheme before you modify individual slides.

FIGURE 13.2
Select a color scheme that you want for your presentation.

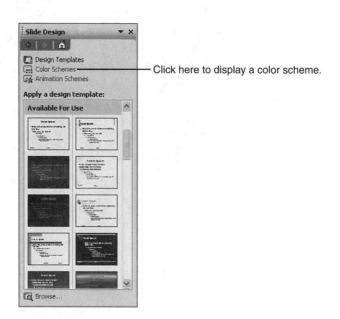

Click here to display a color scheme.

Editing Individual Slides

In most instances, the templates and individual slide layouts and color schemes provide ample variability and style. Rarely do you have to make substantial design edits to your presentation slides; usually you'll change only the text. Unlike most PowerPoint tutorials, this book does not go into great detail about slide editing. You don't need to edit the design of individual slides in most cases because of the detailed layouts that PowerPoint provides.

The major change you must make to the slides for a presentation created with the AutoContent Wizard is to add and edit text on the slides. All the spell-checking and AutoCorrect features that are so important in Word and Excel also work for text you place in a presentation; a red wavy line beneath a word indicates that the Office 2003 spell-checker does not recognize the word. Correct the word, or add it to PowerPoint's dictionary by right-clicking the word.

You can create your presentation's slide text in Word and take advantage of Word's advanced word-processing capabilities. For example, you can import a Word document into PowerPoint. You must, while creating the Word document, use the standard Word styles (such as Heading 1 and Heading 2) and not create your own because PowerPoint uses these standard styles to determine what text converts to slide headings and to bulleted items beneath the headings on the slides. Use Word's File, Send To, Microsoft PowerPoint option to send the Word document to PowerPoint and convert the document to a presentation. You can then select styles that you want to change to add flair to the presentation. Therefore, if you are planning to turn a report into a presentation, save yourself some trouble and use some of the built-in styles in Word, such as the Heading styles, for any headings in your presentation.

  Word documents aren't the only documents you can import into a presentation. You can import an Excel worksheet, HTML-based Web page, chart, or just about any other kind of file (including multimedia files) into a presentation. Beginning with Office 2003, you can insert files with XML content. Select Insert, Object to display the dialog box shown in Figure 13.3, click the Create from File option, and click Browse to locate the document that you want to import.

FIGURE **13.3**

You can insert almost anything into a presen-tation.

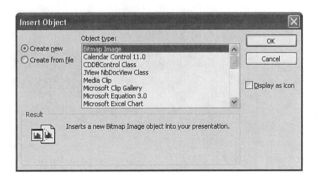

13

Given that PowerPoint 2003 makes quick work of modifying your overall presentation's design and colors, you need to spend some time concentrating on how to edit individual slides. The individual slides take a generic presentation that the AutoContent Wizard generated and turns that presentation into your unique presentation that performs the work you need done.

The Contents of the Master Style

The *Master style* is a collection of headings, colors, and fonts that give a presentation its personality. By selecting View, Master, Slide Master, you can see, and edit, every element defined in your current Master style. Figure 13.4 shows the screen that appears when you display your Slide Master.

You can edit a Slide Master's title style, text styles, and level styles. In addition, you can give your presentation a uniform header and footer appearance from the Master style window. When you change something within the Master style, that element of your presentation changes everywhere it appears.

FIGURE **13.4**

Change the Slide Master to change elements of your own presentation.

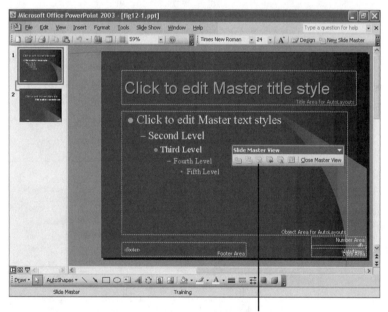

Slide Master toolbar

The following section describes the kinds of edits that you might want to make on individual slides when you need to hone a presentation.

Putting Comments in Your Presentations

The Insert, Comment menu option enables you to insert comments on a slide. The comments appear as small yellow Post-It notes and automatically display your name and the date when you insert the note. After you enter a comment, close the note by clicking outside of it. When you do, it becomes a small box with your initials in it. Later, to read the note, you point to the small comment's icon box to read or edit the comment.

You can add as many comments to a slide or to a presentation as you want. After you add a comment, you can drag the comment to any place on the slide. The comment will not display in the final presentation's slide show.

Comments provide you with a simple annotation tool. You can add to-do notes to yourself for later modifications to the presentation. If you work in a group that is presenting this presentation, each member of the group can add comments for the rest of the group to read as the presentation is passed from worker to worker. This group annotation is perhaps the primary reason why PowerPoint automatically adds the user's name and date to the top of each new comment.

To Do: Add Text and Text Boxes

To add text to a slide, such as text that describes artwork you've placed, you can use a text (or bulleted list) placeholder on a slide. Text placeholders are automatically included as part of some slide layouts. In addition, you can add a text box. A *text box* holds text that you can format. To add a text box, follow these steps:

1. Click the Text Box button on the Drawing toolbar. (The Drawing toolbar is located toward the bottom of your screen. If the Drawing toolbar is not there, select View, Toolbars, Drawing. The ScreenTips that pop up tell you what each tool on the Drawing toolbar does.)

2. Drag your mouse from the text box location's upper-left corner to the text box's lower-right corner. When you release the mouse, PowerPoint draws the text box, as shown in Figure 13.5.

3. Type your text. As you type the text, if your text box is not wide enough to hold the text, the text box will grow to accommodate your text by adding new lines when your typing reaches the right side of the box.

13

4. Use the Formatting toolbar and the Format, Font command to modify the text style and format.

5. Click anywhere outside the text box to deselect the text box and return to the rest of your editing chores.

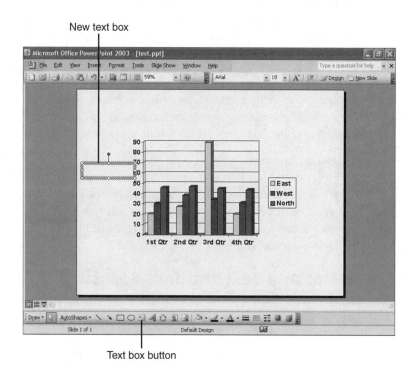

New text box

Text box button

As Figure 13.6 shows, when you click the toolbar's Font drop-down list box, PowerPoint displays each font name in its own font style so that you will see how each font looks before you apply one of them.

FIGURE **13.6**

See a preview of the fonts before you select one.

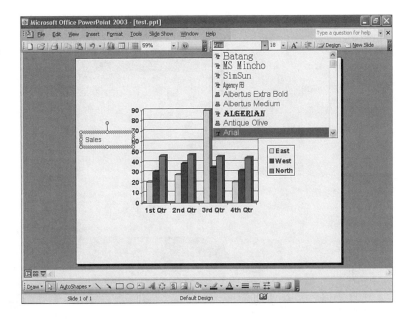

Adding Art

Suppose that you select a slide layout that contains a placeholder for art. Presumably, you have an art image to place on the slide or you would have chosen a different slide layout. When you select a slide layout that includes a placeholder for art, PowerPoint indicates exactly where the art is to go. Figure 13.7 shows an applied slide layout that includes a placeholder for artwork. PowerPoint makes it easy to add the art. Follow the slide's instructions, and double-click within the placeholder to add the art.

When you double-click the art placeholder, PowerPoint displays art from your clip-art collection. (You learned about the clip art and other kinds of clip media files in Hour 5, "Advanced Word 2003.") Your images appear in a dialog box such as the one shown in Figure 13.8. The art can be any graphic image, in addition to other kinds of objects such as video or sound. Scroll down through the clips to see what is available. If you have not yet set up your clip-art collection in another Office product, PowerPoint will first have to locate available clips on your computer. (To add and manage your clips, click the task pane's Clip Art option.)

13

FIGURE 13.7

*PowerPoint indicates
exactly where the art is
to go on the slide.*

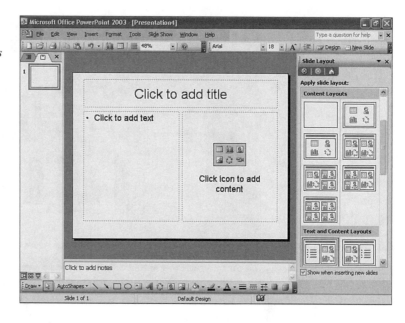

 You can locate clips available online while in the Clip Art window. You are
not limited to clips from your own computer.

If you want to change the slide's clip art, click the image, press Delete, and insert
another one.

Your slide does not need to contain a placeholder for you to insert art. The placeholder
enables you to more easily manage the artwork, however, and to keep the art separated
from the rest of the slide's text and art. If you work with a slide layout that contains a
placeholder, you can move and resize the placeholder while you add the rest of the
slide's elements. When you are ready for the art, double-click the placeholder to insert
the art inside the placeholder's border. Without a placeholder, your artwork overwrites
existing text and graphics that already appear on the slide. You have to move and resize
the inserted art manually to make it fit with the rest of the slide.

Click a clip to select it...

FIGURE 13.8
PowerPoint indicates exactly where the art is to go on the slide.

...and then click OK to insert it in your presentation.

Your art does not have to reside in your clip-art collection for you to insert it. You can insert your own art files, such as logos and pictures, by choosing Insert, Picture, From File and then selecting your file from its directory location.

If you want to import a scanned or digital camera image into a slide, you don't have to exit PowerPoint to scan the image. Select Insert, Picture, From Scanner or Camera. PowerPoint starts your scanner or camera image-loading software. Wait while you scan the image or connect your digital camera to your PC and then insert the image into your slide.

13

Ordering Presentations "To Go"

Once you finish your presentation, you will present it, but you cannot always take your computer with you to your presentation's venue. If you create a presentation on your laptop, you might be able to take your laptop to your meeting, but if you have no laptop, or if you're distributing your presentation to users who might not even have PowerPoint, you need a way to get your presentation in front of your audience.

NEW 2003

PowerPoint 2003 provides a new feature called *packaged presentations* that enables you to save your presentation on a CD and give your presentation on other computers. Even if those computers don't run PowerPoint, your presentation will run fine.

To save your presentation as a packaged presentation, follow these steps:

1. Once you finish your presentation, select File, Package for CD. The Package for CD window shown in Figure 13.9 appears.

FIGURE 13.9

PowerPoint enables you to save your presentation onto CD-ROM to present on other computers.

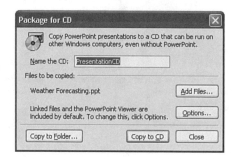

2. To include other presentations, click the Add Files button and select the other presentations you want to save to the CD.

3. Click the Options button if the target computers don't have PowerPoint. Clicking the first option copies a special *PowerPoint viewer* program onto the CD that allows anybody with a computer and the CD to watch your presentation. You can force the viewer to play your packaged presentations in order or let the user select when the playing begins. You must also select the Linked files and the TrueType options if your presentation relies on them.

4. From the Options window, you can also require the end user to enter a password you designate here. (You must type the password twice for verification that you've entered the one you really want to use because the password does not show on the screen as you type it.)

5. Click OK to exit from the Options menu.

6. Insert a blank CD in your writeable CD drive and click Copy to CD. PowerPoint collects the needed files and writes your presentation and optional viewer to the CD. PowerPoint notifies you when the process ends and you can then eject the CD.

> If you want to save your presentation to another computer's folder that is networked to your computer, click the Copy to Folder button and select the target folder instead of the Copy to CD button. (You can even save to Web folders if you have those set up; doing so allows you to save your presentation across the Internet to other computers to which you have access.)

Summary

You learned in this hour how to make presentations look professional and how to modify individual slides when needed. When you work on a presentation with others on a team, the annotated comments provide you a means for distributing notes about the presentation to each other.

Get fancy with your presentation slides by adding graphics and formatting text. As long as your presentation does not get too busy, such distinguishing elements make your presentation more appealing and interesting.

One other technique that can really allow you to show off your presentations is animation. In the next hour's lesson, Hour 14, "Animating Your Presentations," you will learn some of the ways that you can automate your presentation by controlling automatic presentations and determining the way that slides transition from one to the next.

Q&A

Q Why would I add a text box instead of using Outline view to add the text?

A The text on the Outline view is either a title or a bulleted item. If you want to place text outside these areas, you must draw a text box. You can draw a text box anywhere on a slide, and you can even overwrite parts of a clip-art image with a text box. Text boxes are useful for describing figures and for placing extraneous notes on your slides.

Q What if I don't have extensive clip art to embed in my presentations?

A PowerPoint comes armed with many images, so you might not need external graphics-art packages. In addition, PowerPoint includes links to the online world so you can search the Internet for clip-art (as well as picture, video, and sound) files.

13

Hour **14**

Animating Your Presentations

This hour wraps up your PowerPoint tutorial by explaining how to accent and automate your presentation. PowerPoint's Slide Show feature enables you to watch an automated, pre-timed presentation one slide at a time. PowerPoint follows your slide-show instructions and moves the slides forward at the pace and in the style you request. In addition to setting up an automatic presentation, you can control how PowerPoint transitions between slides and spruce up presentations with animation.

The highlights of this hour include the following:

- How a slide show automates your presentations
- How to set up a timed slide show
- How to add voice narration to your slide show
- How to add animated effects to your slides

Using PowerPoint's Slide Show

One of the best ways to see the overall effect of your presentation is to run a simple slide show; that is, walk through your presentation displaying your slides in sequence, moving from one slide to another, transitioning (changing) from one slide to the next without any special effects, but automating the moving at a preset timing that you can control.

An automated slide show is useful for creating self-running demonstrations, product presentations, and conference information distribution. PowerPoint screens use the term *kiosk* to describe the idea of a self-running presentation. Although you can control each and every detail of a self-running slide show, start with the basics and then expand your skills: add a timer to the presentation to control the amount of time each slide is displayed.

To Do: Time Transitions

The Slide Transition task pane is the easiest place to specify slide transition details such as the timing required before the next slide in a presentation appears. Select Slide Show, Slide Transition to display the Slide Transition task pane. Figure 14.1 shows the Slide Transition task pane that appears.

FIGURE **14.1**

Select the transition effect and timing.

Follow these steps to automate the presentation:

1. Towards the bottom of the task pane, you will find an Advance Slide section. Uncheck the option labeled On Mouse Click. Doing so ensures that the presentation speed will not be affected by mouse clicks; the presentation will be fully automated to change slides at a preset time interval.

2. Check the option labeled Automatically After (if it is not already checked).

3. Adjust the value of the minutes and seconds box to 3 seconds (displayed as `00:03`).

4. Click the Apply to All Slides button so PowerPoint does not apply the timed transition just to the current slide. Leave all other values in the task pane alone for now. You have just informed PowerPoint that you want your slide show to run in a kiosk-style with each slide transitioning to the next every 3 seconds.

5. Start the slide show by clicking the Slide Transition task pane's Slide Show button or by pressing F5. The presentation begins. Each slide displays for 3 seconds before the next slide appears. When the final slide displays, PowerPoint displays a blank screen that you can click to exit and return to PowerPoint. During the presentation, click the mouse button and notice that the click has no effect on the presentation's speed. Ordinarily, a mouse click sends the presentation to the next slide.

6. Press Esc to stop the presentation and redisplay your presentation.

Just as Hollywood sometimes fades from one scene to the next, PowerPoint provides some interesting transitional effects that can make your slide transitions more interesting, as you'll learn next.

Transition Effects

If you want more control over the transition, display the first slide in the presentation and select Slide Show, Slide Transition to display the Slide Transition task pane (if it is not still showing from the previous section). The top portion of the task pane determines how your slides can transition from one to the next.

You can control the way an individual slide transitions or the way all slides in your presentation transition. For example, to make the first slide transition to the second by dissolving from the first to the second, click the Dissolve option under the task pane's section labeled Apply to Selected Slides. PowerPoint shows you what the dissolve will look like by dissolving the current slide (as long as the box labeled AutoPreview is checked at the bottom of the task pane). Figure 14.2 shows the dissolve in progress.

To adjust the speed of the transition, click the Speed drop-down list. As soon as you select a speed, PowerPoint dissolves the current slide once more at the new speed so that you can review the speed and adjust again if necessary.

14

FIGURE **14.2**

You can dissolve from one slide to the next.

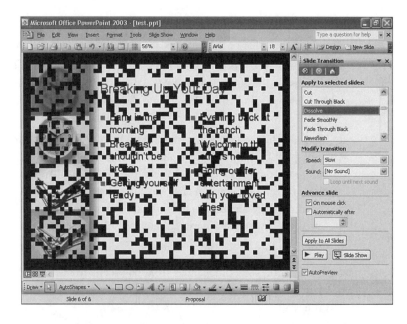

For an even more interesting effect, select a sound as well as a transition. PowerPoint will play the sound, such as applause, when that slide transitions. Some sounds are shorter than the dissolve effect. To repeat the sound until the next sound begins (so that the sound plays during the entire slide's appearance), click the option labeled Loop Until Next Sound.

For both sounds as well as transitions, if you don't click the Apply to All Slides button at the bottom of the task pane, PowerPoint applies the transition and sound only to the current slide.

If you want to use a uniform transition for all slides, click the Apply to All Slides button.

Run through your presentation, using all transitions, before you make your presentation to your audience. Too many transitions can be distracting and can often slow down a presentation and reduce its effectiveness.

Setting Up Shows

PowerPoint provides a Set Up Show dialog box, shown in Figure 14.3, that you display from the Slide Show, Set Up Show menu option. The Set Up Show dialog box lets you control several features of your presentation and is useful whether or not you want to present an automated slide show.

FIGURE **14.3**

The Set Up Show dia-
log box helps you
manage your slide
show.

Table 14.1 explains the various options of the Set Up Show dialog box.

TABLE 14.1   Set Up Show Dialog Box Options

Option	Description
Show Type	Determines whether the presentation is fully automated, controlled by a speaker, or run by an individual at the keyboard. The latter option displays the slide show inside a window, and the other two options display the slide show in full-screen mode.
Show Slides	Determines whether all the presentation slides appear or only a range of slides during the presentation.
Show Options	Enables you to run the slide-show presentation without narration or animation. In addition, you can select a pen color for marking during the slide show and set the slide show to loop continuously until you press Esc.
Advance Slides	Determines whether the speaker or PowerPoint transitions one slide to another.
Multiple Monitors	If your computer has multiple monitors, as might be the case if you use a laptop and connect a projection screen to a second monitor card, you can request that the slide show appear on the second monitor while you control the presentation from the first monitor.
Performance	On slower computers, checking Use Hardware Graphics Acceleration can speed up a slide show, assuming the computer has no system problems with the acceleration. (Errors will appear the first time you try this if the PC will not work.) In addition, you can specify the resolution of the slide show no matter what the screen resolution was before the slide show began.

14

Rehearsing Your Slide Show

If you want your slides to transition at various speeds, you can manually adjust the speed one slide at a time. Some slides might require more time to read than others, and you'll want such slides to remain on the screen longer than others. One of the easiest ways to adjust the timing between slides is to select Slide Show, Rehearse Timings.

As soon as you select the Rehearse Timings option, PowerPoint begins the slide show. As each slide appears (with whatever transition you've applied to that slide's appearance), keep the slide on the screen as long as you think it should remain and then click Next to move to the next slide. Keep clicking through the presentation at the speed you want PowerPoint to move. As you click, PowerPoint records the timing of each slide. At the end of the presentation rehearsal, PowerPoint displays a message box with the total amount of time that the presentation requires. You can save the timings or re-run the rehearsal to specify different timings.

If only one or two slides need their time adjusted, after you walk through the entire rehearsal, you can adjust those slides' transition time individually from the Slide Show task pane.

Voice Narration

If you have a microphone, speakers, and a sound card on your PowerPoint machine, you can add narration to your presentation. Doing so enables you to completely automate all the details of the presentation and not just the slides themselves. Voice animations are great for training sessions, employee orientations, and product demonstrations. They are also helpful for presentations that you distribute via the Web or a company intranet. You can record your voice as you narrate through the slide show, or you can use a sound file you've saved to your disk.

When you select Slide Show, Record Narration, the Record Narration dialog box appears (shown in Figure 14.4). Before you add narration for the first time, click the Set Microphone Level button to let PowerPoint adjust its recording volume as you speak into the microphone. You can also select a higher or lower quality of sound by clicking the Change Quality button. The higher the quality, the more disk space your presentation will require.

After setting up the sound levels and quality, click OK so that PowerPoint will begin the slide show. Even if you've already applied timing to the slides, PowerPoint waits for you to click your mouse button before moving to the next slide. Therefore, when the first slide appears, record the narration that you want your audience to hear on that slide. Then click the mouse when you are ready to see the next slide and record narration for it as well. If you've set up transition effects, PowerPoint retains those effects as the slide show continues. At the end of the narration recording, PowerPoint gives you a chance either to save the presentation with the narration or not save it so that you can have a go at it once again.

FIGURE 14.4

The Record Narration dialog box enables you to add your voice to presentations.

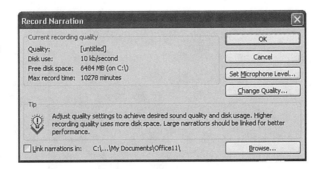

To Do: Use Action Buttons

An *action button* is a button you place on a presentation's slide that, when clicked during the presentation, performs a preset action. To add an action button, follow these steps:

1. Select the Slide Show, Action Buttons menu option. PowerPoint displays a submenu of Action buttons—many of which look somewhat similar to the buttons on a cassette deck. (If you want, you can drag these Action buttons off the toolbar to create a floating toolbar.)

2. Select a button by clicking it.

3. Point to the location on the slide where you want the button to appear and drag your mouse to place the button on the slide. Resizing handles appear around the button (these resizing handles reappear if you select something else on the slide and return to the button) so that you can change the size of the button. You can also move the button by clicking on the button and dragging the button elsewhere on the slide.

4. The button by itself, no matter what the button's icon shows, does nothing. For example, if you placed an action button that looks similar to the Rewind button on a cassette deck, the button will not rewind your presentation. The button does nothing until you specify an *action setting* by selecting Slide Show, Action Settings to display the Action Settings window shown in Figure 14.5.

14

Table 14.2 describes the actions you can apply to the button. For example, if, during your presentation, you want to jump to the Internet and show your audience data from a Web site, you can place an Internet *hyperlink* (also known as a Web address) for the button's action so that when clicked, a Web browser opens and the Web page appears during the presentation. (If you are not connected to the Internet already, the presentation will log you onto the Internet and then display the Web page.)

FIGURE 14.5

Specify exactly what you want the action button to accomplish.

The Mouse Over tab describes the action that occurs when the user points to the button on the screen. In other words, you can apply actions to the user's mouse movement so that certain things happen when the presentation's speaker moves the mouse pointer over the item on the screen without clicking the mouse.

TABLE 14.2 Actions You Can Apply to Slide Elements

Action	Description
None	Removes or keeps any action from occurring.
Hyperlink to	Jumps to another slide or a Web site specified by the hyperlink address when you click the button (the Web address must follow a standard format such as `http://www.samspublishing.com/`).
Run program	Executes the program you select. (Use the Browse button to locate the program if you don't know its exact location or name.)

Action	Description
Run macro	Executes a set of keystrokes you've saved as a macro from the Tools, Macro menu.
Object action	Opens a special object, such as a video file, you've placed on the slide using the Insert, Object menu option.
Play sound	Plays a sound clip when the action occurs.

By the way, if you place action buttons on a slide, you should always specify actions for those buttons. Nevertheless, other elements of your presentation can also take on actions as well as the buttons. Any item you can select, such as a heading, title, or graphic image, as well as a bulleted item on a slide's list, can take on an action that you specify. Therefore, you can simply type the name of a Web site in a slide, select the Web site name, and apply a specific hyperlink to that text from the Action Settings window. You can click the link to display that Web page when you present the Slide Show.

Introducing Animation Schemes

One of the more interesting features of PowerPoint is its ability to animate the various elements of your slides as the slide appears during the presentation. Consider how captivating your presentation could be when any of the following occurs:

- The title flies onto the slide from the side before the rest of the slide's contents appears.
- The top half of the slide falls down from the top while the bottom half of the slide rises up from the bottom of the screen.
- The slide's graphics appear and the text slowly fades into view.
- Each bulleted item in the list comes onto the slide by each letter cart-wheeling into view.
- Paragraphs of text fade in at different moments.
- The title of your slide bounces into view, and when it finally comes to rest at its anchored location, the rest of the slide appears.

The biggest problem with animation is not getting it to work but getting it to work far too well. Don't overdo animation. The animated effects are so fun to work with that it's tempting to add all sorts of fades, cartwheels, wipes, and bounces to the slides. After so many, your presentation will become so top-heavy with animation that the effect will be lost on your audience and the presentation will take on an over-done appearance.

14

To get started with animation effects, select Slide Show, Animation Schemes to display the Slide Design task pane shown in Figure 14.6 with the Animation Schemes option displayed. Read through the different animation options, and you'll see the plethora of effects that PowerPoint provides.

To apply an animation, first display the slide to which you want to apply the animation. Locate the slide by clicking on the slide's thumbnail at the left of the screen or by pressing PageUp or PageDown to display the slide. With the slide showing, click on one of the animation effects.

PowerPoint groups the animation effects by three primary categories: Subtle, Moderate, and Exciting. Each refers to the impact of the effect you choose. Any of the Exciting animation schemes will have far more action than any of the Subtle schemes.

FIGURE 14.6

Specify animation by selecting from the Slide Design task pane.

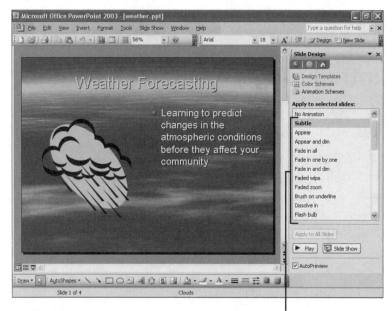

The Animation Schemes

If, after applying a scheme, you decide that you don't want the animated effect, click the No Animation option to remove the animation. If a slide is showing, display the Slide Design task pane and click on different schemes. PowerPoint will show you what the animation looks like.

All animation schemes—as well as transitions, sounds, and other actions you've learned about in this lesson—work whether you manually present your presentation or set up the presentation as a self-running, automated slide show.

Keep in mind that the animation schemes apply to specific elements of your presentation's slides. For example, the Rise Up animation first shows your slide's background image, then the title rises from the bottom of the screen, and then the rest of the slide appears. Unless you've created a slide from a blank slide—keeping all text in the same format and on the same outline promotion level with no animation added—the animation schemes can consistently apply themselves across your presentation if you reuse the same animation on different slides. If you ever change the presentation's Design Template (by clicking on the Slide Design task pane's Design Templates option and choosing a new design), the animations will still work but will be applied to the new design's elements.

Summary

This hour concludes the tutorial on PowerPoint. You can now add animated effects to your presentations to add pizzazz to them and to create attention-grabbing kiosk slide shows. You can select from a wide range of animation effects that automatically and uniformly add animated effects to the elements throughout your slide show.

Hour 15, "Communicating with Outlook 2003," shows you how to manage your contact, calendar, and email with another Office product, Outlook.

Q&A

Q **Should I create an entire, narrated presentation when I give my presentation, or control the presentation myself and narrate live?**

A PowerPoint makes it extremely easy to create a 100% ready-to-go presentation that automatically moves from one slide to the next, in synch with a narrated sound clip that you store. The problem with this is, why would you want to do that if you were there and could give the presentation yourself live? Your audience will surely prefer to hear you give the presentation. You can still use the many slide tools available to give a powerful punch to your presentation, such as animation and transition effects between slides. By giving the presentation live, you can interact with your audience and go at the pace you sense is best for them.

14

People who give the same presentations, however, often have an entire kiosk-style presentation set up, with narration and timed transitions. If that speaker arrives on the scene of a presentation and has a cold or otherwise does not feel up to a live presentation, the audience still gets to hear the show. In addition, Web-based presentations require the automation that the kiosk-style presentations provide. Also, product demonstrations make excellent kiosk-style presentations.

PART V

Organizing with Outlook 2003

Hour

15   Communicating with Outlook 2003

16   Planning and Scheduling with Outlook 2003

HOUR 15

Communicating with Outlook 2003

Outlook contains the biggest assortment of features inside the Office suite due to the number of jobs that Outlook performs. Word is a word processor that is perhaps the most powerful such program with the most features of any word processor ever created, and yet it does one thing, word processing. Outlook, on the other hand, handles many tasks, as you'll see early in this lesson. Outlook helps you manage the details of your life. Not only is Outlook a truly interactive contact, mail, planning, and scheduling program, but it is also fun to use.

The highlights of this hour include the following:

- What Outlook is all about
- How Outlook differs from Outlook Express
- How to read and reply to email messages
- What a contact is
- How to maximize your use of the Outlook 2003 Contacts database

An Outlook Overview

Here is a list that includes just a few of the tasks you can do using Outlook:

- Send and receive all your email.
- Record business and personal contacts.
- Organize your calendar.
- Schedule meetings.
- Manage appointments.
- Track prioritized to-do task lists.
- Keep a journal.
- Write notes to yourself that act as yellow sticky notes when you view them (similar to the comment feature of Word and Excel).

Outlook Is Not Outlook Express

Do not confuse Outlook with *Outlook Express*. Outlook Express is an add-on program that comes with Internet Explorer and Windows. Outlook Express is sort of a slimmed-down version of Outlook but does not contain the scheduling, journaling, and advanced group of features that Outlook contains. Outlook Express does not replace Outlook, so feel free to use Outlook rather than Outlook Express for your contact information.

Outlook Express actually has a feature that Microsoft Outlook does not have. You can work with *newsgroups*, which are a version of massive online electronic bulletin boards organized by topic; with them, you can share files and messages with users from all over the world who are interested in the same topics you are. Microsoft Outlook does not contain a newsgroup reader, but Outlook Express does.

Understanding the Outlook Screen

The opening screen of Outlook can vary considerably depending on how your version is currently set up. The default screen that shows right after installing Outlook is the Outlook Today screen, shown in Figure 15.1. This Outlook Today view is defined by a folder inside Outlook called the Outlook Today folder, and it shows an overview of messages, to-do tasks, and appointments for the current time period. If today's a holiday, Outlook will also tell you that; most major as well as minor holidays appear, and you can adjust, add, and remove other days you want to be reminded of such as birthdays and anniversaries.

If you installed Outlook 2003 over a previous version of Outlook, you will notice that Outlook 2003's screen has changed dramatically. As a matter of fact, Outlook 2003 is the most dramatic change in Office 2003 over Office XP. In addition, Outlook has changed very little since it first appeared in Office 95 until Outlook 2003.

FIGURE 15.1

Outlook's Outlook Today opening screen summarizes your current activities and messages.

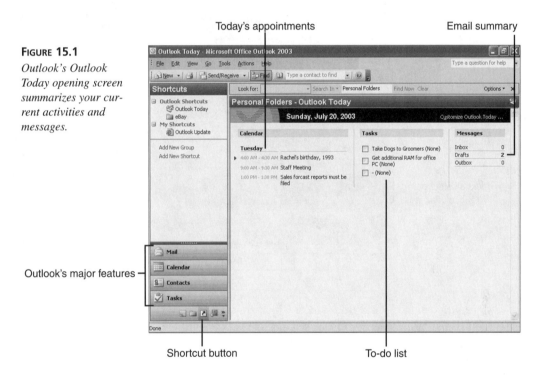

If your Outlook does not open to the Outlook Today screen, but you want it to, select Tools, Options; click the Other tab; and click the Advanced Options button. The drop-down box at the top of the Advanced Options window contains a list of items from which you can select to determine what first appears when you start Outlook. So if you want the Outlook Today screen to appear when you first start Outlook, select Outlook Today from the list. If you want to see your email's *Inbox* (the place where all your mail comes into), select Inbox. You can select from several other opening screens as well. After closing the windows, the next time you start Outlook, the feature you selected will appear.

Figure 15.2 shows the Outlook Calendar folders that you see when you click the Calendar option in the lower-left corner of the screen. You can adjust virtually all screens in Outlook to display data in a format that best suits your preference.

Select time frame.

FIGURE 15.2

The Calendar folder's view shows appointments you've set up.

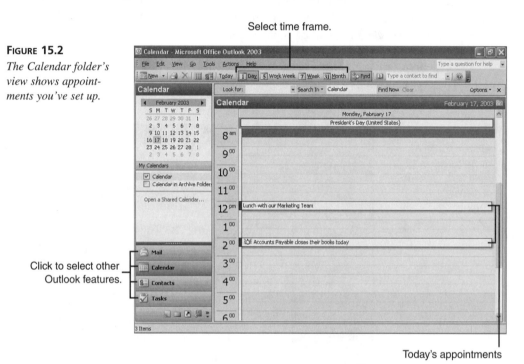

Click to select other Outlook features.

Today's appointments

The different Outlook features, most which are available from the buttons in the lower-left corner of the screen, produce screens that are quite different from each other, more so than the different views of the other Office programs. Here are Outlook screens you'll see:

- Outlook Today—The at-a-glance overview of your current activities that you saw in Figure 15.1. You can view your Outlook Today screen by clicking the shortcut button (shown in Figure 15.1) and then clicking the Outlook Today shortcut that appears in the list at the left of the screen.

- Inbox—A collection of your email messages, organized in topic folders that you set up or contained in the default Inbox folder.

- Calendar—The scheduling screen where you can track appointments, as Figure 15.2 shows.

15

- Contacts—A card catalog of contact name and address information.
- Tasks—Items you have to prioritize and complete.
- Journal—A log of activities you perform on the computer.
- Notes—Notes on any topic that you want to organize.

Outlook's Folders

Outlook stores email and other kinds of data in a series of folders. These folders work much the same way as they do in Windows Explorer; that is, you can move things into the folders, create new folders, rename folders, and delete folders. You can create folders that file Outlook email and other data into compartments where you can easily locate your data later.

Figure 15.3 shows the Mail screen from Outlook (available by clicking the Mail button in the lower-left corner and then clicking your Inbox folder if Outlook does not automatically select the Inbox). You'll see a list of all the folders you've created for Outlook at the left edge of the screen.

The various Outlook screen formats differ quite a bit from that of other Office products. You won't see the typical Formatting toolbar, for example. The Inbox folder (see Figure 15.3) is one of the most common folders you will display. Using Figure 15.3 as a reference, read through these descriptions to familiarize yourself with the Inbox screen elements:

- Inbox folder contents—Lists the email that resides in your Inbox folder. When you want to read a specific message, double-click the message and Outlook opens a message window so that you can read the message.
- Preview pane—Shows the selected email message's contents. You can display, hide, and select the location for the Preview pane from the View, Preview Pane menu option. The Preview pane shows as much of the selected message as will fit; drag the separating window edge between the header list and the Preview pane to change the size of the Preview pane so that you can read more or less of the selected message.

The Favorite Folders area holds a special group of folders that you can add or remove to and from the Favorites list. You'll place the folders you access most in your Favorites list, and then when you need a different folder not shown under Favorites, you can search for the folder you want in the folder area below Favorites.

Favorite folders

FIGURE 15.3
The Inbox folder displays your email messages.

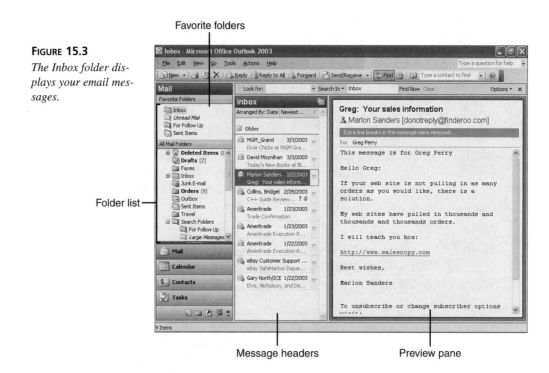

Folder list

Message headers　　　　Preview pane

Viewing Non-Outlook Data

Outlook is a versatile program, as you are beginning to see. Word's primary purpose is to manage documents. Excel's is to manage worksheets. Access's is to manage databases. PowerPoint's is to manage presentations. On the other hand, Outlook manages many different kinds of information. The Outlook screen changes considerably as you work with the various kinds of folders.

While working in Outlook, you can view Web pages within Outlook itself. Outlook provides a Web toolbar with which you can enter a Web page address and view the page from within Outlook, as done in Figure 15.4. When you click the Back button, Outlook returns you to whatever folder you were working in before displaying the page.

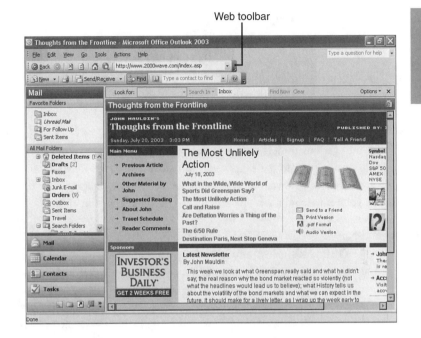

FIGURE 15.4

Display Web pages within Outlook.

Mastering Outlook Mail

Outlook's Mail view displays the following folders:

- Inbox—Holds incoming email messages.
- Sent Items—Displays mail messages you have sent to others.
- Outbox—Holds messages that are queued to be sent.
- Deleted Items—Keeps items, including email messages, that you have deleted but not removed from Outlook. Select Tools, Empty Deleted Items Folder to empty the Deleted Items folder.

In addition to these standard folders, you'll find others. The other folders are what you or someone else created before, either in Office 2003 or a previous Office version that you updated. Outlook also creates and manages some system folders, such as an Archive folder where you can send older data that you no longer need to keep in the forefront but which you might need some day in the future. (Your other option is to delete Outlook data for good.)

Organizing Messages

You can leave all incoming messages that you don't delete inside your Inbox. However, you can organize your email by creating folders for different purposes and then moving email messages (related to those folders) there. For example, you might want to store business-related messages in one folder named Business, and email for your family in one folder named Family.

Outlook manages email from multiple email accounts. The ability to separate messages into various folders comes in handy when you have two or more email accounts. As messages come into the Inbox, you can move those messages to a folder for that email account if you want to save them. Outlook supports a *rules wizard* that will even analyze your email and automatically place email messages in appropriate folders.

Outlook's Hotmail Connection

Outlook 2003 can integrate fully with Microsoft's free, online email account named *Hotmail*, located at http://www.hotmail.com.

You can send and retrieve Hotmail account email messages from any Web browser in the world. Therefore, you don't need your Outlook to get your messages while traveling.

Outlook supports Hotmail accounts so that, when on your own computer, you can use Outlook to send and receive Hotmail email. Therefore, you get the benefits of working in Outlook when in town, but you still get email when you're away.

When you sign up for Hotmail, you can register for a *Microsoft Passport* account, which is a service that enables you to log into different Web sites automatically but safely and securely. With a Passport account, you can take advantage of Hotmail's *Messenger* chat service to talk with other Messenger users around the world. Messenger supports both typed and voice messages for Windows XP users (as long as both users have microphones and speakers—headsets work the best), so you can talk free to anyone in the world. To activate Messenger once you've registered as a Messenger user, select Tools, Options, Other, and check the Instant Messaging option.

If the target folder appears in your Mail folders area, you can drag any message to that folder. You can right-click any message, select Move to Folder, and select any folder to which to move that message even if that folder is not listed on the Mail area's currently displayed folders.

To remove a message, just move the message to your Deleted Items folder. You can also click to select a message and press Delete or click the Delete button on the toolbar. If you change your mind about getting rid of a message stored in your Deleted Items folder,

15

you can move that message from the Deleted Items folder to a different folder. Only when you delete a message from within the Deleted Items folder is that message completely deleted.

> When you remove an item from the Deleted Items folder, Outlook does not send the item to the Windows Recycle Bin; Outlook deletes the item completely from your system.

To Do: Set Up an Email Account

When you first install Outlook on a computer that hasn't had a previous version used for email, you will need to set up an email account so that Outlook can send and retrieve messages. Setting up an email account can, in some situations, be difficult to describe and perform because of the differences among the way email services function.

Fortunately, most current email providers are following email account standards, and email accounts are more uniform than ever before. In addition, many *ISPs* (*Internet Service Providers*, the companies that provide end-user Internet service such as MSN and AOL) automatically set up your Outlook email account when you set up your computer for Internet access. Nevertheless, if you must install your own email account, you can expect to follow these general guidelines:

1. Select Tools, E-mail Accounts.

2. Click the option labeled Add a New E-mail Account and click Next. Outlook displays the E-mail Accounts dialog box that requests your email account's server type.

3. Select the type of email system your ISP uses. Unless you use a Web-based email system such as Hotmail, most of today's email systems follow the POP3 standard, but you *must* get the server type from your ISP to be sure.

4. On the next dialog box, shown in Figure 15.5, assuming that you selected a POP3 email account in the previous step (POP3 is the most common email in use today, other than the various free email sites such as Hotmail that are HTTP based), you specify the most important parameters of your email account. Specify the name that you want to appear as the recipient in messages that you send. Enter your email address as well. You will need to obtain the POP3 and SMTP information from your ISP. Finally, if your email account requires that you specify a name and password, you have to enter that information as well. The information in this dialog box is generally supplied by your ISP, so contact your ISP for the details.

FIGURE 15.5

Set up the specifics of your email system.

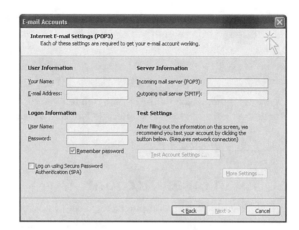

5. Click Next and Finish to finalize your account.

To Do: Create and Send Messages

A task you will perform often is sending a message to a recipient across the Internet. To create an Outlook email message, perform these steps:

1. From the Inbox folder, click the New button (or select File, New, Mail Message) to display the Message dialog box (shown in Figure 15.6).

FIGURE 15.6

Enter the message you want to send.

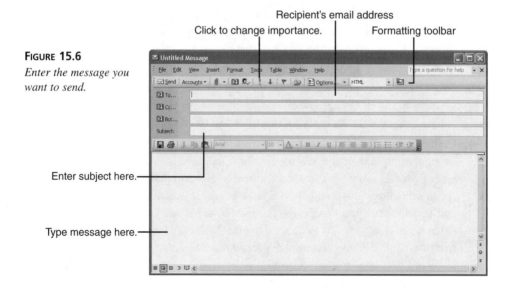

2. Enter the recipient's name in the To (your primary recipient) field. If you enter a name in the Cc (carbon copy) field, Outlook sends a copy of the message to that recipient. After you set up contacts in the Contacts folder (described in a later section entitled, "Keeping Contacts"), you only need to click the To (and Cc) buttons to display a list of contacts from which you can select. Your Contacts folder keeps track of names, phone numbers, addresses, and email addresses so that when you've built a large collection of email contacts, you'll rarely have to type an email address in the To field again.

   If you want to send the same message to multiple recipients, enter the email addresses directly in the To field, separating each with a semicolon (;), or select multiple recipients from the Select Names dialog box that appears when you click the To button.

3. Enter the subject of the message. Your recipient sees the subject in the list of messages that he receives. The subject line is important for organizing email messages in programs such as Outlook, so be sure to include a subject.

> Always enter a subject for your email messages so that your recipient knows at a glance what your message is about. This also makes it easier for you to track sent messages.

4. Type your message in the large message area at the bottom of the Message dialog box. If you've got automatic spell checking turned on (available from the Tools, Spelling and Grammar dialog box just as in Word), Outlook locates spelling problems by flagging them with a red wavy underline.

5. Click the Options tab to select certain message options (such as the message importance level and a delivery date). The recipient, like you, can order received mail by importance level when reading through the messages. The toolbar's Importance button also determines an email's importance.

6. Click the Send button. Outlook sends the message to your folder named Outbox.

7. Select Tools, Send/Receive to send your Outbox messages. Outlook finishes sending your mail and also collects any incoming messages waiting for you. If you are not logged on to the Internet, Outlook displays the Logon dialog box. Always check your Inbox for mail after sending mail from the Outbox using Tools, Send/Receive in case new mail was delivered to you.

Not all messages are text-only, and Outlook works with all file types. To attach another file to your message, such as a Word or Excel document, click the Insert File toolbar button and select a document file from the Insert File dialog box that appears.

You'll notice that the Message window sports a Formatting toolbar just as Word and Excel does. If your recipient can receive formatted email (as most can today, with the exception of some older free email services still in use), feel free to format your message's text.

Figure 15.6 shows the *Bcc* field that your email might or might not show. The Bcc field is the *blind carbon copy* field and enables you to send copies of the current email to multiple recipients without the primary recipient or the other Bcc recipients knowing that you've done so. For example, if you want to send a customer a sales letter and you want to send a copy to your boss, you can put your boss's email address in the Bcc field. Your boss will know that you sent the email to the customer but the customer will not know that your boss got a copy.

If you don't see the Bcc field and you'd like to add it to your email messages in case you want to use it in the future, click the down arrow to the immediate right of your message's Options button and select Bcc from the list that appears. To hide the Bcc field if you don't use it and you want more room to see messages, you can repeat these steps to uncheck the Bcc field.

Checking Mail

Regularly, you need to check your Inbox folder to see what items await you. As mentioned in step 7 of the preceding section, you must select Tools, Send/Receive to send Outbox items and receive Inbox folder items. Outlook logs you on to your Internet provider if needed. Your Inbox folder on the Outlook Bar displays a number indicating how many unread messages require your attention. When you select the Inbox folder, the unread messages appear in bold.

If you use multiple email accounts, select Tools, Send/Receive and select the email account that you want to check. You might use MSN at home and a local Internet provider at work, for example. You can set up both accounts on your home and office computer and select which account's email to retrieve when you select the Tools, Send/Receive option.

Pay attention to Outlook's icons. For example, as you read an email message, the message icon changes to show that the message has been read. Revert the read message flag back to an unread state by right-clicking the message and selecting Mark as Unread from the pop-up menu. A paper-clip icon appears next to each message that contains an attached file. When you open a message with an attached file, Outlook shows the attachment as an icon that you can right-click to save or open.

To read a message, just click on the message header to see the body of the message in Outlook's Preview pane. To open the message in a separate window, double-click it. To reply to the sender (in effect, sending a new message to your Outbox folder), click the toolbar's Reply button and type your reply. You can reply to the sender and all Cc recipients of the sender's message by clicking the Reply All toolbar button.

Outlook's email management system is quite advanced with far too many options to cover in one hour. Generally, however, to send and receive email, two of the most common uses of Outlook, you already have enough Outlook skills to do the job.

Keeping Contacts

Outlook's Contacts area tracks your contacts so that you have a central, uniform repository of information to use when you send email, hold meetings, and record calls. You can add new contacts, delete old ones you no longer need, and change information for a contact from the Contacts folder. The Contacts area maintains name, title, address, phone, and email information on your contacts, and it offers fields that you can use for additional information such as notes, family information, and more. In addition to recording contact information, Outlook uses an intelligent name and address checker to help ensure that your names and addresses are uniform for more accurate searching.

To Do: Record Contacts

When you first use Outlook, you have no contacts entered in the Contacts folder (except for a sample contact that you can click to highlight and press Delete to remove). To record a new contact, perform these steps:

1. Click Contacts in the lower-left area of the screen.
2. Click the New Contact toolbar button at the left of the Contacts screen's toolbar to open the Contact dialog box (shown in Figure 15.7).

Click to enter multiple email addresses.

Click to check name.   Click to add contact's picture.

FIGURE 15.7

Outlook stores contact information for you.

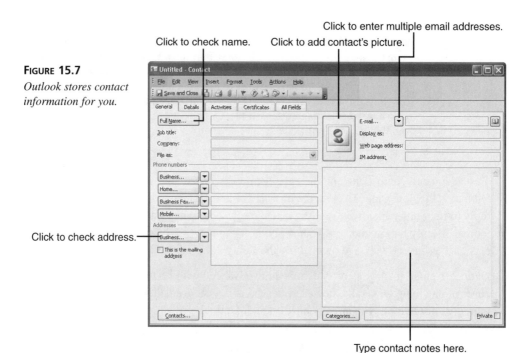

Click to check address.

Type contact notes here.

3. Type the contact's full name. If you click the Full Name button, Outlook displays the Check Full Name dialog box, shown in Figure 15.8, to maintain separate fields for each part of the name (such as title, first name, and last name). The time you take to separate the parts of a name pays off if you use your contact information in form letters and database work.

4. Enter the rest of the contact's information. Click the Address button to track separate parts of the contact's address using a Check Address dialog box similar to the Check Full Name dialog box. Click the drop-down Address list to record multiple addresses for the same contact. You can record a business, a home, or another address, for example, by clicking the appropriate drop-down address type before entering the address. Open the phone number drop-down lists as well to store different kinds of phone numbers for your contacts.

FIGURE 15.8
The Check Full Name
dialog box ensures
that your names are
entered properly.

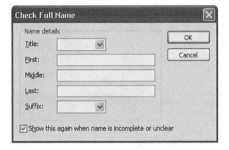

Click an arrow to the left of one of the phone number fields to see how
many types of phone numbers Outlook tracks per contact. In addition to the
four you see on the form, phone numbers for Business, Home, Business Fax,
and Mobile, you can click the down arrow inside each of these fields to display a list box full of additional numbers such as Business 2, TTY/TDD, and
Pager. Today's communication needs often require multiple phone numbers
for the same contact, and Outlook provides all the phone fields that you
might need. Any of the list boxes on the Contact form drops down to provide additional choices. You can enter multiple addresses and email accounts
for each contact, for example, although only one physical address and one
email address shows at any one time.

5. After you enter the phone numbers and email addresses, you can enter a
   Web page site address in case you want to record the contact's Web
   page or the contact's company Web page. A feature added in Outlook 2003 enables
   you to select a picture from a photograph stored on your computer (perhaps one
   you took with a digital camera or scanned from a photograph). Such pictures can
   aid in security systems to identify entry for security guards and will help a sales
   staff better identify clients.

6. The large text box toward the bottom of the New Contact window holds any notes
   you want to keep for this contact.

7. Click the Details tab to record other information, such as a spouse name, with the
   contact. The other tabs are for advanced purposes such as keeping digitally signed
   security IDs, and the All Fields tab enables advanced users to rearrange the fields
   on a contact's form. For most Outlook users, the General and Details tabbed pages
   are more than adequate to hold the information a contact requires.

8. Click the Save and Close button to save the contact information and view your
   contact in your Contacts folder.

When you close the Contact dialog box, your first contact appears in the Address Book. As you add more entries, your Contacts list grows, as shown in Figure 15.9. After you build a collection of contacts, you will click the alphabetic tabs to the right of the Address Book to locate specific contacts.

FIGURE 15.9

Your contacts appear in Outlook's Address Book.

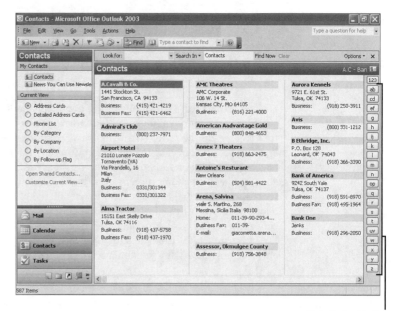

Alphabetical index

 If you want to look up clients by a value different from the name, select from the Current View area at the left of your window.

Selecting Contacts

To select a contact, display your Contacts folder and double-click the contact's entry. After you display a contact, you can do the following things:

- Directly edit the addresses, phone numbers, and email addresses displayed on the page by clicking the appropriate fields.

- Right-click the contact name, select Call Contact, and dial the contact's phone number from the New Call dialog box (shown in Figure 15.10). If you click the Create New Journal Entry option, Outlook adds the call to this contact's Journal; the Journal records the call details. You can use the Journal to track calls such as payment requests so that you have a record of who you called and when you placed the call. The next hour's lesson, Hour 16, "Planning and Scheduling with Outlook 2003," explains more about the Journal feature.

FIGURE 15.10

Outlook automatically dials your selected contact.

15

- Drag the column separators right or left to see more or less of each column. If you prefer to view narrow columns in the Contact folder, you see more contacts but not the full Phone Number and Address field. If you widen the columns, you see more detail for the contacts (but fewer of them at a time).

- Right-click the contact name and select New Message to Contact to write and send an email message to the contact's first email address.

- After you double-click on a contact to open that contact's information window, you can click the toolbar's Display Map of Address button (also available from the Actions menu) to see a graphic map of the contact's general address. Outlook goes to the Web (assuming that you have Internet access), locates the contact's address on a Microsoft Expedia Web map, and shows that location, such as the one shown in Figure 15.11. Not only does the map pinpoint the address, but it also includes links to Web sites related to that area of the country.

FIGURE 15.11

View a map of where your contact resides.

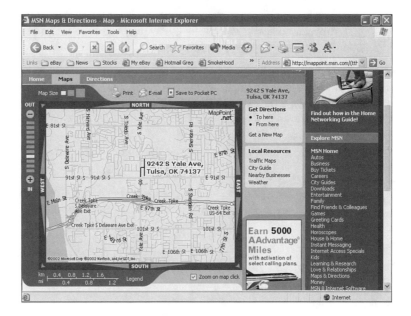

Summary

This hour introduced Outlook and explained Outlook's folders as well as how you can use Outlook to manage all your email accounts. By adding to your contacts, you can place your email recipients just a few mouse clicks away when you want to send them email. When you master the next hour's lesson, you will know enough to manage appointments, schedule meetings, track to-do tasks, and keep notes for reminders you must remember. Additionally, the journal tracks events as they happen, including incoming mail that you receive inside the Inbox. All the features of Outlook work together to help organize your time tasks.

Q&A

Q How does a message reply differ from a forwarded message?

A When you reply to a message, you create a brand new message that contains new information about the recipient's original message. If you forward a recipient's message, you send the message exactly as you first read it to another recipient (or to a list of recipients).

Q Why doesn't Outlook send my messages immediately after I complete them?

A Outlook does not send messages until you select Tools, Send/Receive. (F5 is the shortcut key for sending and receiving from all your email accounts.) If you use the Internet on a high-speed line such as DSL or in an office setting with a T1 connection, you are probably logged on to the Internet most of the time. If you use a modem to access the Internet, however, you have to initiate the logon sequence when you want to check for email.

Dialing and logging on takes time. Instead of logging on to your Internet provider every time you create an Outbox folder message, Outlook waits until you request the check for new mail to get your waiting mail and to send your outgoing mail. By waiting, Outlook only has to log on to the Internet one time to send all your messages.

Hour 16

Planning and Scheduling with Outlook 2003

With Outlook 2003, you can better manage the details of your life. Not only is Outlook an email and contacts manager (as you learned in Hour 15, "Communicating with Outlook 2003"), but Outlook also manages your calendar, to-do tasks, and other items that help you perform your routine duties. In this hour, you'll learn how to use Outlook's calendar for keeping track of appointments and scheduling reminders for those appointments. In addition, you will learn how to use Outlook's secondary features such as journaling and notes management.

The highlights of this hour include the following:

- How to navigate through the Calendar views
- How to schedule meetings and events
- Which tools help you manage tasks
- How to use Outlook to keep notes
- When the Journal tracks items automatically
- How to incorporate smart tags to make it easier to locate and create new Outlook contacts and appointments

Using the Calendar in Outlook

Outlook includes a calendar that not only enables you to organize and record dates, but also enables you to keep track of birthdays and anniversaries (and gives you automatic time-for-a-gift reminders), find open dates, keep a task list, and schedule meetings. It can also remind you of appointments, even if you are working in a different program window. The following sections show you how to use the Outlook Calendar to organize your life.

> Not only does Outlook remind you of specific appointments with an audible and visible reminder, but Outlook also easily sets up recurring appointments, such as weekly sales meetings or annual birthday reminders.

When you are ready to work with Outlook's Calendar, display the Calendar by clicking the Calendar button in the lower-left corner of the window.

Navigating Times and Dates

Notice that the Calendar appears with these major sections:

- Date Navigator—Appears as a monthly calendar pane with one month displayed by default and enables you to move quickly through the calendar year

- Daily Scheduler—Enables you to enter and edit appointments for today or other days

When you first open Calendar, the Date Navigator always highlights the current date (getting its information from your computer's internal clock and calendar) by placing a square outline around the day. The current date's daily scheduler appears at the bottom of the screen, showing the current day's appointments if any exist. You can navigate the Calendar through days and months by following these simple guidelines:

- Change days by first clicking inside the Date Navigator and then clicking either your left- or right-arrow keys; you can also click a specific date with your mouse.

- Change months by clicking to the left or right of the Date Navigator's month name or by clicking the Calendar's month name and selecting from the pop-up month list that appears.

Date Navigator   Click to change daily view.

FIGURE 16.1

Working with the Calendar.

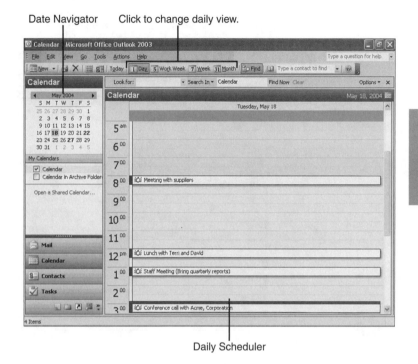

16

Daily Scheduler

Click through the Calendar's days and notice that the daily time planner changes days as you do so. Although you might not have any appointments set yet, you quickly see how you can look at any day's appointments by clicking that day's date in the Date Navigator.

The Calendar also provides a month-at-a-glance format when you click the Month button on the toolbar. (Figure 16.2 shows the month-at-a-glance calendar that appears when you click Month.) When you click any of the month's weekday abbreviations in the Date Navigator area, Outlook displays the schedule for the entire month. If you click either the Work Week or Week toolbar buttons, Outlook shows the week's daily appointments but also still shows the Date Navigator in the upper-right corner. To return to the daily appointment view for today, click Day on the toolbar.

Use the Date Navigator to show the daily appointments you need to see. As Figure 16.3 shows, if you select two days in the Date Navigator, both those days' appointments show in the center of the Calendar screen. The multiple days that you select in the Date Navigator do not have to be contiguous; hold Ctrl and click the days you want to see, and Outlook displays the daily appointments for those days.

FIGURE 16.2

The month-at-a-glance calendar provides a long-range overview of your scheduled appointments.

Selected month   Month button

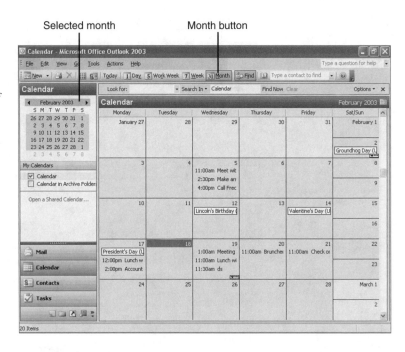

Two selected days

FIGURE 16.3

You can view appointments for two noncontiguous days.

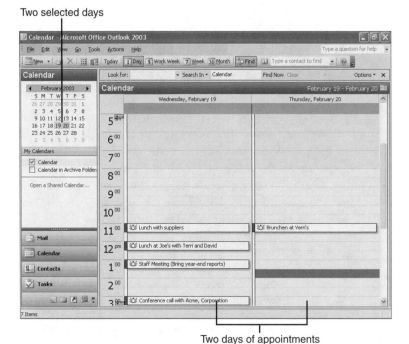

Two days of appointments

As you acquaint yourself with Outlook's Calendar, select from the View menu to customize the screen for your particular needs. In addition, you can drag any bar separating the window panes to provide more or less room to any portion of the Outlook screen that you need.

To Do: Set Appointments

To schedule an appointment, perform these steps:

1. Click the Day button to display a single Day view.
2. Select the day on which you want to schedule the appointment by clicking it in the Date Navigator.
3. Locate the appointment time. You might have to click the daily appointment area's scrollbar or use your up- and down-arrow keys to get to the time you want to use.
4. Double-click the appointment time to display the Appointment dialog box, shown in Figure 16.4.
5. Enter the appointment's subject and location. Outlook keeps track of your locations as you add them, so you don't have to retype them for subsequent appointments. (You need only to select them from the drop-down list that Outlook adds to as you enter new locations.)
6. Set the start and end times or click the All Day Event option if you want to schedule an all-day appointment.

FIGURE 16.4

Scheduling an appointment is easy.

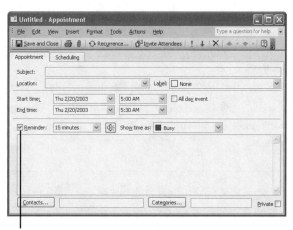

Click to select or deselect a reminder.

16

7. If you want a reminder for this appointment, make sure the Reminder check box is marked and enter the reminder lead time if you want a reminder. Outlook audibly and visibly reminds you of the appointment at whatever time you request.

8. Click the Recurrence toolbar button if the appointment occurs regularly. Outlook displays the Appointment Recurrence dialog box, shown in Figure 16.5. Set the recurrence options to enable Outlook to schedule your recurring appointment.

Instead of opening a daily appointment window first, you can select Actions, New Recurring Appointment from Outlook to go directly to the Appointment Recurrence dialog box when you set up recurring appointments.

FIGURE 16.5
Calendar easily accommodates appointments that occur regularly.

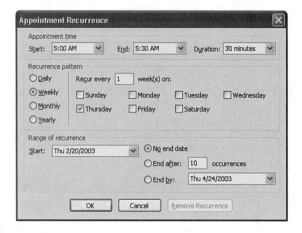

9. Click OK to close the Appointment Recurrence dialog box.

10. Click the Save and Close button. Outlook displays your appointment in the time planner by showing the subject in the daily appointment planner at the time of the appointment.

If you don't always start Outlook as you work on your computer from day to day, Outlook cannot remind you of pending appointments. Therefore, add Outlook to your Windows Startup folder so that Outlook starts automatically every time you start up your computer.

If you need to change a set appointment, double-click the appointment to display the Appointment dialog box, in which you can change the appointment details. Drag the appointment's top or bottom edges from the time planner to increase or decrease the appointment's duration. Drag the appointment's side edges to change the appointment's start time.

You can remove an appointment at any time by right-clicking over the appointment to display a shortcut menu and then selecting Delete. You can also click on an appointment and then click the toolbar's Delete button.

Instead of using the Appointment dialog box to schedule an appointment, you can enter an appointment quickly by clicking the appointment time once to highlight it and entering the text for the appointment directly on the daily appointment pane. When you press Enter, Outlook adds the appointment to the daily planner.

Outlook reminds you of the appointment with an audible alarm 15 minutes before the appointment. In addition, Outlook displays a Reminders window, such as the one in Figure 16.6. From the Reminders window, you can dismiss a reminder or click Open Item to modify the appointment's details. Click the Snooze button to be re-reminded of the appointment and select how much time you want to pass before being reminded once again.

FIGURE 16.6

Outlook reminds you of any appointments.

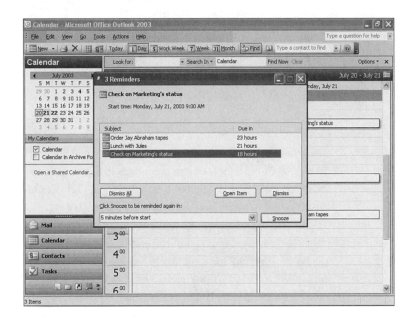

You might not want an audible alarm on all appointments. If you use your laptop in meetings and do not want audible alarms interrupting conversations, for example, you can remove any appointment's audible alarm by double-clicking the appointment and clicking the speaker icon to uncheck the Play This Sound option. (You can also change the sound; play "Happy Birthday" on your spouse's special day if you have a Happy Birthday audio clip on your computer!)

Scheduling Meetings

In Outlook terminology, a *meeting* differs somewhat from an appointment. An appointment is for you; it does not involve other resources (such as people and equipment). A meeting, however, requires that you schedule more people than yourself and perhaps requires that you reserve other resources (such as audio-visual equipment and a room in which to hold the meeting). If you work in a networked environment and others on the network use Outlook, Outlook can scan other people's computer schedules to help you plan meetings that others can attend.

To Do: Schedule a Meeting

Follow these steps to schedule a meeting:

1. Create an appointment for the meeting's day and time.

2. Click the Scheduling tab in the Appointment window. (Figure 16.7 shows the page that appears.)

3. Click the All Attendees box to enter the names of those whom you want to invite.

4. Click the Invite Attendees button and type the names of those attending. If you begin typing a name from your Contacts list and then press Ctrl+K after typing enough of the name for Outlook to locate the contact, Outlook retrieves the name from your Contacts folder and completes it. If two or more names exist that begin with the letters you've entered before pressing Ctrl+K, Outlook lets you select the correct name. Outlook displays the attendee's busy and free time in the grid to the right of the names.

5. Use the scrollbars to view the free and busy times for the people you invite. You must also select the meeting time. Outlook shows you the attendees' available free time when you click AutoPick Next, or you can use your mouse to schedule the attendees even if their free times conflict. (Outlook adjusts for time zones if you invite someone from another time zone.)

FIGURE **16.7**

You can schedule meetings, invite people, and reserve resources.

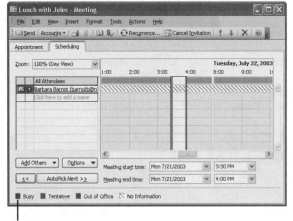

Legend shows grid's meaning.

Obviously, you must be organized and know the attendees quite well to have access to their schedules. Outlook will search your network for the contacts and their free times. If you are not on a network, you do not have access to the free times of the people you invite.

When you click Send, all recipients (if networked or available by email) get invited to your meeting by being sent the appointment's request.

To Do: Schedule an Event

An *event* is an activity not specifically tied to a time frame, such as a holiday or birthday. When you want to record an event, such as your boss's birthday, perform these steps:

1. Select Actions, New All Day Event. The Event dialog box appears (looking very much like the Appointment dialog box) with the tabbed Appointment page displayed.

2. Schedule the event as you would schedule an appointment, but click the All Day Event check box to show that the event lasts the entire day. (Otherwise, the event automatically turns into an appointment.)

3. Select the Show Time As option if you want your calendar to show the time as Free, Tentative, Busy, or Out of Office. Outlook uses this value to send to others on your network who might invite you for an appointment during this time.

4. Select an appropriate reminder time from the Reminder list, such as 2 days, to receive an audible alarm and reminder window entry that informs you of the event so that you can purchase gifts or prepare for the event in some other way.

5. Click the Save and Close button to return to Calendar.

If the event is recurring, click Recurrence to initiate a new recurring event. When you view the event, Outlook shows it in a *banner* (a highlighted heading) for that day in the day planner's views.

Managing a Task List

A *task* is any job that you need to track, perform, and monitor to completion. Outlook tasks (such as appointments and meetings) might be recurring, or they might happen only once. You can manage your Outlook task list by clicking the Tasks button at the left of your Outlook screen.

Unlike appointments, meetings, and events, tasks don't belong to any specific date or time. Tasks are jobs you need to finish but are not linked to a date or time.

To Do: Create a Task

To create a one-time task, perform these steps:

1. Click the New Task toolbar button or select File, New, Task.

2. Enter a task description.

3. Select a due date (the date you must complete the task, but not necessarily the day you perform the task). If you click the Due Date drop-down list, you can select from a calendar that Outlook displays. You can enter virtually any date in virtually any format, including Next Wednesday. Outlook converts your format to a supported date format.

4. Click Save and Close to finalize the task.

After you complete a task, click the task's check box to cross the task from the list. Delete a task by selecting it and clicking the toolbar's Delete button.

If you want to remind yourself of a task's deadline, make an appointment for the deadline on the task's due date. Set the alarm for 24 hours or 2 days. When the deadline draws near, you then are reminded that the task is wrapping up fast.

The Task window's Details page (see Figure 16.8) displays fields you fill out as you complete the task. The Details page even tracks such task-related information as mileage, time involved, companies utilized, and billing information.

FIGURE 16.8

You can track a task's completion details.

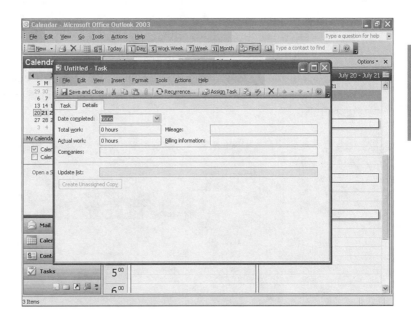

16

Writing Yourself Notes

Outlook notes are equivalent to sticky yellow-paper notes. You can post a note inside Outlook and retrieve, edit, or delete the note later. To see your notes, click the Notes icon at the bottom of the Outlook screen. Double-click any note to see its contents.

To create a new note, click the New Note toolbar button to display a yellow-note window. Type your note and click the note's Close button to close the note. Resize the note by dragging its lower-right corner. Outlook records the note's date and time at the bottom of each note. Change the note's font by selecting a new font from the Tools, Options dialog box and clicking the Note Options button. You can quickly select a different note color by right-clicking the note's icon.

NEW 2003 Turn notes into appointments and tasks easily if you need to. Drag a note from the Notes folder to the Calendar or Tasks buttons. Outlook will open an appropriate window with the note's contents, filling in the task or appointment's description. If you drag a note to your Outbox, Outlook creates an email message with your note's contents and you can select a recipient for the note.

Expanding the Outlook Bar

NEW 2003 The column on the left side of your Outlook screen is called the *Outlook bar*. You can drag the Outlook bar higher and add more buttons to the expanded Outlook bar by dragging the handle at the top of the bar (above the Mail button). As you drag the handle the Outlook bar grows and more buttons appear such as the Notes and Shortcuts buttons.

If you click the arrow at the bottom of the Outlook bar you can add more buttons to the Outlook bar. For example, you can add the Journal button to the Outlook bar as shown in Figure 16.9.

FIGURE 16.9

Select what you want Outlook to track.

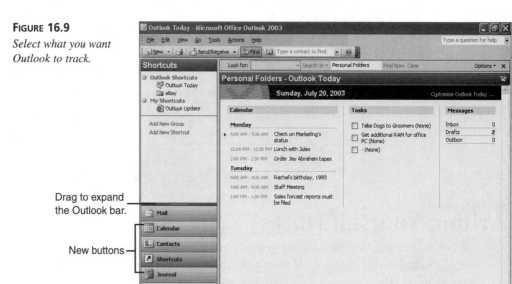

Drag to expand the Outlook bar.

New buttons

Click to add more buttons.

Keeping a Journal

The Outlook *Journal* keeps track of all your interactions with contacts, Outlook items, and activities. Although you can make manual entries, the real power of the Journal appears when you automate Outlook to record the following types of Journal entries:

- Track and record all items (such as email) that you send to and receive from contacts. Depending on the option you selected when you set up a contact, the Journal can automatically record all interactions with that contact, or you can record interactions selectively.

- Keep track of all Office documents that you create or edit. Browse the Journal to find a summary of the documents you created and the order in which you created (and edited) them.
- Track all meetings automatically.
- Track all appointments and tasks manually. (Outlook does not track appointments and tasks automatically; you must enter them yourself every time you add an appointment or task.)
- Manually record *any* activity in your Outlook Journal, including conversations around the water cooler.

Setting Automatic Journal Entry

Have you ever wished that you had recorded a complaint call you made when you got a bad product or service? Let Outlook track all your calls automatically. The Journal records times, dates, and people you called. As you use Outlook to make calls, record notes about the calls and track those notes in your Outlook Journal. You open the Journal by clicking the Journal button if you've added it to your Outlook Bar.

You should review your Journal options by selecting Tools, Options and clicking the Journal Options button. You'll see the Journal Options dialog box shown in Figure 16.10 where you can inform Outlook exactly what to track. Request that Outlook record activities in selected Outlook activities, Office programs that you use, or contacts with whom you send or receive email.

FIGURE 16.10

Select what you want Outlook to track.

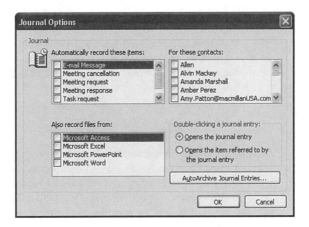

Adding Journal Entries Manually

The Journal cannot automatically record all activity in your life; however, you can add manual entries for any activities you want recorded. If you want to record an appointment, open that appointment (from within the Calendar). If you want to record an item not related to Outlook, such as a conversation, create a note for that item and transport the information from the note to the Journal folder.

To Do: Record a Manual Journal Entry

To record a manual Journal entry from an existing item (such as a new contact you just entered), perform these steps:

1. Double-click the item you want to record to display the Edit dialog box for the item.
2. Select the item's Actions, New Journal Entry option. The Journal now contains an icon that represents the item, such as a phone call to the contact. Double-click the Journal's icon to display the item's details.

Suppose that you wrote a letter to your phone company, for example, and you want to record the complete document in your Journal. If you have set up your Journal to track all Word documents automatically, the document appears in your Journal. If you have not set up the Journal to track Word documents automatically, however, just display the document's icon in the My Computer window on the Outlook Bar and drag the document to the Journal icon on the Outlook Bar.

Periodically, delete older entries from your Journal that you no longer need. The Journal entries add up quickly. When you delete a Journal entry, the files the Journal entry describes are not deleted; only their entries in the Journal are.

The Journal consumes resources quickly. With the Journal recording activities, your use of Office can slow down because your computer will constantly be checking and updating your requested journal entries. Many advanced Office users simply don't use the Journal. They uncheck all activities from the Journal Options window and just use appointments to keep track of activities.

Smart Tags

If you've been working with Office as you've worked through this and the earlier lessons of the book, you have probably seen *smart tags* as you followed along and learned the software. When you enter data in an Office program such as Word or PowerPoint, that Office program underlines the data with a purple dotted line indicating the smart tag. A smart tag is data that an Office product recognizes as data that fits within a category, such as one of these:

- A person's name
- A time (dates, times, even relative dates such as Last Friday)
- Places
- Recent Outlook recipients

The primary purpose of smart tags is to keep you from having to leave your current program to perform a common task related to that smart tag. Outlook is the primary program in question. To clarify, suppose that you were writing a letter to a new client. When you type the client's name, Word displays or changes the name to include a smart tag underline. If you point to the name with your mouse, a smart tag action button appears as an icon above the name. Click the icon to display the menu shown in Figure 16.11.

FIGURE 16.11

You can perform common Outlook-related tasks from a Word document.

Action button's icon   Two additional smart tags

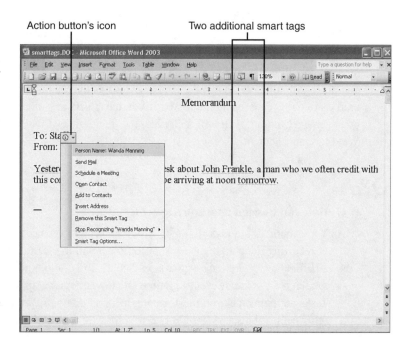

16

The actions on the shortcut menu enable you to add the contact to your Outlook Contacts folder. If the name already resides in your Contacts folder, you can select Open Contact and the contact's window opens so that you can copy and paste information from the contact to your Word document. If the smart tag appears on a date, you can schedule a meeting or show your appointments for that date while still working inside your Word document.

> Without smart tags, you normally have to leave your document to open Outlook, locate the contact, and then copy and paste the contact's information to your document. The smart tags save you some steps in this process. Although you still must work in Outlook's Contact windows, you are still closer to your Word document than you would otherwise be without smart tags.

You can modify the behavior of smart tags by selecting Tools, AutoCorrect and clicking the Smart Tags tab from your Word document. From the dialog box, you can turn off smart tagging, modify the smart tags that are currently active, and download additional smart tags from the Internet.

Summary

This hour explained some of the ways you can use Outlook to check your Calendar; manage appointments, meetings, and events; track tasks; keep notes; and explore your computer. Additionally, the journal tracks events as they happen, including incoming mail that you receive inside the Inbox. If you have used any other personal-information management program, you will really like the integration of Outlook into the Office and Windows environment.

Q&A

Q How can I assign a task to a specific day?

A You cannot assign tasks to days. Tasks transcend days because tasks are one-time or recurring items that you must accomplish within a certain time frame, but not on a particular day. Perhaps you are only confusing Outlook terminology. If you want to assign a particular event to a time and day, assign an appointment or meeting. Tasks are items that you must accomplish and that you can track and assign to other people, but tasks are not tied to a specific time and date.

Q **After I set a reminder, how does Outlook inform me of the appointment, meeting, or event?**

A You must continually run Outlook during your computing sessions for Outlook to monitor and remind you of things you have to do. Outlook is one program that you probably want to add to your Windows Startup folder so that Outlook always starts when you start Windows. Outlook cannot remind you of pending appointments if you are not running it.

Outlook tracks incoming and outgoing events. Also, as you learned in the previous hour, Outlook monitors your electronic mail, faxes, and network transfers and keeps an eye on your reminders to let you know when something is due. The only way Outlook can perform these tasks is if you keep it running during your work sessions.

16

PART VI

Tracking with Access 2003

Hour

17 Access 2003 Basics

18 Entering and Displaying Access 2003 Data

19 Retrieving Your Data

20 Reporting with Access 2003

Hour **17**

Access 2003 Basics

Everyone trudges through data at work and at home. With the proliferation of computers, information overload seems to be the norm. A database manager, such as Microsoft Access 2003, enables you to organize your data and turn raw facts and figures into meaningful information. Access processes data details so you can spend your valuable time analyzing results. Suppose that your company keeps thousands of parts in an Access inventory database, and you need to know exactly which part sold the most in Division 7 last April. Access can find the answer for you.

This hour introduces you to the world of databases with Access. The nature of databases makes Access one of the more involved programs in the Office suite. Generally, people find that they can master Word, Excel, PowerPoint, and Outlook more quickly than they can Access. Access is not difficult to learn and use, but you must understand the structure of database design before you can fully master Access.

The highlights of this hour include the following:

- What a database is
- Which database-related objects Access manages
- Why databases contain tables
- What fields and records are
- How to create and modify tables

Database Basics

Whereas previous hours of this book began by introducing you to the program right away, this hour begins by explaining database concepts. You need to learn how a database management system organizes data before you jump into Access.

A *database* is an organized collection of data. Access is called a *database management system* because it enables you to create, organize, manage, and report from the data stored in databases.

> Database experts have written complete books on database theory. This hour won't give you an extremely in-depth appreciation for databases, but you will learn enough to get started with Access.

A database typically contains related data. In other words, you might create a home-office database with your household budget but keep another database to record your rare-book collection titles and their worth. In your household budget, you might track expenses, income, bills paid, and so forth, but that information does not overlap the book-collection database. Of course, if you buy a book, both databases might show the transaction, but the two databases would not overlap.

Technically, a database does not have to reside on a computer. Any place you store data in some organized format, such as a name and address directory, could be considered a database. In most cases, however, the term database is reserved for organized, computerized data.

When you design a database, consider its scope before you begin. Does your home business need an inventory system? Does your home business need a sales contact? If so, an Access database works well. Only you can decide whether the inventory and the sales contacts should be part of the same system or separate, unlinked systems. The database integration of inventory with the sales contacts requires much more work to design, but your business requirements might necessitate the integration. For example, you might need to track which customers bought certain products in the past.

> Not all database values directly relate to one another. Your company's loan records do not relate to your company's payroll, for example, but both probably reside in your company's accounting database. Again, you have to decide on the scope when you design your database. Fortunately, Microsoft made Access extremely flexible, so you can change any database structure when you begin using your database. The better you analyze the design up front, however, the easier your database is to create.

Database Tables

If you threw your family's financial records into a filing cabinet without organizing them, you would have a mess. That is why most people organize their filing cabinets by putting related records into file folders. Your insurance papers go in one folder; your banking records go in another.

Likewise, you cannot throw your data into a database without separating the data into related groups. These groups are called *tables*; a table is analogous to a file folder in a filing cabinet. Figure 17.1 illustrates a set of tables that hold financial information inside a business's database.

FIGURE 17.1
A database will contain data separated into groups called tables.

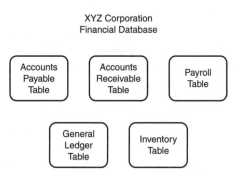

A database might contain many tables, each being a further refinement of related data. Your financial database might contain tables for accounts payable, customer records, accounts receivable, vendor records, employee records, and payroll details (such as hours worked during a given time period). The separate tables help you eliminate redundant data; when you produce a payroll report, Access might retrieve some information from your employee table (such as name and pay rate) and some information from your time tables (such as hours worked).

Access is a *relational database* as opposed to a *flat-file database*. That means Access uses data from multiple tables instead of requiring you to duplicate data in two or more places. Therefore, if you increase a customer's discount, you need to change the discount in only one customer table rather than in the customer table, the pricing table, and the sales table.

Access stores all tables for a single database in one file that ends with the .mdb extension. By storing the complete database in one file, Access makes it easier for you to copy and back up your database. You never have to specify the .mdb extension when you create a database.

You can import data from an Access database table into a Word document or Excel worksheet. The interaction between Access and the other Office products makes creating and reporting data simple. Appendix A, "Sharing Information Between Office 2003 Programs," explains more about sharing data between the Office products.

Records and Fields

To keep track of table data, Access breaks down each table into *records* and *fields*. In some ways, a table's structure looks similar to an Excel worksheet because of the rows and columns in a worksheet. As Figure 17.2 shows, a table's records are the rows, and a table's fields are the columns. Figure 17.2 shows a checkbook-register table; you usually organize your checkbook register just as you would organize a computerized version of a checkbook, so you will have little problem mastering Access's concepts of records and fields.

FIGURE **17.2**

Tables have records (rows) and fields (columns).

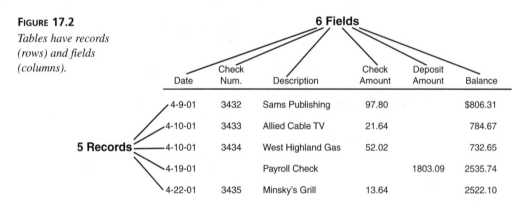

6 Fields

Date	Check Num.	Description	Check Amount	Deposit Amount	Balance
4-9-01	3432	Sams Publishing	97.80		$806.31
4-10-01	3433	Allied Cable TV	21.64		784.67
4-10-01	3434	West Highland Gas	52.02		732.65
4-19-01		Payroll Check		1803.09	2535.74
4-22-01	3435	Minsky's Grill	13.64		2522.10

5 Records

Your table fields contain different data types. As Figure 17.2 shows, one field might hold a text description, whereas another might hold a dollar amount. Every item within the same field must be the same data type, but a table might contain several fields that differ in type. When you design your database, you are responsible for indicating to Access which data type you want for each field in your database tables.

The types of data that you can store in an Access database table are

- *Text*—Text data consists of letters, numbers, and special characters. You only report text data; you cannot calculate with it. A balance-due field would never be a text data type, but addresses, names, and Social Security numbers are examples of text fields. Generally, you store short text items (names, addresses, cities, product names, and part codes) in text fields.

- *Memo*—The memo field can hold an extremely large amount of text, including paragraphs. Memo fields consume a lot of space, and not all tables require them. Memos are great for documenting table entries and adding textual data that is free-form. For example, an Evaluation field for an employee database would be a good Memo candidate because you could then make entries that describe the employee's performance.

- *Number*—A number field holds numbers. Use this field to calculate values.

- *Date/Time*—These fields hold date and time values (similar to the date and time format in Excel). Access enables you to enter data into date and time fields using many formats. Additionally, Access respects your Windows international settings, so you can enter a date in your country's format.

- *Currency*—This field holds dollar amounts. Access keeps the dollar amounts rounded to the correct decimal alignment needed to match your currency designation. Access recognizes your Windows international settings and uses international currency amounts when needed.

- *AutoNumber*—This field holds sequential numbers, a different number for each record in the table.

- *Yes/No*—These fields hold Yes and No (or True and False) two-pronged values to indicate the existence or absence of an item or to indicate the answer to an implied question. For example, some items in an inventory database might be tagged for a special discount whereas others are not tagged.

- *OLE object*—This is an embedded object, such as a graph you create in Excel. Your Access databases can hold any kind of OLE-compatible embedded object.

- *Hyperlink*—This is an Internet Web site address. Such a field can hold an Internet address for a file as well as a network or an intranet address within your system network. When the database user clicks the hyperlink, Access shows the hyperlink's Web page or network file.

> The Internet integration of the other Office products extends to Access. When you click a table's hyperlink to an Internet Web page address, Access sends you to the Web page, logging you on to your Internet provider if necessary.

Using a Key Field

Every Access table requires a *primary key field*. The primary key field (often just called a key) is a field that contains a unique value and no duplicate entries. Whereas a table's city field might contain multiple occurrences of the same city name, a key field must be unique for each record. You can designate an existing data field as the table's key field, or you can use the AutoNumber field that Access adds to all tables as the key field.

> If you access a particular field very often, even if that field is not a key field, designate it as an *index field* in the Design view property settings. Access creates an index for every database and locates the index fields in that index. Just as an index in the back of the book speeds your searches for particular subjects, the index field speeds searches for that field.

If you were creating a table to hold employee records, a good key-field candidate would be the employee's Social Security number because each one is unique. If you are not sure that your data contains unique information in any field, specify the AutoNumber field that Access creates as the key. In the AutoNumber field, Access stores a unique number for each table record.

Access uses the key field to find records quickly. When you want to locate an employee's record, for example, search by the employee's key field (the Social Security number). If you search based on the employee's name, you might not find the proper record; two or more employees might be named John Smith, for example.

> So many companies assign you a customer number because the customer number uniquely identifies you in their database. Although today's computerized society sometimes makes one feel like "just another number," such a customer number enables the company to keep your records more accurate and keep costs down.

Looking at Access

When you start Access, you'll see a screen that looks similar to Word, as Figure 17.3 shows. The New File task pane provides you with links you can use to create a new database or load an existing database. As with Word and Excel, Access supports the use of template files on which you can base new database files that conform to a predetermined pattern.

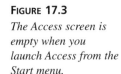

FIGURE 17.3

The Access screen is empty when you launch Access from the Start menu.

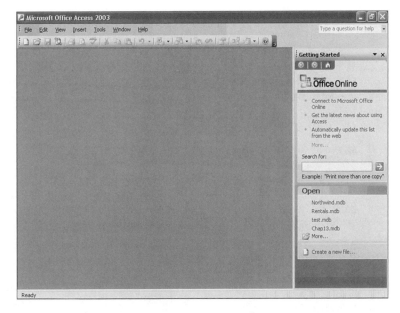

17

Here are the fundamental steps you follow most of the time when you want to work with Access:

- Open an existing database so that you can modify the database structure or work with the database information. Select a database from the list or click the More option to browse a list of existing database files. The section of the New File task pane where you open an existing database is labeled Open.

- Create a new database, which requires that you manually set up the entire database structure, including tables, fields, and other pertinent database-structure information. You can also create a more advanced database *project*, which creates a database system that runs in a networked client/server workspace where the Access database might transfer data to multiple workstations attached to the server. The section of the New File task pane where you create a blank database is labeled New.

- Create a new database that is a copy of an existing database. The New File task pane contains the section for creating a new database file from an existing one. You can get to this option by selecting More. This New File task pane option in effect makes a copy of an existing database file.

- Create a database file based on a template. Access provides templates that create sample blank databases that track data such as asset management, expenses, and inventories. Microsoft provides additional templates on the Web as well.

Creating a Database

Generally, when you need to create a new database, you'll start Access and select Blank Database from the New File task pane. Enter the name of your database in the File New Database dialog box and click Create to generate the blank database file. Access offers the default database filename db1.mdb, but you should give your database a more meaningful name. For example, if you want to track rental property information, you might name the database Rentals. (Access adds the .mdb extension, so your database will be stored as Rentals.mdb.)

When you enter a name and click the Create button, Access displays the *Database window*, shown in Figure 17.4. The Database window title bar includes the name of your database (Rentals in Figure 17.4). As you add to your database, the Database window shows the various components of the database, such as tables.

FIGURE 17.4

The Database window displays a list of your database objects as you create them.

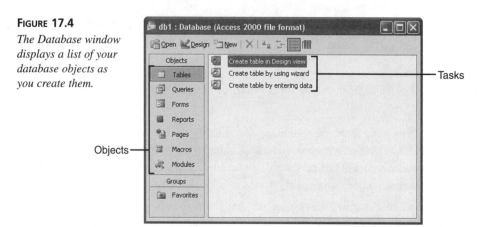

Tables are not the only items that appear in databases. You will generate database reports and other elements, called *objects*, as you work on your database file. The Database window lists the names of all database objects at the left of the window. In the right side, you will see a list of tasks that Access is ready to perform on whatever object you click.

A database object is a piece of an Access database. A table is an object, for example. A database report that prints database data is an object. Your data values, however, are not objects.

In most cases, when you create a database, the first task you want to perform is to create the database's first table. The first Database window task, Create Table in Design View, will help you create a new table to hold data.

Understanding Database Objects

As you create your database, you add objects to the Database window's seven object categories. Any database can contain many objects from each category. The following are brief descriptions of seven kinds of Access objects:

- *Tables*—Related data within a database
- *Queries*—Stored instructions that select data from one or more tables for reporting, analysis, and data-management purposes
- *Forms*—Onscreen representations of paper forms that you and others use to enter data into tables
- *Reports*—Printed listings of database data
- *Pages (also called Data Access Pages)*—Internet-ready data table pages that you can view with Internet Explorer 5 from Web pages
- *Macros*—Stored task lists for Access commands
- *Modules*—Programs written in Visual Basic, a powerful (but advanced for nonprogrammers) programming language with which you can automate any database task

As you create your database, you create one or more instances of the database objects. You might create 25 tables and 50 reports, for example. When you want to create, edit, or work with one of the database objects, return to the Database window to do so. The toolbar always contains a Database Window toolbar button that quickly returns you to the Database window. To create a new instance of one of the objects, click on the object and select the appropriate task that works with the object.

Access provides an Outlook-style grouping mechanism at the bottom-left of the Database window. If you find yourself creating many objects within the same database, you might want to group some objects into new groups that you create. To create a new group, right-click a blank area under the Groups label and select New Group, enter a group name, and click OK to add the new group to the existing group list. For simple databases, you'll probably just keep all the objects ungrouped within the Database window.

To Do: Create a Table

You must create tables before you can enter data in a database. The tables hold the data on which the other objects operate.

When you create a table, you follow these general steps:

1. After creating a new database, select the Database window's option called Create Table in Design View and then click Open to create a new table. The *Design view* window appears (shown in Figure 17.5). You must now describe your table's fields in the Design view dialog box.

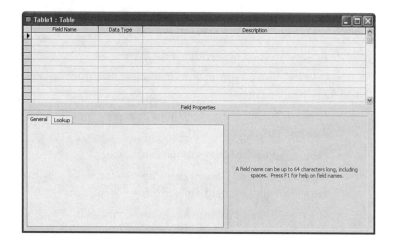

2. Type a field name, such as **First Name** or **Quantity**, for the first field in your database. The names have nothing to do with the data type that you will eventually store in the table's field. The field name enables you to refer to the field as you design your table. Only after you completely design the table do you enter data in the table. The order in which you add fields does not affect the order in which you ultimately enter the table data. Nevertheless, try to add the fields in the general order in which you want to enter the table data.

3. Press Tab and click the drop-down list that appears in the Data Type field to select the field's data type.

4. Press Tab and type a description for the field. Some field names are optional and don't require a description, but the more you document and describe your data, the easier it is to modify your database later.

5. After you enter the first field's name, data type, and optional description, describe the field properties in the lower half of the Design view dialog box. Some fields do not require property settings, but most require some type of setting.

The next section describes in more detail how you set field property values.

Setting Field Properties

The lower half of the Design view contains settings for your field property values. Each field has a data type, as you already know. In addition to describing the field's data type in the Design view's top half, you can further refine the field's description and limitations in the Field Properties section.

You can configure a different set of field property values for each data type. Text fields contain properties related to text data (such as an address or a name), whereas numeric fields contain properties related to numbers (such as decimal positions).

The field properties appear in the lower half of the screen. A few common field property values that you might want to set as you create your table are as follows:

- *Field Size*—Limits the number of characters the field can hold, thereby limiting subsequent data entry of field data.

- *Format*—Displays a drop-down list with several formats that the field's data type can take.

- *Caption*—Holds a text prompt that Access displays when you enter data into this table's field. If you don't specify a caption, Access uses the field name. Access displays the caption in its status bar when you enter data into the table.

- *Default Value*—Contains the field's default value, which appears when you enter data into this table. The user can enter a value that differs from the default if desired. A common default field value would be your company's state. Many of your vendors will be located in your own state so, if this is the case, your vendor database's State field would include your company's state as the default value.

- *Required*—Holds either Yes or No to determine whether Access requires a value in this field before you can save a table's data record. If you don't want the user leaving a field blank, enter Yes for the Required property.

- *Decimal Places*—Holds the number of default decimal places shown for numbers entered into this field.

Figure 17.6 shows a completed table's Design view. The selected field's (the field with the arrow, or *field selector* in the left column) property values appear at the bottom of the dialog box. As you enter your own table fields, edit any information that you type incorrectly by clicking the field name, data type, description, or property value, and move the insertion point to the mistake to correct the problem.

17

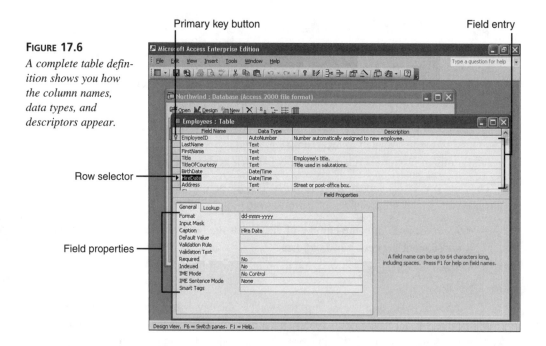

FIGURE 17.6

A complete table definition shows you how the column names, data types, and descriptors appear.

Primary key button

Field entry

Row selector

Field properties

Setting the Key and Saving the Table

After you complete your table's fields, you cannot close the table's Design view without designating a field as the table's primary key field. If you do not designate a key and attempt to close the table, Access warns you that no key exists. Access adds a key field using the AutoNumber format if your data does not contain a key field.

Consider adding your own key field for tables that you access often. The key field enables you to search the table more quickly. The key might be a Social Security number, a phone number, or some other code (such as a unique inventory code or customer number) that is unique for each record in the table. The Key field also prevents duplicate entries.

To specify a key field, select the field by clicking the row selector at the left of the field name and then clicking the Primary Key toolbar button (the button with the icon of the key). Access adds a small key icon to the left of the record, indicating the table's key field.

After you add the key field, save the table by clicking the Save button on the toolbar. (If you attempt to close the table before saving it, Access prompts you for a name.) If you don't specify a new name, Access uses Table1 (and Table2, Table3, and so on as you create additional tables); however, you should use a more meaningful table name, such as Tenants, so that you can easily identify the table. When you close the table, Access returns you to the Database window where you will see the table in the right pane.

Modifying Table Structures

The beauty of Access is that, unlike some other database programs, you can easily change the structure of your tables even after you add data. Access makes it easy to add and delete fields, as well as change field properties.

Some table-structure changes affect table data. After you add data to a table, for example, you lose columns of data if you delete fields, and you lose some data through truncation if you limit a field's Size property after you've entered data. If you add fields to an existing table, you must add the data for the new fields in every existing record in the table.

17

To modify a table, switch to the table's Design view. If you have closed the table and returned to the Database window, select the table name (which now appears in the Database window) and click the Database window toolbar's Design button.

Adding Fields

When you return to the table's Design view, you can add a field to the end of your table just by clicking the first empty Field Name box and entering the field information as you did when adding the table's initial fields.

To insert a new field between two other fields, right-click the row to display the shortcut menu and select Insert Rows. Access opens a new field row and enables you to enter the new field information. Figure 17.7 shows a new field being inserted into a table.

Deleting Fields

To delete a field, right-click over the field name and select Delete Rows from the shortcut menu that appears.

Use Undo (Ctrl+Z) to reverse an accidental field deletion. Access supports multiple levels of Undo so that you can reverse several recent row deletions by issuing Undo multiple times. Once you save your new table design, however, you will not be able to reverse the row deletions.

Room for new field

FIGURE 17.7

*The new field will go
in the empty space.*

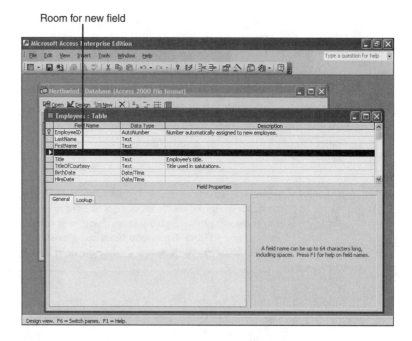

Resizing and Rearranging Fields

Drag your mouse pointer to make minor size adjustments to your table (such as the height of each row and the width of columns). Although the Field Size property determines the exact data storage width of each field in your table, the column widths determine how much of a field you can read while entering and editing table data and the table's structure.

At any time during your table design or subsequent data entry, you can drag a column divider left or right to increase or decrease the width of a column displayed. For example, if your field names are short, you might want to shorten the width of the Field Name column by dragging the right edge to the left to make more room for the field's Description. You can also drag a record divider up or down to increase or decrease a record height.

To rearrange the location of a field, drag the field name by dragging its selector (the gray area to the left of the field) to its new location in the table and release the mouse. Access moves the field to the location you select.

After you make changes to a table's design, Access will prompt you to save your changes when you leave the Design view. Always save any changes you want Access to keep.

The order in which you structure a table's fields has little bearing on the table's use. You can report a table's data in any field order that you want regardless of the physical order in which you entered the fields. Order your fields in whatever way makes the most sense to you.

Viewing Table Design and Entering Simple Data

Until now, you have worked exclusively in the Design view of the table, which describes the table's fields, properties, and key. From the Database window, if you double-click a table name (or select the table and click the Open button), Access displays your table with the Datasheet view, the view shown in Figure 17.8. Unlike the Design view, the Datasheet view enables you to enter and edit data in the table. For a new table, only one table row appears and it's blank because the table has no data. If the table contained data, you would see rows from the table with data. Unlike the Design view, you cannot change the table's structure from the Datasheet view.

FIGURE 17.8

Use the Datasheet view to enter data into your table.

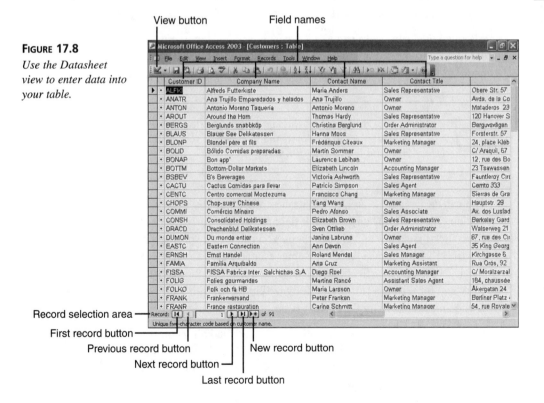

View button   Field names

Record selection area
First record button
Previous record button
Next record button
New record button
Last record button

You can easily switch from Datasheet view and Design view by clicking the Access toolbar's View button. As you design a table and add the table's initial data, the two views help you pinpoint design and data problems.

The Datasheet view enables you to work with your table in row and column format, similar to an Excel worksheet. Until you enter data in the table, the Datasheet view shows only one empty record, but as you add to the table, the Datasheet view grows to resemble an Excel worksheet with cells that represent each table's field.

Although Access offers several ways to enter data into a table, the Datasheet view is the fastest and simplest if you understand records and fields. The Datasheet view is not fancy, however, and some users need more help when entering data. If you build a database application for a video store's inventory, for example, the clerk should not be adjusting the inventory table directly within the Datasheet view when a customer rents a tape. You learn in Hour 18, "Entering and Displaying Access 2003 Data," how to design data-entry forms that walk the user through the data-entry process for specific scenarios so that the user does not inadvertently change information in the wrong record.

Although the Datasheet view is not fancy, it enables you to quickly see your table's design results and to enter data. If you cannot read a full field name, drag the field separator left or right to increase or decrease the field width shown on the screen.

Most of the Database window objects offer two views: a Design view and another view that displays the final object, such as the table's Datasheet view and the form's Form view.

You can design a table from the Datasheet view, but you make more work for yourself if you do. The default Datasheet view field names are Field1, Field2, and so on until you right-click the names and change them. You cannot set specific field properties from the Datasheet view because Access assumes that all fields are text. In addition, you cannot specify a primary key field in the Datasheet view. Use the Datasheet view for simple data entry and for testing your table's design. Skip the Design view phase only if you want to create an extremely simple, all-text table.

So that you can practice manipulating a database and all its objects, Access comes with a comprehensive database called the *Northwind Traders, Inc., Database*, which you can study to learn about advanced database operations. Use File, Open and locate the database in your Office 2003 folder to open and work with the sample database.

Always quit Access and shut down Windows before turning off your computer; otherwise, you might lose data that didn't get saved in your database tables.

Summary

Much of this hour's lesson was theory-based because Access requires more preparation than the other Office products. After you learn about the elements that make up a database—tables, records, and fields—the Access mechanics are easy to understand.

To create an Access database, add tables that describe the database data. Each table contains fields and records. When you design a table, you must describe the field names and data types that the table requires.

Now that you know how to create and edit tables, you are ready to enter data and master forms in Hour 18. By using forms for data entry and editing, you make Access tables easier to manage for you and others who use databases that you create.

Q&A

Q Would I ever want to configure a field with the AutoNumber format?

A Your data might require a unique sequential number for each record, such as an invoice number. Most often, however, Access uses the AutoNumber format for the key field that is added when you don't specify a key field.

Q Can I enter data in the Datasheet view?

A Certainly. As explained in this and the next hour, the Datasheet view is a handy view for entering simple data and for viewing multiple records of data from a table. The Datasheet view offers a worksheet-like view of your data in a row and column format. The Datasheet view gives you quick access to a table's data.

Remember that a Datasheet view shows only a single table's data. It does *not* show the entire database because a database often contains multiple tables of data.

Q Can a key field contain duplicates?

A No. If you have to locate records by field and that field is not unique, you cannot make the field a key. You must decide on another key or let Access add the key field.

HOUR 18

Entering and Displaying Access 2003 Data

You're now ready to enter and edit Access database data. Once you enter the data, you need to print the data to proofread for accuracy and to keep a hard copy as a backup. Although Access provides advanced and fancy reporting tools, you don't have to master those tools to print your Access data, as you will learn in this hour. When you gather a large amount of data, being able to print the data in a meaningful format is important and Access gives you the tools to do just that.

Finally, this lesson explains how to use the Form Wizard to generate forms that match your data. Forms offer a different perspective from datasheets. The Access forms you create resemble printed forms onscreen.

The highlights of this hour include the following:

- How to enter data into tables
- Which table-editing commands Access supports
- How to print tables
- When to use the Form Wizard to generate forms from tables
- How to use forms for data entry and editing
- How to print forms

Entering Table Data

Access gives you two primary means for adding data to tables that you create:

- Datasheet view
- Forms

The Datasheet view that you saw in Hour 17, "Access 2003 Basics," enables you to enter and view several records at one time as well as edit any record that you view. When you use a form, on the other hand, you typically work with only one record at a time. The record takes on the format of a printed form, giving you a better focus on individual records. You learn more about forms in a later section, "Using Forms to Enter and Edit Data." The next section focuses on the Datasheet view.

Using the Datasheet View

In the previous hour, you learned how to display the Datasheet view. The Datasheet view offers one of the simplest ways to enter and edit data in an Access database. The rest of this section shows you how Access makes entering data easy.

Entering Data

To enter data in the Datasheet view after you display the Datasheet view, just click the Datasheet view's first field and enter the field information. When you enter data into the first field, Access opens an additional blank record below the one you are entering. Access always leaves room for additional records. As you enter data, press Tab, Shift+Tab, or the arrow keys to move from field to field. You can also click any field into which you want to enter data. As you enter data, watch the status bar at the bottom of your screen. When you designed your table, if you enter a description for a field, Access displays that description in the status bar as you enter data in that field.

 If, while entering data, you see a number automatically appear in a field, don't panic. Access is automatically entering an AutoNumber into a field defined as an AutoNumber field (such as the key).

Figure 18.1 shows a Datasheet view that contains several records. The record selector always moves as you enter and edit data to show the current record. When you edit one row and then move to another, Access automatically saves that row to the table. As you make an edit, the Editing icon appears to the left of the row to indicate the row being edited. A second kind of record selector, an asterisk, always appears to the left of the next empty record and indicates a new record into which you can enter data.

FIGURE **18.1**

A Datasheet view can show several records of data.

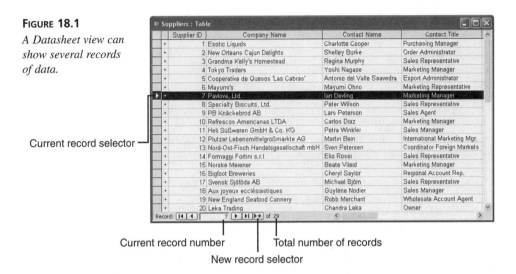

Current record selector —

Current record number   Total number of records

New record selector

Often, multiple records contain the same data in certain fields (as is the case with city and state names in a table). When you are about to enter data in a cell and the previous record contains the same data, press Ctrl+' to copy the previous record's field value into the current field's cell.

As you enter data, take advantage of the Office AutoCorrect feature. Just as Word and Excel support AutoCorrect entries, so does Access. All the Office products share the same AutoCorrect abbreviations you have defined.

When you enter AutoCorrect abbreviations and shortcuts, Access substitutes the shortcut for the AutoCorrect correction. Access does not automatically enable automatic spell-checking as you enter data because much of your table data contains data such as formal names and product codes that would appear to the spell-checker as misspellings. You can check your table's spelling by selecting Tools, Spelling.

To change a mistake, such as a transposed number, click the mistake to display the insertion point inside the Datasheet view's field and correct the entry. You can also press the arrow keys to move to any field and press F2 to edit the field's text.

Formatting Your Data

Access is forgiving when you enter special data such as dates, times, monetary amounts, and memo field values. You can basically enter data in these fields in whatever way seems best to you! You can enter a date in a date field, for example, using any of the following formats:

```
05/12/2005
5/12/2005
May 12, 2005
May 12 2005
```

Access uses a predefined date format to display dates and times in the Datasheet view, so after you type a date, it can be immediately reformatted to match this view. By default, Access uses the date format mm/dd/yyyy.

As with dates, you can enter time in several common ways. Add a.m. or p.m. or use 24-hour clock time. Access, by default, formats your time values to the hh:mm:ss format.

Quickly Entering Date and Time Values

You can press Ctrl+; to enter the current date in a field and press Ctrl+: to enter the current time. Access gets these values from your computer's clock and calendar setting.

Ctrl+; causes the date to display using the format dd/mm/yy (unless your Windows international settings specify a different date format), although Access stores the date using the current four-digit year.

Access currency fields accept a wide variety of formats. You can type a dollar sign (or whatever currency symbol matches your Windows international country setting) and decimals, and you can even place commas in currency values. After you enter a currency amount, Access displays the amount with the default format. The default currency format is based on your International settings. For North America, the default will be a dollar sign. If you fail to type the dollar sign, Access supplies one automatically.

Your Windows Control Panel contains an icon labeled Regional and Language Options. (Pre-Windows XP versions typically call this icon *Regional Settings*.) The language specified in your PC's regional settings determines how Access displays data. Therefore, you can maintain one database for multiple users around the world. The PC running the Access database determines how the data appears on the screen and in reports.

If you need to format a currency amount in a different format from your Windows international settings, you can do so by specifying the format in the Design view's property settings.

If you enter a value that does not meet the Field Properties requirements, such as placing two decimal points inside a single dollar amount, Access displays a dialog box (shown in Figure 18.2), indicating that you should correct the value before entering the next field.

Access does not let you leave a record that contains a bad format. As a matter of fact, Access will not even let you move to another row in the database if a field does not meet the Field Properties requirements. Therefore, when you close your tables, you can be assured that Access saves all the data with the proper data type. Although the data values might not be correct, you will know that the data does fit within the specified formats you declared for the table.

Editing Data

All the editing skills you mastered with the other Office products work with Access. You can rearrange the order of fields and records by dragging the record or field selectors with your mouse. You can select more than one field or record at a time by dragging your mouse through the record or field selectors or by holding down Shift while you click record or field selectors. Press Ctrl+A to select all the records in the table.

To delete one or more records or fields, select the records or fields you want to delete and right-click the record selector to display a shortcut menu. Select Delete Column or Delete Record.

Access provides several shortcut menus that help you perform needed tasks. For example, when you right-click the selected records or fields, the shortcut menu that appears provides familiar Cut, Copy, and Paste commands as well as Insert and Delete commands for records and fields. When you right-click a record selector, a different shortcut menu appears that enables you to work with the rows.

Right-clicking a column selector produces a shortcut menu with the Hide Columns command that temporarily hides fields (they physically stay in the table). These fields stay out of the way while you work with other data, and you can choose Format, Unhide Columns to reveal the data when you are ready to work with the entire table again. Other right-click options can be helpful too, such as the sorting commands. You can sort records in *ascending order* or *descending order* with the shortcut menu's options when you right-click over data in the table.

18

If you often need to adjust the width or height of records and fields, consider changing your table's font size and style (by selecting Format, Font) .

Navigating Large Tables

Use the navigation buttons at the bottom of the Datasheet view (see Figure 18.3) to move through and jump over large blocks of records that don't interest you at the time. The navigation buttons work similar to those on a VCR, enabling you to move forward and backward through your data.

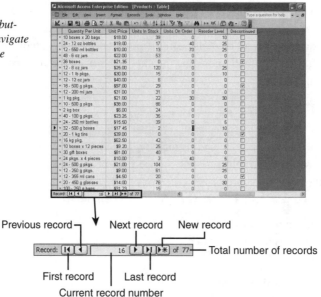

Here are a few pointers:

- Click Next Record to move the record selector to the next record.
- Click Previous Record to move the record selector to the previous record.
- Click First Record to move to the table's first record.
- Click Last Record to move to the table's last record.
- Click the Specific Record box, type a new record number, and then press Enter to jump directly to that record.

Simple Printing

Access includes powerful reporting tools, but they take some time to master. You learn about reporting in Hour 20, "Reporting with Access 2003." If you just want to print a listing of your data, however, you can do so easily from the Datasheet view. Access automatically prints the Datasheet view with field titles.

Perhaps you need to check a table listing for errors, or you want a printed listing (called a *hard copy*) so that you can proofread the data values that you entered. Before printing, display a preview (similar to the one shown in Figure 18.4) by selecting File, Print Preview. Move the magnifying glass mouse pointer over any portion of the preview and click to see a close-up. To close the print preview without closing the table, click the toolbar's Close button.

FIGURE 18.4

Get a preview of printed datasheet tables.

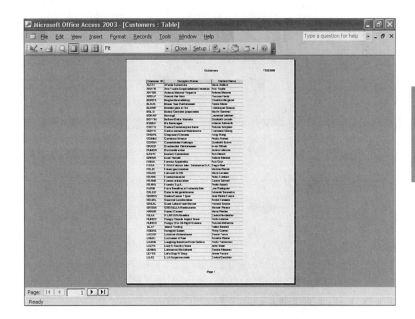

18

To print a Datasheet table, select File, Print (or click the Print button on the toolbar).

Using Forms to Enter and Edit Data

When you computerize your records, you want to make it as easy as possible for people to enter, edit, and view data in your database. Often, Access reduces paperwork. A credit agency might use Access to keep track of loan applications that borrowers fill out, for example. As borrowers bring in their completed applications, a clerk types the data from the application into an Access table. Although a Datasheet view would work fine for the data entry, a form works even better! The form can, while onscreen, mimic the look and feel of paper forms that many people are accustomed to using. You do not have to keep files of paper forms now that you use Access.

To Do: Use the Form Wizard to Generate Forms

You probably want to use the Form Wizard to create your first form. The Form Wizard generates simple forms that work well in most cases.

Follow these steps to start the Form Wizard:

1. Display the Database window with your database open.
2. Click the Forms object to display the tasks you can perform with forms.
3. Click the Database window's New button to display the New Form dialog box (shown in Figure 18.5).

FIGURE 18.5

Creating a new form.

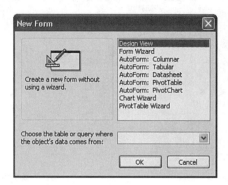

4. Click to select the Form Wizard option.
5. Select the table or query in the lower part of the dialog box to use as a basis for the form. If your database contains multiple tables and queries, each table and query appears in the drop-down list. You must select a table or query before continuing.
6. Click OK to display the opening Form Wizard screen (shown in Figure 18.6). This screen lists the available fields that you can include for your selected table.

You might or might not want to include every field on every form you create. Suppose, for example, that you want to create a form for your company's personnel that contains employee names and extension numbers but not employee pay rates. The next step in creating your form is to indicate to Access which fields to include.

To add table fields to the form, select a field and click the button labeled >. Access adds that field to the selected field list. To include all the fields, click the button labeled >>. The Form Wizard sends all the table's fields to the selected field list.

Click to add field to form

FIGURE **18.6**
*The opening Form
Wizard screen shows
your selected table and
its available fields.*

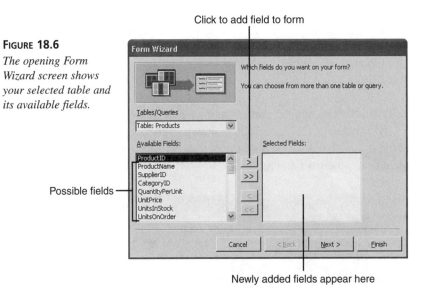

Possible fields

Newly added fields appear here

If you send a field to the form accidentally, select that field and click the button labeled <
to remove the field from the form. Clicking << removes all the fields, so you can start
over if you want to rearrange the fields or copy new ones from scratch.

Click the Next button to display the Form Wizard layout screen (shown in Figure 18.7).
Click the different options to see a preview of how that option changes the form's layout.

18

FIGURE 18.7
*Select a layout for
your form.*

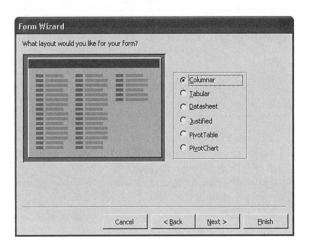

The Tabular and Datasheet form layouts are similar to the Datasheet view. The Columnar and Justified layouts look similar to typical paper forms. As you click each option, Access displays that option's resulting form layout.

When you click the Next button, the Form Wizard displays a screen from which you can select a form style (as shown in Figure 18.8). Click through the style selections to see a preview of those available. Many styles have unique personalities that can add eye-catching appeal to an otherwise dull form.

FIGURE **18.8**

The Form Wizard supports several form styles.

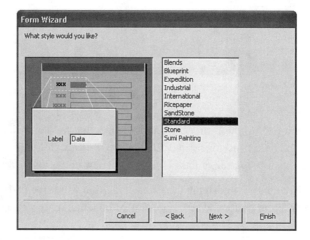

When you click the Next button, you see the Form Wizard's closing screen, which asks for a form title. (The default title is the name of your selected table.) Click Finish to generate the form.

After you learn more advanced Access commands (see Hour 20), such as how to use the form-creation and editing tools, you can open the generated form's Design view and change specific parts of the form. The Form Wizard generates your form, and you can then modify the form to look exactly the way you want it. For now, the Form Wizard's generated forms work well.

In some cases, generated forms contain problems, but you can correct those problems with a little editing from the form's Design view. Figure 18.9 shows a generated form that needs slight editing. The Form Wizard automatically uses field names for the form prompts and data descriptions. If your field names are long, the Form Wizard might not display the entire field name for the prompt. Also, some data might not align properly because the data value's width might be longer than the form's field. In addition, if your table does not contain many fields, the form does not take up the full screen and might look too small. You can maximize the form onscreen or resize the form to a smaller window.

Figure 18.9 displays its form in the Form view. The Form view displays records in the form-like format. Access also contains a form's Design view (not unlike the table's Design view), in which you can edit the form and change its appearance.

FIGURE 18.9

The Form Wizard generates forms for you.

Slight format problem in field name

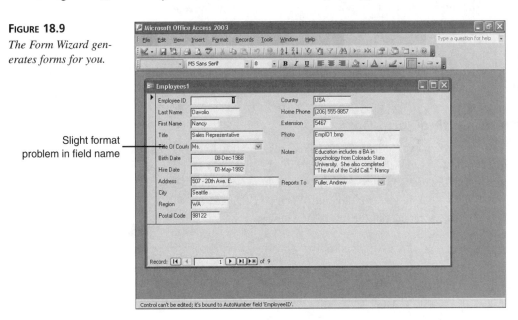

18

When using forms, you must understand how all the data types appear. If your table contains Yes/No data-type fields, those fields appear with an x to indicate the Yes value. If you name a rental property's tenant field `Pet Deposit?`, for example, and assign the Yes/No data type to the field, those owners who pay a pet deposit have an x for this field value.

Memo fields can hold a lot of data, so if you use a memo field, keep typing when the insertion point reaches the right side of the field. Access scrolls the field to enable you to continue. Form views display memo fields with scrollbars so you can look at all the data in the fields.

Navigating Forms

Forms typically show only single records. Unlike the Datasheet view, the form is a much better tool for working with single records. In the Datasheet view, you can often see many records, but not all the fields in those records, because the fields rarely fit on the Datasheet view screen. The form shows only a single record but often manages to include all fields from the records because of the form layout.

Access offers several ways to move through records in the Form view. Press the up arrow, down arrow, Tab, and Shift+Tab to move from one field to another. Press PageUp and PageDown to move to the previous and next table record, respectively. The record number appears at the bottom of the form window's record selection control. As in the Datasheet view, you can click the record selection control to move from record to record.

To jump to a record quickly, press F5, type a record number, and press Enter.

Editing Form Data

As you move through the form records, feel free to change data in the record. The record selector arrow changes to an editing pencil to show that you are editing the record. If you use Tab or Shift+Tab to move from field to field, press F2 when the highlight appears over the field you want to edit. When you change data within the Form view, Access changes the data in the underlying tables.

To add records from the Form view, click the New Record button to display a new one that you can fill out.

Printing Forms

If you select File, Print from the Form view, Access prints the forms. Unlike the onscreen Form view, Access prints as many forms on the page as will fit. (Select the File, Print Preview to see what will print, such as the preview shown in Figure 18.10.)

FIGURE 18.10

Access prints multiple records per form.

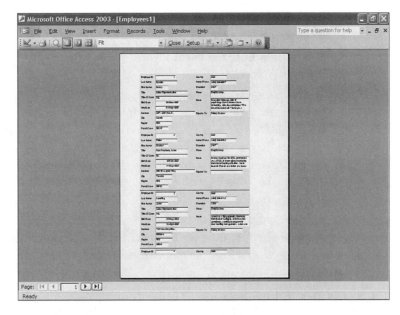

Summary

This hour extended your Access knowledge by showing you how to use the Datasheet view to enter and print data. You also learned how to create and use forms. Access replaces the paper forms you are used to and provides a form-like approach to data entry and editing.

The Form Wizard quickly generates nice forms for you from your table data. The Form Wizard is a great place to start designing your forms because it analyzes your table and generates a form based on your table's fields.

The next hour, "Retrieving Your Data," teaches you how to filter data and use queries so that you can work with subsets of table data.

Q&A

Q When I open a table's Datasheet view, why does the data appear in a different order from the order in which I entered it?

A Access sorts data, in ascending order, according to the table's selected key field. Your Datasheet views always appear in the order sorted by the key field unless you change the sort order by right-clicking the field that you want to sort by and then choosing Sort Ascending or Sort Descending. Access uses the key field to locate records quickly when you search for data.

Q **Why should I use the Form Wizard but not the Table Wizard when I begin learning Access?**

A You must understand tables, records, and fields before you use the Table Wizard to generate tables because you almost always have to modify the Table Wizard's generated table to suit your exact needs. Therefore, it helps, when starting out, to create tables from scratch and learn how tables work. After you learn how to use the table's Datasheet and Design views, you are better equipped to edit tables generated with the Table Wizard.

The Form Wizard looks at tables that you generated and creates simple data-entry forms with the format and layout that you request. Forms require less editing when you generate them from the Form Wizard than tables do. You will be pleased with the Form Wizard from the moment you create your first form.

Q **Can I edit the AutoNumber field?**

A If you let Access create and enter your table's key field, you should also let Access maintain the AutoNumber that it enters for you. When you create reports, you can hide the AutoNumber field so that the field does not appear with the data that others see. The AutoNumber field is Access's bookkeeping field when you fail to designate a key. Access keeps the table sorted in the key order, and you should not bother with this field. If you want, rearrange the table to move the AutoNumber field to the far-right side of the Datasheet view. Then, you rarely see the field when you work with the data.

HOUR 19

Retrieving Your Data

Although your database contains a lot of data, you rarely want to see all that data simultaneously. Generally, you want to see only data subsets. Access filters and queries produce small, meaningful subsets of data from your tables.

When you view data subsets, you prevent unwanted data from getting in the way of the information with which you need to work. The power of queries is that you can select records and fields from multiple tables and view that selected data subset from within a single Datasheet or Form view.

The highlights of this hour include the following:

- What a filter is
- Why you sometimes use Filter by Selection and sometimes use Filter by Form
- When a filter limits you
- Why queries are more robust than filters
- How to use the query wizards
- How to use the Query Design view to create and edit queries
- Where to specify advanced selection criteria

Using Data Filters

A *filter* is a subset of data from a table. Suppose that you want to see only certain records from a table, such as all customers who are past due. Instead of hiding the records that you don't want to see, create a filter. The filter removes unwanted records from view. The records don't go away, and you don't have to unhide the records later (as you do when you actually hide records by right-clicking over a column or row in the Datasheet view and selecting Hide Columns or Hide Row). A filter works similar to a short-term record hider, putting certain records out of the way while you work with the filtered data.

Access supports three filtering approaches:

- *Filter by Selection*—Filters data based on selected table data
- *Filter by Form*—Enables you to choose the data fields that you want Access to use for filtering
- *Advanced Filter/Sort*—Controls advanced filtering options from the Access menu bar

The easiest and most common filter options are Filter by Selection and Filter by Form, which the following two sections describe.

Access includes an Advanced Filter/Sort option on the Records, Filter menu, but you will almost always prefer creating a query to using the advanced filter. In addition, Access supports a Filter Excluding Selection that filters the opposite of Filter by Selection. A query is easier to save and work with in the future than a filter.

Filter by Selection

Filter by Selection works by example. Suppose that you want to display only those table records that contain a specific field value; for example, you need to work only with customer records from Brazil. If your customer table contains a Country field with scattered Brazil entries, you can filter out all those records that do *not* contain Brazil in their Country fields.

You can practice working with filters by opening the sample Northwind Traders database that comes with Access. (You'll locate this northwind.mdb file in your Office Samples folder.) When you first open the Northwind Traders database, a *splash screen* will

appear; a splash screen acts as a title window that appears when you first start an application, and you can designate splash screens for databases that appear when you open
them. Close the splash screen by clicking the window's OK button, and perform the
following steps to design a filter that filters out records that don't contain Brazil:

1. Display the Datasheet view for the Customers table. To do so, click the Tables
   entry inside the Database window and double-click the Customers table.

2. Locate one record with Brazil in the Country field. You might have to click the
   horizontal scrollbar to see the Country field from the Datasheet view.

3. Double-click the single field value that contains Brazil to select that value. If you
   select only the first part of the field instead of selecting the entire field, such as the
   letter *B*, you filter all records that do not start with *B*.

4. Click the toolbar's Filter by Selection button. Access filters out all records that
   don't match your selected *criteria*. Figure 19.1 shows a filtered Datasheet view that
   displays only records containing a Brazil entry in their Country fields. Before the
   filter, this Datasheet view held more than 90 records. By locating the sample field
   and clicking once, you just changed the display to those records that only contain
   Brazil for the Country field value.

5. To return to the full Datasheet view, click the toolbar's Remove Filter button.

As you can see, a filter removes unwanted records; Access filters those unwanted records
from view.

> To filter out records that contain your selected value (instead of all records
> that do not contain a value), select Records, Filter, Filter Excluding Selection.
> The Filter Excluding Selection option works similarly to a reverse filter. Click
> the Remove Filter to revert the Datasheet view to its full table once again.

19

You do not first have to locate a customer record from Brazil to create the previous list's
filter. If you right-click any field value in the table and then type a value in the shortcut
menu's Filter for text box, Access applies the Filter by Selection command to your
entered filter value. Therefore, you can right-click on the Country column, select Filter
By, and then enter Brazil to more quickly create the same filter that the previous steps
created.

For now, remove the filtering by clicking the Remove Filter button on the toolbar.

Filter by selection ─┐   ┌─ Remove filter

FIGURE 19.1

*Filter by Selection fil-
ters out all unwanted
records.*

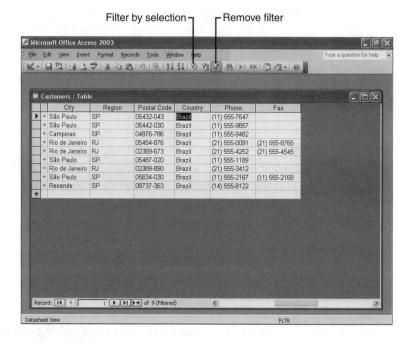

To Do: Perform a Filter by Form

Filter by Form enables you to filter by multiple values rather than by only one value. You
can apply a Filter by Form from both the Datasheet and Form views.

Perform these steps to use Filter by Form:

1. Click the Filter by Form button. Access displays a single blank record. If you have
   recently created a filter, that previous filter's selection value appears in the single
   row that displays. You can erase the value and enter a different one.

2. Scroll to the field you want to filter by or click on the empty field.

3. Click the field's drop-down arrow to display the list. Access displays a scrolling
   drop-down list of every value (without duplicates) that appears in that field within
   the current table.

4. Select the value by which you want to filter.

5. Optionally, click another empty field value and select from that field's drop-down
   list of available values. You can select as many filtering field values as you need.
   Unlike the Filter by Selection, which enables you to filter only by one field value,
   Filter by Form enables you to filter by several fields.

6. Click the Apply Filter button to display the filtered records.

7. Click the Remove Filter button (before you begin filtering, this button is called the Apply Filter button) when you are ready to return to the full-record view.

By filtering on one or more fields, you can easily display only those records you want to see. The filters do not actually remove records from your tables, but they help display the data you need to see at the moment.

If you filter by a date field, Access surrounds the filtered value with pound signs (#). You often see pound signs around dates, such as #7/4/2005#; this designation enables Access to distinguish the date from a formula that might use the forward slash (/) as the divide symbol.

Access can perform an Or filter, meaning that Access filters to find all records that include one or more of your selected filter field values. If you want to find all customers who live in New York or who live in Maine, for example, select New York, click the Or tab at the bottom of the Filter by Form window, and select Maine. You can continue adding Or conditions to select from one of several fields.

Although Access uses an Or condition to select from one of several field values, it uses an *And condition* to select across fields. This means that if you select Brazil for the Country field filter and Rio for the City field filter, Access filters to find all records with both Brazil as a country and Rio for the city. If a record contains the country Brazil but Saõ Paulo for the city, such a filter would not retain that record.

19

Using Queries

A *query* is really nothing more than a question you ask Access about your data. Access does not understand questions the way you generally ask them, so you must ask your question with its special query format. A query differs somewhat from a filter. A query is the request that produces a subset of data. A filter, on the other hand, just temporarily hides certain data from your Access views so that you can see only a subset of data from a table.

A query is an object, just as tables and forms are objects. Therefore, you see the Queries object page on the Database window, and you create, edit, and execute queries from this page. As with other objects, queries have names that you give them. Many queries are nothing more than named filters; however, filters go away when you are finished with them, whereas you can recall a query later by its name. If you want to reapply a filter, you must reproduce it.

> Although you cannot name filters, you can turn a Filter by Form request into a named query. When you enter the Filter by Form request, click the Save as Query toolbar button. Access prompts you for a query name and stores the filter as a query. Often, creating a named query from a Filter by Form is faster than generating a new query from scratch if you only want to create a simple query that filters records.

Queries are often much more advanced than filters. A query enables you to specify selected records from a table or from another query. You can create a query that selects records and fields from multiple tables. The data subset that a query generates often becomes a table-like Datasheet view from which you can report. You can build a query that extracts certain records and fields from three tables, for example, and then generate a report from those extracted records and fields.

Not only can you create a query that extracts fields and records, but also you can specify the exact order of the resulting data subset, sort the subset, and use powerful extraction criteria to select data based on very specific requirements.

Once you generate a query, you can save that query just as you save tables and reports. The saved query will contain all the instructions necessary to once again generate the data so that you do not have to build that query again.

> The created data subset is called a *dynaset*.

Creating a Query with the Query Wizard

Although you can build a query from scratch, the Query Wizard can do the dirty work for you in most cases.

Access includes these four query wizards:

- *Simple Query Wizard*—Extracts fields from one or more tables and from other queries.
- *Crosstab Query Wizard*—Creates a worksheet-like query that summarizes field values and cross-tabulates matching values.

- *Find Duplicates Query Wizard*—Creates a data subset from two or more tables or queries that contain matching values in one or more fields that you select.

- *Find Unmatched Query Wizard*—Creates a data subset from two or more tables or queries that contain no duplicate records.

You use the Simple Query Wizard often because of its general-purpose design. When you create a new query by selecting Queries from the Database window's object list and then clicking New on the toolbar, Access displays the New Query dialog box (shown in Figure 19.2).

FIGURE 19.2

Begin creating your query in the New Query dialog box.

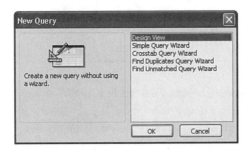

When you create a new query, a list of the four query-based wizards appears and you can select from that list. In addition, a fifth entry appears labeled Design View. The Design View entry is misleading because it is not a wizard but a query-building screen from which you must build the query from scratch without the help from any wizard.

19

To Do: Build a Query with the Simple Query Wizard

Follow these steps to build your first query using the Simple Query Wizard:

1. After opening your database, click Queries in the Database window.

2. Click the Database window's New button to open the New Query window.

3. Select the Simple Query Wizard from the New Query dialog box and click OK. Access starts the wizard and displays the Simple Query Wizard screen (see Figure 19.3).

4. Select a table or an existing query that holds the data you want the query to extract. (You can build queries from tables or from other queries.) Access displays fields from the selected table (or query) in the Available Fields list.

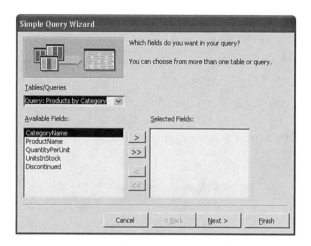

5. Select one or more fields and click the button labeled >. Access includes these fields in the resulting query data subset. If you want the query to extract all customer names and balances from a customer table, for example, select those two fields and click > to send them to the Selected Fields list. The Selected Fields list is the query's resulting structure and holds a description of the data subset that the query eventually produces.

6. Optionally, select another table or query from the Tables/Queries drop-down list and add more fields to the Selected Fields list. If Access prompts you to create a relationship between the tables, click Yes to create the relationship. Access relates the tables automatically if you created the relationship link elsewhere. You are now building a query that extracts data subsets from multiple sources. If you send the wrong field to the Selected Fields list, select the incorrect field and click < to remove it. To remove all your selected fields and begin again, click the button labeled <<.

7. Click Next to select either a detail or summary query. A detail query includes every field of every record; a summary query does not show duplicate selected records and includes summary statistics if you select them by clicking the Summary Options button.

8. Click Next and select a title for the query. Access bases the default name for the new query on the first selected table or existing query.

9. Click Finish to complete the query. Access builds the query and displays the selected records from the query in the Datasheet view. When you close the Datasheet view, you see the new query listed on the Queries page of the Database window. Again, you can often create a filter that produces the same extracted

record subset as a query, but you can later re-extract queries by name instead of rebuilding them from scratch as you must do with filters.

The resulting query is just a smaller table, a subset of the original table, that your query generated. For the first time, you have the power to extract records from multiple tables to create a dynaset, or subset, of your database records.

You can also create a new form (using one of the form wizards) to display the results of a query. When you created a new form in Hour 18, "Entering and Displaying Access 2003 Data," you knew only how to create forms from single tables. If multiple tables contain data you want to display in a form, however, create a query to extract from the two tables and base the form on that query.

To synchronize a multiple-table query, all tables must have a common field (such as a customer number), or you must use advanced Access commands to relate the two tables in some way. Without a relationship, such as a common field, the query cannot combine the fields from the two tables.

Access does not save your query results, just the query structure. Therefore, if you want to see a data subset twice, you must open the Database window's Queries page, select the query, and click Open to generate the query extraction once again. Although the extraction requires a little time to generate (usually the speed is negligible unless the tables contain many records), the query is always fresh. If you change one value in any table and open the query again, your most recent table edit appears in the query.

Another advantage of generating the query every time you need to use the data subset is that Access does not have to store the data twice (once in the source tables and again in the query).

19

If you edit data from the resulting query's Datasheet view (or from the query's Form view), Access updates the data in the original tables. Suppose that you want to edit the pay rate for every employee who works in your company's Northeast division; just create a query to extract only the Northeast division employees, make the edits, and close the query. Find and edit the Northeast employees' pay rates without the other employee records getting in the way.

Using the Query Design View

When you create or edit a query from scratch, you can use the Query Design view (such as the one shown in Figure 19.4).

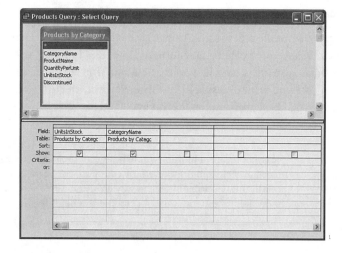

Although the Query Design view looks somewhat strange at first, the view's design is logical. The top of the Query Design view contains the source tables and queries, and the bottom of the Query Design view displays the criteria (the query-selection commands).

You use the Query Design view when you must

- Create an advanced query that the query wizards cannot create.
- Edit an existing query.

After you learn to create a query with the Query Design view, you will also understand how to use the Query Design view to edit existing queries.

To Do: Create a Query from Scratch

To use the Query Design view to create a query, follow these steps:

1. Select Queries in the Database window.
2. Click the New button to open the New Query dialog box.
3. Select Design View and click OK to open the Query Design view. Access displays the Show Table dialog box that contains all your table and query details (similar to the one shown in Figure 19.5).

FIGURE 19.5

Select from your database's tables and queries for the new query.

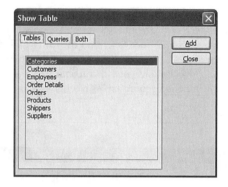

4. Click the table or tables that you want to include in the query and then click Add. As you add tables to the query, Access displays a new table in the Query Design view showing in the background. If you want to base your new query on another query, click the Queries tab to display a list of them from which you can choose and then add the selected query. If you want to add both tables and queries, click the Both tab to display all your database tables and queries and then select the ones you need.

5. Click Close to close the Show Table dialog box.

You have yet to build the entire query, but you have selected tables, existing queries, or both on which to base your new query. Next, enter the query's criteria so that Access knows which records and fields to select from your tables and existing queries.

It's easy to accidentally add the same table twice to a query. If you do, just click the "extra" table in the upper pane of the query and press Delete.

Figure 19.6 shows the start of a new query. This query extracts from two tables, one named Customers and one named Employees. The line connecting the tables' common field, City, appears when you drag your mouse between the common field, as you do when you want to create a relationship. You might recall from the preceding section that Access must base queries on related tables and queries, and the common field relates the two tables.

Think of the top half of the query's design window as starting the request, "Given these tables and queries…" and the lower half of the window as finishing that request, "…extract all data that meets these conditions." The Query Design view contains your instructions when you want Access to extract data from one or more tables or queries and display the result in a table subset.

FIGURE 19.6

This query can now extract from two related tables.

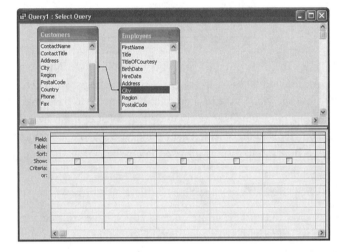

Each column in the Query Design view's lower half contains the resulting query's fields. Therefore, if you want the resulting data subset to contain four fields, you fill in four of the Query Design view's lower columns. These columns contain the instructions that indicate to the query how to extract the data from the table, tables, query, queries, or combinations of tables and queries that you have specified for the query.

To Do: Work with Complex Queries

To complete the query, follow these steps:

1. Click the first column's row labeled Table and select the table that contains the resulting query's first field. If you want the query's data subset to start with a field from the Tenants table, for example, you select Tenants from the drop-down list.

2. Click the first column's row labeled Field and select the field that you want to place first in the resulting data subset. You might select Customers from the list, for example.

3. If you want to sort the resulting query's subset based on the first field, select either Ascending or Descending from the row labeled Sort. You don't have to sort on the first field that you add to the query; you can sort on any field that you add. The query sorts all the resulting data based on the value of the field by which you sort. If you sort on two or more fields, Access sorts the data in the leftmost Sort column first.

4. Leave the Show option checked if you want the field to appear in the resulting query's data subset. Generally, you want the field to appear. If you want to sort the subset on a field but not send that sort field to the resulting extracted subset, uncheck the Show option for that field.

5. Click the first column's row labeled Criteria and enter a criterion. If you type a value, such as JJ1, Access extracts only those records with a field containing JJ1. You can continue adding criteria values beneath the first one. You can type the values JJ1, BR1, BR2, and BE1 for five rows of criteria (still in the first column). It is like asking Access to extract only those tenants whose Tenant ID is JJ1, BR1, BR2, or BE1, for example. If the field is a text-data type, Access encloses the criteria in quotation marks (like the fields shown in Figure 19.7). Access encloses dates inside pound signs (#1/6/1898#, for example) if you enter dates in the criteria.

FIGURE 19.7

This query must match several criteria values for Customer ID.

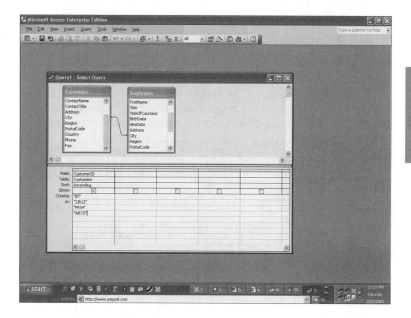

19

6. It gets fun here. Instead of selecting the field from the second column's drop-down list labeled Field, drag the field name from a table in the upper half of the Query

Design view (such as the Order Date field in the Orders table). Access automatically fills in the table and field name in the second column of the query! (You might also double-click a field name from the table in the upper portion of the Query Design view to use that field name in the query.)

7. Enter the selection criteria for the new field. The criteria indicate exactly how you want to pull records from the table. If you want to extract all the records (all that fall within the criteria of the first field that you have entered), leave the second field's criteria blank. You can further limit the extraction by entering an additional criterion for the second field. Suppose that you not only want customers with the IDs listed in the first criteria, but you also want to limit the selection to any of those five who have an order date of January 6, 2005. You enter #1/6/2005# for the criteria.

8. Continue adding fields that you want to appear in the resulting query. When you execute your query, these fields appear in the resulting table.

As you work with the query, you might want to add more tables. Add the tables in the Query Design view by selecting Query, Show Table. Add as many tables (or queries) as you prefer to the query from within the Query Design view, but remember that the tables and queries must relate somehow. Remove a table or query from the Query Design view by right-clicking the table name and selecting Remove Table.

> You can use all the cut, copy, and paste methods that you learned earlier in the book for the query-extraction fields. You can move a field from one location to another by selecting, cutting, and pasting it, for example. You can also resize column widths by dragging the field column edges, and you can change any value by clicking that value in the Query Design view.

If you really want to get fancy, use the relational operators in Table 19.1 to add to your extraction power.

TABLE 19.1   Access's Relational Operators

Operator	Description
>	Greater than
<	Less than
>=	Greater than or equal to
<=	Less than or equal to
<>	Not equal to
=	Equal to (not needed for simple matches)

Suppose that you want to include customer-order details in a query, but you only want to include orders with more than 19 units. Enter >19 for the Quantity field's criterion to limit the selection to those records that match the other criteria and that have order quantities of more than 19 units. The relational operators work with numbers, text values that fall within a range of words, and dates.

The Between keyword is useful when you want to extract values that fall between two other values. If you type Between #1/1/2005# And #1/31/2005# for a date criterion, for example, Access extracts only records whose date falls between 1/1/2005 and 1/31/2005 (including the days 1/1/2005 and 1/31/2005).

Access uses an implied Or when you specify multiple criteria. Instead of typing five separate Customer IDs such as 101, 102, 103, 104, and 105, for example, you could enter 101 Or 102 Or 103 Or 104 Or 105. (Of course, entering Between 101 And 105 is even easier.)

Be sure to save your query when you finish with it. Click the Query Design view's Close Window button and name the query so that you are able to refer to it later. When you select the query and click Open from the Queries page of the Database window, Access runs the query, extracts the data, and displays the result in your Datasheet view.

Although Access queries are useful and not extremely complex, the screens might seem daunting at first for Access newcomers. The Access online help screens provide many examples and explanations that you might want to peruse to familiarize yourself better with database queries.

Summary

19

This hour showed you how to narrow your data and form subsets. Often, a table contains many more fields and records than you want to work with at any one time. Access's filter and query powers enable you to create subsets of data to make your work more manageable.

Filters provide quick subsets, but queries provide more power and flexibility. After you run a filter or query to create a subset of your data, you can make changes to the subset and modify data in the underlying tables. Although the Query Design view takes some getting used to, it enables you to specify powerful query extraction criteria so that Access searches for and finds the data with which you need to work.

Now that you can produce subsets of data, you need a way to report that data. The next hour, "Reporting with Access 2003," explores some of the reporting capabilities. The Report Wizard makes quick work of report generation from your tables and queries.

Q&A

Q Should I use a filter or a query?

A When you quickly want to see a subset of a table, use a filter. You sometimes use the subset in another way (as input to a report, for example), so creating a query that you can name and execute makes more sense.

Q If I save a filter as a named query, what does the query's Query Design view look like?

A Filters are less powerful than queries, but they are easier to designate. As you create more queries and get used to your data needs, you will find that many of your queries are little more than filters. Instead of messing with the Query Design view to design the query, generate a simpler Filter by Form filter and save it as a query. If you then want to modify the filter-based query or add more complex criteria, open the query's Query Design view and you can see that Access selected the proper source table and field names for you. You can then add to the criteria lines and request additional fields if you want.

Q Does the row on which I place criteria make a difference?

A Yes, although you are getting into some confusing logic. The way you specify criteria between two fields often indicates how you want the combined criteria to work. If you place one field's criterion on the same row as another field's, an implied *and* relation takes place, and Access extracts only those records that contain a match for both criteria values. If you place one field's criterion on a different row from another field's, an implied *or* relation takes place between them.

Q How can I see my data in two ways, say, with the field names arranged alphabetically and with the fields arranged in the order of my table's design?

A Create a query that extracts all the fields from your table. The query's output, or data subset, will contain all data that the original table contains. (The subset will be the same size as the table.) Set up the query's output for ordering the fields alphabetically. Queries aren't just for creating smaller subsets of tables; you can create a query to report table data in an order that differs from a table's original design order.

HOUR 20

Reporting with Access 2003

This hour shows you how to create custom Access 2003 reports. Access includes several reporting tools, both automatic and manual, that produce complex reports. You can create a simple report by clicking a toolbar button. If you spend a little time developing the report with a report wizard, you can create extremely professional-looking reports.

You do not have to master the Report Design view, an extensive and complex report-creating tool, to create most of your reports. Some people have never used the Report Design view to design an Access report from scratch because of the report wizards' power. The report wizards give you complete control over a report's design.

The highlights of this hour include the following:

- How to create report queries
- How AutoReport creates simple reports
- Which report wizards Access supports
- How to use the main report wizard to generate virtually any report you need by making a few selections
- When to request summary statistics
- Why you should preview reports

Introducing Access Reports

You often want printed listings of your data, and the Access reporting tools enable you to produce professional reports with ease. This hour introduces you to the report wizards and discusses the different reporting styles and options available. You learned how to produce printed listings in Hour 18, "Entering and Displaying Access 2003 Data." In this hour, you learn how to add flair to your reports. Keep in mind that discussions of Access's reporting wizards could fill an entire book. Although you will not be a complete master at the end of this hour, you'll have a better idea of what reporting tools you can use.

Unlike forms, a report often displays multiple records in a view that resembles the Datasheet view. The difference between the Datasheet view and a printed report is that the report provides summary statistics, fancy headings, footers, page numbers, and styles that accent your data. In addition, you can pick and choose exactly what data the report is to include as well as group that data to subtotal and total certain pieces of data in the database.

> A *report* is not only a listing of multiple data values. Anytime you need to send Access data to paper, you must create a report. Therefore, a report might be a series of checks or mailing labels that you print.

Before you print any report, use the Print Preview to see the report on your screen. Often, you notice changes that you need to make, so previewing a report can save you time and paper. Your computer's print *spooler* (the area of memory that holds your report while printing) is too fast to stop quickly, so you usually end up printing the first few pages of a report even if you attempt to stop the printing.

When you are about to print a report, click the Reports object in the left pane of the Database window, select a report, and click the Preview button on the Database window's toolbar. Access can generate nice reports (see Figure 20.1).

Rarely do you report all the data from a single table. Except for detailed reports, such as inventory listings and master customer listings, you almost always report part of a table or values from multiple tables.

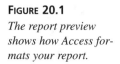

FIGURE 20.1

The report preview shows how Access formats your report.

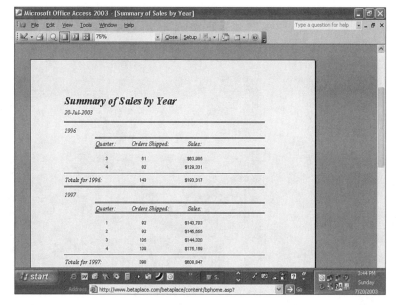

Almost all reports that you generate, therefore, get their data from queries that you have created. If you need to report from part of a table's data or from multiple tables, create a query on which to base the report. Your queries can order the data the way you want to see it, and Access can then print your query's results.

Generating Simple Reports Using AutoReports

Access includes an *AutoReport* feature, which quickly generates reports from your Datasheet views. As Figure 20.2 shows, the AutoReport feature is just a listing of field names and their corresponding field values.

Unlike the printed listings you get when you select File, Print from the Datasheet view, AutoReport formats your data in a readable manner without squeezing too much information on a single page.

To Do: Produce Quick Reports

If you need to run a quick report from a table, follow these steps to enable AutoReport to generate the report:

1. Display your data in a Datasheet view. If you want to report from a subset of data or from a collection of multiple tables, display the query's Datasheet view or apply a filter to the data.

20

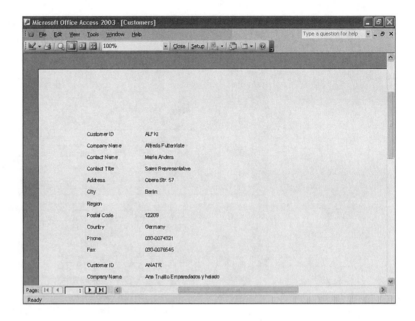

FIGURE 20.2

AutoReport generates simple reports.

2. Click the down arrow next to the New Object button on the toolbar.

3. Select AutoReport from the button's drop-down list. Access generates a report from the current Datasheet view and shows a preview of the report (shown in Figure 20.2).

4. If the preview shows what you want, click the Database toolbar's Print icon to print the report.

5. Click the Design button to close the AutoReport preview and to display the Report Design view (shown in Figure 20.3). The Report Design view can be difficult to understand when you first see it. (The Form Design view looks similar.) For now, don't worry about the specific screen elements. AutoReport created the report's design and saved you from having to use the Report Design view tools that you see in Figure 20.3.

6. Close the Report Design view and enter a report name if you want to save the AutoReport's design. If you think you will ever edit an AutoReport design later or generate the same report often, save the report. Generally, you use AutoReport only to generate quick reports. You will use the report wizards (described next) to generate more standard reports.

> AutoReport generates reports using Access's report-designing tools. After you learn how to modify a Report Design view, you can use AutoReport to generate the foundation of a report and then change the report to make it look the way you want.

FIGURE 20.3

AutoReport enables you to avoid using the Report Design view.

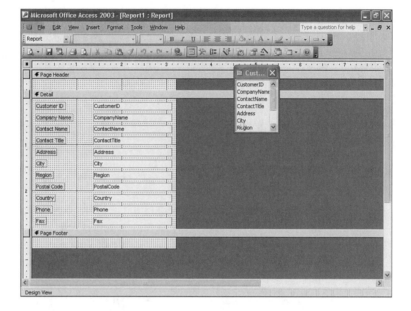

If you like using AutoReport for quick reports, check out the AutoForm feature. AutoForm creates fast and simple forms from your Datasheet views.

Generating Reports Using the Report Wizards

Access includes several report wizards that design reports according to the specifications you give. Select one of the report wizards by opening the Database window, clicking the Reports object (which displays the reports currently defined in the database), and clicking the New button to create a new report. The New Report screen (see Figure 20.4) appears.

20

The New Report dialog box enables you to access the following reporting components:

- *Design View*—A blank Report Design view on which you can add a new report's headers, footers, detail, and *summary* requests. When you want to generate a report from scratch, use the Design View in the New Report dialog box.

- *Report Wizard*—Walks you through the report-generation process by enabling you to select the source tables and queries as well as the fields that you want in the final report. You will probably run Report Wizard more often than the other options because it generates less specific reports than other reporting wizards. The next section, "To Do: Use Report Wizard," explains how you can use Report Wizard to create reports.

FIGURE **20.4**

*Request a report
from the New Report
dialog box.*

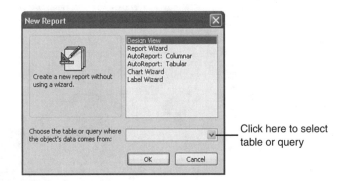

Click here to select
table or query

- *AutoReport: Columnar*—Generates a report that contains all the fields from the underlying table or query. The columnar report resembles the AutoReport, except that the columnar report makes better use of your report's page space and designs a more routine report. A columnar report can include titles and special fonts and can emphasize field data.

- *AutoReport: Tabular*—Generates a report that displays on a single line the record of each source table or query by adjusting the font size to fit your report page. The tabular report looks much better than a simple Datasheet view and is often more useful than the generic AutoReport you learned about in the previous section. Figure 20.5 shows a sample of the wizard's tabular report. As you can see from the figure, Access is not always able to fit the complete field name at the top of a column of data. You can adjust the report's design to allow more room for the field name if you prefer.

- *Chart Wizard*—Produces graphs from your data. Access graphs resemble Excel graphs, and you can control the format and style as well as the table from which Access graphs.

- *Label Wizard*—A generic mailing-list report that produces mailing labels for all common labels. The mailing-label industry has a standard numbering system (the *Avery numbering system*, after the company that is perhaps best known for computerized mailing labels). Most office-supply stores sell mailing labels with an official Avery number, so you can format a report for your labels.

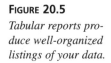

FIGURE 20.5
Tabular reports produce well-organized listings of your data.

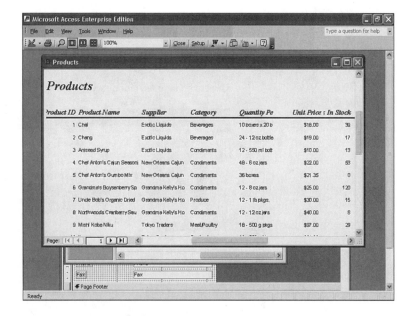

To Do: Use the Report Wizard

The second New Report screen option, Report Wizard, is probably the most common selection you make when you generate customized reports. The Report Wizard walks you through a series of steps to create a custom report from your tables and queries, and it includes many common reporting styles and special features that you need.

> You must create a named query before generating a report based on that query. You cannot create a report based on a query that you have not yet written.

20

To start the Report Wizard, follow these steps:

1. Display the Database window.

2. Click the Reports object to display any database reports you've defined and to generate new ones.

3. Click the New button to display the New Report screen.

4. Select Report Wizard.

5. Open the New Report's drop-down list box to select from a list of tables and queries that reside in your database.

6. Click the OK button to display the Report Wizard's field selection screen (shown in Figure 20.6). The field selection screen displays a list of fields from your selected table or query that you can select for use as the report's data.

FIGURE 20.6

Select the fields you want for your report.

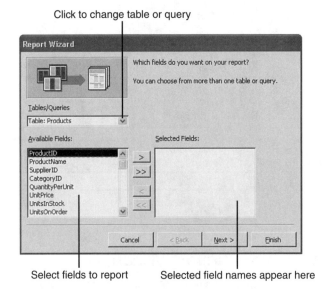

Click to change table or query

Select fields to report   Selected field names appear here

7. Select the fields that you want in the final report by clicking the field in the Available Fields list and then clicking > to send the field to the Selected Fields list. You can also double-click a field name to send it to the Selected Fields list. As you can see when you open the Tables/Queries drop-down list box, you can select fields from several tables and queries in addition to the primary source you selected in step 5.

8. After you select the fields for the report, click Next.

Grouping Report Summaries

Now that you have selected the report fields, you must indicate how the report is to be summarized. Rarely will you want to print a data listing without requesting a *report summary* that includes totals and subtotals. Depending on the type of numeric fields you have selected for the report, the Report Wizard prompts you for subtotal and total summary information or grouping information. If your report contains numeric data, the Report Wizard lets you choose the grouping options (shown in Figure 20.7). Use this dialog box to indicate how you want Access to group your report subtotals.

FIGURE 20.7

Indicate how Access is to produce the subtotals and totals.

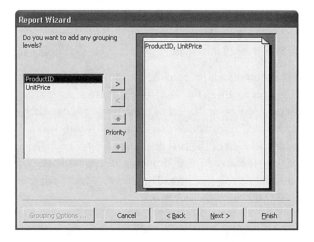

Access totals and subtotals reports based on a group's numeric fields, not text fields. The numeric fields enable the Report Wizard to produce subtotals and total summaries, whereas no such summaries are possible with text fields.

If Access does not display the Summary dialog box, the Report Wizard prompts you for grouping information, and you can select the field on which you want your data grouped. When you request grouping, you are telling Access how to sort your report. If you grouped by a City field, for example, the report would sort the report in City order. The subtotals are then summed for each city in the report data.

You might have to run the Report Wizard a couple of times to group the report the way you prefer. Be sure to select only those numeric fields that produce proper subtotals. If you report a division number field and that field is numeric, for example, you wouldn't want Access to subtotal and total the division number. If you print a report with customer past-due balances, however, you do want to print a subtotal for each customer and an overall grand total of past-due balances.

The grouping field should be nonnumeric groups, such as customer IDs, for which you are printing a detailed list. Although the same customer might appear on several report lines, you want Access to subtotal only when the customer ID changes to the next customer in the report. The grouping doesn't total or subtotal the customer IDs, but the totals and subtotals that appear all break (stop) when the customer ID changes. The grouping capability keeps multiple customer IDs from appearing down the column when you print multiple records for the same customer.

20

As you click each field that you selected, the grouping dialog box displays a preview of your report, showing how the grouping will fall out. Generally, the grouping options and preview give you enough information to decide on a grouping scheme.

If you want to group on multiple fields, the group order you select determines the priority that Access uses to group the data. The highest priority grouping level (if you select multiple groups) appears on the left of the report. You can change the highest priority level by clicking the Priority button on another grouping level. The second grouping level appears to the right of the first one, and so on. Generally, multifield grouping gets confusing. If you want to add such grouping levels, click every group level from the series of fields that Access displays. The Report Wizard prioritizes the multifield groups in the order that you select the fields.

You can group by a maximum of four field-grouping levels. If you need to group by more than four fields, you have to edit the report design or create a report from scratch. Rarely do you need more than four groups.

If the Report Wizard has presented you with the grouping view screen rather than the subtotal and total summary screens described here, you need only click the field by which you want to group the report. If you are producing a customer balance report, for example, the Report Wizard might enable you to group by either the Customer ID field or the Customer Order Number field.

After you set up the grouping levels that you need, click Next to select a sort and summary order for the report.

The Report's Sort and Summary Order

When you see the sorting and summary screen (see Figure 20.8), you are almost done creating your report. Select from one to four fields that you want Access to use for sorting your data. If you are reporting from a query that already contains sorted data, and if you generate the report so that the data groups in the order of those sorted fields, don't select any fields by which to sort. If you want to sort by one or more fields that do not enter the reporting system already sorted, however, select up to four fields and click the button labeled Ascending to sort in ascending order.

The Ascending button changes to Descending when you click it, so you can then select a descending sort.

FIGURE 20.8

Select from one to four
fields by which to sort.

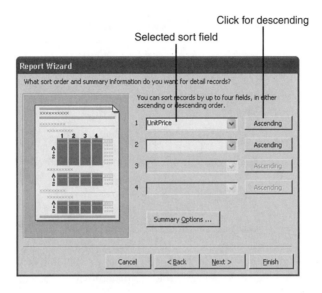

If you requested totals and subtotals in earlier Report Wizard steps, you will see a Summary Options button. These options display the Report Wizard's Summary Options screen. Each of your report's numeric fields appears in the box, so you can select any or all these summaries for that field:

- *Sum*—Requests a total for the field
- *Avg*—Requests an average for the field
- *Min*—Requests that Access highlight the minimum value in the field
- *Max*—Requests that Access highlight the maximum value in the field

 You cannot display summaries if your report has no numeric fields or if you are grouping by the numeric fields.

20

Choosing a Report Layout and Style

Click OK to close the Summary Options screen and then click Next to choose a report layout. Click through the various layouts to select one that fits your needs. As you click layouts, Access displays thumbnail sketches of those layouts. If you click the Block style, for example, you see that Access displays boxes around your report fields.

After you select the layout, click Next to select from the Report Wizard's style screen (shown in Figure 20.9). From this dialog box, you can add the finishing touches to your report.

FIGURE 20.9

The Report Wizard's style screen determines the overall appearance of your report.

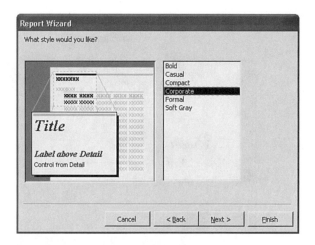

Click Next, enter a report title if you don't want to use the original source table or query name, and click Finish to generate the completed report. Sometimes Access takes several minutes to generate the report, especially if the source tables and queries contain many records and your report contains several grouping levels. When finished, Access prints a preview of your report so that you can look at your handiwork.

Summary

Access is certainly a powerful program. Despite its ease of use, it does take some getting used to before you fully master all its features. You will probably use the Access wizards more than any other wizard in any other Office product.

At this point, you are ready to begin generating sample databases and practicing with Access. As you create more databases, you will learn how to partition your data properly into tables and generate data-entry forms and reports.

Hour 21, "Office 2003 and the Internet," begins the part of the book that explains how the Office programs interact with the Internet.

Q&A

Q How does the toolbar's AutoReport differ from the AutoReport entries I see on the Report Wizard's opening screen?

A The AutoReport entries on the Report Wizard's opening screen create more finished reports than the AutoReport toolbar button. Use the AutoReport toolbar button to quickly generate a report from your Datasheet and Form views. Use the

Report Wizard AutoReport entries to produce more complete reports without taking the time to set up summary and sorting features. Not all reports require summaries, and the two AutoReport wizards suffice for many reports that you will generate.

Q What is the largest page size that I can produce in an Access report?

A Access report pages can be as large as 22 inches wide by 22 inches long.

Q Do I subtotal on numeric fields or fields that I want to group by, such as Customer ID numbers?

A When you specify grouping instructions, the field that you group by is usually a nonnumeric field, such as a Customer ID field. Access collects all the customer ID records together and reports each customer's information in one group. When Access finishes reporting a customer's records (when the ID changes), Access subtotals the numeric fields in that group before starting the next group.

20

PART VII

Combining Office 2003 and the Internet

Hour

21 Office 2003 and the Internet

22 Creating Web Content with Word, Excel, and PowerPoint

HOUR 21

Office 2003 and the Internet

Microsoft ensured that all the Office products integrate well within an Internet world. The Internet is so much a part of computer users' lives, and Office needs to help users access and use information from the Internet. The individual Office products all provide some level of Internet connectivity.

The highlights of this hour include the following:

- How to access the Internet from within Office products
- How to view Office documents from within Internet Explorer
- How to include Web links in your Office documents

How Office Products Combine with the Web

Office offers a complete set of tools that integrate the Office products and the Internet. From any Office product, you can access files and Web pages on the Internet. The following sections describe how you can access the Web from Office.

To Do: View Web Pages from Within Office Programs

You don't have to start Internet Explorer to view a Web page from within an Office program. All you need to do is display the Web toolbar and type the address you want to see. While creating an Excel worksheet, for example, you might need to locate financial information from your company's Web site. Follow these steps to surf the Web from Excel:

1. Select View, Toolbars, Web to add a new Web-browsing toolbar to Excel. Figure 21.1 shows what the Web toolbar looks like.

FIGURE 21.1

Use the Web toolbar to access Internet information from any Office program.

Type Web address here

2. Click the Address text box on the Web toolbar.
3. Enter the Web address that you want to see. (Alternatively, you can click the Favorites list on the Web toolbar to view and select the Web page that you want to view.) If you access the Internet from a modem, Excel dials your Internet service provider (ISP) to get Internet access. If you're already connected to the Internet, Excel immediately goes to the Web page.
4. Excel's menus and toolbars change to match that of Internet Explorer, the Microsoft Web browser, and Excel displays the Web site that you want to view. You can switch between the Web and Excel by pressing Alt+Tab. In addition, you can copy and paste information from Web pages to your Excel worksheet.

Figure 21.2 shows what you see when you view a Web page from Excel. Notice that the program doesn't look much like Excel anymore! Actually, Excel triggered the start of Internet Explorer and your Excel worksheet is still in another window that you can get to through Alt+Tab or by clicking the Excel window's button on your Windows taskbar.

Viewing Documents in Internet Explorer

In addition to launching Internet Explorer from an Office product, you can view Office documents directly from within Internet Explorer. Whenever you are browsing the Internet, select File, Open and type the full path and filename you want to view (or click Browse to locate the path and file) from within Internet Explorer.

FIGURE 21.2

You can go straight from any Office program, such as Excel, to a Web browser simply by typing a Web address in your program's Web toolbar's address text box.

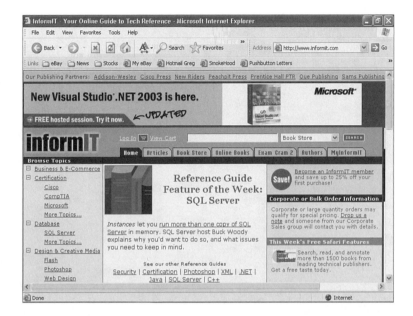

Internet Explorer opens and displays the file within the browser window. Not only does Internet Explorer display the file, but all Internet Explorer menus change to enable full editing capabilities for that Office document. If you open a Word document, for example, Internet Explorer menus change to Word menus; you can then insert a table or format the text as if you were using Word. If you click the Internet Explorer Tools toolbar button while viewing the Office document, the Word toolbars appear beneath the Internet Explorer toolbar so that you have full Word toolbar capabilities within Internet Explorer.

Figure 21.3 shows an Excel worksheet viewed by starting Internet Explorer from the Windows Start menu and opening the worksheet from the Internet Explorer program. When Internet Explorer senses that the file is an Excel worksheet file, Internet Explorer triggers Excel's launch (just as Excel triggers Internet Explorer when you view a Web page from within a worksheet) and the worksheet loads. As you can see, the result is the full set of Excel buttons and menus.

Being able to launch Web pages from Office programs and Office programs from Internet Explorer saves you a step over having to start the second program. In other words, if you're editing an Access database and you need to look at a Web page for some data, you don't have to first start Internet Explorer and then find the Web page. You only need to access that page from the Access Web toolbar and Access takes care of loading Internet Explorer for you, while keeping your current position inside Access.

21

FIGURE 21.3

*You can view a work-
sheet within Internet
Explorer.*

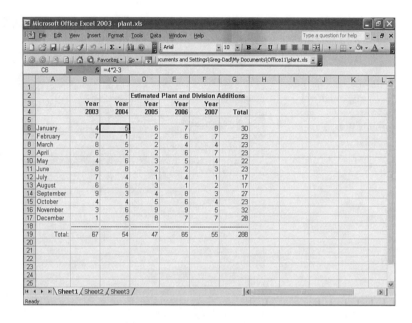

FIGURE 21.3

*You can view a work-
sheet within Internet
Explorer.*

Excel as a Browser?

You might wonder why Excel displays browser menu options and toolbar buttons when a Web page appears, but Excel reverts back to a worksheet program when you view worksheets in Excel. What is Excel: a Web browser, a worksheet program, or both?

Remember, Excel actually does not access the Web; for that, you need a Web browser such as Internet Explorer. Nevertheless, the Web toolbar that you find in all the Office products does enable you to navigate between Office files and the Web without changing programs. Through *DLLs* (for *Dynamic Link Libraries*) and *ActiveX controls*, the Office programs are able to borrow some characteristics of a Web browser as long as the browser resides on your computer.

Perhaps someday, the only program you will need is a Web browser. The browser menus and toolbars would change depending on the document with which you want to work. Internet Explorer integrates with Windows itself so that the browser becomes part of your Windows environment. The Internet is so important to computing today that companies such as Microsoft are incorporating Web technology into all products as well as operating systems.

Creating Links in Office

As you learned how to use Office programs throughout the previous hours, you learned that you can type a Web address in an Office document to create a link to that address.

When you type a Web address in a PowerPoint presentation, for example, that address becomes a link to an active Web site address. If you click that address, the Office program starts Internet Explorer, logs you on to the Internet if needed, and displays the Web page located at that address.

Keeping Current

The Office programs help you utilize the Internet to its fullest. Conversely, the Internet helps you keep your Office applications running smoothly as well. For example, from any Office program, you can select Help, Office on Microsoft.com to view the latest information about the topic on which you're requesting help.

In addition, you can use the Web to download the latest updates, bug fixes, and patches to your Office programs. When you browse `http://office.microsoft.com/`, you will see a Web page similar to the one in Figure 21.4. (Figure 21.4 lists information about Office XP, the Office version that predates Office 2003, because no Office 2003 Web pages were publicly available at the time of this writing.) You will be able to read the latest news about Office products; see how others use Office; and download sample files, templates, and updates to your software.

FIGURE 21.4

Microsoft maintains a huge Office-based Web site.

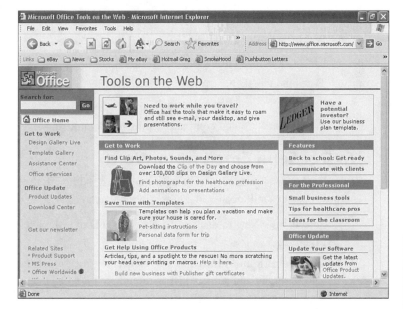

21

If you click on the Web page's Product Updates link, you'll be able to install an automatic update feature that instructs Office to check the Internet regularly. If updates are posted that will bring your installation up to date, the update process starts automatically so that you can keep current.

> Notice that the Office Web site not only has news and advanced advice and help for your Office programs, but the site also provides links to clip art, photos, and sounds. If you want to add sound to the opening or closing screens of your PowerPoint presentations, for example, you can check the Office site to see whether any sound clips interest you. If so, you can download those clips and start them at the beginning or end of your presentation. The Office Web site also has numerous templates that you can use as a foundation for all kinds of special-purpose Office documents you might want to create, such as invoice worksheets, greeting card–like Web sites, and collectibles and hobby-related Access database applications.

Word Sends Email

Too many times, someone using Word needs to send an email, so that person does the following:

1. Starts Outlook.
2. Waits for Outlook to begin.
3. Creates a new email message in Outlook.
4. Types the message.
5. Sends the message from Outlook.
6. Returns to Word and continues typing the document.

To Do: Send Email from Word

There's a better way and it's built right into Word. Although the actual process described in these six steps still occurs, the user's job is much easier if he or she does this:

1. Selects File, New to display the New Document task pane shown in Figure 21.5.

2. Click the E-Mail Message link. A new email message opens, complete with fields for the sender and subject just as though you'd created a new, blank email message within Outlook.

3. Complete the email message. Clicking the To field will display your Outlook contacts just as though you'd created this email within Outlook.

FIGURE 21.5

You can send an email from within Word.

Click to start a new email message

4. Click the Send button to send the message. Word sends the message to the recipient, dialing your Internet provider if needed first to establish a connection.

5. Word then returns to the position in your document where you last left it.

To Do: Send Office Documents as Email

Perhaps you don't want to send a regular email, but you want to send your Office program's document to a friend or associate over the Internet. You can send your current Word document, Excel worksheet, Access database, or PowerPoint presentation to any email recipient in your Outlook Contacts list or to anyone whose email address you know by following these steps:

1. Once you complete the Office document, worksheet, database, or presentation you want to send to someone, select File, Send to. Depending on what Office program you're sending from, you will be able to send this document in one of several ways.

2. Select how you want to send the document. For example, you can often send Word documents as email attachments or as the actual body inside the email. You can only send an Access database as an email attachment.

21

3. Depending on what kind of email attachment you send, Office might ask you for a data type that it can convert your file to. For example, if you send an Access database to an email recipient, Access displays the Send dialog box shown in Figure 21.6. Select the data type you want Access to convert the database to before sending the database to your recipient.

FIGURE 21.6

Select the format you want to convert the database to before sending it as an email attachment.

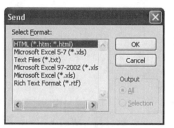

4. Once you select the conversion data type, your Office program sends the email and returns to where you were before you sent the email.

The format you select depends on how your recipient will use the database and what kind of program the recipient has. You might have to ask which of the conversion file formats your recipient prefers to receive from the list available to you.

Summary

This quick hour showed you some of the ways you can combine the Office programs with Internet technology. Office and the Internet work together. Not only can you view Web pages with Internet Explorer, but you can also view other kinds of files such as Office documents and data. Your Web browser might already be part of your daily computing routine. One day, you will find that you do most of your work from Web-browsing software such as Internet Explorer, including editing your Office documents directly from a single screen that acts both as a Web browser and as a controller for your Office data.

The next hour, "Creating Web Content with Word, Excel, Access, and PowerPoint," continues the Internet discussion by explaining how to create simple Web pages from within the Office products. Once you do that, you'll be prepared to learn a new program designed to work alongside the Office programs: Publisher, starting in Hour 23, "Publishing with Flair Using Publisher 2003."

Q&A

Q How do I know whether I should send an Office document as an email or email attachment?

A The kind of Office data you send might dictate how you can send it. For example, you can often send a Word document as an email directly, meaning the Word document will comprise the actual email body of the message. You should send a presentation or database, however, as an attachment. Those kinds of Office data documents do not always conform to a linear, text-centered single document that can comprise the body of an email.

Q Does all Internet information appear on Web pages?

A The Internet's information appears in many forms, sometimes in a form known as an FTP site or a newsgroup. The Web page standard, however, has become one of the most popular ways to organize and view Internet information. As more people used the Web-page standard, more modern technology enabled that standard to evolve into a uniform container of multimedia-based information. Therefore, with a Web browser, you can view all kinds of information over the Web.

21

HOUR 22

Creating Web Content with Word, Excel, Access, and PowerPoint

You don't just have to be a user of Web pages. You can create them yourself with the tools available in Office. With the Office design tools, you can quickly create Web pages that equal those from the pros. You can hone text, graphics, and data tables and present that data to the world on the Web.

Most Office users who do not learn FrontPage implement Word as their primary Web page development tool and import other Office product data into their Word Web pages. All the Office products are Internet-aware; they all enable you to convert their data to Web pages.

The highlights of this hour include the following:

- What you need to publish pages on the Internet
- How to save Word documents as Web pages
- How to use the various Office templates to generate your initial Web pages
- How to export Excel and Access data to your Word-based Web pages
- Why you should limit the amount of Access information that goes into your Web page

- How to save individual Access objects in a data access page
- How to modify the way a PowerPoint presentation looks and behaves on the Internet

Preparing to Publish Web Pages

Before you can publish pages on the Web, you must have access to a *Web server*. Perhaps your company uses a Web server for its site; if so, you can store your Web pages on that computer. If you have access to an online service, such as MSN, your online service might offer an area for one or more Web pages that you can copy to the online site's Web server free or for a small charge. Several free Web hosting sites, such as `http://www.geocities.com/` and `http://www.brinkster.com`, allow you to post Web pages that others can view. Most of these free services require that you and your users view ample advertisements to pay for the free services the host offers, although you can often upgrade these free ad-based sites to a monthly paid service for a small fee. Brinkster.com provides free Web space without advertisements, so you might want to check out that site.

If you want to publish a personal Web page for fun, you will enjoy telling the world your stories and sharing your family photos with others. If you want to start a business on the Internet, however, or offer timely information that you want others to visit often, you need to be aware that Web-page *maintenance* is costly and time-consuming. You don't just create a Web page, load the page on the Web, and expect to keep people's interest if you don't keep the material up-to-date. In addition, performing *e-commerce* (selling goods and services over an Internet connection) often requires the help of an outside agency such as a bank or credit-card service, so you might want to get help when you first go online with your organization. In addition, the free Web hosts typically offer only to serve personal Web pages and not business Web pages, so you will always have to factor in extra costs for hosting.

Many homes and small businesses are now getting fast Internet connections. Many of these connections, such as *DSL* (*Digital Subscriber Line*), enable you to set up a fixed *IP address*. An IP address, or *Internet Protocol address*, anchors your position on the World Wide Web so that you can set up your own Web server and host your Web pages directly from your own computer, if you're inclined to do such a thing. Keep in mind that you need to address storage, speed, and security issues (the dreaded s's of Web hosting) before you can safely and successfully host your own site.

Perhaps you are beginning to realize that data communications, by its very nature, is technical. When you begin to develop Web pages and manage Web sites, you will see that you must master some network terminology and phrases just to understand what is taking place.

22

Office and the Web

One of the reasons you should consider using Office to create Web pages is that you already have the Office tools. Office offers several templates that you can use to create your Web pages. Nevertheless, Office is not necessarily the best tool you can use to create Web pages. Office offers good tools with which you can create and maintain a Web page. If your Web page generates a lot of interest, however, you might want to use a more specific tool for Web-page creation such as Microsoft FrontPage and Internet Explorer. FrontPage is to Web pages what Access is to databases; FrontPage offers specific Web-page tools that create advanced Web pages with very little effort on your part.

All the Web-related aspects of Office support both the Internet and *intranets*. Therefore, if your company maintains an intranet (which is an in-company Web site viewed only from computers on your company's network), you can save Web pages to that intranet as easily (and sometimes more easily) as on the Internet.

Each of the following sections describes how you can use Word, Excel, Access, and PowerPoint to generate Web-page information. If you connect to your Web server with your PC, you can offer live content on the Internet. In other words, as soon as you update your database, viewers of your Web site who access that database see the updated values.

Most of your early Web page creations will probably take place in Word until you master a full-featured Web-page creation program such as FrontPage. Even if you embed an Access database on a Web page, you will probably do most of that Web-page design in Word. Therefore, most of this hour focuses on Word's Web-editing tools. The final sections describe how to integrate the other Office products into your Word Web pages.

Word and Web Pages

You can create Web pages with Word, although FrontPage and Publisher give you far more design tools to do the job.

Saving Word Documents as Web Pages

One of the easiest ways to create a Web page from a Word document is to save the document in *HTML format*. Suppose you create a company report that you want to publish on your Web server. All you have to do is select File, Save As Web Page and then click OK. Word then saves the file in an HTML Web page-compatible format that you then can transfer to the Web server. The Web page will have the extension .mhtml, which your browser can read as an HTML page.

You can view your document from the Internet Explorer Web browser by selecting File, Web Page Preview. By viewing the document from the Web browser, you see how your Web page will appear to other Internet users. The format will differ slightly from the document in its native Word format (especially italicized fonts).

Figure 22.1 shows a Word editing session for a rather complex Web page. Figure 22.2 shows how that same Web page looks when viewed from Internet Explorer when you select from Word's File, Web Page Preview menu option. The lines and other editing marks inside the Word document help distinguish the Web page's alignment and table cells that work together to form the final page.

Page design's formatting lines

FIGURE 22.1

When editing a Web page with Word, the page's alignment grids and other element marks show.

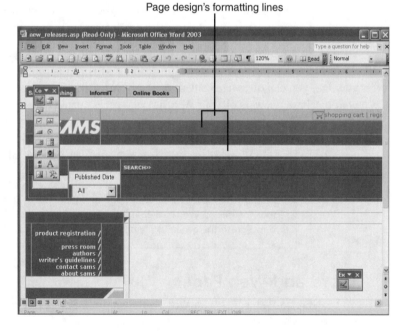

FIGURE 22.2
By viewing your document as a Web page, you learn how the document will look as a Web page.

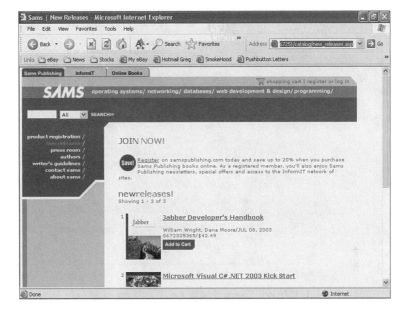

22

When formatting your Web page, keep your end user in mind and write for the largest audience possible. You can select a fancy font for your Web page text. If you stick with the standard fonts that come with Windows (such as Courier, Times New Roman, and Arial), however, you ensure that all viewers of your Web page will have those same fonts and the page will look the way you intend for it to look on their browsers.

Remember that Web pages are often colorful. Color fonts can spruce up a Web page dramatically as long as you don't overdo the colors. Use the toolbar's Font Color button to select a new font color quickly.

For Web Masters Only

If you have written HTML code before, you can embed HTML commands in your Web page from within Word. Format your HTML code with the HTML markup style, and Word embeds it as HTML code. The code does not appear on the Web page, but the browser that displays the Web page formats the page according to your HTML-based instructions.

Figure 22.3 shows HTML code for a Web page being edited in Word. (Word displays HTML inside a special window called the *Script Editor*.) The HTML code can be tedious if you are unfamiliar with it, but Word does offer itself as a text editor (as opposed to a word processor that would incorrectly wrap words inside the HTML code) when you work with HTML code.

FIGURE 22.3

*You can view the
HTML code for your
Web page.*

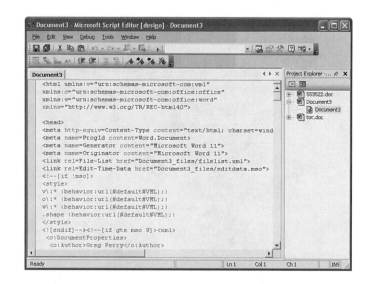

Using a Word Template to Create a Web Page

If you want to use a Word template to create a Web page, select File, New. From the
New Document task pane's Templates section, select On My Computer. The Templates
window appears, as shown in Figure 22.4. Click the Web Page icon and then OK to start
the Web page document.

FIGURE 22.4

*Word can generate
a blank Web page
for you.*

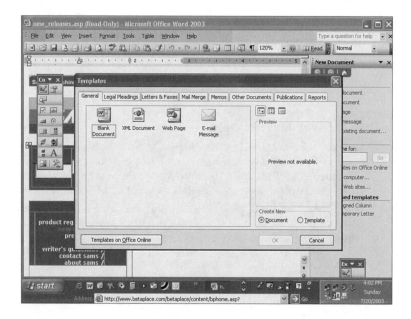

If you first apply a theme to your Web page document, your headers, *link bars* (an area of your Web page that links to other pages on your site and other sites), headings, text, colors, horizontal lines, and borders all take on a uniform look. To apply a theme, select Format, Theme. The Theme window appears from which you can select a theme for your Web, such as the Willow theme shown in Figure 22.5.

FIGURE 22.5
Word offers several themes for your Web pages.

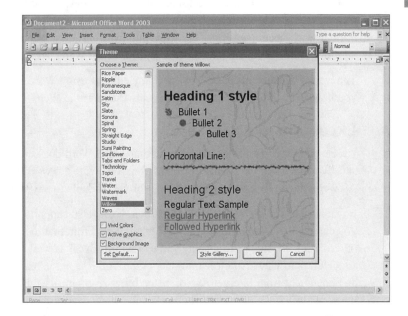

After you create the basic design for your Web page in Word, save the page. Word automatically adds a Web page filename extension to your document so you can view the document in a Web browser.

Word's Web page creation tools are rather limited. As long as you don't require fancy Web pages with many elements, you'll be fine using Word for simple Webs. Nevertheless, the tools in FrontPage are far more advanced and actually many times easier to use when adding advanced Web page elements to your documents, such as link bars. In many instances, you can generate a simple Web page in Word, apply a theme, add your text, save the page, and then open it in FrontPage to add the extras later.

Now that you have seen how to use Word to create Web pages, you already know a lot about how the other Office products create Web pages. Many of the Web-page features in the other Office products work the same way as in Word. You can save an Excel worksheet as a Web page, for example. When saving Office documents as Web pages, most of the formatting and editing features you get with the products' native formats remain. In other words, an Excel worksheet that you save as a Web page contains all the same elements that the worksheet contains when you save that worksheet as an Excel file with the normal worksheet extension, .xls. Revision markings do not appear in Web pages, but all other Office document elements do appear in the Web page.

The remaining sections build on your knowledge of using Word and the Web by showing you how Excel, PowerPoint, and Access also support the Web.

Excel and Web Pages

Excel supports most of the same Web features that Word does, including the capability to save worksheets in the HTML format. After you create the worksheet, select File, Save As Web Page to save the worksheet in a format readable to any browser.

In addition to the Web-based HTML format, Excel also supports the Web toolbar that you can display by selecting View, Toolbars, Web. From that toolbar, you can select other Office documents to display and edit within Excel as well as enter an Internet Web site address to view. All Office products support the Web toolbar, and you can display any document from Internet Explorer (the browser engine used by all Office products when you work with Web-based objects and pages). Because of these two facts, all Office products enable you to view any of the other Office products' documents or any Web page just by typing that document or Web-page address in the address text box of the Web toolbar.

If your company stores worksheets on the Internet or on an intranet, the File, Open option in Excel can open those worksheets. When you select File, Open and then enter the URL and filename, such as http://www.mycompany.org/accts.xls, Excel opens that worksheet. (Excel launches the Internet Log On dialog box if you are not already logged on to the Internet.)

If you type a hyperlink Web address or a hyperlink to another Office document in an Excel cell, Excel takes you to that document and displays the Web toolbar automatically (if the toolbar is not already displayed). When you click the Web toolbar's Back button, Excel takes you to the preceding Web page.

22

Rarely does a Web page contain just an Excel worksheet. Web pages contain other text and graphics; that's why you probably want to create the general Web page in Word (or FrontPage) and then import (using the Windows Clipboard or Insert menu) your Excel data into the Web page. If you insert a link to your Excel data instead of inserting a copy of the worksheet, your published Web page always contains "live" worksheet data that changes as you update the worksheet.

If you use an online service to publish your Web page and not a local Web server networked to your PC, you have to update the Web page manually each time you want to update the worksheet data.

Access and Web Pages

Access supports hyperlinks in its database forms, reports, and fields in datasheets. Access supports Word, PowerPoint, Excel, as well as Internet or intranet hyperlinks. In addition to other documents, the hyperlink can point to other Access tables, forms, and

One reason you might want to store hyperlinks in a database field is to store Web pages for vendors, competitors, and customers in tables. When you

view forms that display the hyperlink to those tables, you can click the hyperlink to see the Web site.

Obviously, a hyperlink is not active when it appears in a printed report or onscreen in Preview mode. If you import the report into a Word document, Excel worksheet, or an HTML page, however, the hyperlink is active.

The Hyperlink data type is one of the Access data types that you can designate as you create your table (shown in Figure 22.6).

As you know, Access databases contain several objects, tables, forms, reports, and queries. A simple File, Save As Web Page option cannot, without more information, determine exactly how you want to export the objects to the HTML document. You could use such an option for the other Office documents because they had fewer objects than an Access database. Therefore, to save a table or other object to its own Web page, select

File, Save As
and select
Data Access
Page for the

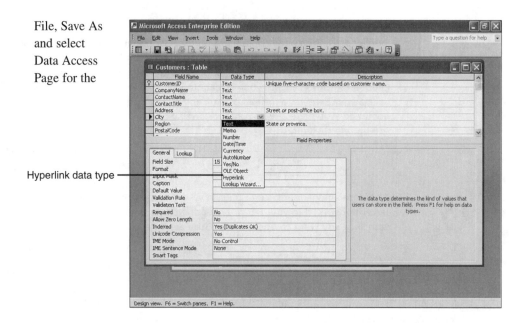

Hyperlink data type

type of file to save. Access stores the object as a Web page using the HTML format.

FIGURE 22.6
Access offers the data type when you design your tables.

PowerPoint and Web Pages

When you save a PowerPoint presentation as a Web page, PowerPoint presents you with the Save As dialog box and a Publish button that, when you click it, produces the dialog box shown in Figure 22.7. The dialog box determines how your presentation appears over the Internet when a remote site displays the presentation's Web page. If you don't click Publish, PowerPoint saves the document with a Web page filename extension, and your Web browser can read it.

PowerPoint actually lends itself well for Internet presentations. When generating a pre-

22

sentation for display on the Internet, keep your graphics to a minimum so that the

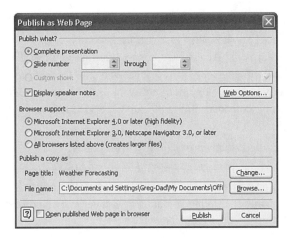

slides load quickly inside the user's browser. The user can control the presentation by clicking the mouse or pressing PageDown.

FIGURE 22.7
The Publish as Web Page dialog box determines how your presentation will appear on the Internet.

Summary

This hour showed you how to use Office products to create Web pages. Word certainly offers the advantage in your initial Web page design, unless, of course, you want to put a PowerPoint presentation on the Web—in which case, the PowerPoint templates offer the best place to start your Web page design.

You can use Word as your primary Web-page development tool and import other Office products as needed to add their elements to the Web page that you save from Word. PowerPoint offers a unique Web page design wizard that designs Web-based presentations with the same look and feel as other Web pages.

Now that you have seen how to use Word, Excel, Access, and PowerPoint to create Web pages from your Office data, you're ready to move to a new Office 2003 program, Microsoft Publisher. With Publisher, you will be able to create, edit, and arrange a publication such as a newsletter, flyer, or even rather complicated Web pages with ease. Hour 23, "Publishing with Flair Using Publisher 2003," explores Publisher.

Q&A

Q Can I use my Windows Me or Windows XP PC as a Web server?

A Several programs now turn just about any computer into a Web server. One of the most popular is the Apache server software that you can download from `http://www.apache.com`, the Apache Web site. Depending on how much computing power you have, you might not want to tie up your PC by using it as a Web server. If not, consider renting the server service from one of the many Web-hosting companies that exist.

Q Can I include Excel graphs on my Web pages?

A Certainly. You can copy the graph to your Windows Clipboard and then paste it directly into your Word- or PowerPoint-based Web page. An Excel graph is no different from any other kind of data that you can copy and paste into a Web page from any of the Office products.

Windows supports *OLE (Object Linking and Embedding)* technology that enables you to insert virtually any object inside any other kind of document. If you want to insert an Excel graph or a video file with sound into a Web page, you can do so by using the Insert menu from the Office product's menu bar.

PART VIII

Publishing Eye-Catching Documents

Hour

23   Publishing with Flair Using Publisher 2003

24   Adding Art to Your Publications

HOUR 23

Publishing with Flair Using Publisher 2003

This hour introduces Publisher 2003 and shows you how to create eye-catching publications within Publisher. Also, you'll learn how to turn documents you created in other Office products into polished, professional publications. Publisher 2003 is the latest in a series of Publisher versions that Microsoft has produced over the years. In keeping with Publisher's tradition, Publisher offers new and simpler ways of producing documents that look better than ever before.

Publisher was the first product to offer wizards, the technology that everyone familiar with Microsoft products has used. You've worked with wizards throughout this book and you know how wizards can help guide you through the document-creation process. Publisher actually starts its wizards for you and creates sample publications that you then can edit to suit your own needs. Publisher creates samples for almost any publication you need; you'll rarely have to create a document from scratch again. Once you create a publication, Publisher generates the initial publication and you then can begin your work to change that publication's specific elements.

The highlights of this hour include

- Why you might use Publisher (as opposed to Word) for your publications

- How to use the Publisher's sample technology to create initial publication designs
- When to add details to the publication's design
- Why use a text box to hold text you'll need to edit later
- How to make text flow from one newsletter column to another, even if that column appears on another page

All Kinds of Publications

Publisher creates just about any kind of publication you can imagine. Here is just a sample:

Advertisements	Greeting cards
Banners	Labels
Business cards	Letterheads
Calendars	Newsletters
Catalogs	Postcards
Email backgrounds	Résumés
Envelopes	Signs
Flyers	Web sites

Not only does Publisher assist in the creation of all these kinds of publications and more, Publisher is one of the most graphical of all the Office programs. As Figure 23.1 shows, Publisher displays a thumbnail image of all documents from which you can choose. You'll always know in advance what your publication's general look will be.

Publisher enables you to combine text, art, and headlines and put them together in the way you want them to look. Just a few years ago, print shops were paid big bucks to use scissors, photos, paper, and glue to do what you can make Publisher do with a mouse click!

When you want to combine text and graphics, as you'd do for a newsletter or many other publications, you work within a *what-you-see-is-what-you-get* environment (called *WYSIWYG* in computer lingo and pronounced *"wizzy-wig"*). It's important to get a sense of how all your publication elements fit together, and you need to see all the various elements on the screen where you can make adjustments and additions.

Figure 23.2 shows the early stages of an editing session for a catalog. The screen shows the first page. The margins, text, and pictures are all laid out in such a way that you can select and edit any of those elements. You can drag the sizing lines between the elements to move or resize any part of the publication. If a picture is too large, you can shrink it, and when you do, any text that might surround the picture adjusts automatically.

FIGURE 23.1
Publisher always gives you a preview of the publication you can create.

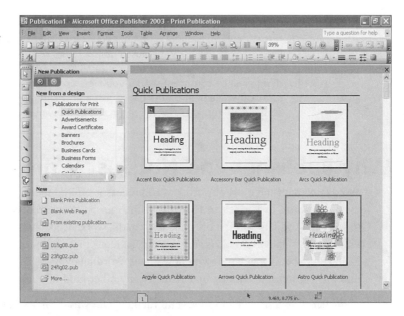

Editing area

FIGURE 23.2
When you work on a publication, you see all the elements so that you can make adjustments.

Toolbox

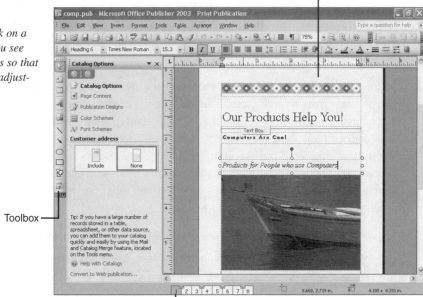

Page 1 is selected

Not a graphic designer? Didn't get your typesetting degree? With Publisher's help, nobody will know because Publisher aims to keep your publication looking good and attempts to balance all the elements so that the final design will be consistent. And if you mess up the publication's margins or some other element on the pages, just adjust and reprint. Publisher makes edits simple for you, as you'll see in this and the next hour.

Why Publisher and Not Just Word?

Word is perhaps the most powerful word processor offered today. Word works with more than just words, as you learned starting with Hour 5, "Advanced Word 2003." In addition to words, Word lets you import graphics, charts, worksheets, and just about every other kind of data, including videos (represented as icons that you or the reader of your document can click to watch). As you now know, Word lets you easily create documents with multiple columns, headlines, and virtually any other kind of publication you'll need.

Publisher differs from Word in several fundamental ways. First and foremost, Publisher focuses more on your publication's design, whereas Word focuses more on your publication's words. Despite the fact that you *can* create publications with Word, and quite powerful publications at that, Word's strengths do lie in its ability to manage the words you type. To complement Word (instead of competing with Word), Publisher lets you manage the layout of those words, along with graphics and the other design elements you want to put in your finished publication.

Microsoft includes both Word and Publisher in some versions of Office because these two products work so well together. If you want to create attention-getting publications that contain exactly the information that's important to you, *first* write your publication's text (perhaps more than one article if your publication requires multiple articles) with Word's powerful word-based editing tools. Hone your words to perfection in Word. Once you are satisfied with your writing, import that Word document into Publisher. Publisher then takes over and, with Publisher's help, you can turn your words into a publishable product.

 Of course, Publisher imports files from Office programs other than Word. For example, you can import an Excel worksheet to use as a table in your publication.

Getting Acquainted with Publisher

NEW 2003 Start Publisher by selecting Microsoft Publisher from the Windows Start, Programs, Microsoft Office option. The opening screen, shown in Figure 23.3, makes it clear what you do first. Select the kind of publication you want to create: a print publication, a Web site and email, a *design set*, or a blank publication where you design all the elements. You can click on any of the categories in the New Publication task pane to expand that item into a more specific kind of publication within that category. For example, if you want the create an award certificate to give to a star employee, you can click the item labeled Publications for Print in the task pane to expand the items beneath Publications for Print and select the Award Certificate to see a list of awards you can create.

23

New publication task pane

FIGURE 23.3

Publisher makes it clear where you begin when you want to create a publication.

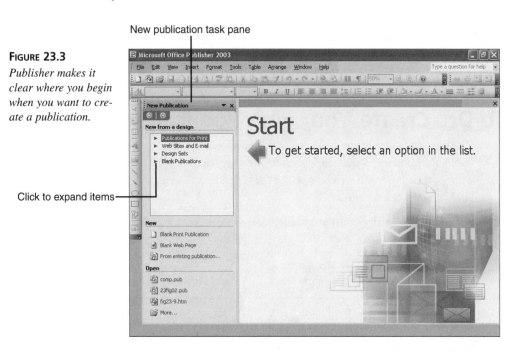

Click to expand items

A design set is a collection of publications that all have a similar look. For example, a restaurant might create a main menu and daily special menus that differ in content and form but that must share a similar look as their primary menu. A catalog company might want a design that that keeps consistency in its catalogs, advertisements, and business cards. A design set helps ensure that different kinds of publications share a similar overall look.

The blank publications provide page layouts for all the various kinds of publications that Publisher works with. Publisher does not, however, fill those pages with a color scheme or suggest where a picture or graphic design element such as a border should go. Therefore, if you want to design a business card from scratch but do not want to worry with specifying the size of a routine business card, you click Blank Publications and select the Business Card entry to create the layout for a business card without any of the elements that Publisher would normally suggest.

You'll notice that Publisher's task pane appears on the left side of the editing window. The task pane normally appears on the right side of the screen in Excel and the other Office products.

If you have children, click the Publications for Print entry in the New Publication task pane, scroll down, and click Paper Folding Projects, and you'll see publications you can print that show you and your kids how to create airplanes and origami paper-folding artwork.

To Do: Create Your First Publication

Publisher generates samples so that you then can create almost every publication in Publisher. Publisher's built-in wizard technology handles most needs, and once you start a publication, your job will be to enter the text, import the graphics, and fine-tune the publication to meet your needs.

Get acquainted with Publisher by following these steps to create your first publication:

1. Start Publisher.

2. Click Publications for Print to open the list if it's not already open.

If you click the toolbar's New button instead of starting Publisher from scratch or instead of selecting File, New to start a new publication, Publisher does not show the large To get started, select an option in the list notice that appears when you first start Publisher. Instead, Publisher shows the New Publication task pane with a blank publication in the editing area of your screen.

3. Click Newsletters. Publisher displays a list of newsletter design choices in your editing area. More choices appear than will fit inside the editing area, so you can

scroll down to see additional newsletter designs. The dialog box's preview area shows what the design will look like once you create the publication.

4. For this example, click to select the Floating Oval Newsletter design. Publisher creates a sample document and places sample text, graphics, and titles on the document. Figure 23.4 shows this newsletter's initial design.

FIGURE 23.4

Publisher generates an initial design and helps you finish the publication.

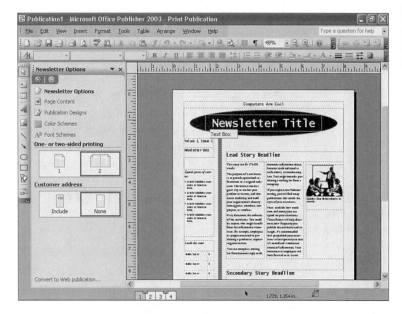

5. Click the Zoom control's plus sign inside the magnifying glass to zoom closer into the sample publication to see the details better. The minus sign takes you further out so you can see the overall design once again.

At the bottom of the screen is a series of pages with page numbers. Many of your publications will span multiple pages, and you traverse through the pages by clicking on the page number you want to see.

6. You can edit the newsletter's elements directly, but you can also select areas to edit within the Newsletter Options task pane. For example, click Color Schemes to select from a list of color sets for the newsletter's elements.

You can change the color scheme for your publication at any time, even after you have added all the other details to your publication. You don't have to stick with any color scheme you select during your publication's design. Experiment and see what looks best.

7. Click different color schemes to see the effect of the color schemes applied to the sample newsletter in the editing area pane. For this example, select the Prairie color scheme to apply it to your publication.

8. Click the task pane's Page Content to see the choice of column offerings. Select the icon that indicates a two-column page. When you move your mouse pointer over the icon, a down arrow appears that gives you the option of applying the column change to the current page or to all pages within your multipage publication. Figure 23.5 shows what the two-column newsletter would look like if you keep the two-column format.

FIGURE 23.5

Publisher can adjust your newsletter to a different number of columns.

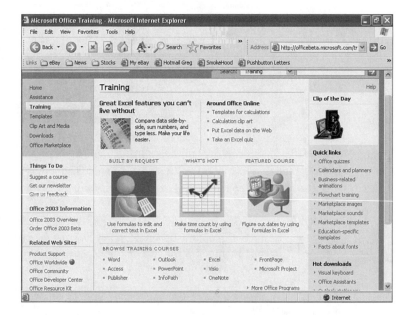

9. You can continue selecting options from the task pane and adjust your publication's details. The publication in the editing area always reflects your latest selections.

Publisher Adds Initial Content for Placeholders

How can Publisher create an initial newsletter with graphics and text when Publisher doesn't know what you want to say in your newsletter?

Remember that Publisher initially creates your newsletter designs for you but not the actual newsletter's details. Normally, the hardest part of producing a publication is laying out the picture and text properly so they remain appealing to your readers. Publisher eases this burden by generating a sample publication for you when you select the kind of publication you want to create. Once Publisher creates the layout that you want for your publication, you fill in the details.

23

Microsoft Gives Some Online Training

NEW 2003 If you want more help about a particular Publisher process, Microsoft provides some online training. Although the training is not overly detailed, you can work through training courses by selecting Help, Microsoft Publisher Help. The task pane changes to show a list of help topics. Click Training, and Publisher takes you to the Microsoft Office online training site shown in Figure 23.6. Clicking the Publisher link takes you through one or more short, interactive courses about things you can do in Publisher.

FIGURE 23.6

Microsoft offers a few Web-based, interactive, self-guided tutorials from the Help menu.

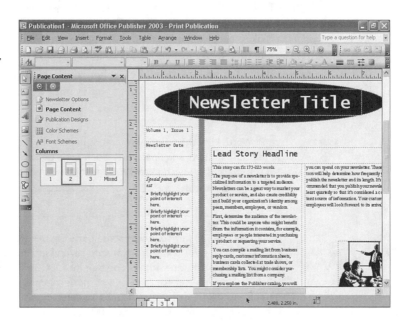

Filling in the Details

Once Publisher lays out the newsletter's design, the sample newsletter publication offers more help. You can change any part of your newsletter's design, such as the font scheme (the set of fonts used in your documents, all of which were selected to look good together), by editing that part of the publication.

Now that you've laid out your publication with Publisher's help, your publication is ready for the details. Those details are the titles, text, graphics, and pictures that make your newsletter unique.

Adding Text

One of the first elements you'll add to any design is the text. The simplest text to add is the text that you type directly into your publication. Click over one of the newsletter's columns to highlight the column. When you begin typing, the highlighted text will automatically disappear. (In the Office programs, as well as most other Windows programs, when you select text and start typing new text, the new text always replaces the selected text.)

Therefore, now that you've selected the first newsletter's column by clicking the column, you can begin typing the text that you want to appear in that column. The first thing you'll notice, as soon as you begin typing, is that you might not be able to read what you are typing! That's okay because you can press F9 or the toolbar's Zoom in button (with the plus sign) at any time to zoom into the text that you type. Figure 23.7 shows zoomed text being entered into the first column. Use the horizontal and vertical scrollbars to bring whatever zoomed text area into view that you want to work with.

As in Word, Publisher supports paragraph indention. Select Format, Paragraph, Indents and Spacing to open a dialog box from which you can set the spacing for each paragraph's first line indention.

If you use the Tab key to indent some parts of your text, you'll see that Tab probably moves the text cursor forward several more characters than you prefer. The default tab width is one-half inch. One-half inch is rather wide when your newsletter contains two or more columns. You can change the default tab width, or set specific tabs, by selecting the Format, Tabs menu option and entering specific tab values as well as a default tab width measurement.

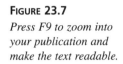

FIGURE 23.7

Press F9 to zoom into your publication and make the text readable.

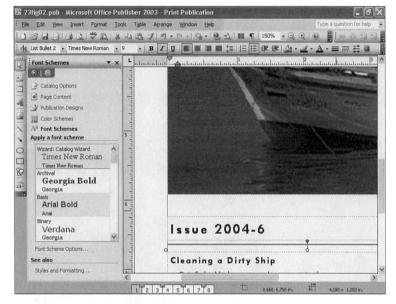

23

As you type, you'll notice that Publisher automatically hyphenates for you. You can turn off the automatic hyphenation by selecting Tools, Language, Hyphenation. In addition to turning automatic hyphenation on and off, you can control when the hyphenation occurs from the Hyphenation dialog box.

Publisher performs background spell-checking as you type in the same way that Excel and Word do. Also, you can select Tools, Spelling, Spelling (F7 is the shortcut key) to check the spelling of the entire document one final time. Publisher has no grammar-checking abilities. If you create the text in Word, however, you can use the Word writing tools to create accurate text and then bring the text into your publication once you've designed the initial publication. If you make a mistake while typing, Publisher supports multiple levels of undo just as Word and Excel do.

Continue entering text and you'll notice that Publisher supports the same AutoCorrect entries you set up in Word. Use the F9 key to zoom in and then back out of your Publisher. When looking at the overall publication, you can click on any column, title, or banner with text and type new text. If you click over an area where you've already entered text, Publisher lets you edit that text.

All of the character-formatting options from Word and Excel are available. If you don't like a font, select Format, Font and choose a new font (although selecting one of the font schemes from the Font Schemes entry in the task pane ensures a more consistent set of fonts in most cases).

If you want to add a *drop cap* (a large character that begins a paragraph's first sentence) to a paragraph, select Format, Drop Cap. (The drop capital letter cannot follow a tab.) Select the type of drop cap that you want to see, click OK, and you'll see the drop cap such as the one shown in Figure 23.8.

FIGURE **23.8**

Add pizzazz to your introductory para-graphs with a fancy first letter.

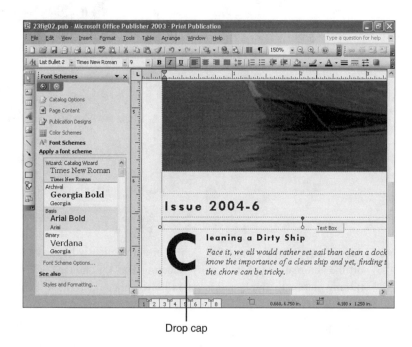

Drop cap

Importing Text into Your Documents

You won't always want to type text directly into a publication. As mentioned earlier in this hour, you'll often create the text in Word and then transfer that text to Publisher. To bring text from other sources, you'll almost always do one of two things:

- Copy text from the Windows Clipboard
- Import the text from its original application's document file

Suppose you write a travel book that teaches people how to travel through Europe the fun way, as a traveler who meets the people and not as a tourist who views the sites from a bus 50 yards away. To help promote your book, you create a newsletter that acts as a sales flier for your book. You might want to copy some text from the book's manuscript into the newsletter. You certainly don't want to copy the entire book, just a paragraph or two.

Start Word (you don't have to exit Publisher to start Word, of course—just click the Start button and start Word as you normally do). Load the book's document into Word, select the paragraph you want to copy to the newsletter, and select Edit, Copy (Ctrl+C) to copy that paragraph to the Windows Clipboard. Switch to Publisher (press Alt+Tab to switch to Publisher or click the Publisher button on your Windows taskbar), click the area that is to receive your text, and select Edit, Paste (Ctrl+V) to put the Clipboard's text into your publication.

23

Some people find that they can paste text (and perform other text-related operations) more easily by right-clicking over the area to receive the text and selecting Paste to paste the text at the cursor's location.

Although the Clipboard is useful for copying small portions of text into your publication, you might want to import long columns of text into Publisher from a full Word document. If you work with others who write for the publications you produce, you will be able to lay out an initial publication and then import the other writers' document files directly into the newsletter columns.

To import a file from Word, select Insert, Text File from the menu to display the Insert Text File dialog box. Select the document from whatever folder contains that text document, and Publisher then imports that file directly into your publication. You can format the text, such as adding a drop cap and making other font and character spacing changes if you want.

Don't import a file over a column's title. Type all titles so you can be sure that the title fits within the area you've designated for the title. Import only into the body of a column of text.

Using Text Boxes

As you type, you enter text into publication elements called *text boxes*. The figures you've seen throughout this hour have shown their text inside text boxes, outlined rectangular areas that contain text.

If you use Publisher to generate samples of all publications before you add any text, as opposed to creating new publications from blank ones, you don't need to be as concerned about adding text boxes as you have to be if you create a publication from scratch.

Publisher adds all the text boxes for you. You can also add more. Publisher always adds text boxes where text is to go so that you can easily type or insert text at that location. Text boxes keep the text in columns within your publication instead of allowing text from one article to bleed incorrectly into another.

By putting text in a text box, and by separating the text from the other elements such as the art, Publisher lets you return to that text and edit the text using the standard insert and delete text-editing tools you are accustomed to. You can format the text, spell-check the text, and so on.

If Publisher did not put your text into a special text box but simply put the text in your publication without distinguishing text from art, you would not have text-editing access to the text. Some art is textual in nature, such as fancy lettering boxed within a flowery border. You would only be able to edit that kind of art-based text as you would edit art-work, one *pixel* (a screen's dot, from the words *picture element*) at a time.

To add a text box to a publication, as you would do if you were to create a publication without the help of a Publisher's initial samples, click the Text tool on the toolbox at the left of the Publisher screen. (The Text tool is the button with a small document and a letter *A* showing in the upper-left corner of that little document, usually the second tool on your toolbox.) Once you select the Text tool, drag your mouse anywhere inside a publication to create a rectangular text box that works just like the text box you used to enter text in the previous section. You can add multiple columns inside a single text box or use a different text box for each column in your publication.

To add multiple columns to a text box, right-click over a text box and select Format Text Box to display the Format Text Box dialog box. Click the Text Box tab to display the dialog box shown in Figure 23.9. Notice the options labeled `Include "Continued on Page"` and `Include "Continued from Page"` that add connecting messages to columns that continue on subsequent publication pages.

Click the Columns button on the Format Text Box dialog box to adjust the number of columns that appear inside the selected text box. You can adjust both the number of columns as well as their width from the Columns dialog box shown in Figure 23.10. Publisher displays a preview of that text box as you make adjustments to the columns.

FIGURE 23.9
The Format Text Box dialog box determines how the text in your text boxes will appear.

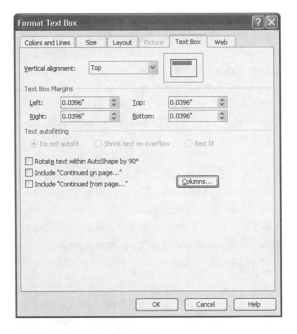

23

FIGURE 23.10
Publisher enables you to determine how many columns a text box will contain.

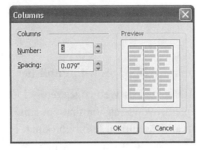

Linking Text Boxes to One Another

If you want text to wrap across columns, continuing into subsequent columns as you type, you need to connect two text boxes together. Click inside the first text box and then click the top toolbar's Create Text Box Link button with a chain link on it. The mouse pointer changes to an overflowing cup. Click the cup on the second text box that is to be linked to the first to create the link.

You will first need to select the text box's page number if the text is to continue into a text box on a different page. Once connected, Publisher ensures that overflowed text from the first text box flows into the connected text box, even if that text box is on a different page. You can break such a link by clicking on either text box and then clicking the Break Forward Link toolbar button with the broken chain link.

When typing text directly into a text box, if you type more text than that text box will hold, Publisher will not automatically expand the text box. Doing so without your express approval would violate any surrounding publication elements, such as other text and graphics you've applied. If you begin to type more text than will fit inside the text box, Publisher displays a message asking if you want to use *autoflow*, where Publisher automatically flows the text to another text box. If you answer yes, Publisher locates an empty text box or creates a new one to hold your extra text.

Summary

This hour introduced you to Publisher 2003. You now know about all of the many kinds of publications Publisher helps you produce. Publisher's strength lies in its ability to help you format text and graphics. Many publishers first use Word to compose their publication's text and then import that text into their Publisher publications, where they then can wrap the text from column to column and format the text in a way that catches the reader's eye.

There is so much more you can do with Publisher. In the next hour, "Adding Art to Your Publications," you'll explore ways to use graphics to spruce up your publications with Publisher.

Q&A

Q Why would I want to create Web pages with Publisher?

A The simple answer is that Publisher's Web pages really look good! By starting with Publisher's sample Web pages, you'll ensure that your sites have an appealing and consistent look. Although another Office family product, FrontPage, is perhaps the most powerful tool within Office to create and manage Web pages, you now can develop fairly complex Web pages in Publisher. Once you generate your initial Web site with Publisher, you later can import that Web site into FrontPage if your Web-site needs become more advanced.

HOUR 24

Adding Art to Your Publications

In the previous hour, you learned what Publisher can do for you, and this hour spruces up your publications graphically. Attention-getting publications use artwork and pictures effectively, and Publisher provides the perfect tools for putting those graphics into your publications. Publisher works with hardware devices such as digital cameras and scanners to get your images into your publications quickly and easily.

The highlights of this hour include the following:

- What types of graphics are available for you to use within Publisher
- How to use the Clip Art task pane to insert graphics into your publication
- How to make text wrap around photos and graphics
- Where to locate graphics for your publications
- How Publisher's drawing tools help you add accenting images and designs to your publications
- How to add fancy borders around artwork

Your Publication's Art

Graphics typically come in two flavors: *bitmap graphics* such as pictures and *vector graphics* such as drawings, art, and the kinds of art that often comprise fancy borders. You usually create and edit these two different kinds of graphic images in two different kinds of programs. You'll need a photo-editing program to edit your photos and a drawing program that enables you to edit and manipulate graphics such as cartoons and other vector graphics. Many such programs are available, and even the least expensive ones handle all common graphic-creation and editing tasks.

In Publisher, working with art is actually simpler than working with text. Art resides inside art frames just as text resides inside text boxes. You can easily change the art, resize, and move art within its frame.

When Publisher finishes designing a sample publication for you to work with, you need to change the sample's art to the artwork you want to use. Publisher makes replacing artwork simple. When you click to select sample artwork to replace in a publication, one place you can get another image is from Publisher's collection of clip art. After selecting the art frame, select Insert, Picture, Clip Art to display the Clip Art task pane shown in Figure 24.1.

FIGURE 24.1

Publisher's clip art supplies graphics that you can place in your own publications.

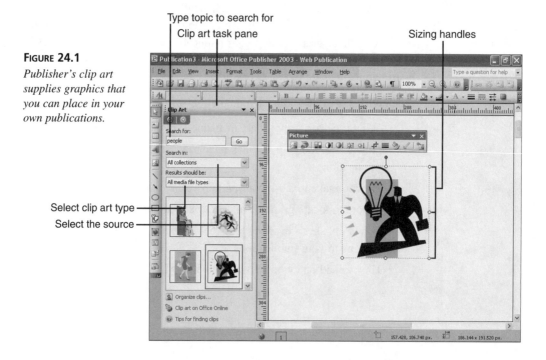

When you select a clip art image, Publisher places that image in your selected art frame. You then can resize the image to fit the publication's boundaries as needed. The Clip Art task pane provides multiple kinds of files, including video and audio files, but for a publication you want to insert just fixed graphics. (If you use Publisher to create Web sites, you might want to select an audio or video clip, though.)

If you want to use artwork from another source, such as a scanned image, you can select Insert, Picture, From Scanner or Camera. Publisher then accepts your scanned or digital camera's image, assuming you've got the proper hardware connected and ready to go.

Publisher inserts all major picture formats, including GIF, JPEG, Kodak Photo CD, TIFF, and just about all other image formats in use today.

24

Once you load the image you want to place in your publication, you can move or resize that image. When you click inside an art frame, eight sizing handles appear around the frame's borders. By dragging any of the resizing handles in or out, you can shrink or expand the art frame, and the image size changes along with the frame.

If you point to the art frame's edge without pointing to a resizing handle, the mouse cursor changes to a Move cursor. You then can drag the image (and its frame) to any location on the publication. If you move the art frame over text, Publisher formats the text around the art frame so that the art does not cover the text, as Figure 24.2 shows.

Justify both margins to get newspaper-like columns where the text aligns evenly on both sides of the column. When you then move artwork into the text, as shown in Figure 24.2, the text flows more gracefully around the artwork.

As with text, you can copy pictures from the Windows Clipboard that you have copied there from another application.

If you've got images and photos stored on your computer, select Insert, Picture, From File and locate the graphic you want to insert into your publication.

Text wrapped around image

FIGURE 24.2

When you move an art frame into text, Publisher wraps the text around the art.

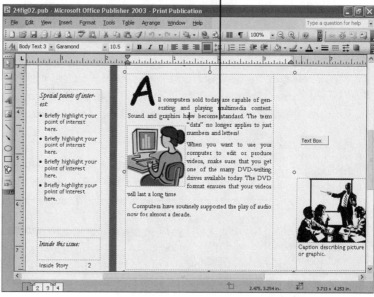

Instead of moving or resizing a graphic image, you might need to *crop* an image. Cropping cuts off part of an image, removing from the graphic whatever area you crop. Whenever you click over a graphic image, Publisher displays a floating Picture toolbar with tools that you can use to edit the image. If you select the Crop tool, Publisher places cropping lines around the image that you can drag inward to crop parts of your picture away.

Extra Shapes

The Publisher toolbox, the set of tools on the left side of your screen, includes a few drawing tools with which you can add shapes to your publication. Although these tools are not good enough to use for original artwork, you can use the drawing tools to add lines, circles, boxes, and other simple shapes to your drawing. Many of these shapes make good borders or highlighters to accent special points inside your publication. You can also add special text as you might for emblems and callouts that you want to add to your publication.

The shapes don't require art frames. You can place the shapes anywhere on a publication, including over text. For example, you can use the Line tool to add separating lines between columns and under banners.

To access the shapes, click the line, oval, or box drawing tools. A collection of special shapes appear when you click the *AutoShapes tool*, as shown in Figure 24.3. AutoShapes are predesigned shapes that you might want to use, such as arrows and stars. To draw any shape, whether that shape is a line, oval, or AutoShape, select the shape and then click and hold your mouse at the shape's starting point in your publication. As drag your mouse while holding down your mouse button, the shape appears in your publication. To place the shape, release your mouse. Any time you click over the shape, the sizing handles appear so you can resize or move the shape to another location in your publication.

24

FIGURE 24.3

Select an AutoShape from the collection of shapes available from the toolbox.

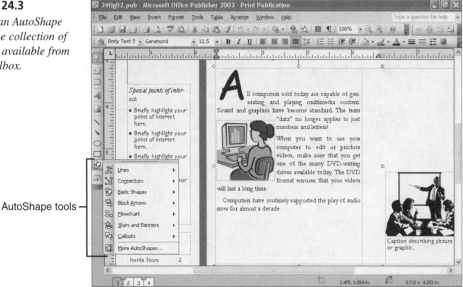

AutoShape tools

Designing with the Design Gallery

Publisher includes a design feature called the *Design Gallery*. The Design Gallery acts as a repository of predesigned elements that you can place in your publications. For example, you might need a special banner to spruce up a newsletter's featured column. Although you can design your own eye-catching banner, why not check the Design Gallery to see whether you like an example that's already there?

One of the most beneficial features of the Design Gallery is that you can store additional design elements in the Design Gallery collection. Therefore, you can create headline banners for each division's newsletter within your company and store each of those banners in the Design Gallery. When the time comes to begin work on the next issue for a particular division, you can grab the banner that you created before and re-use the banner to maintain consistency across your newsletter issues.

To Do: Explore the Design Gallery

You can explore the Design Gallery contents by following these steps:

1. Click the Design Gallery Object button on the toolbox. The Design Gallery Object button is the button at the bottom of your toolbox. The Design Gallery window opens as shown in Figure 24.4.

   Like the Clip Gallery, the Design Gallery is organized in categories listed down the left edge of the Design Gallery window. (When you add your own items to the Design Gallery, you can create new categories that will appear on the tabbed page labeled My Objects.) Each category has its own design.

2. Click on different Design Gallery categories to see the designs available in them.

3. Once you locate the picture that represents the Design Gallery item you want to insert, double-click the item to insert it into your publication. Publisher places the item on the Publisher editing area and closes the Design Gallery window. You can move, resize, and edit the item as if you had designed and drawn the item yourself from the shape and text tools on the toolbox.

Your design gallery collection

FIGURE 24.4
*The Design Gallery
contains graphic ele-
ments you can include
in your publication.*

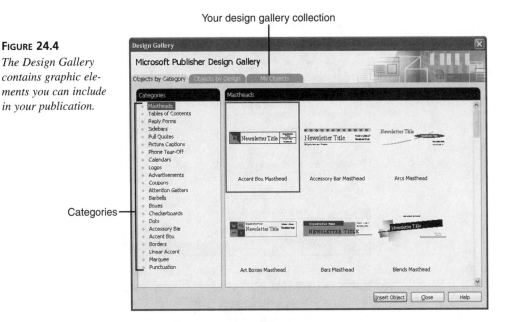

Categories

Getting Help with the Design Checker

Publisher includes a special design tool called the *Design Checker* that you use *after* you
create your publication. The Design Checker analyzes your publication and offers suggestions on how to improve it. When you select Tools, Design Checker, Publisher opens
the Design Checker task pane. To learn what kinds of design elements that Design
Checker analyzes, click the Design Checker Options link at the bottom of the task pane
and then click the Checks tab to select from the kinds of publication elements you want
the Design Checker to critique. You can uncheck one or more of the options if you want
to limit the Design Checker to just those items you've selected. By default, Publisher
checks for any and all possible problems with your publication, such as text that flows
into an overflow area which you have not properly linked.

When you start the Design Checker by clicking the Design Checker button on your toolbox, the Design Checker analyzes your publication and searches for the problems listed
within the Options dialog box (shown in Figure 24.5).

FIGURE 24.5

The Design Checker analyzes your publication for common design problems.

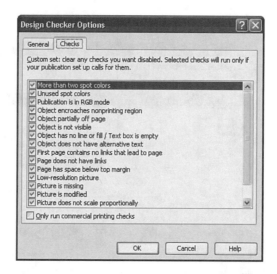

Use Design Checker to look over your publication after you've completed the initial design, added your text, and placed your figures. The Design Checker acts like a last-minute proofreader that finds mistakes that are easy to overlook. For example, the Design Checker can locate text that will not fit within its text box but continues into a special overflow area, meaning that a text box is not large enough to hold all the text that's there.

The Design Checker does not leave you hanging once it finds a problem. Point to any problem shown in the Design Checker task pane and a down arrow appears to the right of that problem. The Explain option gives you detailed instructions on how you might go about correcting the problem that Publisher's Design Checker just located.

Even if Design Checker finds multiple problems with your publication, you don't have to wait for the Design Checker to find them all before you correct the problems. Sometimes, the Design Checker can take a while to locate everything. You can leave the Design Checker task pane and begin correcting problems as the Design Checker lists them. Once you fix the problem, go back to the Design Checker task pane and handle any remaining problems that Publisher might have found.

Putting Borders Around Your Publications

You might want to place a border around your entire publication or perhaps around a single text box or art frame. A border looks nice around smaller publications you create, such as placeholders for dinner guests. You might want to create your own business cards and place a border around your company's name.

Publisher makes it easy to place borders, either before or after you finish creating the material that is to go within the border. Placing a border requires only that you format an element, such as an art frame, and specify the border you desire.

To Do: Add a Frame

To add a border to a publication's art frame, follow these steps:

1. Click the frame that holds the art where you want a border to appear. You can add an empty art frame if you want to add a border before adding the art.

2. Right-click the art frame and select Format Picture. The Format Picture dialog box appears.

3. Click the Border Art button to display the BorderArt dialog box shown in Figure 24.6.

24

FIGURE 24.6

The BorderArt dialog box determines the size, color, number of sides, and thickness of your border lines.

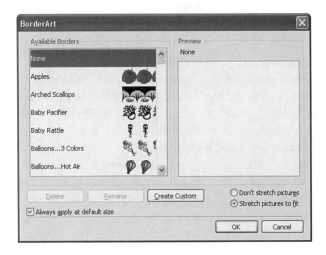

The BorderArt dialog box page lets you specify the kind of border you want as well as its properties. In addition, you can determine whether artwork that will go inside the border (if you plan to place art inside the border) is to stretch to fit the border or whether the border's picture is to retain its size even if the border is much larger than the figure.

4. You can click the Create Custom button to make your own border art. Once you enter the name of a picture (from the Clip Gallery or other image), Publisher repeats that image to build a border that you can name and save in the list of borders that appear.

5. Click OK to save the border art on your editing area. You now can resize the border as you would any other box or graphic image on the publication.

Summary

Although the past two hours have been a quick tour of Publisher, that's really all you need to get started. In many ways, Publisher tries to appeal to a wider audience than the other Office products. Publisher offers many guides and examples that get you started. Placing and managing your publication's artwork is relatively simple and often requires little more than resizing or adjusting the location of an image once you place that image in your publication's editing area.

Q&A

Q How can I place a background on my publication?

A A background image can appear on the back of your publication, acting like a lightly hued watermark image that shows through the other text and pictures. By placing the background on every page in your multipage publication, you can add consistency to your publication's look.

You have to add the graphic image (the image can be any picture or graphic image such as a corporate logo) and then select Format Picture after right-clicking it. Click the Picture tab and under Image Control select Washout from the Color list. Select Recolor, pick a color that you want for the watermark, and then click Apply. You have now turned the image into a lightly hued image. You now must display Publisher's Arrange menu and select Order, Send to Back. This places the watermark behind all other text and images on your page. Where blank spots appear on the page, the background image will lightly show through.

PART IX

Appendixes

A   Sharing Information Between Office 2003 Programs

B   Business Contact Manager and Office Extras

APPENDIX A

Sharing Information Between Office 2003 Programs

This appendix explores how Office products work together. Office programs integrate so well that it is hard to know where to start describing the possibilities. Generally, if you need to combine two or more Office files, you are able to load or embed one product's file within another even though the Office programs that created the two files are completely different.

From inserting links in Word documents to combining an Access table and an Excel worksheet into a PowerPoint presentation, Office supplies the interaction you need. You can also add your own graphics to your Office documents by drawing with the Office drawing tools.

Sharing Data Between Applications

Office's cornerstone is data sharing among its programs. Office offers several ways to share information among products. Almost all the Office products support the inclusion of other Office files. For example, Word includes the Insert Microsoft Excel Worksheet toolbar button that inserts any Excel worksheet in a Word document.

Besides inserting entire files, you might want to insert part of a document in another Office application. The following sections explain the most common methods to embed part of one application's file inside another.

To Do: Drag and Drop

Suppose that you want to use part of an Excel worksheet inside a Word document. You might want to do this if you are preparing a report for management on last quarter's sales figures. If you have both Excel (with the relevant data loaded) and Word running at the same time, these steps quickly insert the worksheet into the Word document:

1. Resize your Excel and Word program windows so that you can see both the *source file* (the Excel worksheet) and the *destination file* (the Word document).

2. In the Excel worksheet, select the cells that you want to copy and transfer to Word.

3. You can use the keyboard or mouse to make the transfer. Select Edit, Copy to copy the selected cells to the Office Clipboard; click on the Word document's location where you want the cells to go; and select Edit, Paste to place the worksheet into Word. You can also hold the Ctrl key and drag one edge of the highlighted worksheet cells directly to the location in your Word document where you want to place the table and release the mouse to finalize the transfer. Figure A.1 shows the result of such a copy.

If you use the mouse and do not first press Ctrl before dragging the cells, Excel will move the table from the Excel worksheet to the Word document instead of copying the table.

Depending on the size and style of your Word document, you might want to format the copied table differently from Excel's format. Right-click the table and select Format Object to display the Format Object dialog box. You can apply colors, lines, shading, and other formatting attributes to the copied object from the Format Object dialog box.

A

FIGURE A.1

This table in Word came from Excel.

From here in Excel...

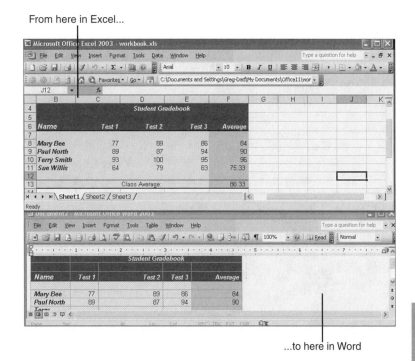

...to here in Word

Creating Links

Suppose that you create a monthly sales report using the same Word document and the same Excel worksheet every time. Although the data within the Excel worksheet changes to reflect each new month's figures, the structure and formulas remain the same. You don't have to drag the updated Excel table to your Word document before printing the Word document each month. Instead of copying or moving the cells, you can create a *link* to the cells. A link points to another file.

As long as you have inserted a link to the Excel worksheet in your monthly report document's template, you need only change the Excel worksheet each month, start Word, create a report document from the template, and print the document. You won't have to copy or move the actual Excel cells into the report because the link points to the cells and displays their contents. The report always points to the worksheet cells via the link that you inserted when you created the Word document.

To Do: Link to a Worksheet

To create such a link, perform these steps:

1. Arrange and resize your two program windows so that you can see both the source document (the Excel worksheet) and the destination document (the Word document).

2. Select the cells in the Excel worksheet that you want to link and transfer to Word.

3. With the right mouse button, drag the edge of the highlighted cells to the location in your Word document where you want to place the table. You might have to practice doing this for a while if you are not accustomed to using the right mouse button for dragging.

4. Release the right mouse button. Word opens a shortcut menu with these options: Move Here, Copy Here, Link Excel Object Here, Create Shortcut Here, Create Hyperlink Here, and Cancel.

5. Select Link Excel Object Here to indicate to Word that you want to create an object link (as opposed to a move or a copy of the cells). Although the cells appear as though Office copied them into the Word document, the cells represent only the link that you created between the Excel source file and Word's destination document. Whenever you change the data in Excel's source file, the linked information in Word is automatically updated.

The destination file (in this case, the Word document) always reflects the most recent changes to the source file (in this case, the Excel worksheet). Therefore, if you must keep archives of old reports with the previous monthly values, you want to copy the cells instead of creating a link.

After inserting one or more links, select Edit, Links. The Links dialog box contains every link in your document and enables you to change, break, or lock any link. When you break a link, the data becomes embedded in the document and no longer updates when you update the source. When you lock a link, you temporarily prevent the link from being updated when its source is updated.

To watch the real-time nature of the links, change a value in the source Excel worksheet. The Word document immediately reflects your change. If the Word document does not reflect the change, select Edit, Links and make sure that the Automatic Update option is set. If Manual Update is set, Word will not update the link to reflect any changes in the Excel worksheet until you select Edit, Links and click the Update Now button.

Creating Shortcuts

Instead of inserting a copy or a link, you can insert a *shortcut* in the destination document.

You probably use shortcuts less often than links and embedded copies when producing reports because you usually want the reports to show actual data and not icons. If you often work with data from one program while in another program, however, the shortcuts are nice. The data does not get in your way until you are ready to work with it because you see only icons that represent the shortcut data. In addition, the icon loads much faster than the underlying data would load, and speed becomes an issue if you work on older computers.

> When you create a shortcut from one Office program to another, Office displays a shortcut icon. If you double-click the data, Office opens the appropriate program and enables you to edit the original data using the source program that created the data. If you insert a shortcut into a non-Office program, however, Office inserts a shortcut icon that represents the data. If you double-click the icon from within the other program, the appropriate Office program begins, and you can edit the data.

Several scenarios exist where a link might work well. Suppose that you are working in Excel, modifying weekly salary figures for a large worksheet that you maintain. Each week you must study the salary amounts and enter a 10-line explanation of the salaries. Instead of typing the definition each week or (worse) using Excel as a limited word processor and editing the text each week, you could embed a shortcut to a Word document that contains a template for the text. When you double-click the shortcut, Excel starts Word, which automatically loads the template. You can create the final text in the template, copy the Word text into your salary worksheet (replacing the shortcut), and save the worksheet under a name that designates the current week's work.

A

To Do: Insert Shortcuts

To insert a shortcut, perform these steps:

1. Arrange and resize your program windows so that you can see both the source document (the Word template document) and the destination file (the Excel worksheet).

2. Select the Word template text that you want to use for the shortcut. (Press Ctrl+A if you want to select the entire Word template document.)

3. With the right mouse button, drag the edge of the highlighted template text to the location in your Excel worksheet where you want to place the shortcut.

4. Release the right mouse button.

5. Select Create Shortcut Here from the pop-up menu. Office creates the shortcut. As with a link, the shortcut data does not actually appear in the destination document. Unlike a link, you can drag the shortcut to your Windows desktop, to Explorer, or to another program to create additional copies of the shortcut.

Before inserting an Access table into another Office program, run a query to filter data that doesn't interest you. Hour 19, "Retrieving Your Data," explains how to develop data queries. Later in this appendix, the section titled "Using Word and Access" describes how to insert Access data into a Word document.

Inserting Hyperlinks

Thanks to the Internet, more and more users are accustomed to using hyperlinks. A hyperlink is text (or an object) that describes the link to another document or to a Web page on the Internet. When you point to the hyperlink, the mouse pointer changes to the shape of a hand. When you click the hyperlink, that linked document appears.

Perhaps you want to insert a hyperlink to a corporate Web site that an employee can click to locate information on a product's specifications. You can insert hyperlinks to other Office products, but in reality, hyperlinks are typically used for Web pages.

The nature of hyperlinks means that you will use hyperlinks most often to point to Web pages. Office 2003 makes inserting hyperlinks extremely simple if you display the actual Web page address inside your Office 2003 files. For example, if you want to embed a hyperlink inside an Excel worksheet, you only need to type the hyperlink itself and Excel automatically turns that address into a hyperlink. As soon as you type the Web address, Excel underlines the Web address and turns the address into a hyperlink to that site.

> You can turn the automatic conversion of Web addresses into hyperlinks on and off. Select Tools, AutoCorrect and click the tab labeled AutoFormat as You Type. Uncheck the option labeled Internet and Network Paths with Hyperlinks when you want to type Web addresses without the Office product converting that address to a hyperlink.

Remember that you don't have to use Web addresses for hyperlinks in Office documents. You can enter path and filenames that reside on your own PC. When you or another user clicks the link, the Office product displays that link's file. Therefore, you can easily link documents together, even documents from different products within Office.

Perhaps you want something other than the Web address to appear. In other words, one of your PowerPoint presentation slides might include the text `Click here to view our informative Web page`, and when clicked during the presentation, the slide changes to show the actual Web page.

To Do: Convert Hyperlinks to Text

To change a hyperlink to customized text, follow these steps:

1. Type the Web address or path to the Office file that you want to display when the user clicks the hyperlink.
2. Select the hyperlink.
3. Press Ctrl+K to display the Insert Hyperlink dialog box shown in Figure A.2. The toolbar also displays an Insert Hyperlink button that displays the Edit Hyperlink dialog box.
4. Type a new value in the text box labeled Text to Display.
5. Click OK. Your text appears in place of the hyperlink's address.

A

Use the Insert
Hyperlink dialog box
to change the text on
the hyperlink.

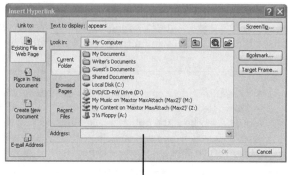

Enter hyperlink text here

Turning a Word Document into a Presentation

Word and PowerPoint share a special link that enables you to turn a set of notes into a presentation. As you create your notes in Word, be sure to use the Heading 1 through Heading 5 styles. PowerPoint uses the Heading 1 style for each slide's title and uses the Heading 2 through Heading 5 styles for the slide's subsequently indented text.

> If your Word document contains styles other than Heading 1 through Heading 5, PowerPoint ignores those paragraphs.

You can easily apply Heading 1 through Heading 5 styles to a Word document that you have already created by clicking a paragraph (or by moving the mouse pointer anywhere within the paragraph), clicking the Style box's drop-down arrow, and selecting Heading styles from the drop-down list box. You can also select the style by opening the Style drop-down list box and scrolling to the heading style that you want to select.

After you create the Word document, open the document within PowerPoint and save the presentation. From Word itself, you can convert your document to a presentation by selecting File, Send to, Microsoft PowerPoint.

Using Word and Access

A database can be extremely large with many tables. Often, you want to export a portion of an Access database to a Word document. The drag-and-drop method does not always offer exactly what you need to get the data you want into a Word document.

> If you want to use an Access table in a PowerPoint presentation, load the table into a Word document and then convert the Word document to a PowerPoint presentation as described in the previous section.

To Do: Use an Access Table in Word

To load Access data into a Word document, perform these steps:

1. Display the Database toolbar in Word. (Select View, Toolbars and then click Database.)

2. Click the Insert Database toolbar button. Word displays the Database dialog box.

3. Click the Get Data button to begin locating the database to import. Before specifying the data to be imported into Word, you must locate the database.

4. Browse to the database file you want to import. When you locate the database, select the database and Word displays the Select Table dialog box shown in Figure A.3.

FIGURE A.3

Indicate exactly which table Word is to use.

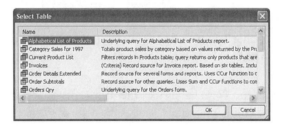

5. Select the table or query that you want to load into the Word document, and click OK to return to the Database dialog box.

6. Click the Query Options button if you want to limit the table's records or fields. (If you don't select the Query Options button, Word imports the entire table.) Word displays an Access query window, from which you can select records and fields using normal Access database-selection criteria. Select one or more fields that meet the criteria you specify. You can specify additional tables if you want Word to import data from multiple tables.

7. Click the Insert Data button to insert your selected data.

8. You now can format the data and use it in your Word document as if you typed the data yourself.

A

Outlook Letters

Users often keep Outlook loaded throughout the day, making appointments, calling contacts, and planning meetings. Outlook includes a handy feature that enables you to write a letter to any contact quickly and easily. A wizard makes the connection between Outlook and Word.

To Do: Write a Letter from Outlook

The following steps explain how to access this often-overlooked feature from Outlook:

1. Click to select any Outlook contact.

2. Select Actions, New Letter to Contact to start Word's Letter Wizard shown in Figure A.4.

3. Select a page design and letter style from the dialog box.

4. Click the Recipient Info tab to display the letter's recipient information. The wizard will have already filled in the contact's name and address. Select or type the salutation that you desire on the Recipient Info tab.

5. Click the Other Elements tab to define other aspects of the letter such as the reference line and subject if those items are to appear.

6. Click the Sender Info tab to enter information about you, the sender. You can put your return address information as well as a company name and closing, such as "Best wishes."

7. Click Finish and Word builds the letter using the elements you selected. Your only job now is to fill in the details such as the body of the letter and to complete the elements such as the attention and subject lines.

In a similar manner, you can send a letter you're writing in Word to an email recipient. With your Word document loaded, select File, Send to, Mail Recipient. Word opens an email message and copies your document to the message body. You then can click the To button to select a recipient who is to receive the emailed document.

FIGURE A.4

The Letter Wizard takes care of the letter's formatting and address details.

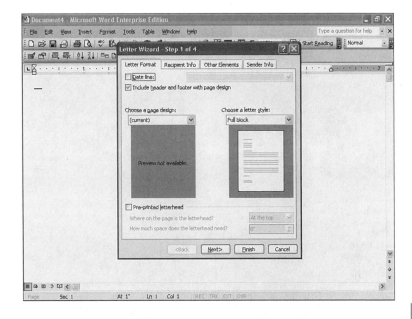

Sending Attachments

When you work on an Office file, such as a Word document or Excel worksheet, you can easily send the document to one of your Outlook recipients. Simply select File, Send to, Mail Recipient (as Attachment). Office automatically opens a new email message with your document attached to the message. You then can click the To button or type a recipient's email address, enter a subject, and send the email with your file attached. The user on the other end can then open your email message from within her mail program and save or view your attachment.

Summary

This appendix described how to integrate Office products by sharing data files among the programs. One of the most elegant ways to copy or move data from one Office program to another is to use drag and drop. By holding your right mouse button, you can control how the drag-and-drop operation sends the data from one document to another.

Word and PowerPoint share data files easily as long as you use the proper heading styles. Presenters often use Word documents as a basis for a PowerPoint presentation, and you will appreciate the automation Office provides. After you convert your Word document to a PowerPoint presentation, you can adjust the presentation's format and add slides if you want.

When importing Access data into Word, you must be selective. Databases are often huge, and you usually want to import only a small part of the database into your Word document. Make sure to indicate to Word what data from what table you want to import so that you get only the data you need.

APPENDIX B

Business Contact Manager and Office Extras

Depending on which version of Microsoft Office 2003 you get, your collection of programs that compose your Office suite will differ from that of others'. The primary purpose of this appendix is to give you a quick, descriptive overview of some of the newer Office add-on programs that might be unfamiliar to you even if you've worked in previous versions of Office. You won't master these programs in this appendix, but you'll certainly know more about how you might be able to use them if the need arises.

You'll see that most of these new add-on programs are most effectively used inside businesses and other organizations where many people work jointly on projects and share corporate information.

New Office Programs

As you read through this appendix, keep in mind that it's only an overview, or a guide, so that you can more accurately decide whether you need these additional programs. Each of these programs could have its own 24-hour tutorial, but because they are new, just learning what these products can do for you will benefit your decision-making.

Microsoft Office InfoPath 2003

 Microsoft Office InfoPath 2003 was known for many months before its final release as *XDocs*. (Perhaps Microsoft got tired of people confusing XDocs with Microsoft's Xbox game console!) InfoPath is for members of teams and organizations to help them gather and share information within their organization. InfoPath supports dynamic, Extensible Markup Language (XML) forms. (A later section entitled "What Is XML?" introduces you to the XML technology.)

InfoPath helps business users collect, access, and reuse information so that fewer actual paper documents are handled, fewer copies get out when security is a concern, and all team members can more easily keep track of what the others are doing. InfoPath is often a forms-based system so that you can get to organizational data inside forms when working inside a team. These XML-based forms can interact and update just about any corporate information (as long as that data is stored in a compatible XML format). The forms allow for optional fields (such as notes and comments that some forms might need when another might not need a place for notes and comments).

These InfoPath forms support the standard Office AutoComplete feature so when entering data common to the form, the InfoPath form can fill in the rest of a field for you when you type the first few letters. In addition to AutoComplete, InfoPath checks forms against databases and ensures that the data users in the organization enter follows pre-designed rules such as those that must fall within a certain price ranges if the checked field holds such data.

Figure B.1 shows an InfoPath form. The form supports background spell-checking just as the other Office products do. Although InfoPath is more than just a form generator and data-entry program, thinking in those terms does give you a general introduction to what InfoPath can do.

FIGURE B.1

Your employees can enter information into dynamic forms with InfoPath.

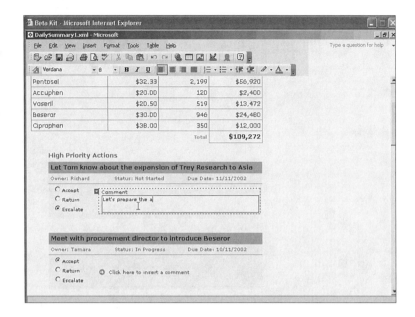

Microsoft Office OneNote 2003

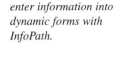

OneNote is a program that captures and organizes information in a variety of formats, including handwriting. The capture of handwriting is becoming increasingly more important due to the proliferation of tablet PCs. With a tablet PC, the notes you write on the screen turn into text that you can edit with Word. In addition to handwriting, OneNote captures audio and even enables you to sequence handwriting with the audio so you can replay the audio and see the handwriting appear at the exact point you wrote the notes. This dual-capture feature comes in handy during meetings, for example. You can record the meetings and your notes at the same time and play back the combination later.

Of course, OneNote also captures text you type at the keyboard as well as handwriting, audio, and other forms of data input. The notes you make are freeform, meaning you can write just about anywhere and mix drawing, handwriting, and typing. OneNote tracks the timing of each of those input elements for later playback. Figure B.2 shows you one such session.

B

FIGURE B.2

OneNote keeps track of typing, handwriting, and even audio.

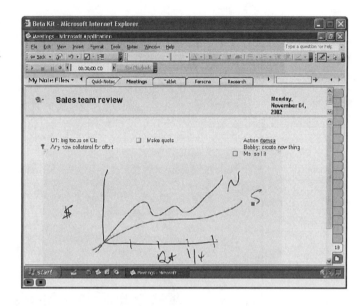

The fact that your notes are freeform doesn't mean that OneNote is disorganized. You can search through all your notes (no matter what the format is) and perform keyword searches. You can, in effect, instantly locate information by letting OneNote search through all your meeting notes, files, and other activities.

Microsoft SharePoint Portal Server

One of the more confusing Office products is the SharePoint Portal Server. Meant to be used by layers of groups within a larger organization, the SharePoint Portal Server enables an organization to create and serve up a major Web site, with departments inside the company sharing resources from that larger site to manage their own sites. Even teams and individual employees can have their own Web sites (either Internet-based or *intranet*-based, meaning limited to the network inside the company and not accessible to the outside world).

Each layer is a *portal* managed by the SharePoint Portal Server software. Security is integral at every layer, as are the reporting and statistical analysis of all the portal layers' usage. SharePoint Portal Server provides a universal answer for an organization that needs consistency among its internal and external Web sites.

Microsoft Office Outlook 2003 with Business Contact Manager

NEW 2003 Microsoft Outlook has developed into an important email client, contact manager, appointment reminder, scheduler, journal, and note-taker as you saw in Hours 15, "Communicating with Outlook 2003," and 16, "Planning and Scheduling with Outlook 2003." If you have Outlook with the Business Contact Manager, you have a tool that helps small businesses keep better track of their clients and sales contacts.

All businesses depend on their income, and sales drive income. Tracking potential customers, former customers, and current customers is vital so that sales information can get to the right people at the right time. A salesperson must be able to locate sales contacts quickly and look up information about those contacts, such as previous purchases, and even personal history, such as family information, to get better rapport for the sale.

One of the best things about Business Contact Manager is that it's really just Microsoft Outlook with a few extra bells and whistles that manage business contacts more effectively than Outlook does alone. Therefore, Business Contact Manager is simple to learn because, unlike a comprehensive program such as InfoPath or the SharePoint Portal Server software, you already know how to use Outlook.

As an overview, here are a few things Business Contact Manager does well:

- Tracks business accounts, contacts, and sales opportunities (such as every time in the past a customer was called upon).
- Reports on prioritized comprehensive sales activities and contacts.
- Stores business contacts separately from regular Outlook contacts so you can track business-specific data, such as leads, income, sales history, sales calls, and returns.
- Scans all activities available for any one specific business contact or business account.
- Links documents to your accounts and sales contacts to you can view, edit, and manage them easily.
- Manages follow-up appointments that you set so your sales staff can return to the customer at a given time.
- Allows your company to purchase target sales leads and import those leads directly into your Outlook Business Contact Manager files.

Figure B.3 shows a business contact. The contact is for a business account and not for an individual person. As you can see, the format is similar to any other Outlook contact

B

except you'll notice fields for the account's financial information, multiple contact entries available at this account's location, and a history of the account's activities sorted by most recent date.

FIGURE B.3

Outlook lets you keep multiple items about your business contacts.

The Flavors of Microsoft Office 2003

The programs that come with your Microsoft Office suite are determined by what you purchased. The Microsoft Office 2003 Enterprise Edition, generally bought only by large organizations that provide companywide services powered by Office, will include all the add-on programs described here and more—such as the Visio graphics program with which you can create and manipulate vector graphics such as blueprints, flowcharts, and other graphics that a company often needs for planning and other purposes.

The typical Microsoft Office suite sold is the Microsoft Office Professional. With the Pro edition, you'll get all the standard Office applications as well as Access, which doesn't come with the student or regular Microsoft Office edition.

Most of the Office programs, including OneNote and InfoPath, are available for you to purchase individually. Therefore, you can get the kind of Microsoft Office suite you need now to get started and add other products to your customized suite later.

What Is XML?

One of the industry buzzwords used and often overused in the past few years is *XML*. Microsoft provides more XML integration into Microsoft Office 2003 than ever before. Microsoft provided very light support for XML in Office XP, although the implementation was so light that many chose to wait until Microsoft integrated XML more closely into Office.

One of the first places to use XML is to begin converting data files to an XML-based set of data. Microsoft Word 2003, Excel 2003, and Access 2003 recognize the XML format and enable you to save documents in the XML format if your application calls for it.

The entire XML concept is cloudy for many people. If you want to take a few moments to understand XML better, you can then determine, along with the computer-support staff at your business, whether XML and Office make a good fit for your applications yet. The rest of this appendix gives you a fast-paced but thoroughly introductory lesson on XML.

Introduction to XML

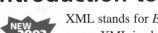 XML stands for *Extensible Markup Language*. As you might guess from its name, XML is closely tied to HTML (the language behind Web pages), and both look very similar. As a matter of fact, all XML code resides inside HTML code, so without HTML, XML would not be possible.

Even XML support inside of Office 2003 is still not as complete as some would prefer, but Microsoft has made it clear that XML support will certainly be with Office and will play a role in each succeeding version.

HTML includes a set of specific commands, known as *command tags*. These command tags determine how that part of a Web page will look.

Here is a line of HTML code:

```
They say cars sometimes are <i>racy</i> in Indianapolis!
```

If this line appears on a Web page, you would see the following on your screen when you viewed the Web page:

```
They say cars sometimes are racy in Indianapolis!
```

Your Web browser would see the starting command tag <i> and know to show all text in italics until the terminating command tag, </i>. Terminating command tags, as you can see, usually begin with a forward slash indicating that a particular format or hyperlink is being completed and that the Web browser is to stop formatting at that point.

B

Whereas HTML deals with formatting Web pages and handling hyperlinks from one Web page to another, XML is a set of command tags that describe actual data and not just how the name of the data is to look in a Web browser.

> Strictly speaking, XML commands are not called "command tags," but for now that's the best way of viewing them. They're always enclosed in angled brackets, such as <PartNo> just as HTML tags are.

XML and Its Impact

How important is XML? In 1999, the Gartner Group, an Internet research company, said that 80% of business-to-business (also known as *B2B*) traffic used XML.

The user and author of a file of XML code can define and use, on-the-fly, brand new command tags that are also available to other Web pages. In defining new XML command tags, you use the extensible portion of XML.

As mentioned in the previous section, HTML describes the *format* of a Web page; XML describes the *content* of a Web page. XML does more than just tell the Web browser where and how to place Web page elements.

Consider the following possible XML section from a Web page:

```
<CARMAKE>Swifty</CARMAKE>
<CARMODEL>Dove</CARMODEL>
<ENGINEPARTNO>546-32Xs</ENGINEPARTNO>
<WHOLESALE>$21,039</WHOLESALE>
<SUGGESTEDRETAIL>$32,483</SUGGESTEDRETAIL>
```

Over time, industries will begin to standardize their XML tags. Therefore, <ENGINEPARTNO> might be standardized by automobile Web-site designers to designate any automobile manufacturer's engine part number. As other automobile Web developers standardize and use <ENGINEPARTNO> (and its corresponding ending tag of </ENGINEPARTNO>), Web pages can be combined, borrowed, and used as the basis of other Web pages that also contain such parts.

When learning XML, you would not learn a <CARMAKE> tag because no such tag exists. As soon as a Web site uses <CARMAKE>, however, the tag is defined and should be used in that context. As a Web designer, you will learn the standard XML tags being used for the type of Web site you are developing. Your XML tags then define data categories, not actual data specifics.

One problem at this time is that XML is too new for globally agreed upon definitions to exist. Even within industries, one company might create XML tags that differ greatly from another's. The move toward organization will come only as companies that support XML begin to agree on a standard and that standard grows. For example, if your company's Web site is to interact with a vendor's XML-based Web site, one of you must adopt the other's XML tags or you must put into place a combined system. This agreement process will continue and grow as more companies move to XML.

> For the first time, Web search engines can begin to search across industries for categories of items instead of performing time-consuming, tedious, and resource-grabbing searches for specific text embedded in Web pages. A search engine could scour Web page tags for the exact tag <ENGINEPARTNO> to locate specific engine parts for automobile manufacturers quickly, instead of wasting search time and resources scanning nonautomobile Web-site inventories.

HTML has a defined set of formatting and hyperlink tags, and you could very easily learn all of them. XML is defined as Web designers use it. You'll never learn all the XML tags, because new tags will continue to be developed as long as the language is in use.

Office and XML

You can select XML format when saving any Office program's data. When you do, Office converts that document from its native format, such as a Word document, to XML-readable code. If your company wants to publish a document on last year's sales, for example, on its Web site and you are assigned to write the report, your company's technical people might request that you save the document in XML format.

One reason to do so is that your company's Web developers can insert proper XML tags that label key pieces of your document. They might want to place industry-standard XML tags around your important inventory remarks, for instance, so that when XML-aware search engines, such as Google.com, scan your document, the search engines will better be able to place your company's Web-site documents in the proper search-results pages. Without XML, the search engines will have little way to file your site's documents properly except by exact word matching. Word matching does not always produce accurate results. XML tags, as described in the previous sections, allow your documents to become richer in content when viewed by other people and programs across the Web.

B

PART X

Bonus Hours

Hour

25 Using FrontPage 2003 for Web Page
   Design and Creation

26 Managing Your Web with FrontPage

HOUR **25**

Using FrontPage 2003 for Web Page Design and Creation

With FrontPage 2003, you can create and edit your own Web pages as well as manage your entire Web site. Although you can create Web pages with Word, Excel, Access, and PowerPoint, FrontPage takes your Web pages to a much higher level of performance and design than the other products can provide.

FrontPage 2003 works much like a word processor with advanced graphics-placement abilities for any Web pages you want to develop or edit. Not only can you create and edit your own Web pages, but you can edit Web pages of others that appear on the Internet. (You won't be able to put the edited content back on another's Web site, however, unless you have permission to do so.)

The highlights of this hour include

- How FrontPage hides the job of HTML coding from your Web-page designing job
- Where to store Web pages
- How to use FrontPage's tools to edit Web pages

- When and why you adjust the relationship between text and pictures so both go well together on the same area of the Web page

- How to add a background image or graphic pattern to the Web pages you create

Introduction to FrontPage 2003

FrontPage 2003 is a program that graphically enables you to edit Web pages. Behind all Web pages is *HTML, Hypertext Markup Language*. HTML is a language that contains commands to format the text, graphics, video, sound, and applets that you place on your Web page. Listing Web 1.1 shows a partial HTML listing of a Web page. As you can see, the HTML language can be cryptic.

LISTING WEB 1.1   HTML Commands Can Be Difficult to Decipher

```
<HTML>
<HEAD>
 <META HTTP-EQUIV="Content-Type" CONTENT="text/html" />
 <TITLE>Microsoft Corporation</TITLE>
 <META http-equiv="PICS-Label" content="(PICS-1.1 &quot;
  http://www.rsac.org/ratingsv01.html&quot; 1 gen true r
  (n 0 s 0 v 0 l 0))" />
<META NAME="KEYWORDS" CONTENT="products; headlines;
  downloads; news; Web site; what's new; solutions;
  services; software; contests; corporate news;" />
<META NAME="DESCRIPTION" CONTENT="The entry page to
 Microsoft's Web site. Find software, solutions, answers,
 support, and Microsoft news." />
<META NAME="CATEGORY" CONTENT="home page" />
<STYLE TYPE="text/css">
    A:link {color:#003399}
    A:visited {color:#800080}
    A:hover {color:#FF3300}
    TD {font-family: Verdana,Arial; font-size: xx-small;}
</STYLE>
<xml id="hpflyout">
<menu site="microsoft" subsite="Homepage">
</BODY>
</HTML>        'A.nodec:visited {color:#000000;text-decoration:
```

When you view a Web page, the computer serving the Web page to you sends you only the HTML commands, and your Web browser, such as Internet Explorer or Netscape Navigator, interprets the HTML codes and builds a Web page on your screen. The browser knows where to place, size, and format all the graphics, text, hyperlinks, and other elements such as buttons from the HTML code.

So an HTML page comes to your browser; your browser interprets the HTML formatting commands and displays the resulting Web page in a format useful for the person viewing the page. Figure Web 1.1 shows the resulting Web page from the full set of HTML commands contained in Listing Web 1.1, the home page of Microsoft. In other words, the figure is the result of the strange HTML language shown in Listing Web 1.1 (and Listing Web 1.1 shows only a part of the long HTML code that Microsoft.com's home page contains). The Web page, once your browser formats it by obeying the HTML codes, is easy to read and work with. The HTML is for the browser to interpret, not for the person viewing the Web page.

FIGURE WEB 1.1

Once your browser interprets all the HTML commands, the resulting Web page looks nice.

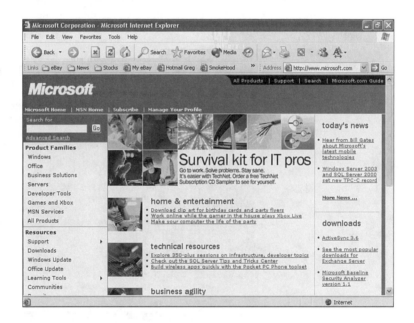

Before Web-page editors such as FrontPage, you'd have to master the HTML language before you could create or edit a Web page. Fortunately, FrontPage and other programs like it enable you to bypass HTML by putting a buffer between you and the underlying HTML code. If you want to draw a line or place a graphic image in a particular location on the Web page you're designing, you'll be able to drag that item onto the page with your mouse and with a little help from FrontPage.

25

To Do: Work in FrontPage

To start FrontPage 2003 and familiarize yourself with its interface, perform these steps:

1. Select the Start menu's Programs, Microsoft FrontPage menu option. FrontPage loads and displays a blank editing area.

2. Select File, Open, and a dialog box appears that enables you to select a file from your disk or from the Internet.

3. Type `http://www.informit.com` in the text box to inform FrontPage that you want to edit that site's Web page.

4. Click OK and FrontPage loads the Web page from the Internet. After a brief pause, depending on the speed of your Internet access, you'll see the Web page inside FrontPage's editing area, as shown in Figure Web 1.2. The four tabs at the bottom of the screen labeled Design, Split, Code, and Preview, show four different views of the Web page. The Web page appears similar to the way it looks in your browser to simplify editing. Use the scrollbars to see more of the Web page if you need to adjust the display.

FIGURE WEB 1.2

FrontPage 2003 works graphically with Web page content.

5. You can select File, Exit to close the Web page and leave FrontPage for now.

FrontPage enables you to edit Web pages located on your own PC or on the Web. The pages you view or edit don't have to reside on your PC as you saw here, but you can modify a Web site in place on the Internet. And unlike previous versions of FrontPage, with FrontPage 2003 you can work very easily with HTML and sophisticated features with advanced Web-page elements such as frames, tables, and imagemaps, all of which you'll learn more about as you master Web-page development.

FrontPage 2003 does not actually edit Web pages in place; the changes you make can reside only on your own PC unless you have server access to the Web page you change. For example, if you make changes to the Informit.com Web page you loaded, those changes will not take place on the actual Informit.com site. You must save your changes back to the Web page's server before the actual Web page is changed for all others to see. You will not have permission to change the Informit.com home page by saving it back to the Informit.com server, but using Informit.com works well as an example here.

Preparing for Web-Page Publishing

Before you can publish pages on the Web, you must have access to a W*eb server*. Perhaps your company uses a Web server for its site; if so, you can store your Web pages on that computer. If you have access to an online service, such as America Online, it might offer an area for one or more Web pages that you can copy to the online site's Web server. Many Internet service providers offer free but limited storage for their customers' Web pages.

If you want to publish a personal Web page for fun, you will enjoy telling the world your stories and sharing your family photos with others. If, however, you want to start a business on the Internet, or offer timely information that you want others to visit often, you need to be aware that Web-page *maintenance* is time-consuming. You don't just create a Web page, load the page on the Web, and expect to keep people's interest if you don't keep the material up-to-date. Use FrontPage's tools to maintain your Web pages and keep the viewers' interest.

FrontPage 2003 supports both the Internet and *intranets*. Intranets are networked computers that use Internet protocol, such as Web page technology, to communicate. Therefore, if your company maintains an intranet, you are able to create, edit, and save Web pages to that intranet as easily (and sometimes more easily) than on the Internet.

25

Working with FrontPage 2003

Two Web chapters are not nearly enough time to master FrontPage 2003, but you can gain a quick understanding of the product in this and the next Web hour and learn what's in store if you want to further your skills.

When you want to create a Web page, you can select File, New. You then have the option of creating a single Web page or a complete *Web site* (a collection of Web pages, the first of which is called the *home page*).

Figure Web 1.3 shows the many wizards and design templates that appear when you want to create a new Web page. These design options appear when you select File, New and then select One page Web site from the task pane. The resulting Web site you create does not have to remain a single page, but it begins as one. Some of the Web pages you can create are

- *One Page Web*—Creates a blank Web page
- *Corporate Presence Wizard*—Begins a step-by-step wizard that generates a Web-site structure for a large organization
- *Discussion Page Wizard*—Helps you create a Web page that enables users to chat back and forth in a bulletin-board text format
- *Customer Support Web*—A Web page designed for a Help support staff to help users of products and services
- *Database Interface Wizard*—A Web page that connects to Access and other types of databases so that you can manage and display database information over the Internet, such as an inventory or product-order system

FIGURE WEB 1.3
FrontPage 2003 offers several Web-page templates and wizards.

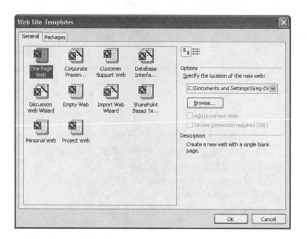

All Web pages you create with FrontPage contain basic HTML editing tags that enable the Web page to operate in an Internet browser. You can see the bare-bones minimum, HTML-based, blank Web page contents in Listing Web 1.2. These HTML commands form the basis of all Web pages. FrontPage adds even more HTML tags when you create a Web page. As you can see, many HTML commands, called *tags*, are enclosed in angled brackets. Often, a command begins with an opening tag (such as `<title>`) followed by a closing tag (such as `</title>`), indicated with a forward slash. Fortunately, you do not have to be a master of HTML specifics when you first begin learning FrontPage; you only need to be aware of them and be able to recognize what HTML is at this point.

LISTING WEB 1.2   All Web Pages Contain These Fundamental HTML Commands

```
<html>
  <head>
  </head>
  <body>
  </body>
</html>
```

Although HTML is rather simple compared to major programming languages such as C++, HTML is cryptic and you can already see that working in the graphical environment that FrontPage 2003 provides is much simpler than mastering HTML commands.

The initial tags shown in Listing Web 1.2 are only sufficient to define a blank Web page, and it's your job to fill in the page with text, graphics, and other elements. As you add these elements, FrontPage adds all the necessary HTML command tags that will produce the page you desire inside your users' Web browsers.

To Do: Create Your First Web Page

To get an idea of how simple it is to create Web pages with FrontPage 2003, and to see how much work FrontPage does behind your back that you don't have to, you can create a simple Web page from scratch to watch FrontPage in action.

Follow these steps to begin your Web page:

1. Select File, New to display the New Page or Web Site task pane.

2. Select Blank Page to generate a blank Web page. As Figure Web 1.4 shows, FrontPage begins in Design view and shows your blank page.

3. Click the Code button in the lower-left corner to select the Code view. You see that FrontPage shows any and all HTML code behind the blank page. Listing Web 1.3 shows this code that appears on your screen. Even though the Web page is still blank, HTML code is behind the page. FrontPage has added a few extra codes that go beyond the minimum shown in Listing Web 1.3, but basically the HTML is sparse because the Web page is still blank.

25

FIGURE WEB 1.4

FIGURE WEB 1.4

FrontPage begins in Design view.

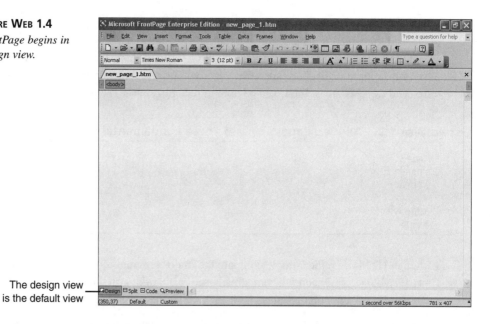

The design view is the default view

LISTING WEB 1.3 FrontPage Adds Some HTML Codes Automatically, but Your Blank Web Page Does Not Have Much HTML at This Time

```
<html>

<head>
<meta http-equiv="Content-Type" content="text/html;
 charset=windows-1252">
<title>New Page 1</title>
</head>

<body>

</body>

</html>
```

Although this seems like much discussion about HTML, the goal is to demonstrate that a few short years ago you had to write your own HTML code to generate a blank Web page, whereas FrontPage generates the code for you and makes things much easier. As you add text and more to this Web page between now and the rest of the chapter, you will better appreciate that FrontPage does so much for you.

Adding a Title to Your Web Page

This chapter continues introducing you to FrontPage by walking you through a sample Web page that you build. Unlike the other Office programs, FrontPage will make much more sense to you if you learn about FrontPage while you use it as you're doing now.

Click the Design View button once more to return to the blank Web page. Now, select File, Properties and click the Title field to enter a title. Type **My Home Page** in the field and click OK. This will make sure that My Home Page appears in the title bar of any user's Web browser that views your page later.

Select the Code tab to view the HTML window, and you'll see My Home Page between the <title> and </title> HTML command tags. You now know that the text between <title> and </title> displays in the Web browser's title bar at the top of the browser window when your Web page is viewed over the Internet. Without FrontPage, you would have typed this title inside the HTML tags.

The title is not the only property that the Properties dialog box can help you manage. If you select File, Properties once again and click the tabs to see the other dialog box property sheets, you'll find these tabbed sheets that help you quickly place Web page elements on your page:

- *Background*—Select an image or colors to form your Web page's background.
- *Margins*—Specify the top and left margins of your Web page.
- *Custom*—Advanced Web-page designers can create variables that hold content that is placed in the variables when the Web page is displayed on the Internet.

As you add to your Web page, watch your status bar at the bottom of the FrontPage window. FrontPage estimates the amount of time required, in seconds, for your Web page to load on an Internet user's PC using a 56Kbps modem connection. As you add elements to your Web page, the estimated download time will increase. You want your users to see your Web page as quickly as possible without sacrificing quality or attention-getting graphics and other Web-page components.

25

Web Pages Can Hold Many Kinds of Elements

FrontPage's menus and toolbars go a long way towards helping you create, edit, and add content to your Web pages. Figure Web 1.5 shows one set of FrontPage's options that appear when you select Insert, Web Component. You can add such items as an Excel worksheet to the Web page you are creating or editing.

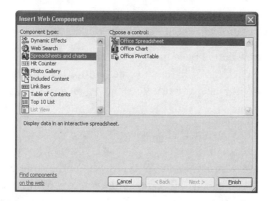

FIGURE WEB 1.5

Use the FrontPage tools to add special elements to your Web page.

To add one of the objects anywhere on your Web page, select the object and FrontPage places the object on the Web page. You then can drag the object to its proper location and size the control to the size you require. Unlike desktop-publishing programs and visual programming systems such as Visual Basic, FrontPage does not initially place the control in the center of the form but places the controls side-by-side as you choose them. You then can drag and resize them as needed.

The Insert, Form menu option produces a large set of items you can include on your Web page. Here is a description of each item that you can include:

- Form—A rectangular form that acts as a separate table on your Web page
- One-line text box—An area where the Internet user can type and edit information on the Web page
- Scrolling text box—A multiline text box the user can scroll left, right, up, or down to read the full contents (select Insert, Form, Text Area to locate the scrolling text box)
- Check box—An option the user can click to add (select) or remove (deselect) a check mark
- Radio button—An option the user can click to select or deselect the option; only one radio option button can be selected in a single page frame, not unlike the old car radios that allowed for only one radio station button to be pressed in at any one time
- Drop-down menu—A menu that opens from its one-line station on the Web page

- Push button (sometimes called a command button)—A button the user can click to trigger an action such as the playing of a sound clip

- Picture—A graphic image you want to place on the page

- Label—A text box into which you can place and format text, such as a title or instruction header

> FrontPage requires that you master some programming skills to operate command buttons and respond to the option selections properly. This text cannot go into the advanced processing required for more complex Web pages that include interactive applets and multimedia segments.

Without programming in HTML, you can place tables, graphics, and hyperlinks (links to other Web pages that the user can click to select) by clicking the Insert Table, Insert Graphic, and Create or Edit Hyperlink toolbar buttons that appear on the toolbar beneath the menu. More advanced Web-page components, such as animation and sound clips, still require that you master HTML.

To Do: Finish Your First Simple Web Page

The rest of this chapter takes you a little further in using FrontPage by adding some text and graphics to your Web page. Although the next Web chapter continues building your FrontPage skills, no advanced material is presented. There is no way to make you a Web-page master in 2 hours, even with a tool as powerful as FrontPage 2003, but you can get insight into what Web-page creation by working through examples, even simple ones.

Follow these steps to add more material to the Web page you created earlier:

1. To see how many of FrontPage's menus and toolbars work like those of the other Office products, type the following text in the Web page you're creating and then click the Bold toolbar button: The more books you read, the taller you grow!

2. Select the entire sentence you just typed and click the Center toolbar button and then the Bold button to center and format the text.

3. Select the text (if you don't still have it selected) and increase the font size by dropping the Font Size list and selecting 6 (24 pt). Click anywhere on the page to remove the selection from the text. Your screen should look like the one in Figure Web 1.6.

25

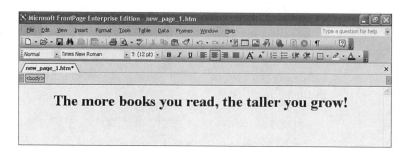

 Web pages don't allow as many font-size choices as Word documents and
Excel worksheets. You're limited to 7 sizes, as the Font Size toolbar drop-
down list shows. The actual sizes might change from computer to computer
when viewed in a Web browser because they are based on the target Web
browser's default font size.

4. Insert a horizontal line below the heading. To do this, click at the end of the heading's exclamation point to anchor the text cursor there and press Enter to move the
cursor to the next line. Select Insert, Horizontal Line. FrontPage places a horizontal
line below the heading.

5. Why not place a picture on the page? You can use the Office clip-art collection to
get the art. Select Insert, Picture, Clip Art. In the Search for text box, type **books**
and click Go. Several images will appear. Scroll down until you get to one you
like. If you see the Mother Goose character reading, select her by clicking on her
picture. Otherwise, pick a different one. When you select the picture, it appears in
the center of the Web page.

6. Leaving the text cursor to the right of the centered picture, type the following text
(don't worry about the length or how the text looks): Reading is a lifelong
pursuit because learning is a lifelong pursuit. Neither should end
when you finish school. As you type, the picture moves around to adjust itself.

7. Select all the text but not the figure.

8. Change the text size by selecting 6 (24 pt) from the toolbar.

9. Click the Left Align toolbar button.

10. Right-click over the picture and select Picture Properties. Click the large Left button (one of three buttons toward the top of the dialog box with the icon), and you'll
see the text adjust to the picture and look more planned than before, as Figure Web
1.7 shows. You've just instructed FrontPage to place the picture to the left of the

text instead of trying to take a position on the same line as the first line of the text. Your font might or might not look smoother than that in Figure Web 1.7, depending on your FrontPage default font setting.

Indicates the beginning of the Web page's body

FIGURE WEB 1.7
Your first Web page is looking better.

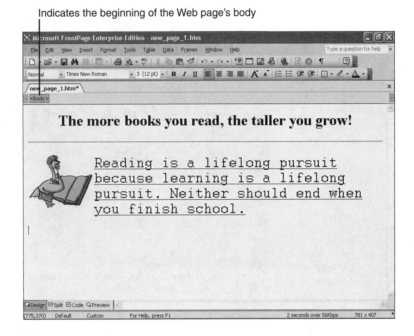

Different Views

NEW 2003 The `<body>` HTML command tag appearing toward the top of the page indicates the part of the Web page you're currently viewing. After you add elements such as graphics and text to your Web page, you can click over anything on your Web page and FrontPage will show the HTML tags for whatever you click on.

NEW 2003 To get an idea of the kind of HTML FrontPage has generated for you as you placed the picture and text, click the Split view button. As Figure Web 1.8 shows, this displays the HTML in the top window pane and your resulting Web page in the bottom. The Split view becomes helpful as you get more advanced and begin modifying some HTML code yourself.

25

You might wonder why much of this chapter has been discussing HTML along with FrontPage. A Web-page designer is never far away from HTML, and no matter how powerful FrontPage is, sometimes viewing the HTML code and making adjustments there is a needed skill. Although programs such as FrontPage make extensive HTML editing no longer necessary, HTML is the key to Web pages and understanding its presence is essential.

This HTML code...

FIGURE WEB 1.8

Your first Web page is looking better.

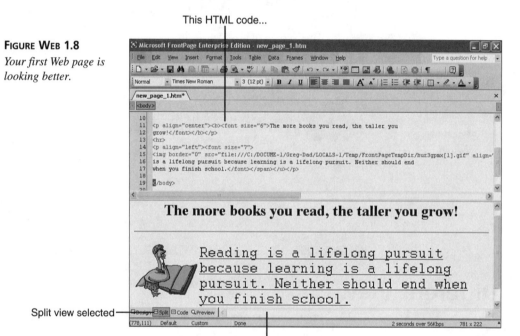

Split view selected

...produces this Web page

Adding a Background

There's time to learn one more FrontPage skill, and then you'll need to take a short break and start the next Web chapter to finish your FrontPage introduction.

FrontPage makes it easy to add a background to any Web page. Backgrounds can be a solid color or perhaps a pattern or picture, not unlike the background wallpaper that you can set for Windows.

Before adding a background to any Web page, keep in mind these two considerations:

- Backgrounds can add considerable time for a Web page to load. Keep an eye on the time gauge in FrontPage's lower-right corner. If a page takes too long to load, your Web audience will likely just move to a different Web site without waiting for yours to load.
- Backgrounds can make your Web page look far too busy. Always balance content and form so your page looks inviting and doesn't look too cluttered.

To add a background pattern, right-click anywhere on your Web page and select Page Properties from the pop-up menu. Click the Formatting tab and then click the Background picture option. You now can locate a picture on your computer or on your network server to place as a background on the page. You'll find some possibilities in your c:\Windows folder because that's where Window stores the desktop wallpaper samples. When you select a picture and close the dialog boxes, your Web page's formerly plain background now takes on a more finished look, as Figure Web 1.9 shows.

FIGURE WEB 1.9

The simple Web page is getting more complex with its background.

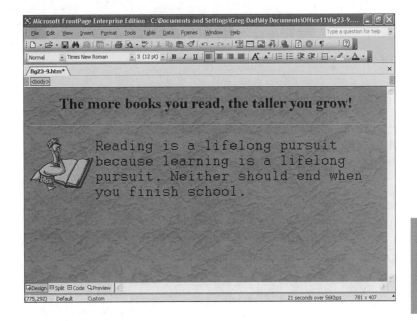

Please keep in mind that this chapter is flying through FrontPage options, and not only is there much more to learn, but there are a lot of features you don't have time to learn in one book. Nevertheless, the goal here is to give you an idea of how FrontPage works.

25

You must place any art that you end up using for a Web page on the same server computer as the rest of the Web page. If you've included a graphic file from your computer (as done here), other computers will probably be unable to view those figures over the Internet. Most Web developers create a folder named images to store all their Web picture files. As you learn more about Web-page creation, you'll learn more about the proper storage locations of items on your Web pages.

Summary

This chapter introduced you to FrontPage 2003. You now have some idea of what it takes to create and edit Web pages. Although much of FrontPage is simple to use, FrontPage is full of both simple and highly advanced features.

FrontPage makes it unnecessary to master HTML commands right away. The HTML language was the original formatting language of Web pages. Although all Web pages contain HTML code, programs such as FrontPage hide the underlying HTML code from you so that you can create simple and even fairly advanced Web pages from the graphical elements without working in HTML at all.

Q&A

Q How can users find my site?

A If you put a business on the Web, you certainly want to make it as easy as possible for users to locate your site. One of the best ways to do that is to register your site with search engines such as *Google* (www.google.com). The search-engine sites will include your site, indexed by keywords that you suggest, and you can contact any search engine for more information on how to get a high-ranked listing.

Q Do the FrontPage wizards and templates make Web-page development easier than starting from scratch?

A FrontPage's wizards and templates make creating Web pages *far* easier than starting from scratch. Although this chapter could have taught you to create your first Web page from a template or by using an Office wizard, you have a much better understanding of what is required to produce Web pages now that you have created a simple one from scratch. The next Web chapter quickly explains the process for creating Web pages from templates and the FrontPage wizards.

HOUR 26

Managing Your Web with FrontPage

There is so much you can do with FrontPage to create eye-catching Web sites. Although it would take a complete book just to teach FrontPage fundamentals, you already have a basic understanding of FrontPage from the other Web chapter lesson, and this chapter continues that tutorial by showing you more ways to update and create pages.

One of FrontPage's most powerful features that newcomers appreciate is its wide assortment of template and wizard-based Web pages and Web sites. By using these templates and wizards, you can quickly create a new site from a list of predesigned sites and then customize your site for your specific needs.

The highlights of this hour include

- How to include hyperlinks to other Web pages in your own Web pages
- When to use templates and wizards for Web design
- Why FrontPage's Navigation view is critical for understanding a Web site's structure
- What XML is designed to do
- Why Microsoft incorporated XML into the Office products

Hyperlinking to Other Web Pages

As your Web presence grows and you create more Web pages, some of your Web pages will refer to other Web pages. Part of the reason HTML grew so popular so quickly, and part of the reason early Web-page designers chose HTML as the engine behind the pages, is that HTML provides a vehicle for hyperlinks to other Web pages. The Web-browsing viewers can view one Web page, go to another simply by clicking a hyperlink, and then press the browser's Back button and go right back to where they started.

To Do: Add a Link to a Web Page

Inserting a hyperlink in a FrontPage Web page is as simple as doing so in Word and other Office 2003 programs. You saw how to add a hyperlink to PowerPoint presentations in Hour 14, "Animating Your Presentations." To add a link to the Web page you created in the previous Web hour, you would follow these steps:

1. Click at the end of the last word you typed, `school`. This places the text cursor at the end of the sentence.

2. Press Enter twice to place two blank lines at the end of the text.

3. Type the following: `Click here for great books!`

4. Select the sentence you just typed.

5. Select Insert, Hyperlink from the menu. The Insert Hyperlink will appear.

6. In the text box to the right of the Address label toward the bottom of the dialog box, type this Web address: `http://www.samspublishing.com`.

7. Click OK.

8. Click anywhere on the page to eliminate the selection of the text. The text will be underlined and appear in a different color to indicate that the text is now a link to another Web page. Figure Web 2.1 shows what your Web page looks like now.

If you click the link, nothing will happen except the FrontPage will display a message telling you that you must click your Ctrl key and the link to move to that page. This is because you're editing the page in the Design view. If you were to display the page in Preview mode, you only need to click the hyperlink with your mouse to see the linked Web page. Obviously, once your Web page is placed on your server, all visitors to your Web page will be able to jump to the link by clicking on the text without having to hold their Ctrl keys when they do.

FIGURE WEB 2.1

*The page now links to
another Web page.*

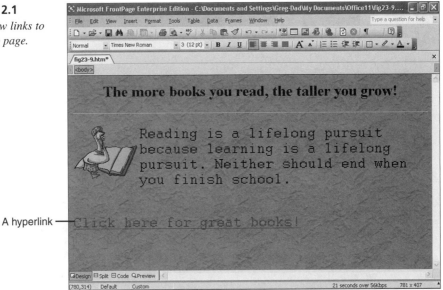

A hyperlink

One very good question often asked about now is, "How do I get my Web
page onto the actual Web?" The way you do it depends on many factors. If
you work on Web pages inside a company that has a Web site, your company's Web-site expert can help you get your page onto the site. If you want
your own domain name (your own .com name), you'll need to find one that
is currently not being used (which is not always a simple task), rent the
name, and then have a Web-hosting service connect that new domain name
to your Web pages that you store on the host's server. If all this sounds
tedious, it is; fortunately, you can locate many services that act as one-stop
locations where you can get set up from scratch. Search one of the Internet
search engines for *web hosting*, and you'll find many companies who can
help you.

Save your Web page and close the page so you can begin a new Web page in the next
section.

26

To Do: Use a FrontPage Wizard to Create a Web Page

Instead of designing a Web page from scratch, now that you've seen the basics of Web-page creation, you are ready to accept more help from FrontPage. Using FrontPage's wizards and templates enables you to generate a predesigned page or complete site (with a collection of similar pages) that you can edit to suit your specific needs.

Therefore, to get some experience in creating a Web page using a FrontPage wizard, the next few steps walk you through the initial creation of a simple Web page using one of FrontPage's Web-page wizards.

1. Select File, New to open the New Page or Web Site task pane.
2. Select Web Package Solutions to display the Web Site Templates dialog box shown in Figure Web 2.2. Some of these entries are templates for Web sites where you will type in placeholders for text, graphics, and headers, whereas other entries are wizards that walk you through a step-by-step query process that builds the Web site based on your answers.

FIGURE WEB 2.2

Creating a Web site with a template or a wizard.

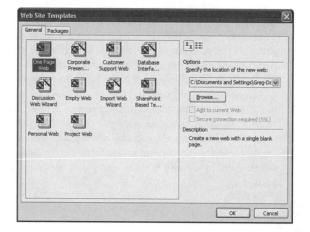

 The icons that show a wand with stars around it are icons that represent wizards, and the rest are templates.

3. Select the Corporate Presence Wizard to start the wizard that creates a simple Web site for a business. FrontPage displays the wizard's opening window shown in Figure Web 2.3.

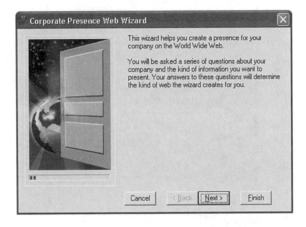

4. Click Next and the wizard will offer a list of Web content choices that you can put on the site you are creating. Keep in mind that the wizard is creating a general Web page set, not just a single home page.

5. Click Next to determine the items you want on your home page.

6. Click Next to determine the items you want to appear on your remaining pages.

7. Keep clicking Next and answer the prompts. Eventually, the wizard prompts you for your company name, address, and other demographic information.

8. When you finish the wizard, FrontPage 2003 follows the wizard's instructions and produces the site's Web pages that you specified. A table summarizes each page in the site. Appearing in the left-hand column of your screen is a list of files that compose the site. Double-click the page named index.htm, and you will see the home page that you can change and add graphics and text that fill your specific needs. All Web-site home pages are named either index.htm or index.html.

One of the most helpful views you can show for a multipage Web site is the Navigation view, obtained by selecting View, Navigation. As Figure Web 2.4 shows, the Navigation view shows the hierarchical structure of your complete Web site beginning with the home page. The full structure probably will be too large to fit in the window so use the scrollbars to scroll left and right to see the full navigation of the site.

26

FIGURE WEB 2.4

The Navigation view shows the structure of your Web site's pages.

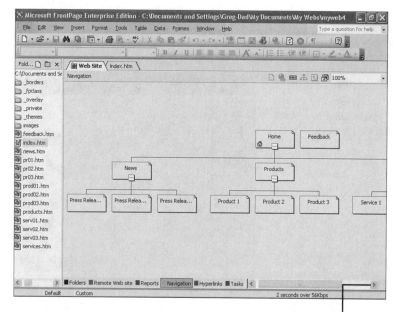

Click here to scroll

Scroll through your new home page to see the elements on it. You can add text boxes, check boxes, and options to the page; rearrange elements of the page; and add graphics and other elements. You can select the HTML view tab to see the HTML code that you might want to edit as well.

Publishing Your Web Page

Once you finalize your Web page with FrontPage, FrontPage can help you publish your page on the Web or on your local network server as an intranet using the Web Publishing Wizard. The wizard translates your Web page from the FrontPage format to HTML format to be compatible with Web browsers.

To start the wizard, select File, Publish Site. The wizard begins and collects information that your Internet provider needs about your Web pages and sends that information, along with your Web pages, to your provider. (You'll need proper Internet access and a browser to use the wizard.) Once you complete the wizard, your Web page should be available for use.

Although the Web Publishing Wizard helps gather information and makes publishing your Web page simpler than would otherwise be the case, you still might have to contact your Internet provider (the provider sponsoring your Web page) to determine some of the answers to the Web Publishing Wizard's questions. For example, you'll need to tell the wizard the URL where your Web page will reside and the type of provider you use.

To use some of the sophisticated Web-management tools included with FrontPage, the server that hosts your site will need to install the proper FrontPage Web-server extensions. In other words, your Internet service provider's Web server must be equipped with FrontPage extensions for you to take full advantage of FrontPage's Web-management capabilities. Most if not all of today's Web-hosting companies provide these extensions automatically due to the popularity of FrontPage.

Introduction to XML

XML is a term that stands for *Extensible Markup Language*. As you might guess from its name, XML is closely tied to HTML, and both look very similar. As a matter of fact, all XML code resides inside HTML code, so without HTML, XML would not be possible.

Although the version of Office that preceded Office 2003 (Office XP) offered some support for XML, that support was limited. Even XML support inside of Office 2003 is still not as complete as some would prefer, but Microsoft has made it clear that XML support will certainly be with Office for the foreseeable future.

Although XML is not strictly a part of FrontPage 2003 but rather part of all the Office 2003 products, introducing you to XML makes sense here in the FrontPage chapters because it was in the Web chapters that you learned about HTML.

HTML is a set of specific commands, known as *command tags*, as you learned in the previous chapter, whereas XML is a set of command tags that each user can create and work with.

26

Strictly speaking, XML commands are not called "command tags," but for now that's the best way of viewing them. They're always enclosed in angled brackets, such as <PartNo>, just as HTML tags are.

XML and Its Impact

How important is XML? Almost four years ago, the Gartner Group, an Internet research company, said that 80% of business-to-business (also known as *B2B*) traffic used XML. XML is much like HTML and in some ways is identical.

The author of XML code can define and use, on-the-fly, brand new command tags that are also available to other Web pages. In defining new XML command tags, you use the extensible portion of XML.

Whereas HTML describes the *format* of a Web page, XML describes the *content* of a Web page. XML does more than just tell the Web browser where and how to place Web page elements.

Consider the following possible XML section from a Web page:

```
<CARMAKE>Swifty</CARMAKE>
<CARMODEL>Dove</CARMODEL>
<ENGINEPARTNO>546-32Xs</ENGINEPARTNO>
<WHOLESALE>$21,039</WHOLESALE>
<SUGGESTEDRETAIL>$32,483</SUGGESTEDRETAIL>
```

Over time, industries will begin to standardize their XML tags. Therefore, <ENGINEPARTNO> might be standardized by automobile Web-site designers to designate any automobile manufacturer's engine part number. As other automobile Web developers standardize and use <ENGINEPARTNO> (and its corresponding ending tag of </ENGINEPARTNO>), Web pages can be combined, borrowed, and used as the basis of other Web pages that also contain such parts.

When learning XML, you would not learn a <CARMAKE> tag because no such tag exists. As soon as a Web site uses <CARMAKE>, however, the tag is defined and should be used in that context. As a Web designer, you will learn the standard XML tags being used for the type of Web site you are developing. Your XML tags then define data categories, not actual data specifics.

One problem at this time is that XML is too new for globally agreed upon definitions to exist. Even within industries, one company might create XML tags that differ greatly from another's. The move toward organization will come only as companies that support

XML begin to agree on a standard and that standard grows. For example, if your company's Web site is to interact with a vendor's XML-based Web site, one of you must adopt the other's XML tags or you must put into place a combined system. This agreement process will continue and grow as more companies move to XML.

> For the first time, Web search engines can begin to search across industries for categories of items instead of performing time-consuming, tedious, and resource-grabbing searches for specific text embedded in Web pages. A search engine could scour Web page tags for the exact tag <ENGINEPARTNO> to locate specific engine parts for automobile manufacturers quickly instead of wasting search time and resources scanning nonautomobile Web-site inventories.

HTML has a defined set of formatting and hyperlink tags, and you could very easily learn all of them. XML is defined as Web designers use it. You'll never learn all the XML tags, because new tags will continue to be developed as long as the language is in use.

Office and XML

You can select XML format when saving any Office program's data. When you do, Office converts that document from its native format, such as a Word document, to XML-readable code. If your company wants to publish a document on last year's sales, for example, on its Web site and you are assigned to write the report, your company's technical people might request that you save the document in XML format.

One reason to do so is that your company's Web developers can insert proper XML tags that label key pieces of your document. They might want to place industry-standard XML tags around your important inventory remarks, for instance, so that when XML-aware search engines, such as Google.com, scan your document, the search engines will better be able to place your company's Web-site documents in the proper search-results pages. Without XML, the search engines will have little way to file your site's documents properly except by exact word matching. Word matching does not always produce accurate results. XML tags, as described in the previous sections, allow your documents to become richer in content when viewed by other people and programs across the Web.

26

Summary

This hour extended your FrontPage 2003 tutorial to add hyperlinks to your Web pages. Even though FrontPage 2003 is simple to use for creating brand new Web pages, you can use FrontPage's wizards and templates to create predesigned Web pages and sites and then edit those pages to add your own graphics and other components to the page. By integrating XML into the Office 2003 programs, Microsoft has assured that the documents and data you create will be more accessible to the rest of the Internet. Many search engines scan XML-based documents more accurately than documents of other formats, including standard text documents.

Q&A

Q Can you tell me exactly how I can use XML today to improve my Web sites?

A To put it bluntly, no. XML is actually an evolving set of tag-like commands that industries are developing and standardizing upon still and will be for a long time. For now, it's important that you understand the overview of XML and that it enables HTML-like tags to describe your data, not just format your data. Later, when another program or Web site scans your documents and Web sites that contain XML, those sites will be better able to automatically understand the type of content your site and documents hold and don't have to base their assumptions on perfect keyword matches, which is error-prone at best.

Q Should I host my own site?

A If you have a high-speed Internet connection, a very fast second computer that you don't need to use exclusively, and an Internet connection that is set up with a fixed *IP address (Internet Protocol address)* so when you link a .com domain to your location, that location won't change, you can host your own Web site, as well as charge others to host theirs. But really your work has just begun. You must be completely on top of backing up the server constantly or you could very easily lose your (and your clients') Web data due to an electrical problem (rare) or a hacker attack (less rare). You must constantly update your security to have the latest security patches so the latest hacker breaches don't successfully enter your server's files from somewhere else in the world. You'll need to understand networking protocols deeper than you think you do as well.

If you're willing to devote the time and resources just described, sure you can host your own site. Many people do just that. Nevertheless, the majority of Web-site owners like the freedom of paying a hosting service a monthly fee and let them handle the hosting headaches. You can then concentrate on what is truly important, and that is the content that you place into your Web site's pages.

INDEX

Symbols

' (apostrophe), Excel worksheets, 111
* (asterisk), 128, 296
, (comma), Excel, 118
$ (dollar sign), relative cell referencing, 131
= (equal sign), Excel formulas, 128
/ (forward slash), 313
(pound sign), 141, 313

A

Abs() function, 137
absolute cell referencing, Excel formulas, 130-131
Access, 8, 283
    asterisk (*), 296
    AutoNumber, 296
    currency fields, 298

data retrieval
    filters, 310-313
    queries, 313-323
Database window, 284
databases, 278
    creating, 284-285
    data types, 280-281
    fields, 280-281,
        287-288
    index fields, 282
    objects, 284-285
    primary key fields,
        281-282, 288
    records, 280-281
    tables, 279-280,
        285-293
dates, entering, 298
filters, 313
overview, 16-17
records, removing. *See* filters
relational operators, 322
reports
    generating, 327-332
    layout, 335-336

naming, 328
printing, 326-328
report summaries,
  332-335
sorting, 334-335
styles, 335-336
shortcut menus, 299
tables
  data entry, 296-297,
    301
  data formatting,
    Datasheet view,
    297-299
  data modification,
    Datasheet view,
    299-300
  fields, hiding/showing,
    299
  fonts, 300
  forms, 302-306
  loading in Word,
    401-402
  navigating, 300
  printing, 301
  records, sorting, 299
  records/fields, deleting,
    299
times, entering, 298
viewing in Outlook,
  244-245
Web pages, creating,
  359-360
accessibility features, 23-24
accessing Web pages, 342
**Accounting format (Excel
worksheets), 142**
accounts
  email (Outlook), 247-250
  Microsoft Passport, 246
**action buttons (PowerPoint),
231-233**

**Action Buttons command
(Slide Show menu), 231**
**Action Settings command
(Slide Show menu), 231**
**Action Settings dialog box,
204**
Actions menu commands
  New All Day Event, 265
  New Journal Entry, 270
  New Letter to Contact,
    402
  New Recurring
    Appointment, 262
active cells, Excel, 114
ActiveX controls, 344
Add Files button, 222
**Add to Dictionary option
(Spelling dialog box), 73**
addresses, IP, 352
**Advance Slides option (Set
Up Show dialog box), 229**
Advanced Filter/Sort, 310
**alarms, appointments
(Outlook), 264**
Align Left button, 53
Align Right button, 53
aligning tabs (Word), 55
**alignment, Excel work-
sheets, 165-166**
Alignment tab, 165
**All Day Event check box,
265**
**anchor points, ranges
(Excel), 126**
**And conditions, Access fil-
ters, 313**
**Animate! option (Office
Assistant), 21**
**animation, PowerPoint slide
shows, 233-235**
**apostrophe ('), Excel work-
sheets, 111**

applications, data sharing
  drag-and-drop, 394
  hyperlinks, 399-400
  links, 395-397
  shortcuts, 397-399
**Apply to All Slides button,
227**
**Apply to Selected Slide
option, 213**
**Appointment dialog box,
261**
**Appointment Recurrence
dialog box, 262**
**appointments, scheduling
(Outlook), 261-264**
Area chart (Excel), 173
**arguments, Excel functions,
134**
arrows, toolbar options, 32
asterisk (*), 128, 296
attachments
  email (Outlook), 250
  files, sending as, 403
audio. *See* sound
AutoComplete, 23, 406
**AutoContent Wizard,
188-191**
AutoCorrect, 43-44, 297
  Cut/Copy/Paste, 148-149
  data, clearing, 149
  search-and-replace,
    146-148
  symbols, adding, 84
**AutoCorrect command
(Tools menu), 43-44, 146,
272, 399**
AutoCorrect dialog box, 44
**AutoCorrect option
(Spelling dialog box), 73**
AutoFill, 152-153
**AutoFill Options button,
133**

AutoFill series (Excel work-sheets), 156
autoflow, Publisher, 380
AutoFormat (Excel), 113, 118
AutoFormat as You Type tab, 44, 399
AutoFormat command (Format menu), 118, 162
AutoFormat dialog box, 118, 162
AutoFormatting, 43, 161-162
Automatic Bulleted Lists check box, 51
automatic hyphenation
    turning off, 375
    Word, 69, 75-76
Automatic Numbered Lists check box, 51
Automatically Use Suggestions from the Spelling Checker option (AutoCorrect), 43
AutoNumber, 282, 296
AutoReports, 327, 329
AutoReport: Columnar, 330
AutoReport: Tabular, 330
AutoShapes tool, 385
AutoSum, 135-136
AutoText command (Insert menu), 88
AutoText entries, 23, 88-89
AutoText tab, 88
Average() function, 134, 137
Avery numbering system, 330

B

background images, Excel charts, 178-180
backgrounds, adding (Web pages), 425, 431-432
banners, Outlook events, 266
Bar chart (Excel), 173
bars (Outlook), expanding, 268
Bcc (blind carbon copy), email, 250
Between keyword, 323
blind carbon copy (Bcc), email, 250
blue dotted lines, 70
boilerplate text. See AutoText entries
Bold button, 48
boldface formatting (Word), 48
books, eBooks (Word), 31
border art (publications), creating, 390
Border dialog box, 167
Border tab, 166
BorderArt dialog box, 389
borders
    adding (publications), 389-390
    cells (Excel worksheets), 166-167
boxes, Style, 60. See also check boxes; dialog boxes; text boxes
Brochure Wizard, 63
browsers (Web), Excel, 344
Bubble chart (Excel), 173
bulleted lists (Word), insert-ing, 51-52
Bullets and Numbering command (Format menu), 52
Bullets button, 52
business cards, creating (Publisher), 370
Business Contact Manager, 409-410
buttons
    action (PowerPoint), 231-233
    Add Files, 222
    Align Left, 53
    Align Right, 53
    Apply to All Slides, 227
    AutoFill Options, 133
    Bold, 48
    Bullets, 52
    Calendar, 258
    Center, 53
    Change Quality, 230
    Chart Type, 180
    Collapse Dialog, 174
    Comma Style, 118
    command, Web pages (FrontPage), 427
    Copy, 38
    Copy to Folder, 223
    Custom Dictionaries, 72
    Cut, 39
    Decrease Font Size, 204
    Decrease Indent, 52
    Display Map of Address, 255
    Draw Borders, 167
    Expand Dialog, 174
    Font Color, 49
    Format Painter, 61
    Full Name, 252
    Highlight, 50

Increase Font Size, 204
Increase Indent, 52
Insert Function, 138
Invite Attendees, 264
Italic, 48
Justify, 53
Legend, 180
Merge and Center, 140
Modify, 164
Multiple Pages, 61
New Contact, 251
New Note, 267
New Record, 306
New Slide, 193, 200
New Style, 60
New Task, 266
Note Options, 267
Numbering, 51
Paste, 38
Paste Options, 38
Primary key, 288
Publish, 360
Recount, 69
Recurrence, 262
Redo, 45
Select Picture, 179
Set Microphone Level, 230
Shortcut Key, 84
Show Toolbar, 69
Slide Design, 212
Start Reading, 31
Switch Between Header and Footer, 95
Symbol, 97
Tables and Borders, 92
Tabs, 54
Text box, 217
toolbars, 23
Transition, 205
Underline, 48

C

calculating Excel worksheets, 133
Calculation tab, 134
Calendar (Outlook), 242
    appointment scheduling, 261-264
    Daily Scheduler, 258
    Date Navigator, 258-259
    dates/times, 258-261
    event scheduling, 265-266
    meeting scheduling, 264-265
    tasks, 266-267
Calendar button, 258
camera images, inserting
    PowerPoint, 221
    Word, 87
Caption property (Access database fields), 287
CDs, saving PowerPoint presentations to, 222
cell pointers (Excel worksheets), 108
cell reference (Excel worksheets), 108, 130-131
cells (Excel), 108. *See also* ranges
    active, 114
    borders, 166-167
    comments, adding, 157-158
    correcting mistakes, 123
    editing 123
    inserting, 123-124
    moving, 124
    relative cell referencing, 117
    selecting, 122
    shading, 167

Cells command (Format menu), 141-142, 165
Cells command (Insert menu), 124
Center button, 53
center justifying text (Word), 53
Change All option (Spelling dialog box), 73
Change option (Spelling dialog box), 73
Change Quality button, 230
character formatting (Word), 48-51
characters
    leader, 55
    special (Word), inserting, 84-85
Chart toolbar, 180
Chart Type button, 180
Chart Wizard, 330
    chart type, choosing, 172-173
    charts, modifying, 176-177
    data series, choosing, 173, 176
    data tables, 174
    labels, 175
    legends, 174
Chart Wizard dialog box, 172
charts (Excel)
    background images, 178-180
    creating, 177-178
    data series, choosing, 173, 176
    data tables, 174
    legends, 174-175
    modifying, 176-177
    types, choosing, 172-173

Check Address dialog box,
252
check boxes
   All Day Event, 265
   Automatic Bulleted Lists,
    51
   Automatic Numbered
    Lists, 51
   Check Grammar as You
    Type, 70, 73
   Check Spelling As You
    Type, 70
   Different Odd and Even or
    Different First Page, 96
   Keep Lines Together, 59
   On Mouse Click, 226
   Reminder, 262
   Show AutoComplete, 89
   Suppress Line Numbers,
    59
   Use Hardware Graphics
    Acceleration, 229
Check Full Name dialog
box, 252
Check Grammar as You
Type check box, 70, 73
Check Spelling as You Type
check box, 70
checking spelling, 297, 375
Choose Assistant option
(Office Assistant), 21
Clear command (Edit
menu), 150
clearing data, Excel work-
sheets, 149
clip art
   downloading (Web), 346
   inserting (Word), 86-87
Clip Art task pane, 86, 382
Clipboard, 38, 148
Clippit, 19
Code view, 423

code. *See* **syntax**
Collapse Dialog button, 174
color
   applying (Word), 49-51
   tabs, Excel worksheets,
    168
color schemes, publications,
372
Column chart (Excel), 173
columns
   Excel worksheets
    deleting, 124-125
    formatting, 140-141
    inserting, 124
   text boxes, adding (publi-
    cations), 378
   Word tables, 92-95
Columns command (Format
menu), 93
Columns command (Insert
menu), 124
Columns dialog box, 93, 378
comma (,), Excel, 118
Comma Style button, 118
command buttons, Web
pages (FrontPage), 427
commands
   Action menu
    New All Day Event,
     265
    New Letter to Contact,
     402
    New Journal Entry, 270
    New Recurring
     Appointment, 262
   Edit menu
    Clear, 150
    Copy, 38, 377
    Cut, 39, 125
    Delete, 125, 150
    Fill, 152
    Fill, Series, 155

    Find, 40, 146
    Go To, 35
    Links, 396
    Paste, 38, 117, 377
    Replace, 41
    Undo, 45
   File menu
    Exit, 420
    New, Mail Message,
     248
    New, Task, 266
    Package for CD, 222
    Page Setup, Layout, 96
    Picture, From Scanner
     or Camera, 88
    Print, 207, 301, 306
    Print Preview, 61, 208,
     301
    Properties, 68, 425
    Publish Site, 438
    Save, 107
    Save As Web Page,
     354
    Web Page Preview, 354
   Format menu
    AutoFormat, 118, 162
    Bullets and
     Numbering, 52
    Cells, 141-142, 165
    Columns, 93
    Font, 49, 203, 218,
     300, 375
    Paragraph, 55-57
    Style, 163
    Style, Formatting, 60
    Theme, 357
    Unhide Columns, 299
   Help menu
    Microsoft Publisher
     Help, 373
    Show Office Assistant,
     21

HTML, Web pages, 423
Insert menu
    AutoText, 88
    Cells, 124
    Columns, 124
    Comment, 157, 217
    Date and Time, 85
    Form, 426-427
    Functions, 138
    Hyperlink, 434
    Page Numbers, 85
    Picture, Clip Art, 86,
        382, 428
    Picture, From File, 86,
        221, 383
    Picture, From Scanner
        or Camera, 221, 383
    Reference, Footnote,
        97
    Rows, 124
    Slide, 200
    Symbol, 84
    Text File, 377
    Web Components, 426
Query menu, Show Table,
    322
Records menu, Filter, 310
Slide Show menu
    Action Buttons, 231
    Action Settings, 231
    Record Narration, 230
    Slide Transition, 226
Table menu
    Insert, Table, 89
    Select, 92
    Table AutoFormat, 92
Tools menu
    AutoCorrect, 43-44,
        146, 272, 399
    Customize, 78
    Customize, Options, 11
    Design Checker, 387

E-Mail Accounts, 247
Language,
    Hyphenation, 75, 375
Language, Thesaurus,
    77
Letters and Mailings,
    99
Options, Spelling &
    Grammar, 70, 73
Options, View, 34
Send/Receive, 249
Spelling, 297, 375
Word Count, 69
View menu
    Full Screen, 62
    Header and Footer, 95
    Master, Slide Master,
        216
    Notes Page, 206
    Task Pane, 38
    Toolbars, 78
    Toolbars, Chart, 180
    Toolbars, Customize,
        32
    Toolbars, Database,
        401
    Toolbars, Drawing, 217
    Toolbars, Outlining,
        201
    Toolbars, Web, 342,
        358
Commands tab, 78
Comment command (Insert
    menu), 157, 217
comments
    adding (Excel), 157-158
    slides (PowerPoint), 217
Compatibility option
    (Options dialog box), 79
conditional formatting,
    Excel worksheets, 168
Conditional Formatting dia-

log box, 168
conditions, And/Or, 313
Cone chart (Excel), 173
Contact dialog box, 251-252
Contacts (Outlook), 243
    displaying, 249
    recording, 251-254
    selecting, 254-255
Contents option (Properties
    dialog box), 68
Convert to Number option
    (Excel worksheets), 112
converting
    data to XML, 413, 441
    Word files into presenta-
        tions, 400-401
Copy button, 38
Copy command (Edit
    menu), 38, 377
Copy to Folder button, 223
Corporate Presence Wizard,
    422, 437
corrections, grammar, 45
Count() function, 137
CountBlank() function, 137
crash-recovery features, 23
cropping images, publica-
    tions, 384
Crosstab Query Wizard,
    314
currency fields (Access), 298
Currency format (Excel
    worksheets), 142
Custom Dictionaries button,
    72
Custom format (Excel
    worksheets), 142
custom lists, creating (Excel
    worksheets), 154-155
Custom Lists tab, 154
Custom Mark text box, 97
Custom option (Properties

dialog box), 68
customizations (Word),
    78-80
Customize command (Tools
    menu), 78
Customize dialog box, 23,
    78-79
Customize, Options com-
    mand (Tools menu), 11
customizing
    Office Assistant, 20-22
    toolbars, 23
Cut button, 39
Cut command (Edit menu),
    39, 125
cutting
    data, Excel worksheets,
        148-149
    Word text, 38-39
Cylinder chart (Excel), 173
Daily Scheduler (Outlook),
    258

D

data
    converting to XML, 413,
        441
    Cut/Copy/Paste (Excel
        worksheets), 148-149
    search-and-replace
        (Excel), 146-148
data entry, Access tables
    databases, 291-293
    Datasheet view, 296-297
    forms, 296, 301
data fills, Excel worksheets,
    151-152
data filters. See filters
    (Access)
data formatting, Access
    tables, 297-299
Data Labels tab, 175
data modification, Access
    tables
    Datasheet view, 299-300
    forms, 306
data retrieval (Access)
    filters, 310-313
    queries, 313
        creating, 314-323
        display results, 317
        dynasets, 314
        naming, 314
        sorting subsets, 321
        synchronizing, 317
data series, choosing (Excel
    charts), 173, 176
data sharing
    between Word and Excel,
        401
    drag-and-drop, 394
    hyperlinks, 399-400
    links, 395-397
    Outlook, writing Word let-
        ters, 402-403
    shortcuts, 397-399
data source, Mail Merge
    (Word), 98
data tables, Excel charts,
    174
data types, Access databas-
    es, 280-281
Database dialog box, 401
Database Interface Wizard,
    422
database management sys-
tems. See Access
Database window (Access),
    284
databases
    Northwind Traders,
        310-311
    relational database sys-
        tems. See Access
    relational versus flat-file,
        279
databases (Access), 278
    creating, 284-285
    data types, 280-281
    fields, 280-288
    index fields, 282
    objects, 284-285
    primary key fields,
        281-282, 288
    records, 280-281
    tables, 279-280
        creating, 285-286
        data entry, 291-293
        design, 291-293
        fields, 289-291
        modifying structure,
            289
        saving, 288
Datasheet form, 304
Datasheet view, 291-292
    data entry, 296-297
    data formatting, 297-299
    data modification, 299-300
    table navigation, 300
    tables, printing, 301
Date and Time command
    (Insert menu), 85
Date format (Excel work-
    sheets), 142
Date Navigator (Outlook),
    258-259
Date series (Excel work-

sheets), 156
dates
    Calendar (Outlook),
        258-261
    entering
        Access, 298
        Excel worksheets,
            113-114
        Word, 85
**Decimal Places property
    (Access database fields),
    287**
**Decrease Font Size button,
    204**
Decrease Indent button, 52
**Default Value property
    (Access database fields),
    287**
**Delete command (Edit
    menu), 125, 150**
Delete dialog box, 125, 150
demoting elements,
    PowerPoint outlines, 201
design, tables (Access data-
    bases), 291-293
**Design Checker (Publisher),
    387-388**
**Design Checker command
    (Tools menu), 387**
**Design Gallery (Publisher),
    385-387**
design sets (Publisher), 369
design templates
    (PowerPoint), 192-194
Design view, 329
designing PowerPoint pre-
    sentations, 212-214
destination files, 394-396
dialog boxes
    Action Settings, 204
    Appointment Recurrence,
        262

Appointment, 261
AutoCorrect, 44
AutoFormat, 118, 162
Border, 167
BorderArt, 389
Chart Wizard, 172
Check Address, 252
Check Full Name, 252
Columns, 93, 378
Conditional Formatting,
    168
Contact, 251-252
Customize, 23, 78-79
Database, 401
Delete, 125, 150
E-mail Accounts, 247
Edit Hyperlink, 400
Event, 265
File New Database, 284
Fill Effects, 179
Find and Replace, 35,
    40-43, 146
Font, 49, 141
Footnote and Endnote, 97
Format Cells, 143,
    164-165
Format Chart Title, 176
Format Object, 394
Format Picture, 389
Format Text Box, 378
Go To, 114
Help, 20
Hyphenation, 76, 375
Insert, 124
Insert File, 250
Insert Function, 138
Insert Hyperlink, 400, 434
Insert Picture, 86
Insert Table, 89
Journal Options, 269
Links, 396
Message, 248

New Call, 254
New Form, 302
New Office Document, 18
New Query, 315, 318
New Report, 329-330
Options, 79-80
Page Numbers, 85
Page Setup, 53, 57
Paragraph, 55
Print, 207
Properties, 68
Publish as Web Page, 360
Record Narration, 230
Series, 155-156
Set Up Show, 228-229
Show Table, 318-319
Spelling, 72-73
Style, 163
Summary, 333
Symbol, 84
Tabs, 54-55
Theme, 64
Web Site Templates, 436
Zoom, 62
**dictionaries, removing
    words, 72**
**Different Odd and Even or
    Different First Page check
    box, 96**
digital camera images,
    adding
    PowerPoint slides, 221
    Word, 87
**Display Map of Address
    button, 255**
dissolving transitions,
    PowerPoint slide shows,
    227
**Discussion Page Wizard,
    422**
DLLs (Dynamic Link

Libraries), 344
documents (Word). *See also*
    worksheets
    creating, 33
    destination, 394-396
    extensions, 33
    main documents, Mail
        Merge, 98
    multiple, editing, 34
    navigating, 35-36
    properties, 68-69
    saving, 33
    sending as attachments,
        403
    sending as email, 347-348
    source, 394-396
    tables
        columns, 92-95
        creating, 89-91
        drawing, 92-93
        inserting, 89
        rows, inserting, 92
        traversing, 91-92
    viewing in Internet
        Explorer, 342-344
dollar sign ($), relative cell
    referencing, 131
Doughnut chart (Excel), 173
downloading Web elements,
    345-346, 425
drag-and-drop
    sharing data between
        applications, 394
    Word text, 39
drag-and-drop editing
    (Excel), 149
Draw Borders button, 167
drawing Word tables, 92-93
drop caps, text (publica-

tions), 376
drop-down lists
    Font Size, 49
    Print What, 208
    Style Name, 164
Dynamic Link Libraries
    (DLLs), 344
dynasets, queries (Access),
    314

E

email
    Hotmail, 246
    Outlook
        accounts, 247-250
        attachments, 250
        blind carbon copy, 250
        checking, 250-251
        creating, 248-250
        moving to folders, 246
        organizing, 246-247
        sending, 248-250
    sending from Word,
        346-347
    sending Office files as,
        347-348
E-Mail Accounts command
    (Tools menu), 247
E-mail Accounts dialog
    boxes, 247
E-Mail Message link, 346
eBooks, reading (Word), 31
Edit Hyperlink dialog box,
    400
Edit in Formula Bar option
    (Excel worksheets), 112
Edit menu commands
    Clear, 150

Copy, 38, 377
Cut, 39, 125
Delete, 125, 150
Fill, 152
Fill, Series, 155
Find, 40, 146
Go To, 35
Links, 396
Paste, 38, 117, 377
Replace, 41
Undo, 45
Edit option (Options dialog
    box), 79
effects, transitions
    (PowerPoint), 227-228
endnotes (Word), inserting,
    97-98
entries, Journal (Outlook),
    269-270
equal sign (=), Excel formu-
    las, 128
Error Checking Options
    option (Excel worksheets),
    112
errors, correcting, 43-45
events, scheduling
    (Outlook), 265-266
Event dialog box, 265
Excel, 8
    active cells, 114
    AutoFormat, 113, 118
    charts
        background images,
            178-180
        creating, 177-178
        data series, choosing,
            173, 176
        data tables, 174
        labels, 175
        legends, 174
        modifying, 176-177
        types, choosing,

172-173
comma (,), 118
comments, adding,
157-158
data sharing with Word,
401
drag-and-drop editing, 149
formulas, copying/pasting,
116
navigating, 114
overview, 12-13
pound sign (#), 141
printing, 156-157
relative cell referencing,
117
starting, 106
viewing in Outlook,
244-245
Web browsers, 344
Web pages, creating,
358-359
workbooks, 106-108
Excel worksheets, 106
apostrophe ('), 111
AutoCorrect, 146-149
cells, 108, 122-124
columns, 124-125
creating, 115
data fills, 151-152
dates/times, entering,
113-114
fills, creating, 154-156
formats, 142-143
formatting, 116-119
AutoFormatting,
161-162
conditional, 168
fonts, 141-142
justification, 140
rows/columns, 140-141
special alignment,

165-166
special cell borders,
166-167
special cell shading,
167
styles, modifying,
163-164
tab colors, 168
formulas, entering,
112-113
asterisk (*), 128
cell referencing,
130-131
copying, 132-133
equal sign (=), 128
math operators, 129
operator-hierarchy
model, 129
ranges, 129-130
functions
advanced, 138
arguments, 134
AutoSum, 135-136
Average(), 134
modifying, 137
Sum(), 134-135
labels, 111
links, creating, 396-397
naming, 107
numbers, entering,
112-113
opening, 25, 107
ranges, 126-127
recalculating, 133
rows, 124-125
saving, 107
series, creating, 154-156
smart fills, 152-153
storing, 107
text
deleting, 110

entering, 109-112
**Exit command (File menu),
420**
Expand Dialog button, 174
Explorer. *See* **Internet
Explorer**
**Extensible Markup
Language.** *See* **XML**
extensions. *See* **file exten-
sions**

F

**Favorites Folder (Outlook),
243**
features
Access, 8, 16-17
accessibility, 23-24
AutoComplete, 23
AutoCorrect, 43-44
AutoFormatting, 43
Excel, 8, 12-13, 118
FrontPage, 8
Go To (Excel), 114
integration, 10-11
Outlook, 9, 14-15
PowerPoint, 8, 14, 208
Print Preview, 61-62
Publisher, 9, 17-18
Undo, 43-45
Word, 8, 11-12, 98-100
**Field Size property (Access
database fields), 287**
fields, Access
currency, 298
databases, 280, 28
adding to tables, 289
deleting from tables,
289
index, 282
primary key, 281-282,

288
tables, 299
    forms, adding, 302
    rearranging, 290-291
    resizing, 290-291
file extensions
    FrontPage, 439
    .mdb, 279
    .pot, 187
    .ppt, 194, 207
    Word documents, 33
    .xls, 107
File Locations option (Options dialog box), 79
File menu commands
    Exit, 420
    New, Mail Message, 248
    New, Task, 266
    Package for CD, 222
    Page Setup, Layout, 96
    Picture, From Scanner or Camera, 88
    Print, 207, 301, 306
    Print Preview, 61, 208, 301
    Properties, 68, 425
    Publish Site, 438
    Save, 107
    Save As, 354
    Web Page Preview, 354
File New Database dialog box, 284
files. *See* **documents; worksheets**
Fill Color palette, 179
Fill command (Edit menu), 152
Fill Effects dialog box, 179
Fill, Series command (Edit menu), 155
fills, Excel worksheets
    creating, 154-156
    data, 151-152

smart, 152-153
Filter by Form, 310-313
Filter by Selection, 310-311
Filter command (Records menu), 310
Filter Excluding Selection, 310-311
filters (Access). *See also* **queries (Access)**
    / (forward slash), 313
    # (pound sign), 313
    Advanced Filter/Sort, 310
    And/Or conditions, 313
    Filter by Form, 310-313
    Filter by Selection, 310-311
    Filter Excluding Selection, 310-311
Find All Word Forms option (Find and Replace dialog box), 42
Find and Replace dialog box, 35, 40-43, 146
Find command (Edit menu), 40, 146
Find Duplicates Query Wizard, 315
Find Unmatched Query Wizard, 315
Find Whole Words Only option (Find and Replace dialog box), 42
find-and-replace, 146-148
flat-file databases versus relational databases, 279
folders (Outlook)
    Favorites Folder, 243
    Inbox Folder, 243
    Mail view, 245
    moving email to, 246
Font Color button, 49
Font command (Format menu), 49, 203, 218, 300,

375
Font dialog box, 49, 141
Font Size drop-down list, 49
Font tab, 141
fonts
    Access tables, 300
    applying, Word, 49
    formatting, Excel worksheets, 141-142
    text, publications, 375
    Web pages (FrontPage), 428
footers (Word), creating, 95-96
Footnote and Endnote dialog box, 97
footnotes (Word), inserting, 97-98
Form command (Insert menu), PDF:10-PDF:11
Form Wizard, 302-305
Format Cells dialog box, 143, 164-165
Format Chart Title dialog box, 176
Format menu commands
    AutoFormat, 118, 162
    Bullets and Numbering, 52
    Cells, 141-142, 165
    Columns, 93
    Font, 49, 203, 218, 300, 375
    Paragraph, 54-57
    Style, 163
    Styles, Formatting, 60
    Theme, 357
    Unhide Columns, 299
Format Object dialog box, 394
Format Painter, 60-61
Format Picture dialog box,

389

Format property (Access database fields), 287

Format Text Box dialog box, 378

formats, Excel worksheets, 142-143

formatting. *See also* **templates; wizards**
  AutoFormatting feature, 43
  data (Access), 297-299
  Excel worksheets, 116-119
    AutoFormat, 161-162
    conditional, 168
    fonts, 141-142
    justification, 140
    rows/columns, 140-141
    special alignment, 165-166
    special cell borders, 166-167
    special cell shades, 167
    styles, modifying, 163-164
    tab colors, 168
  Outlook screens, 243
  Web pages, 355

formatting (Word)
  bulleted lists, inserting, 51-52
  character, 48-51
  numbered lists, inserting, 51-52
  paragraph, 52
    indentation, 55-57
    justifying text, 53
    line breaks, 57-59
    margins, 53
    page breaks, 57-59
    ruler, 57
    spacing, 55-57
    tabs, 54-55
    styles, 60, 65
    themes, 64-65
    viewing, 59

Formatting toolbar, 32

forms
  Access tables
    adding fields, 302
    data modification, 306
    generating, 302-305
    navigating, 306
    printing, 306
  data entry, 296, 301
  Datasheet, 304
  Tabular, 304

formulas (Excel worksheets)
  asterisk (*), 128
  cell referencing, 130-131
  copying, 132-133
  copying/pasting, 116
  entering, 112-113
  equal sign (=), 128
  math operators, 129
  operator-hierarchy model, 129
  ranges, 129-130

forward slash (/), 313

Fraction format (Excel worksheets), 142

FrontPage, 8, 418-419
  extensions, 439
  interface, 419, 421
  intranets, 421
  launching, 419, 421
  Web pages
    background, adding, 425, 431-432
    command buttons, 427
    creating, 421, 423, 425, 436-438
    download time, esti-mating, 425
    fonts, 428
    hyperlinks, 434
    images, adding, 427-429
    margins, adding, 425
    modifying, 420
    objects, adding, 426-427
    publishing, 421, 435, 438-439
    text, adding, 427-429
    titles, adding, 425
    views, 430-431
  Web sites, creating, 422

full justifying text (Word), 53

Full Name button, 252

Full Screen command (View menu), 62

Function command (Insert menu), 138

functions, Excel worksheets
  advanced, 138
  arguments, 134
  AutoSum, 135-136
  Average(), 134
  modifying, 137
  Sum(), 134-135

G

General format (Excel worksheets), 142

General option (Options dialog box), 79

General option (Properties

dialog box), 68
Go To command (Edit menu), 35
Go To dialog box, 114
Got To feature (Excel), 114
Grammar Checker, Word, 69, 73-75
graphics. *See* **images**
graphs. *See* **charts (Excel)**
green triangles, 112
green wavy lines, 45, 70, 73
grouping (Access)
  objects, 285
  report summaries, 332-334
Growth series (Excel worksheets), 156

H

hanging indents (Word), 56
Header and Footer command (View menu), 95
headers (Word), creating, 95-96
Help. *See also* **Office Assistant**
  Design Checker (Publisher), 387-388
  questions, typing, 23
  Web, 345
Help dialog box, 20
Help menu commands
  Microsoft Publisher Help, 373
  Show Office Assistant, 21
Help on This Error option

(Excel worksheets), 112
Hide option (Office Assistant), 21
hiding
  fields, Access tables, 299
  task panes, 33
Highlight button, 50
highlighting Word text, 36-37
home task panes (Excel), 106
Hotmail, 246
HTML (Hypertext Markup Language)
  commands, Web pages, 423
  tags, 411, 423, 439
  Web documents, saving, 354
  Web pages, 355, 418
Hyperlink command (Insert menu), 434
Hyperlink to action, 232
hyperlinks, 24
  Access, Web pages, 359
  inserting, 25
  sharing data between applications, 399-400
  Web pages, adding, 434
Hypertext Markup Language. *See* **HTML**
hyphenation
  automatic, 69, 75-76, 375
  zones, 76
Hyphenation dialog box, 76, 375
hyphens, 75-76

I

icons
  Outlook, 251
  paper-clip, 251
  Regional and Language Options, 298
  shortcut, 398
  toolbars, enlarging, 79
Ignore All option (Spelling dialog box), 73
Ignore Error option (Excel worksheets), 112
Ignore Once option (Spelling dialog box), 73
images
  adding
    PowerPoint slides, 219-221
    Web Pages, 427-429
    Word, 86-87
  background, Excel charts, 178-180
  cameras (Word), inserting, 87
  downloading (Web), 346
  modifying (PowerPoint slides), 204
  publications, 382-384
importing text, publications, 376-377
Inbox (Outlook), 241-243
Increase Font Size button, 204
Increase Indent button, 52
indentation (Word)
  bulleted lists, 52
  numbered lists, 52
  setting, 55-57
  text, publications, 374

index fields, Access databas-
    es, 282
InfoPath 2003, 406
Insert dialog box, 124
Insert File dialog box, 250
Insert Function button, 138
Insert Function dialog box,
    138
Insert Hyperlink dialog box,
    400, 434
Insert menu commands
    AutoText, 88
    Cells, 124
    Columns, 124
    Comment, 157, 217
    Date and Time, 85
    Form, 426-427
    Function, 138
    Hyperlink, 434
    Page Numbers, 85
    Picture, Clip Art, 86, 382,
        428
    Picture, From File, 86,
        221, 383
    Picture, From Scanner or
        Camera, 221, 383
    Reference, Footnote, 97
    Rows, 124
    Slide, 200
    Symbol, 84
    Text File, 377
    Web Components, 426
Insert mode (Word), 35
Insert Picture dialog box, 86
Insert Table dialog box, 89
Insert, Table command
    (Table menu), 89
insertion point, 34-35
integration feature, 10-11,
    24-25
Intelliprint, 157

interfaces, FrontPage, 419,
    421
Internet Explorer, 24-25,
    342-344
Internet Protocol (IP)
    addresses, 352
intranets, FrontPage, 421
Invite Attendees button, 264
IP addresses, 352
Italic button, 48
italicized formatting
    (Word), 48

J-K

Journal entries (Outlook),
    243, 268-270
Journal Options dialog box,
    269
justification
    Excel worksheets, 140
    Word, 53
Justify button, 53

Keep Lines Together check
    box, 59
key fields, primary (Access
    databases), 281-282, 288
keyboards (Excel), navigat-
    ing, 114
keys. See shortcut keys
keywords, Between, 323

L

Label Wizard, 330
labels, Excel, 111, 175

Language, Hyphenation
    command (Tools menu),
    75, 375
Language, Thesaurus com-
    mand (Tools menu), 77
languages, translations
    (Word), 77-78. See also
    HTML; XML
layouts, reports (Access),
    335-336
leader characters, 55
left justifying text (Word),
    53
Legend button, 180
legends, Excel charts, 174
letters (Word), writing for
    Outlook, 402-403
Letters and Mailings com-
    mand (Tools menu), 99
Line and Page Breaks tab,
    58, 76
line breaks (Word), insert-
    ing, 57-59
Line chart (Excel), 173
line spacing (Word), setting,
    55-57
Linear series (Excel work-
    sheets), 156
lines
    blue dotted, 70
    green wavy, 45, 70, 73
    red wavy, 45, 70-72
links. See also hyperlinks
    E-Mail Message, 346
    Organize Clips, 86
    Product Updates, 346
    sharing data between
        applications, 395-397
    text boxes (publications),
        379
    updating, 397
    Web, creating in Office,
        344

Links command (Edit menu), 396
Links dialog box, 396
lists. *See also* drop-down lists
   bulleted/numbered (Word), inserting, 51-52
   custom, creating (Excel worksheets), 154-155

M

Mail Merge (Word), 98-100
Mail view (Outlook), 245
   email
      accounts, 247-250
      attachments, 250
      Bcc (blind carbon copy), 250
      checking, 250-251
      creating, 248-250
      organization, 246-247
      sending, 248-250
   folders, 245
mail. *See* email
main documents, Mail Merge (Word), 98
managers, Business Contact Manager, 409-410
margins
   adding (Web pages), 425
   setting (Word), 53
Master styles (PowerPoint slides), 216
Master, Slide Master command (View menu), 216
Match Case option (Find and Replace dialog box), 42

math operators, Excel formulas, 129
Max() function, 137
.mdb file extension, 279
meetings, scheduling (Outlook), 264-265
menus
   personalized, 10, 32
   shortcut
      Access, 299
      Word, 396
      Word, removing items, 78
Merge and Center button, 140
merge fields, main documents (Word), 98
Message dialog box, 248
messages. *See* email
Messenger, Hotmail, 246
microphones (PowerPoint), adjusting volume, 230
Microsoft Access. *See* Access
Microsoft Excel. *See* Excel
Microsoft FrontPage. *See* FrontPage
Microsoft Office 2003 Enterprise Edition, 410
Microsoft Office Professional, 410
Microsoft Outlook. *See* Outlook
Microsoft Passport accounts, 246
Microsoft PowerPoint. *See* PowerPoint
Microsoft Publisher Help command (Help menu), 373
Microsoft Publisher. *See* Publisher
Microsoft Word. *See* Word
Min() function, 137

Modify button, 164
multiple email accounts (Outlook), 250
Multiple Monitors option (Set Up Show dialog box), 229
Multiple Pages button, 61
multiple Word documents, editing, 34
multiplication, Excel formulas, 128

N

naming
   queries (Access), 314
   ranges (Excel), 127
   reports (Access), 328
   worksheets (Excel), 107
narration, voice (PowerPoint), 230-231
navigating
   Access tables, 300, 306
   Design Gallery (Publisher), 386-387
   Excel, 114
Navigation view, 437
New All Day Event command (Actions menu), 265
New Call dialog box, 254
New Contact button, 251
New Document task pane, 33, 63, 107
New File task pane, 282
New Form dialog box, 302
New Journal Entry command (Actions menu), 270
New Letter to Contact command (Action menu), 402
New Note button, 267

New Office Document dia-
log box, 18

New Page or Web Site task
pane, 423

New Presentation task pane,
187

New Publication task pane,
369-370

New Query dialog box, 315,
318

New Record button, 306

New Recurring
Appointment command
(Actions menu), 262

New Report dialog box,
329-330

New Slide button, 193, 200

New Style button, 60

New Task button, 266

New, Mail Message com-
mand (File menu), 248

New, Task (File menu), 266

newsgroups, Outlook
Express, 240

newsletters (Publisher), creating, 370-371

nonbreaking hyphens, 76

None action, 232

Normal view
PowerPoint, 198
Word, 30

Northwind Traders data-
base, 310-311

Note Options button, 267

Notes
OneNote 2003, 407-408
Outlook, 243, 267
presentations
(PowerPoint), 199

Notes Page command (View
menu), 206

Notes Page view, 199,
206-207

Number format (Excel
worksheets), 142

Number tab, 142

numbered lists (Word),
inserting, 51-52

Numbering button, 51

numbers, 112-113

O

Object action, 233

objects. *See also* forms;
queries
Access databases, 284-285
Web Pages, adding,
426-427

Office Assistant
Clippit, 19
Conditional Formatting
dialog box, 168
customizing, 20-22
Grammar Checker, 73-74
moving, 20

Office Clipboard, 38, 148

On Mouse Click check box,
226

OneNote 2003, 407-408

operator-hierarchy model,
Excel formulas, 129

operators
math, Excel formulas, 129
relational, Access, 322

optional hyphens, 76

Options dialog box, 79-80

Options option (Office
Assistant), 21

Options option (Spelling
dialog box), 73

Options, Spelling &
Grammar command
(Tools menu), 70, 73

Options, View command
(Tools menu), 34

Or conditions, Access filters,
313

Organize Clips link, 86

orphans, paragraphs, 58

Outline tab, 191

outlines (PowerPoint),
200-201

Outlook, 9
Business Contact
Manager, 409-410
contacts
displaying, 249
recording, 251-254
selecting, 254-255
email, moving to folders,
246
folders, 243
Hotmail, 246
icons, 251
Journal, 268-270
Mail view
email, 246-251
folders, 245
non-Outlook data, view-
ing, 244-245
notes, 267
overview, 14-15
Preview pane, 243
screens
Calendar, 242, 258
Calendar, Daily
Scheduler, 258
Calendar, Date
Navigator, 258-259
Calendar, dates/times,
258-261

Calendar, scheduling, 261-266

Calendar, tasks, 266-267

Contacts, 243

formatting, 243

Inbox, 241-243

Journal, 243

Notes, 243

Outlook Today, 240-242

Tasks, 243

smart tags, 271-272

spell checking, 249

Word letters, writing, 402-403

Outlook bar, expanding, 268

Outlook Express, newsgroups, 240

Outlook Today, 240-242

Overtype mode (Word), 35

P

Package for CD command (File menu), 222

packaged presentations (PowerPoint), 221-223

page breaks (Word), inserting, 57-59

page numbers (Word), inserting, 85, 95

Page Numbers command (Insert menu), 85

Page Numbers dialog box, 85

Page Setup dialog box, 53, 57

Page Setup, Layout command (File menu), 96

pages. *See* **Web pages**

palettes, Fill Color, 179

panes, Preview, 243. *See also* **task panes**

paper-clip icon, 251

Paragraph command (Format menu), 54-57

Paragraph dialog box, 55

paragraph formatting (Word), 52

indentation, 55-57

justifying text, 53

line breaks, 57-59

margins, 53

page breaks, 57-59

ruler, 57

spacing, 55-57

tabs, 54-55

paragraphs, 58

Passport (Microsoft), accounts, 246

Paste button, 38

Paste command (Edit menu), 38, 117, 377

Paste Options button, 38

pasting

data, Excel worksheets, 148-149

Excel formulas, 116

Word text, 38-39

Patterns tab, 167

PCs, tablet, 407

Percentage format (Excel worksheets), 142

Performance option (Set Up Show dialog box), 229

personalized menus, 10, 32

Pi() function, 137

Picture, Clip Art command (Insert menu), 86, 382, 428

Picture, From File command (Insert menu), 86, 221, 383

Picture, From Scanner or Camera command (File menu), 88

Picture, From Scanner or Camera command (Insert menu), 221, 383

pictures (Word), inserting, 86-87

Pie chart (Excel), 173

placeholders (PowerPoint slides), 219-220

Play sound action, 233

portals, SharePoint Portal Server, 408

.pot file extension, 187

pound sign (#), 141, 313

PowerPoint, 8, 185

microphones, adjusting volume, 230

overview, 14

presentations, 186, 225

action buttons, 231-233

animation, 233-235

AutoContent Wizard, 188-191

creating, 187-189

design, 212-213

modifying, 198

notes, 199

outlines, 200-201

packaged, 221-223

planning, 188-190

printing, 207-208

rehearsing, 230

saving, 194, 207-208

setting up, 228-229

slides, adding, 193, 200

templates, design,
192-194
thumbnails, 198
transitions, 226-228
viewing, 194
voice narration,
230-231
slides, 186-187, 201
comments, 217
design, 213-214
images, adding,
219-221
images, modifying, 204
modifying, 191, 198-
201, 214-217
moving, 202
Notes Page view,
206-207
objects, modifying, 202
placeholders, 219-220
Slide Sorter view,
205-206
sorting, 199
text, 203-204, 215-218
text boxes, 217-218
transitions, 206
templates, 187, 190
viewing in Outlook,
244-245
views, 198-199
Web pages, creating,
360-361
Word, importing, 215
.ppt file extension, 194, 207
presentations (PowerPoint),
186, 225
action buttons, 231-233
animation, 233-235
AutoContent Wizard,
188-191
creating, 187-189
design, 212-213

modifying, 198
notes, 199
outlines, 200-201
packaged, 221-223
planning, 188-190
printing, 207-208
rehearsing, 230
saving, 194, 207-208
setting up, 228-229
slides, adding, 193, 200
templates, design, 192-194
thumbnails, 198
transitions, 226-228
viewing, 194
voice narration, 230-231
Word files, converting to,
400-401
Preview pane (Outlook), 243
previewing
printing (Word), 61-62
Web pages, 354
Primary Key button, 288
primary key fields, Access
databases, 281-282, 288
Print command (File menu),
207, 301, 306
Print dialog box, 207
Print Layout view (Word),
30
Print option (Options dialog
box), 79
Print Preview command
(File menu), 61, 208, 301
Print Preview feature, 61-
62, 208
Print What drop-down list,
208
printing
Access
reports, 326-328
tables, 301, 306
Excel, 156-157

PowerPoint
presentations, 207-208
slide notes, 206
Word, previewing, 61-62
Product Updates link, 346
Product() function, 138
promoting elements,
PowerPoint outlines, 201
proofreading (Word)
automatic hyphenation,
69, 75-76
Grammar Checker, 69,
73-75
Spell-Checker, 69-73
Thesaurus, 69, 77
properties
fields, setting (Access
databases), 287-288
Word documents, 68-69
Properties command (File
menu), 68, 425
Properties Custom tab, 69
Properties dialog box, 68
Properties Summary tab, 69
publications
borders, 389-390
color schemes, changing,
372
creating, 369-373
images, 382-384
modifying, 374
shapes, adding, 384-385
text, 374-377
text boxes, 377-380
Web pages, 352-353
Web pages (FrontPage),
435, 438-439
Publications tab, 63
Publish as Web Page dialog
box, 360
Publish button, 360

Publish Site command (File menu), 438
Publisher, 9
 autoflow, 380
 business cards, creating, 370
 Design Checker, 387-388
 Design Gallery, 385-387
 design sets, 369
 newsletters, creating, 370-371
 online training, 373
 overview, 17-18
 publication types, 366-368
 starting, 369
 versus Word, 368
Pyramid chart (Excel), 173

Q

queries (Access), 313
 creating
  Query Design view, 318-323
  Query Wizard, 314-317
 dynasets, 314
 naming, 314
 results, displaying, 317
 subsets, sorting, 321
 synchronizing, 317
Queries tab, 319
Query Design view, 318-323
Query menu commands, Show Table, 322
Query Wizard, 314-317
questions, typing (help), 23
quoted passage styles, 61

R

Radar chart (Excel), 173
ranges, (Excel)
 cells, 122
 formulas, 129-130
 naming, 127
 worksheets, 126
Reading Layout view (Word), 31
Record Narration command (Slide Show menu), 230
Record Narration dialog box, 230
recording (Outlook)
 contacts, 251-254
 Journal entries, 270
records (Access)
 databases, 280-281
 removing. *See* filters (Access)
 tables, 299
Records menu commands, Filter, 310
Recount button, 69
recovery, crashes, 23
Recurrence button, 262
red wavy lines, 45, 70-72
Redo button, 45
Reference, Footnote command (Insert menu), 97
Regional and Language Options (Regional Settings) icon, 298
rehearsing slide shows, PowerPoint, 230
relational databases versus flat-file databases, 279
relational database systems. *See* **Access**
relational operators (Access), 322

relative cell referencing, Excel, 117, 130-131
Reminder check box, 262
reminders, appointments (Outlook), 262-263
Replace command (Edit menu), 41
Replace Text As You Type option (AutoCorrect), 43
Report Design view, 328
Report Wizard, 330-331
 report summaries, 332-335
 reports, 334-336
Report Wizards, 329-330
reports (Access)
 generating, 327-332
 layout, 335-336
 naming, 328
 printing, 326-328
 report summaries, 332-335
 sorting, 334-335
 styles, 335-336
 summaries (Access), 332-335
Required property (Access database fields), 287
Reveal Format task pane, 59
right justifying text (Word), 53
Roman() function, 138
rows
 Excel worksheets
  deleting,124-125
  formatting, 140-141
  inserting, 124
 Word tables, inserting, 92
Rows command (Insert menu), 124
ruler (Word), 57
rules wizard, 246

Run macro action, 233
Run program action, 232

S

Save As Web Page command (File menu), 354
Save command (File menu), 107
Save option (Options dialog box), 79
saving
  Excel worksheets, 107
  PowerPoint presentations, 194, 207-208
  tables, Access databases, 288
  Word documents, 33, 354-355
scanned camera images (PowerPoint), inserting, 221
scanned images (Word), inserting, 87
scheduling (Outlook)
  appointments, 261-264
  event, 265-266
  meetings, 264-265
Scheduling tab, 264
Scientific format (Excel worksheets), 142
scientific notation, 112
screens, splash (Northwind Traders database), 310-311
screens (Outlook)
  Calendar, 242
    appointment scheduling, 261-264
    Daily Scheduler, 258

Date Navigator, 258-259
dates/times, 258-261
event scheduling, 265-266
meeting scheduling, 264-265
tasks, 266-267
Contacts, 243
formatting, 243
Inbox, 241-243
Journal, 243
Notes, 243
Outlook Today, 240-242
Tasks, 243
ScreenTips, 79
scrolling Word documents, 35
search engines, 413, 441
Search option (Find and Replace dialog box), 42
search-and-replace, 146-148
searches, Word text, 40
Security option (Options dialog box), 80
Select command (Table menu), 92
Select Picture button, 179
Select Style options (Format Cells dialog box), 167
Send/Receive command (Tools menu), 249
series, creating (Excel worksheets), 155-156
Series dialog box, 155-156
servers
  SharePoint Portal Server, 408
  Web, 352, 421
Set Microphone Level button, 230

Set Up Show dialog box, 228-229
shading cells (Excel worksheets), 167
shapes, adding (publications), 384-385
SharePoint Portal Server, 408
sharing data (between applications)
  drag-and-drop, 394
  hyperlinks, 399-400
  links, 395-397
  Outlook, writing Word letters, 402-403
  shortcuts, 397-399
  Word and Excel, 401
shortcut icons, 398
Shortcut Key button, 84
shortcut keys
  assigning, 24
  Ctrl+1, 165
  Ctrl+A, 37, 93, 299, 398
  Ctrl+B, 48
  Ctrl+C, 38, 116, 148, 377
  Ctrl+D, 152
  Ctrl+F, 40, 146
  Ctrl+F6, 34
  Ctrl+G, 35
  Ctrl+H, 41
  Ctrl+I, 48
  Ctrl+K, 264, 400
  Ctrl+O, 33
  Ctrl+S, 33
  Ctrl+U, 48
  Ctrl+V, 38, 117, 148, 377
  Ctrl+X, 39, 125, 149
  Ctrl+Z, 43, 289
  Shift+F5, 35
  symbols, 84

shortcut menus
  Access, 299
  Word, 396
shortcuts, sharing data between applications, 397-399
Show AutoComplete check box, 89
Show Formula Auditing Toolbar option (Excel worksheets), 112
Show Office Assistant command (Help menu), 21
Show Options (Set Up Show dialog box), 229
Show Slides option (Set Up Show dialog box), 229
Show Table command (Query menu), 322
Show Table dialog box, 318-319
Show Toolbar button, 69
Show Type option (Set Up Show dialog box), 229
showing
  fields, Access tables, 299
  task panes, 33
Shrink to Fit option (Format Cells dialog box), 165
Simple Query Wizard, 314-317
sites, Web hosting, 352. See also Web sites
sizing handles, Excel charts, 176
Slide Design button, 212
Slide Design task pane, 187, 212
Slide Layout task pane, 192

Slide Show menu commands
  Action Buttons, 231
  Action Settings, 231
  Record Narration, 230
  Slide Transition, 226
Slide Show view (PowerPoint), 199
slide shows. See presentations (PowerPoint)
Slide Sorter toolbar, 205
Slide Sorter view, 205-206
Slide Sorter view (PowerPoint), 199
Slide tab, 191
Slide Transition command (Slide Show menu), 226
Slide Transition task pane, 205, 226
slides (PowerPoint), 186-187
  adding, 193, 200
  comments, 217
  design, 213-214
  images, 204, 219-221
  Master, 216
  modifying, 191, 198-201, 214-217
  moving, 202
  Notes Page view, 206-207
  objects, modifying, 202
  placeholders, 219-220
  Slide Sorter view, 205-206
  sorting, 199
  text, 203-204, 215-218
  text boxes, 217-218
  transitions, 206
Slides command (Insert menu), 200
smart fills, Excel worksheets, 152-153

smart tags
  Outlook, 271-272
  Word, 70
sorting
  Access
    query subsets, 321
    records, 299
    reports, 334-335
  PowerPoint slides, 199
sound
  adding (PowerPoint slides), 219-221
  downloading (Web), 346
  inserting (Word), 86-87
  transitions (PowerPoint slides), 228
Sounds Like option (Find and Replace dialog box), 42
source files, 394-396
spacing (Word), setting, 55-57
special characters (Word), inserting, 84-85
Special format (Excel worksheets), 142
speed, transitions (PowerPoint slides), 227
spell checking, 297
  Outlook, 249
  Publisher, 375
Spell-Checker (Word), 69-73
Spelling & Grammar option (Options dialog box), 79
Spelling command (Tools menu), 297, 375
spelling corrections, 45
Spelling dialog box, 72-73
spelling dictionaries, removing words, 72

splash screens, Northwind Traders database, 310-311

spreadsheets. *See* worksheets (Excel)

Sqrt() function, 138

Standard toolbar, 32

Start Reading button, 31

starting Excel, 106

startup, 18-19

Statistics option (Properties dialog box), 68

Stdev() function, 138

Stock chart (Excel), 173

storing
  Excel worksheets, 107
  Web pages, 352

Style box, 60

Style command (Format menu), 163

Style dialog box, 163

Style Name drop-down list, 164

styles
  Access reports, 335-336
  Excel, modifying, 163-164
  quoted passage, 61
  Word, 60, 65

Styles and Formatting task pane, 60

Styles, Formatting command (Format menu), 60

Sum() function, 134-135, 138

summaries, reports (Access), 332-335

Summary dialog box, 333

Summary option (Properties dialog box), 68

Suppress Line Numbers check box, 59

Surface chart (Excel), 173

Switch Between Header and Footer button, 95

Symbol button, 97

Symbol command (Insert menu), 84

Symbol dialog box, 84

symbols (Word), inserting, 84-85

synchronizing Access queries, 317

synonyms, Thesaurus (Word), 77

syntax
  blank Web page, 424
  HTML, Web page listing, 418
  Web pages, HTML commands, 423

system crashes, recovery, 23

T

Table AutoFormat command (Table menu), 92

Table menu commands
  Insert, Table, 89
  Select, 92
  Table AutoFormat, 92

tables (Excel), data tables, 174

tables (Access), 279-280
  creating, 285-286
  data entry, 291-293, 296-297, 301
  data formatting, Datasheet view, 297-299
  data modification, Datasheet view, 299-300
  design, 291-293
  fields, 289-291
  fields, hiding/showing, 299

fonts, 300

forms, 302-306

loading in Word, 401-402

modifying structure, 289

navigating, 300

printing, 301

records, sorting, 299

records/fields, deleting, 299

saving, 288

tables (Word)
  columns, 92-95
  creating, 89-91
  drawing, 92-93
  inserting, 89
  rows, inserting, 92
  traversing, 91-92

Tables and Borders button, 92

Tables and Borders toolbar, 78

tablet PCs, 407

tabs
  Alignment, 165
  AutoFormat As You Type, 44, 399
  AutoText, 88
  Border, 166
  Calculation, 134
  color, Excel worksheets, 168
  Commands, 78
  Custom Lists, 154
  Data Labels, 175
  Font, 141
  Line and Page Breaks, 58, 76
  Number, 142
  Outline, 191
  Patterns, 167
  Properties Custom, 69
  Properties Summary, 69

Publications, 63
Queries, 319
Scheduling, 264
setting (Word ruler), 57
Slide, 191
Text Box, 378
Word, setting, 54-55
Tabs button, 54
Tabs dialog box, 54-55
Tabular forms, 304
tags
    HTML, 411, 423, 439
    smart (Word), 70
    XML, 412, 440
Task Pane command (View menu), 38
task panes
    Clip Art, 86, 382
    Design Checker, 387
    hiding, 33
    home (Excel), 106
    Mail Merge, 99
    New Document, 33, 63
    New Document (Excel), 107
    New File, 282
    New Page or Web Site, 423
    New Presentation, 187
    New Publication, 369-370
    Office Clipboard, 38
    Reveal Format, 59
    showing, 33
    Slide Design, 187, 212
    Slide Layout, 192
    Slide Transition, 205, 226
    Styles and Formatting, 60
    Thesaurus, 77
    Translate, 78
    Word, 31
Tasks (Outlook), 243, 266-267

templates,
    PowerPoint, 65, 187, 190-194, 212-214
    Word, 33, 356-358
text
    Excel
        deleting, 110
        entering, 109-112
    PowerPoint
        modifying, 203-204, 215
        slides, 217-218
    publications, 374-377
    Web Pages, adding, 427-429
    Word, 34
        AutoCorrect feature, 43-44
        AutoFormatting feature, 43
        copying, 38-39
        cutting, 38-39
        deleting, 37
        document navigation, 35-36
        drag and drop, 39
        Find and Replace feature, 40-43
        finding, 40
        justifying, 53
        modifying, 40
        pasting, 38-39
        selecting, 36-37
        typing, 34-35
    zooming, 374
Text Box button, 217
Text Box tab, 378
text boxes
    Custom Mark, 97
    publications, 377-380
    slides (PowerPoint), 217-218

text cursor. *See* **insertion point**
Text File command (Insert menu), 377
Text format (Excel worksheets), 142
Text tool, 378
Theme command (Format menu), 357
Theme dialog box, 64
themes (Word), 64-65, 357
Thesaurus (Word), 69, 77
thumbnails, PowerPoint presentations, 198
Time format (Excel worksheets), 142
times
    Access, entering, 298
    Excel, entering, 113-114
    Outlook, Calendar, 258-261
    Word, inserting, 85
timing transitions, PowerPoint slide shows, 226-227
titles, adding (Web pages), 425
Today() function, 138
toolbar buttons. *See* **buttons**
toolbar icons, enlarging, 79
toolbar options arrows, 32
toolbars
    Chart, 180
    customizing, 23
    ScreenTips, 79
    Slide Sorter, 205
    Tables and Borders, 78
    Web, 24-25, 342, 358
    Word, 32
    Word Count, 69
Toolbars command (View menu), 78

How can we make this index more useful? Email us at indexes@samspublishing.com

Toolbars, Chart command (View menu), 180
Toolbars, Customize command (View menu), 32
Toolbars, Database command (View menu), 401
Toolbars, Drawing command (View menu), 217
Toolbars, Outlining command (View menu), 201
Toolbars, Web command (View menu), 342, 358
tools
   AutoShapes, 385
   Text, 378
Tools menu commands
   AutoCorrect, 43-44, 146, 272, 399
   Customize, 78
   Customize, Options, 11
   Design Checker, 387
   E-Mail, 247
   Language, Hyphenation, 75, 375
   Language, Thesaurus, 77
   Letters and Mailings, 99
   Options, Spelling & Grammar, 70, 73
   Options, View, 34
   Send/Receive, 249
   Spelling, 297, 375
   Word Count, 69
Track Changes option (Options dialog box), 80
Transition button, 205
transitions, PowerPoint slide shows, 203, 226-228
Translate task pane, 78
translation (Word), 77-78
traversing Word tables, 91-92

triangles, green, 112
typing text (Excel worksheets), 109-112

U

Underline button, 48
underline formatting (Word), 48
Undo command (Edit menu), 45
Undo feature, 43, 45, 289
Unhide Columns command (Format menu), 299
updates
   links, 397
   Web, downloading, 345-346
Use Hardware Graphics Acceleration check box, 229
Use Wildcards option (Find and Replace dialog box), 42
User Information option (Options dialog box), 80
Var() function, 138

V

video, inserting
   PowerPoint slides, 219-221
   Word, 86-87
View menu commands
   Full Screen, 62
   Header and Footer, 95
   Master, Slide Master, 216

Notes Page, 206
Task Pane, 38
Toolbars, 78
Toolbars, Chart, 180
Toolbars, Customize, 32
Toolbars, Database, 401
Toolbars, Drawing, 217
Toolbars, Outlining, 201
Toolbars, Web, 342, 358
View option (Options dialog box), 79
viewing
   PowerPoint presentations, 194
   Word formatting, 59
views
   Code, 423
   Datasheet, 291-292
      data entry, 296-297
      data formatting, 297-299
      data modification, 299-300
      table navigation, 300
      tables, printing, 301
   Design, 329
   Navigation, 437
   Notes Page, 206-207
   PowerPoint, 198-199
   Query Design, 318-323
   Report Design, 328
   Slide Sorter, 205-206
   Web pages (FrontPage), 430-431
   Word, 30-31, 62-63
views (Outlook), Mail, 245
email
   accounts, 247-250
   attachments, 250
   Bcc (blind carbon copy), 250
   checking, 250-251

creating, 248-250
organization, 246-247
sending, 248-250
folders, 245
voice narration, PowerPoint slide shows, 230-231
volume, microphones (PowerPoint), 230

W

watermarks (Word), inserting, 87
Web, 341
clip art, downloading, 346
email, sending from Word, 346-347
Help, 345
latest updates, downloading, 345-346
links, creating in Office, 344
Office files
sending as email, 347-348
viewing in Internet Explorer, 342-344
search engines, 413, 441
sound, downloading, 346
Web browsers, Excel, 344
Web Components command (Insert menu), 426
Web hosting, 352, 435
Web Page Preview command (File menu), 354
Web pages
Access, creating, 359-360
accessing, 342
creating, 353
Excel, creating, 358-359

formatting, 355
HTML code, 355, PDF:2
PowerPoint, creating, 360-361
previewing, 354
publishing, 352-353
storing, 352
viewing in Outlook, 244-245
Word
creating, 353, 356-358
saving as, 354-355
themes, applying, 357
Web pages (FrontPage)
background, adding, 425, 431-432
blank, syntax, 424
command buttons, 427
creating, 421, 423, 425, 436-438
download time, estimating, 425
fonts, 428
HTML commands, 418, 423
hyperlinks, P434
images, adding, 427-429
margins, adding, 425
modifying, 420
objects, adding, 426-427
publishing,421, 435, 438-439
text, adding, 427-429
titles, adding, 425
views, 430-431
Web Publishing Wizard, 438-439
Web servers, 352, 421
Web Site Templates dialog box, 436

Web sites (FrontPage), creating, 422
Web toolbar, 24-25, 342, 358
widows, paragraphs, 58
windows, Database (Access), 284
wizards
AutoContent Wizard, 188-191
Brochure Wizard, 63
Chart Wizard, 172-173, 330
Corporate Presence Wizard, 422, 437
Database Interface Wizard, 422
Discussion Page Wizard, 422
Form Wizard, 302-305
FrontPage, creating Web pages, 436-438
Label Wizard, 330
Mail Merge Wizard, 99
modifying, 173-177
Query Wizard, 314-317
Report Wizard, 330-331
grouping report summaries, 332-334
report summaries, 334-335
reports, 334-336
Report Wizards, 329-330
rules wizard, 246
Web Publishing Wizard, 438-439
Word, 63
Word, 8, 29
Access tables, loading, 401-402
AutoText entries, creating, 88-89
camera images, inserting, 87

clip art, inserting, 86-87
converting files to presentations, 400-401
customizing, 78-80
data sharing with Excel, 401
dates/times, inserting, 85
documents, 33-34
    properties, 68-69
    saving as Web pages, 354-355
email, sending, 346-347
eBooks, reading, 31
editing area, 30
endnotes, inserting, 97-98
footers, creating, 95-96
footnotes, inserting, 97-98
Format Painter, 60-61
formatting
    bulleted lists, inserting, 51-52
    character, 48-51
    numbered lists, inserting, 51-52
    paragraph, 52-59
    styles, 60, 65
    themes, 64-65
    viewing, 59
grammar corrections, 45
headers, creating, 95-96
importing to PowerPoint, 215
Insert mode, 35
letters, writing for Outlook, 402-403
Mail Merge, 98-100
menu items, removing, 78
modes, 35
Overtype mode, 35
overview, 11-12
page numbers, inserting, 85, 95

personalized menus, 32
printing, previewing, 61-62
proofreading
    automatic hyphenation, 69, 75-76
    Grammar Checker, 69, 73-75
    Spell-Checker, 69-73
    Thesaurus, 69, 77
vs. Publisher, 365
shortcut menu, 396
smart tags, 70
sound clips, inserting, 86-87
special characters, inserting, 84-85
spelling correction, 45
spelling dictionaries, removing words, 72
styles, quoted passage, 61
tables
    columns, 92-95
    creating, 89-91
    drawing, 92-93
    inserting, 89
    rows, inserting, 92
    traversing, 91-92
task pane, 31
templates, 33
text
    AutoCorrect feature, 43-44
    AutoFormatting feature, 43
    copying, 38-39
    cutting, 38-39
    deleting, 37
    document navigation, 35-36
    drag and drop, 39
    Find and Replace feature, 40-43

    finding, 40
    modifying, 40
    pasting, 38-39
    selecting, 36-37
    typing, 34-35
toolbars, 32, 79
translation, 77-78
Undo feature, 45
video clips, inserting, 86-87
viewing in Outlook, 244-245
views, 30-31, 62-63
watermarks, inserting, 87
Web pages, 353-358
wizards, 63
Word Count command (Tools menu), 69
words, removing (spelling dictionaries), 72
workbooks. *See* **worksheets (Excel)**
worksheets (Excel), 106
    AutoCorrect, 146-149
    cells, 108, 122-124
    columns, 124-125
    creating, 115
    data fills, 151-152
    dates/times, entering, 113-114
    fills, creating, 154-156
    formats, 142-143
    formatting, 116-119
        AutoFormatting, 161-162
        conditional, 168
        fonts, 141-142
        justification, 140
        rows/columns, 140-141
        special alignment, 165-166

special cell borders,
166-167

special cell shading,
167

styles, modifying,
163-164

tab colors, 168

formulas

asterisk (*), 128

cell referencing,
130-131

copying, 132-133

entering, 112-113

equal sign (=), 128

math operators, 129

operator-hierarchy
model, 129

ranges, 129-130

functions, 134-138

advanced, 138

arguments, 134

AutoSum, 135-136

Average(), 134

modifying, 137

Sum(), 134-135

labels, 111

links, creating, 396-397

naming, 107

numbers, entering,
112-113

opening, 25, 107

ranges, 126-127

recalculating, 133

rows, 124-125

saving, 107

series, creating, 154-156

smart fills, 152-153

storing, 107

text, 109-112

**Wrap Text option (Format
Cells dialog box), 165**

X-Z

XDocs. *See* **InfoPath 2003**
.xls file extension, 107
**XML (Extensible Markup
Language)**

InfoPath 2003, 406

Office data, converting to,
413, 441

overview, 411-412,
439-440

tags, 412, 440

**XY (Scatter) chart (Excel),
173**

Zoom dialog box, 62
Zoom feature, 374

Your Guide
to Computer
Technology